# THE ARCHITECT'S HISTORY OF ARCHITECTURE

Second Edition

Hans Morgenthaler
*University of Colorado*

**KENDALL/HUNT PUBLISHING COMPANY**
4050 Westmark Drive    Dubuque, Iowa 52002

# CONTENTS

*Introduction* ..............................................................................................................................xiii

**CHAPTER 1**    *Origins* .........................................................................................................................1

Stonehenge (2750-1500 BCE) ........................................................................................................1

Ziggurats ...........................................................................................................................................3

    White Temple, Uruk (3500-3000 BCE) .....................................................................................3

    Ziggurat, Ur (2150-2050 BCE) ....................................................................................................3

Pyramids .............................................................................................................................................3

    Mortuary Complex of King Zoser, Imhotep, Saqqara (2750 BCE) ..........................................4

    Pyramids, Giza (2750-2500 BCE) ..............................................................................................4

**CHAPTER 2**    *Houses, Cities, and Gardens* ..........................................................................................9

House, Ur .............................................................................................................................................9

    House, Banpo (3rd Millenium BCE) ............................................................................................9

    Jericho ............................................................................................................................................9

    Çatal Hüyük .................................................................................................................................10

    Babylon (612 BCE) .....................................................................................................................10

    Hanging Gardens-Babylon ........................................................................................................10

    Ishtar Gate (575 BCE) ...............................................................................................................10

    Mohenjo Daro, Indus Valley (3rd Millenium BCE) ...................................................................11

    Panels, Nineveh (668-627 BCE) ...............................................................................................11

Additional Buildings and Monuments .........................................................................................12

    Persepolis (518-460 BCE) .........................................................................................................12

**CHAPTER 3**    *Egyptian Temples* .........................................................................................................15

Mortuary Complex of Queen Hatshepsut, Senmut, Deir-El-Bahari (15th C. BCE) ....................15

Temple Complex, Karnak (ca. 1991-670 BCE) ............................................................................15

Temple of Amon (Rameses II) and Temple of Hathor (Nefertiti), Abu Simbel (1250 BCE) ...................16

Construction .....................................................................................................................................17

Expression ........................................................................................................................................17

Excursus: Wilhelm Worringer's *Abstraction and Empathy* (1910) ...........................................17

**CHAPTER 4**    *Non-Western Architecture* ...........................................................................................19

India ...................................................................................................................................................19

    Vedic Culture................................................................................................................................19

    Caves, Barabar Mountains (ca. 250 BCE) ...............................................................................19

    Ajanta (2nd C. BCE)....................................................................................................................20

    Stupas, Sanchi (5th C., 237-232 BCE) ....................................................................................20

    Chaitya Hall, Karli (1st C. CE) ...................................................................................................20

    Kandariya Mahadeva Temple, Khajuraho (11th C. CE) ...........................................................20

Indonesia and Cambodia ...............................................................................................................21

    Stupa, Borobudur (8th C., ca. 760-847 CE) ............................................................................21

    Temples at Angkor (12th-13th C. CE) .......................................................................................22

Japan .................................................................................................................................................22

    Shinto Shrines, Ise .....................................................................................................................22

    Horyuji Monastery, Nara (607 CE) ...........................................................................................22

**CHAPTER 5**    *Minoan and Mycenean Architecture* ...........................................................................25

    Historical and Cultural Background ...........................................................................................25

    Early Palatial Period 2000-1700 BCE) .....................................................................................25

    Palace, Knossos (1600-1400 BCE) ..........................................................................................25

    Citadel, Tiryns (1400-1200 BCE) .............................................................................................26

Citadel, Mycenae, with Lion Gate (1250 BCE) ..................................................27
Treasury of Atreus (1300 BCE) ..................................................27

**CHAPTER 6**   *Greek Architecture* ..................................................29

Urban and Landscape Design ..................................................29
Athens ..................................................29
Miletus, Hippodamus of Miletus (479 BCE) ..................................................30
Priene (350 BCE) ..................................................30
Sanctuary of Apollo, Delphi (350 BCE) ..................................................30
Siphnian Treasury (CA. 524 BCE) ..................................................31
Treasury of the Athenians (510-490 BCE) ..................................................31
Theater (4th-3rd C. BCE) ..................................................31
Stadium and Gymnasium ..................................................31
Sanctuary of Athena Pronaia at Marmaria ..................................................31
Tholos, Theodoros of Phokaia (380 BCE) ..................................................31
Public Buildings ..................................................32
Theater, Epidaurus (350 BCE) ..................................................32
Choragic Monument of Lysicrates, Athens (335 BCE) ..................................................32
Mausoleum, Hallicarnassos (353 BCE) ..................................................32
Temples ..................................................32
Construction Technique ..................................................33
Optical Refinements ..................................................33
Proportions ..................................................33
Orders ..................................................33
Temple of Neptune, Paestum (450 BCE) ..................................................34
Acropolis, Athens ..................................................34
Temple of Athena Nike (449/8, 427-424 BCE) ..................................................34
Propylaea (437-432 BCE) ..................................................34
Erechtheion (421-405 BCE) ..................................................35
Parthenon (447-432 BCE) ..................................................35
Sculptural Decoration ..................................................35
Meaning, Expression ..................................................36

**CHAPTER 7**   *Roman Architecture* ..................................................39

Introduction ..................................................39
Sanctuary of Fortuna Primigenia, Palestrina [Praeneste] (80 BCE) ..................................................40
Maison Carrée, Nîmes (20 BCE) ..................................................40
Temple of Vesta, Tivoli (late 1st C. CE) ..................................................40
Pantheon, Rome (118-128 BCE) ..................................................40
Pont du Gard, (14 CE) ..................................................41
Urban Design ..................................................41
Pompeii (7th C. BCE-79 CE) ..................................................41
Forum, Rome (6th C. BC-2nd C. CE) ..................................................42
Forum of Augustus ..................................................42
Forum of Trajan, Rome (106-113 CE) ..................................................42
Basilica Ulpia (98-117 CE) ..................................................42
Trajan's Market (100-112 CE) ..................................................42
Colosseum, Rome (72-80 CE) ..................................................42
Baths of Caracalla, Rome (211-217 CE) ..................................................43
Basilica of Maxentius, Rome (307-312 CE) ..................................................43
Residential and Landscape Design ..................................................43
Houses and Villas, Pompeii ..................................................43
Apartment Building, Ostia ..................................................43
Hadrian's Villa, Tivoli (118-134 CE) ..................................................44
Aesthetics ..................................................44

**CHAPTER 8**  *Sustainability and Ecology in Architecture*..............................................47
Introduction............................................................................................47
Africa......................................................................................................48
    Kenya...............................................................................................48
    Togo.................................................................................................48
    Uganda .............................................................................................48
    Niger................................................................................................49
    Nigeria .............................................................................................49
    Great Zimbabwe, Zimbabwe (1000-1500) .......................................49
    Christian Churches, Lalibela (Ethiopia)...........................................50

**CHAPTER 9**  *Early Christian and Byzantine Architecture*................................................51
Christian Building, Dura Europos (231) .................................................51
Catacombs, Rome (4th C.)......................................................................52
Old St. Peter's, Rome (319-329) .............................................................52
S. Appollinare in Classe, Ravenna (532-549) ..........................................52
S. Vitale, Ravenna (526- ) ......................................................................53
Hagia Sophia (532-537) .........................................................................53

**CHAPTER 10**  *Romanesque Architecture* ..................................................................57
Medieval Design Theory and Principles ..................................................57
    Palatine Chapel, Odo von Metz, Aachen (796-805) ........................57
Monasticism ..........................................................................................58
    Plan of a Monastery, St. Gall (820).................................................58
    St. Michael, Hildesheim (1001-1022) .............................................58
    St-Sernin, Toulouse (1080-1120) ...................................................59
    Cathedral, Pisa (1063-13th C.).......................................................59
    S. Miniato al Monte, Florence (1062-1200) ....................................59
    Cathedral, Durham (1093-1133) ....................................................60
Structural Systems ..................................................................................60
Meaning .................................................................................................60

**CHAPTER 11**  *Pre-Columbian Architecture* ..............................................................61
Serpent Mound, Locust Grove, Ohio (1200-900 BCE) ...........................61
Native American Architecture .................................................................61
    Southwest ........................................................................................61
    Hohokam .........................................................................................62
        Casa Grande Ruins, Arizona (1300-1450) ..............................62
    Anasazi ............................................................................................62
        Cliff Dwellings, Mesa Verde, Colorado (1100) .......................62
        Pueblo Bonito, Chaco Canyon, New Mexico (1100) ...............62
South American and Central American Cultures......................................62
    Olmec (2000-200 BCE) ..................................................................62
        La Venta (900-400 BCE).........................................................63
    Aztec................................................................................................63
        Teotihuacán............................................................................63
    Maya ................................................................................................63
        Chichén Itzá...........................................................................63
    El Castillo (late 12th century) .........................................................63
    Tikal (100 BCE - 9th c. CE) ...........................................................63
    Inca ..................................................................................................63
        Saqsaywaman Fortress, Cuzco (1400) .....................................63
        Machu Picchu (1450-1540).....................................................64

**CHAPTER 12**  *Gothic Architecture*............................................................................67
Origins....................................................................................................67
Early Gothic Architecture .......................................................................67

Abbey Church, St.-Denis (1130-1144) ..................................................................67
Structure ...........................................................................................................68
Parts .................................................................................................................68
Spatial System ..................................................................................................68
Cathedral, Laon (1160-1225) ...........................................................................68
Cathedral of Notre-Dame, Paris (1163-1250) ...................................................68
Cathedral, Chartres (1194-1220) ......................................................................69
High Gothic Architecture ...................................................................................71
Reims Cathedral, Jean d'Orbais (1211-1287) ....................................................71
Amiens Cathedral, Robert de Luzarches, Thomas de Cormont,
    Renaud de Cormont (1220-88) ...................................................................71
Ste-Chappelle, Thomas de Cormont, Paris (1241-1248) ....................................71
Cathedral of Ste-Cécile, Albi (1276-1397) .........................................................72
Cathedral, Salisbury (1220-1260) ......................................................................72
St. Elisabeth, Marburg (1235-83) ......................................................................72
Santa Maria della Fiora, Arnolfo di Cambio, Florence (1296- ) ..........................72
Meaning .............................................................................................................73

**CHAPTER 13**    *Islamic Architecture* ......................................................................................79
Background ........................................................................................................79
General Characteristics ......................................................................................79
Dome of the Rock, Jerusalem (691-692) ...........................................................79
Great Mosque, Cordoba (786-987) ....................................................................80
Alhambra, Granada (1238- ) .............................................................................81
Court of Myrtles ................................................................................................81
Court of Lions (1378- ) .....................................................................................81
Friday Mosque, Isfahan .....................................................................................82
Tomb, Mosque, and Madrasa of Sultan Hasan, Cairo (1356) ............................82
Mosque, Qayrawan ...........................................................................................82

**CHAPTER 14**    *Early Renaissance Architecture* .......................................................................85
Background ........................................................................................................85
Filippo Brunelleschi (1377-1446) ......................................................................85
Baptistry Door Competition (1401-2) .............................................................85
Dome of Cathedral, Florence (1418-1436) ........................................................86
Foundling Hospital, Florence (1419-24) ............................................................86
Santa Spirito, Florence (1436-82) ......................................................................86
Leone Battista Alberti (1404-1472) ....................................................................86
Palazzo Rucellai, Florence (1455-1470) .............................................................87
Sant'Andrea, Mantova (1472-1493 [nave and western entrance]) .......................87
Spatial System ...................................................................................................87
Early Renaissance Outside Italy ..........................................................................88
France ...............................................................................................................88
Castle, Domenico da Cortona, Chambord (1519-1550) ...................................88
Castle, Blois (1498-1638) ................................................................................88
Square Court, Louvre, P. Lescot, Paris (1546- ) ..............................................89
Spain .................................................................................................................89
History ............................................................................................................89
England .............................................................................................................89
Longleat House, Smythson, Wiltshire (1572-80) .............................................89
Wollaton Hall, Smythson, Nottinghamshire (1580-88) ...................................90
Hardwick Hall, Smythson, Derbyshire (1590-96) ...........................................90

**CHAPTER 15**    *Far-Eastern Architecture* .................................................................................93
Imperial Palace (Forbidden City), Beijing (1403 begun) ....................................93
Golden Pavilion, Kyoto (End 14th C.) ............................................................93

**CHAPTER 16**  *High Renaissance* ...................................................................................................................95
Historical Background ...................................................................................................95
Artistic Characteristics ...................................................................................................95
Tempietto, Donato Bramante, Rome (1502-04) ...................................................95
St. Peter's, Rome (1504-1590) ...................................................................................96
Palazzo Farnese, Rome (1515- ) ...................................................................................96
Venice ...................................................................................................97
Library of San Marco, Sansovino, Venice (1536- ) ...................................................97
Spain ...................................................................................................97
Escorial, Toledo (d. 1567) and Herrera, nr. Madrid (1562-84) ...................................97
Germany ...................................................................................................98
St. Michael's, Sustris, Munich (1583-97) ...................................................................98
Andrea Palladio (1508-80) ...................................................................................98
San Giorgio Maggiore, Venice (1559-1610) ...................................................................98
Il Redentore, Palladio, Venice (1577-1592) ...................................................................99
Villa Barbaro, Maser (1549-57) ...................................................................................99
Villa Rotonda, Palladio, Vicenza (1566-70) ...................................................................100

**CHAPTER 17**  *Mannerism* ...................................................................................................................105
Capitol Square (Campidoglio), Rome, Michelangelo (1538-1664) ...................................105
Laurentian Library, Florence, Michelangelo (1524-1534; Finished by Vasari in 1559) ...................106
Palazzo del Te, Mantua, Romano (1527-34) ...................................................................106

**CHAPTER 18**  *Baroque Architecture in Rome* ...................................................................................109
Completion of St. Peter's, Bernini, Rome (1624-1667) ...................................................110
Sant'Andrea al Quirinale, Bernini, Rome (1658-70) ...................................................110
San Carlo alle Quattro Fontane, Borromini, Rome (1638-39, 1665-67) ...................110
Sant'Ivo della Sapienza, Borromini, Rome (1643-48) ...................................................111
Chapel of SS. Sindone, Turin Cathedral, Guarini (1667-90) ...................................111
Santa Maria della Salute, B. Longhena, Venice (1631-32) ...................................................112
Castle, Vaux-le-Vicomte, Le Vau (1657-61) ...................................................................112
Castle, Le Vau, Hardouin-Mansart et. al., Versailles (1661-1750) ...................................112
Louvre East Façade, Perrault, Paris (1667-70) ...................................................................113
St. Paul's Cathedral, London, Wren (1675-1709) ...................................................................114
Town Hall, Elias Holl, Augsburg (1615-20) ...................................................................115
Meaning ...................................................................................................115

**CHAPTER 19**  *17th-Century Global Architecture* ...................................................................................119
Japan ...................................................................................................119
Katsura Imperial Villa, Kobori Enshu, Kyoto (1620-1658) ...................................................119
India ...................................................................................................120
Taj Mahal, Agra (1631-1648) ...................................................................................120
North American Colonies ...................................................................................120
Governor's Palace, Santa Fe (1610-14) ...................................................................120
S. Francis of Assisi, Rancho de Taos (18th C.) ...................................................................120
Parson Capen House, Topsfield (1683) ...................................................................120
Old Ship Meeting House, Hingham (1681) ...................................................................120
Bacon's Castle (1655) ...................................................................................120
St. Luke's (1632) ...................................................................................121
John Brocket, Plan, New Haven (1638) ...................................................................121
Plan, Wm. Penn, Philadelphia (1682) ...................................................................121

**CHAPTER 20**  *Compositional Innovation and Stylistic Changes in Late Baroque Architecture* ...................123
Enlightenment ...................................................................................................123
Stylistic Changes ...................................................................................................124
Superga, Juvarra, Torino (1719-31) ...................................................................124
Spanish Steps, F. de Sanctis, Rome (1723-25) ...................................................................124

Fountain of Trevi, N. Salvi, Rome (1732-62) .................................................................125
Blenheim Palace, Vanbrugh and Hawksmoor, Oxfordshire (1705-22) ................................125
Christ Church, Hawksmoor, Spitalfields (1714-29) ...........................................................125

**CHAPTER 21**    *Rococo: Sensuality in Architecture* ...........................................................127
Stylistic Sources .......................................................................................................127
Hôtel de Soubise, Interior, G. Boffrand, Paris (1735-40) ...................................................128
Austria and Southern Germany .....................................................................................128
Amalienburg, F. Cuvilliés the Elder, Munich (1734-39) ......................................................128
St. John Nepomuk, Asam Brothers, Munich (1733-46) .......................................................128
Vierzehnheiligen, J. B. Neumann (1743-72) ...................................................................129
Wieskirche, Dominikus Zimmermann (1746-54) ..............................................................129

**CHAPTER 22**    *Historicism I: 18th-Century Neoclassicism* .................................................131
Johann B. Fischer von Erlach (1656-1723) ....................................................................131
St. Charles Borromeo (Karlskirche), Vienna (1715-37) ......................................................131
Palladianism ...........................................................................................................132
Chiswick House, London (1725-30) ..............................................................................132
Colonial Georgian Architecture in the American Colonies ....................................................133
Governor's Palace, Williamsburg (1749-51) ...................................................................133
Redwood Library, Harrison, Newport (1748-50) ..............................................................133
Virginia State Capitol, Jefferson & Clérisseau, Richmond, VA (1785-89) ................................133

**CHAPTER 23**    *Historicism II* ..................................................................................137
Theory ...................................................................................................................137
Carlo Lodoli (1690-1761) ..........................................................................................137
Marc-Antoine Laugier (1713-69) .................................................................................138
Giovanni Piranesi (1720-78) .......................................................................................138
St. Sulpice, Oppenord and Servandoni, Paris (1646-1732) ................................................138
Ste-Genevieve (Panthéon), Soufflot, Paris (1756-90) ........................................................139
Petit Trianon, Gabriel, Versailles (1761-68) ....................................................................140
Kedleston Hall, Derbyshire (1760-70) ..........................................................................140
Syon House, Adam, Middlesex (1762-63) ......................................................................140
Greek Revival ..........................................................................................................140
Brandenburg Gate, Langhans, Berlin (1789-94) ..............................................................141

**CHAPTER 24**    *Visual Arts and Architecture* ...................................................................143
Picturesque .............................................................................................................143
English Garden .........................................................................................................144
Chiswick House, Gardens (1717-24) ............................................................................144
Stourhead, Hoare & Flitcroft (1744-65) .........................................................................144
Circus (Wood the Elder), Royal Crescent (Wood the Younger), and
Landsdowne Crescent (Palmer), Bath (1764-93) ..............................................................145
Gothic Revival ..........................................................................................................145
Strawberry Hill, R. Adam, et al., Twickenham (1749-77) ...................................................145
Fonthill Abbey, Wyatt, Wilshire (1796-1807) ..................................................................146
International Style .....................................................................................................146
Piet Mondrian (1872-1944) ........................................................................................147
Basic Philosophy ......................................................................................................147
The Red Tree (1908) .................................................................................................147
The Grey Tree (1912) ................................................................................................147
Flowering Apple Tree (1912) ......................................................................................147
Composition (1916) ..................................................................................................147
Composition with Red, Blue, and Yellow (1930) ..............................................................148
Villa Savoye, Le Corbusier, Poissy (1929-31) .................................................................148
Purism ...................................................................................................................148
Vers une Architecture (1923) ......................................................................................148

Five Points of a New Architecture (1927) ................................................................148
Transparency in Modern Architecture ...................................................................149

**CHAPTER 25**   *Architecture and Industry*..................................................................................151
Severn Bridge, Coalbrookdale, T. Pritchard & A. Darby III (1777-79) ...................151
Royal Pavilion, Brighton, J. Nash (1811-23) ...........................................................152
Bridge, Menai Straits, Telford (1818-26)..................................................................152
Brooklyn Bridge, John & Washington Roebling, New York (1867-83) ...................152
Crystal Palace, Paxton, London (1850-51)................................................................152
Meunier Chocolate Factory, Sulnier, Noisiel-sur-Marne (1869-72).........................153
Eiffel Tower, Gustave Eiffel, Paris (1887-89) ..........................................................154

**CHAPTER 26**   *Architecture and Revolution* ...............................................................................157
Etienne-Louis Boullée (1728-99).............................................................................157
Newton Cenotaph (1783) ........................................................................................158
Claude-Nicholas Ledoux (1736-1806) .....................................................................158
   Salt Works, Arc-et-Senans (1775-79) ..................................................................158
   Ideal City of Chaux (1790) .................................................................................159
   Oikéma.................................................................................................................159
   Barrières, Paris (1785-89) ...................................................................................159
Modernism...............................................................................................................160
   Adolf Loos (1870-1933) ......................................................................................160
   "Ornament and Crime" (1908) ............................................................................160
   Steiner House, Vienna (1910) .............................................................................160
International Style ....................................................................................................161
Russian Constructivism ...........................................................................................161
Suprematism ............................................................................................................161
   Monument to the 3$^{rd}$ International, Tatlin (1919-20) ........................................161
Deconstruction ........................................................................................................162
   House II (Falk House), Eisenman, Hardwick, VT (1969-71) ..............................162

**CHAPTER 27**   *19$^{th}$-Century Neoclassicism*..................................................................................165
Arc de Triomphe, J.-F.-T. Chalgrin, Paris (1806-1836) ...........................................165
La Madeleine, A.-P. Vignon (1807-45) .....................................................................166
State Theater, Schinkel, Berlin (1819-21).................................................................166
Altes Museum, Schinkel, Berlin (1824-28) ..............................................................166
Walhalla, von Klenze, Regensburg (1831-42) ...........................................................167
British Museum, Smirke, London (1824-47).............................................................167
Travelers' Club, Barry, London (1829-31).................................................................168
Reform Club, Barry, London (1837-41) ...................................................................168
Monticello I, Jefferson, Charlottesville (1769-82) ...................................................168
Monticello II (1793-1809) .......................................................................................169
University of Virginia, Jefferson, Charlottesville (1804-17).......................................169
Girard College, Walter, Philadelphia (1833-47) .......................................................170

**Chapter 28**   *Gothic Revival*....................................................................................................175
Augustus Welby Pugin (1812-52).............................................................................175
   Houses of Parliament, Barry & Pugin, London (1836-60) ...................................176
High Victorian Gothic..............................................................................................176
   All Saints', Butterfield, Margaret Street, London (1849-59)................................176
   Keeble College, Butterfield, Oxford (1866-83) ..................................................176
   University Museum, Deane & Woodward, Oxford (1855-60) ..............................177
   St. Pancras Station (1863-67) and Midland Hotel (1866-74) Scott, London ......177
   Eugène-Emanuel Viollet-le-Duc ..........................................................................177
   Restoration of Notre-Dame, Paris (1844-66) .....................................................177
   De Courmont House, Paris (1846-9) ...................................................................177
United States Historical Background ........................................................................177
   Memorial Hall, Ware & Van Brunt, Cambridge (1870-78)...................................178

**CHAPTER 29**    *Second Empire and Structural Rationalism* ........................................................................179
The Transformation of Paris..........................................................................................................179
    Louvre Extension, Visconti & Lefuel, Paris (1852-7) ..............................................................180
    Opera House, Garnier, Paris (1861-75)....................................................................................180
Victor Hugo's Architectural Theory..............................................................................................180
Henri Labrouste...............................................................................................................................181
    Bibliothèque Ste-Geneviève, Paris (1842-50) ..........................................................................181
United States....................................................................................................................................182
    City Hall, John MacArthur, Philadelphia (1874-) ...................................................................183

**CHAPTER 30**    *Theory, Philosophy, and Architecture*..............................................................................185
Ecoles des Beaux-Arts.....................................................................................................................185
    Antoine Quatremère de Quincy (1755-1849)...........................................................................185
    Jean-Nicolas-Louis Durand (1760-1834).................................................................................185

**CHAPTER 31**    *Domestic Revival*..............................................................................................................187
Red House, Webb, Bexleyheath (1859-60).....................................................................................187
Leyeswood, R.N. Shaw, Sussex (1868-69)......................................................................................187
Voysey House "The Orchard," Voysey, Chorleywood (1899-1900) ..............................................188
Stoughton House, Richardson, Cambridge (1882-3)......................................................................188

**CHAPTER 32**    *Chicago School and the Skyscraper*.................................................................................189
History and Origin in New York ....................................................................................................189
Tribune Building, R.M. Hunt, New York (1873-75) .....................................................................189
Chicago School.................................................................................................................................189
    Home Insurance Building, Jenney, Chicago (1883-86).............................................................190
    Marshall Field Wholesale Store, Richardson, Chicago (1885-7) ..............................................190
    Sullivan and Adler ....................................................................................................................190
    Auditorium, Chicago (1887-89) ...............................................................................................190
    Guaranty Building, Buffalo (1895) ...........................................................................................191
    Carson Pirie Scott & Co. Store, Chicago (1899-1904) ............................................................191

**CHAPTER 33**    *Art Nouveau*......................................................................................................................193
Tassel House, Victor Horta, Brussels (1892-3) ..............................................................................193
Glasgow School of Art, Mackintosh, Glasgow (1897-1909) .........................................................193
Antonio Gaudi (1852-1926) ...........................................................................................................194
    Casa Battlò, Barcelona (1905-7) ...............................................................................................194
    Casa Milá, Barcelona (1905-10)................................................................................................195
    Sagrada Familia, Barcelona (1884-1926) ..................................................................................195
Metro Stations, Hector Guimard, Parish (1899-1904) ..................................................................195
Palais Stoclet, Hoffmann, Brussels (1905-11) ...............................................................................195

**CHAPTER 34**    *Modernist Beginnings*.......................................................................................................201
Preconditions for Modern Architecture..........................................................................................201
Stock Exchange, Berlage, Amsterdam (1897-1903)........................................................................201
Secession Building, Olbrich, Vienna (1898-99)..............................................................................202
Post Office Savings Bank, Wagner, Vienna (1904-06)....................................................................202
Robie House, Wright, Chicago (1908-09)......................................................................................203
AEG Turbine Factory, Behrens, Berlin (1909)................................................................................203
Fagus Factory, Gropius, Alfeld (1911-3) ........................................................................................204
Century Hall, Max Berg, Breslau (1912-13) ..................................................................................204
Futurism...........................................................................................................................................205
    Antonio Sant'Elia (1888-1916) ................................................................................................205
    Studies for Architectural Forms (1912-13) ...............................................................................205
    Città Nuova (1913-14) ..............................................................................................................205

**CHAPTER 35**   *International Style*..................................................................................................209
Schröder Schräder House, Rietveld, Utrecht (1924) ...............................................209
Bauhaus Building, Gropius, Dessau (1925-26)........................................................210
German Pavilion, Mies van der Rohe, Barcelona (1929) .........................................210
Tugendhat House, Mies van der Rohe, Brno (1929-30) ..........................................211
Wittgenstein House, Wittgenstein & Engelmann, Vienna (1926-28)........................211
Lovell Beach House, R. Schindler, Newport Beach (1922-26)..................................212
PSFS Building, Howe & Lescaze, Philadelphia (1931-32).......................................212
   Commission..................................................................................................212
   Client ...........................................................................................................213
   Building........................................................................................................213
Casa del Fascio, Terragni, Como (1932-36)............................................................213

**CHAPTER 36**   *Countermodernism*....................................................................................217
Expressionism ......................................................................................................217
   Glass Pavilion, Bruno Taut, Cologne (1914)....................................................217
   Einstein Tower, Erich Mendelsohn Potsdam (1917-21).....................................218
   Grosses Schauspielhaus, Hans Poelzig, Berlin (1919 begun)..............................218
   Goetheanum II, Steiner, Dornach (1924-28).....................................................218
Romanticism and Traditionalism...........................................................................219
   Urban Plan, Lutyens, New Delhi (1912-31)......................................................219
   Viceroy's House, New Delhi (1920-31).............................................................219
   Woolworth Building, Cass Gilbert, New York (1911-13)....................................219
   Chrysler Building, Van Alen, New York (1928-30)............................................220
   Rockefeller Center, Hood et. al., New York (1931-39).......................................220
   Totalitarian Architecture during the 1930s.......................................................220
   Zeppelin Field, Speer, Nuremberg (1936).........................................................220
   New Chancellory, Speer, Berlin (1937-8)..........................................................220
   Plan for Berlin, Speer (1937-40)......................................................................220
F.L. Wright's Second Career ...................................................................................221
   Fallingwater (Kaufmann House), F.L. Wright, Bear Run (1937)........................221
   Guggenheuim Museum, F.L. Wright, New York (1943, 1956-59).......................221

**CHAPTER 37**   *Structuralist Architecture*................................................................227
Alvar Aalto (1898-1976)........................................................................................227
   Villa Mairea, Noormarku (1938-39)................................................................228
   Civic Center, Säynätsalo (1949-52) .................................................................228
Louis Kahn (1901-74) ...........................................................................................228
Design Philosophy.................................................................................................228
   Richards Medical Center, Philadelphia (1957-64).............................................229
   Jonas Salk Institute, La Jolla (1959-65) ...........................................................229
Notre-Dame-du-Haut, Le Corbusier, Ronchamp (1950-55)....................................230
Querini-Stampaglia Foundation, Carlo Scarpa, Venice (1961-63)...........................230
Aldo Van Eyck (1918-).........................................................................................230
   Orphanage, Amsterdam (1957-60) .................................................................230
Herman Hertzberger (1932-).................................................................................231
   Centraal Beheer, Apeldoorn (1968-72) ............................................................231
Participatory Architecture......................................................................................232
   Student Housing, Lucien Kroll, Louvain (1969-73)..........................................232
Ralph Erskine.......................................................................................................232
   Byker Wall, Newcastle (1968-75).....................................................................233
James Stirling (1926-92) ........................................................................................233
   Neue Staatsgalerie, Stirling, Stuttgart (1977-84) ..............................................233

**CHAPTER 38**   *Post-War International Style*..........................................................237
Seagram Building, Mies van der Rohe & Philip Johnson, New York (1954-58).........237
Engineering Faculty Building, Stirling, Leicester University (1959-63)......................238

**CHAPTER 39**   *Postmodernism* ..................................................................................................241
        Guild House, Venturi, Philadelphia (1960-65) ..................................................241
    Charles Moore ..........................................................................................................242
    Condominium I, Sea Ranch (1965-72)......................................................................242
        Piazza d'Italia, Moore, New Orleans (1975-80)...............................................243
    AT&T Building, Philip Johnson, New York (1978-84)..............................................243
    Public Services Building, Graves, Portland, OR (198-82).........................................244
    Autonomous Architecture..........................................................................................245
        Cemetery, Rossi, Modena (1971-83)..................................................................245
    Mario Botta ...............................................................................................................245
        Single-Family House, Riva San Vitale (1972-3)................................................245
        Secondary School, Morbio Inferiore (1972-77) ...............................................246
    Casa Tonini, Reichlin & Reinhardt, Torricella (1972-74).........................................246
    German Museum of Architecture (1979-84)...............................................................246

**CHAPTER 40**   *Deconstructivist Architecture* ...........................................................................253
    Background.................................................................................................................253
    Formal Architectural Source......................................................................................253
    Society ......................................................................................................................253
    Philosophy.................................................................................................................253
        Centre Pompidou, Piano & Rogers, Paris (1971-77).........................................254
        Austrian Travel Agency, Hollein, Vienna (1978).............................................254
        City Museum, Hollein, Mönchengladbach (1972-82) .......................................254
        Gehry House, Gehry, Santa Monica (1979)......................................................255
        Wexner Arts Center, Eisenman, Columbus (1983-89).......................................255
        Parc de la Villette, Tschumi, Paris (1984-95) ...................................................256
        Vitra Fire Station, Hadid, Weil am Rhein (1987-1993).....................................257
        Berlin Museum Extension for Jewish Museum, Berlin (1989, 1992-98)................258

**CHAPTER 41**   *Contemporary Developments* ...............................................................................265
    United States Holocaust Memorial Museum, Ingo Freed, Washington (1993)...............265
    Museum of Technology Culture, Asymptote, New York (1999-2005) .......................266
    Dodger Stadium, Los Angeles (1999)........................................................................266
    Calputta Sogn Bendetg, Sumvigt (1985-88) ..............................................................266
    Thermal Bath, Zumthor, Vals (1996) ........................................................................266
    Footbridge over the Mur; Marcel Meili, Markus Peter,
        Jürg Conzett, Murau (1996) .............................................................................267
    *Glossary*....................................................................................................................269

# INTRODUCTION

Architects must know the history of their discipline in order to become successful practitioners. This book aims to provide architects with a presentation of architectural history that is useful to their future task.

Why do architects need history? History provides a focus, a center for everybody. Our world has become complex: cybernetics, information glut, advances in communications and bio-technology, and globalism have created a physical and psychological environment that is rather anti-human. Fighting alone against these forces, we can no longer find our own center. Society has become pluralistic, without strong communal beliefs. We are agnostics and no longer capable of recognizing the transcendental grounds and reasons for our existence. This led to a crisis of content. Architects no longer know what values and meanings to express in their designs. As a result, during the last three decades of the 20th century, architectural design to a large degree has become totally impersonal and influenced by mass media.

Already in the 1980s, Charles Jencks proposed that architects—together with the public—need to establish the public realm collectively. Architecture is the exemplary public art. Buildings, squares, and streets establish the places where we conduct our lives, and these must be shaped collectively and articulated in a language that everybody can understand. However, the public realm should not be surrounded by purely superficial nostalgic concoctions found in amusement parks. Instead, buildings should possess a memorial quality and express the craftsmanship and permanence associated with things that last longer than just one mortal life. He admonished architects to design in a language he called "abstract representation," clarifying that architectural messages are conveyed best when slightly veiled.

The history of architecture also offers architects valuable advice. The rules, laws, and methods of architecture are deeply rooted in the past. Even though we use new materials and new technologies today, our buildings are still heavily influenced by the past. Churches today still look like churches in the Middle Ages. So, the history of the discipline still informs the present practice of the discipline. The significance of today's buildings is still determined to a large degree through their relationships to buildings of the past. Architecture should reflect its "nature," and history presents a way to understand this nature. New meanings are better understood if they allude to familiar meanings from the past.

In a way, one could compare the need of history for architects with our own need of memories and experiences. Just as we rely on them to guide us in our everyday behavior, so knowing historical buildings will guide architects in making their own designs. However, no one should become a slave to history. Theodor Adorno's advice to Germans about how to deal with their Nazi past also applies to how architects should deal with the history of architecture. He posited that one could either end the past, simply forgive and forget, or consciously process and digest the past. Ending one's past destroys memory and questions historical continuity. Such a total loss of history means that mankind has no memory, and that concrete time disappears. We would then become strangers to ourselves. A better strategy is to process and digest the past, because processing will strengthen the individual. He or she sees itself as part of the objective world and less as part of a collective.

Familiarity with history assists architects in becoming better at what they are doing. A survey conducted among architectural practitioners in Europe asked them what qualities they preferred in their new hires. The survey resulted in the following top ten:

1. Capacity to think and understand critically and analytically
2. Skills in expression and communication
3. Work in interdisciplinary team
4. Work with both autonomy and collaboration
5. Create designs that are both esthetically and technically proficient
6. Capacity to apply knowledge in practice
7. Design skills to meet user requirements within budget and building regulations
8. Evaluate evidence and draw conclusions
9. "Learning to learn" ability
10. Ability to develop transdisciplinary understanding

Design skills do not even make it into the top ten. This suggests that architectural firms do value interpersonal and communal attitudes and character traits. Such abilities are best taught in history classes, as it is there that architectural students learn about the economical, social, and technological relationships that ultimately turn a design into reality.

This book provides a perspective on architectural history geared towards architects, not historians. Its explanations emphasize buildings first, laying out the historical background second. In this approach, it is heavily influenced by Walter Benjamin's "Theses on the Philosophy of History." There, Benjamin advocates that

> history should be mediate through the present
> history is not a continuum, but rather a chain of "now-times"
> historical events should be understood as authentic moments, that interrupt the continuum and are isolated from past, present, and future
> these instances of now-time are created by applying a shock to the continuous system of history
> an epoch is blown out of the homogeneous course of history
> a life is blown out of the epoch
> an individual work is blow out of the life work of an artist

Through this, one becomes historically responsible. That is, one begins to anticipate the new by remembering the past. Ultimately, Benjamin advises us to feel historical events, or as he put it, to understand through redemption. (See Walter Benjamin, "Theses on the Philosophy of History," in *Illuminations,* pp. 253–264)

The concept of the "world in front of the work" is an important tool in achieving such a personal interpretation of a work of architecture. Just as a musician performs a piece from a sheet of musical notations, without advice on how to play each note, so we stand in front of buildings without a manual on how to interpret it. Musicians use their experience to guide them in their performances. Architects use intuition tempered through criticism. Of course, this act of interpretation separates the work from its (historical) background, just like Benjamin advises. The world in front of the work is our world, not the work's one. The personal interpretation confronts the intentions of the creative mind and times that produced it in the first place. (Stephen Parcell, "The Work in Front of the Work," *Journal of Architectural Education,* Vol. 46 [May 1993] pp. 249–259)

**FIGURE 1.** Civic Centre, Jones and Kirkland, Mississauga, Canada (1987), This façade looks like the stage scenery for an opera, and does not project the solid impression one would expect of a building that should represent the civic values of the citizens of Mississauga.

**FIGURE 2.** Neue Staatsgalerie, James Stirling, Stuttgart (1977-1984), This building has inserted itself gracefully into the public realm by not only providing museum spaces, but also offering itself as a foot path to lead people from the busy street in the foreground to the residential quarter behind.

# Chapter 1

# Origins

The year 2750 BCE was a spectacular year for architecture. In Southern England, the first stages of Stonehenge were erected. In Mesopotamia, ziggurats were built in the first large cities. In Egypt the great pyramids introduced straight lines and vertical extension into architecture. These three geographic locations were at different stages of evolution, and demonstrate a telescoped image of the beginning of architecture. Significant architectural activity began after the melting of the last Ice Age, around 12,000 BCE.

Architecture may actually have already existed, in ridges, valleys, hills, caves, and so on. Such topographical features brought the concept of boundary into building. Apart from defining space in this manner, architecture for human use primarily provided shelter. One of the main problems associated with the origins of architecture is whether it arose from the crafts or from an artistic sense. In painting, the earliest examples are naturalistic, indicating their origin in the imitation of life, not in abstract principles. Gottfried Semper (1803-79) proposed in the 19th century that architecture originated in the crafts. He defined the essential elements of architecture and the craft in which they originated as: the hearth (ceramics, metalworking), the platform (masonry), the frame and roof (joinery/carpentry), and the walls (weaving). Wilhelm Worringer (1881-1965) believed that art is different from nature. He suggested that a simple urge to imitate does not produce genuine art. Instead, artistic volition, especially the urge to abstract living beings and objects, is at the beginning of art. This urge stems from a deep inner worry about the phenomena of the world. The transition of man from animal relying on touch to human relying on vision produced a spiritual fear of space. Through abstraction, a living object is removed out of its natural context, and placed in an ideal, non-threatening sphere. This isolation restored the unities of the external world. Thus, while art protected against the spirits and powers of the environment, architecture provided physical shelter.

Monumental architecture begins with abstract designs that indicate a process of intellectualization and rationalization. At Carnac (3000 BCE), when Paleolithic hunters evolved into Neolithic farmers, large stones were placed upright as markers into an alignment consisting of ten to thirteen rows of granite megaliths running for several miles. This constituted an act of organization that fixed space as a place under the sky. The alignment was different from the common world of experience, and contrasted to it an abstract, regular super-world. Such megaliths seem liberated from the earth, instead tracing the movement of the clouds in the sky in the form of circumscription. Taken individually, they embody the philosophy of the cool. In their commanding posture, they manifest correct physical and mental comportment: stiff, spiritual, and upright. They stress a generalized humanity, not individual and personal ambition.

Large upright stones may have stood for the dead, in a form of stylization, and were also used for tombs consisting of an enclosure of upright stones for walls and horizontal ones for roofs. Forms were box- (dolmen), gallery-, and passage-like. In the latter, the burial chamber is round and covered by corbelling. Tombs were covered with earth, having thus rather an interior emphasis. In this, they already expressed the enclosure of space. The Chapel at Ronchamp (1950-55) by Le Corbusier uses a similar form.

## STONEHENGE (2750-1500 BCE)

Stone circles were erected in the period from circa 2500 to 1000 BCE, primarily in the British Isles. Most probably they arose out of the circular ritual enclosures known to date from early on in the Neolithic period (in the form of cairns, heaps of stones piled up as memorials). These arose from the intention to propitiate the dangers of nature: elements, wild animals. The pits underneath were filled with earth and charcoal. These monuments were intended to secure man and woman's well-being now and in the afterlife. Art assisted in controlling the environment and in intervening in the cause of events, especially those that man cannot control himself.

These circles were possibly meeting places to be attended at particular times of the year. They had more than one purpose. Trading, religious rites, tribal meetings, and moots may have been conducted at these monuments. Architecturally, they form sacred precincts, enclosures.

The first written record of the circle at Stonehenge dates from 1130 CE, in Henry of Huntington's *History of England*. In 1136, a historian claimed Merlin had built it as a tomb, with stones brought from Ireland. In 1620, Inigo Jones proposed that it was a Roman building. At the same time, Celtic priests, the Druids, were named as builders, referring to the pre-Roman inhabitants of Britain. In the late 17th century, John Aubrey first dated this monument to prehistoric times, since similar circles were found in places known not to have been occupied by historically recorded invaders. Aubrey also discovered the holes lining the outside of Stonehenge. However, the Celts were an Iron Age culture that lived long after Stonehenge was begun. 19th- and 20th-century excavations, especially of the surrounding burial mounds, have suggested that Stonehenge was built by people who came to England during the Early Stone Age from the European mainland. They traveled by boat and reached the Salisbury Plain via the river Avon. During the next few centuries, this culture changed from a hunting-and-gathering tradition to a herding-and-farming tradition. For these people, the Northern direction seemed significant, indicating a connection to the moon, most probably relating the moon to death. The sun, in contrast, was associated with the seasons, and hence with life.

Stonehenge was built in stages. The first building activity was probably completed in 3200 BCE. It was started as an ordinary henge, a circular earthen enclosure with bank and outer ditch. Four stones were placed upright in the direction of the northernmost moonrise. At the center of this ring may have been a timber building. Just inside this original henge fifty-seven pits–the so-called Aubrey holes–were dug. They contain artifacts, human remains, earth, and charred wood. An avenue was built from the river Avon to the monument, lined by the same banks as the original circle.

Between 3200 and 2500 BCE, a double concentric circle of bluestones was erected inside. These stones came from a quarry in Wales, and were either transported to the site by boat or brought there naturally through glaciation. By 2500 BCE, the horseshoe of five trilithons was erected. The technical refinement of this building campaign is impressive. The alignment changed from the moon to the sun. An entrance, flanked by two stones, was left in the northeast, with an outlier, the heel stone beyond. Standing in the center at summer solstice, the heel stone marked the point where the sun appeared. Four additional station stones describe a rectangle perpendicular to the midsummer sunrise axis. This part of Stonehenge was built by the first generation of the Bronze Age culture.

During the late 3rd millennium BCE (ca. 2150 BCE), the interior of Stonehenge was transformed, and a ditch (immediately refilled) was dug around the heel stone.

Around 1500 BCE, the bluestones were reused for an additional stone circle between the horseshoe trilithons and the sarsen circle. Further out, two fresh rings of pits (the Y and Z holes) were added.

Thus ends the long building campaign of this monument. It was probably abandoned circa 1100 BCE.

From its beginning, this monument had definite sightlines built into it, which points to its designers' concern for them. The heel stone is placed on the sightline from the center toward the position of the sun at midsummer (summer solstice) sunrise. In addition, there are fifty-three stake holes across the entry, in eleven rows, six deep, which are oriented to the midwinter rising of the moon. Three post holes to the northwest, outside the henge, may have served as alignments on midsummer sunset and midwinter moonset. Furthermore, the henge seems to have been located in this place because the extreme northern and southern risings and settings of sun and moon are at right angles to one another. There are four stations inside the circle enclosing a rectangle whose side provides the lines toward these celestial points (the rectangle is perpendicular to the axis of the midsummer sunrise). The height of particular stones was set differently, so that they matched the visible horizon line.

Originally, the monument was aligned along the lunar points. In the beginnings of agriculture, the moon was regarded as a goddess. She was the giver of life and all that promotes fertility. Later on, the alignment changed to solar, to indicate a change in religious orientation to sky and earth gods.

Another theory holds that Stonehenge lies at a significant point on one of the energy lines that distribute the sun's energy through the earth. This line extends from Stonehenge to the Great Pyramid at Gizah.

Stonehenge was probably an open-air observatory where a wide range of astronomical phenomena could be predicted with marvelous precision. However, the care and effort spent on its construction make it more than that. Here, celestial events were more celebrated than predicted. It was a sacred center of community for the tribes that used it. It provided a setting for ritual that makes of each user, for a brief moment, a larger person than he or she is in daily life, filling each one with the pride of belonging. In modern terms, it accommodated the epiphany (appearance or manifestation of a divine being) of gods in relation to the calendar. This was architecture as a power. The emphasis was on use, not on looking at something. Whether something was working was more important than whether it was beautiful.

Standing at the altar stone and facing the avenue, one's view crossed a series of concentric rings, from the stone circles to the earthen embankment. Thus, Stonehenge provides a measure of aesthetic pleasure.

# ZIGGURATS

Geographically, Mesopotamia is divided into three parts: in the north a hilly terrain with deep river valleys and strips of desert and steppe, in the middle a flood plain, and in the south a lagoon. The fertile valleys of the Euphrates and Tigris Rivers enabled human beings to become sedentary, which in turn led to the establishment of cities and the organization of ceremonies and rituals.

Architectural forms were determined by the conditions of the land: climate, available building materials, and economic structure, as well as the demands of religion, state, and society. Local materials were reeds, clay, and sand. Wood and stone had to be imported. Mesopotamian building technology relied on massive walls, flat roofs, and cubical building forms. Articulation of the flat façades became an important aspect of architecture.

## White Temple, Uruk (3500-3000 BCE)

This temple was placed in the center of the city, and marks the evolution from open-air sanctuary to enclosed one. It is placed on a forty feet tall platform with sloping sides of paneled brickwork with protruding buttresses. This articulation imitated vernacular architecture, as it is still found today in the reed huts in the deltas of the Euphrates and Tigris rivers.

The temple was of rammed earth construction, and also had wood ornament inserted in the recesses between the buttresses. Worshippers entered the temple through a side chamber. The imposing doorways at either end of the sanctuary were entrances for the gods. Inside the long cella, an altar niche and offering table faced the main entrance. Lateral chambers extended from the main room. This plan would later be repeated for many religious interiors, including the Christian basilica.

The temple placed on a tall platform indicates the reconciliation of heaven and earth as the locations of the primary forces of prehistoric religion. Here, the concept was that the earth gods dwell in the mountain platform; the sky gods use the top as a resting place. The main feature of the early religious buildings was the long central hall. Walls were generally decorated with cone mosaics made of clay arranged in geometric patterns and consisting of the colors red, white, and black.

## Ziggurat, Ur (2150-2050 BCE)

King Ur-Nammu, ruling in the last phase of the Mesopotamian civilization, established the characteristic ziggurat form. This monument features the characteristic massive walls, flat roof, and cubical building form that the available building materials in Mesopotamia allowed. This ziggurat (the first known one) consists of three successive platforms, which were climbed through a complicated system of stairs. The temple corners were oriented to the cardinal points of the compass. Construction was of a core of mud bricks with an exterior cover of burnt brick. The base measures 200 by 150 feet.

Ziggurats were symbolic stairs into heaven. Here, for the first time, a large building mass is oriented according to the vertical direction. An additional symbolism is that of the mountain.

# PYRAMIDS

Like Mesopotamia, Egypt relied on the Nile River for its continued fertility. Its water irrigated the fields and its yearly floods fertilized the fields. It dictated the main seasons of the ancient Egyptians, *Inundation* (June - October), *Emergence of the Fields from the Water* (November - February), and *Drought* (March - May). Every year, the floods swept away the field boundary markers, and the people had to perfect a system of geometry and mathematics, so that these boundaries could be redefined to everyone's satisfaction. The Nile gave the Egyptians an eternal north-south axis, which complemented the east-west axis of the sun.

Egyptians understood their world as an unchanging continuum, not as subject to the whims of gods. Their view of life was very conservative. They worked to ensure a continuously pleasurable life, both here and in the afterlife.

Farming villages existed as early as 5500 BCE. Two cultures developed in Upper and Lower Egypt. They were united by Menes in 3100 BCE. There followed a peaceful period from 2700 - 2200 BCE, the Old Kingdom. The pharaos (kings) ruled absolutely, and a centralized government was responsible for control of the water. After a breakup of absolute power, in the First Intermediate Period, 2200 to 2052 BCE, there followed the Middle Kingdom, 2052 - 1786 BCE. The capital shifted from Memphis to Thebes, and the priests became more powerful. After the Second Intermediate Period, 1786 - 1575 BCE, the New Kingdom began in 1575 and lasted till 1087 BCE. By 1000 BCE, the Empire had ended, and a slow decline began until it was conquered, first by the Persians, then by Alexander the Great, and finally by the Romans.

## MORTUARY COMPLEX OF KING ZOSER, IMHOTEP, SAQQARA (2750 BCE)

Egyptian stone architecture began as imitation of earlier traditions used to serve the royal cult of the dead. The post-and-lintel structure of the temples probably derived from the same structure used in the earlier tents. Flat terraces are a characteristic feature of Egyptian monumental architecture.

This sanctuary is revolutionary: it was built of limestone, and introduced the pyramid form to architecture. The complex was enclosed by a niched wall, thirty-four feet high. It covers an area measuring 1788 by 909 feet. The true entrance is in the southeast, although there are many false gates. Upon passing, one enters a columned hall in the form of a corridor, with spur walls terminating in engaged columns. This hall leads to a large courtyard with two altars in the central North-south axis. The court is bounded by masonry walls on the east (with stepped terraces) and west sides, and the pyramid on the northern one. On the southern wall is a dummy tomb. The stepped pyramid began as a simple mastaba. To accommodate more burial chambers, the original mastaba was enlarged, and a new one put on top. Entry to the underground burial chambers (ca. 100 feet below the base of the pyramid) is on the northern side. In front of this entrance was the original mortuary temple. Still farther north, just inside the enclosing wall, was an altar that was cut into existing rock, and originally covered in marble veneer.

Off the entrance corridor one also entered a second courtyard with a temple and dummy chapels on either side. Most buildings were sham structures, with niches or corridors for cult statues. The only useable structures were the entrance hall, the sacristy, and the living quarters for the dead king on the north side of the pyramid. There were additional courtyards in the complex, and two buildings identical in shape, the "House of the South" and the "House of the North." Both consist of dummy chapels and forecourts. These are imaginary palaces, and symbolize the pharaoh's reign over both Upper and Lower Egypt. They are decorated with engaged fluted papyrus columns. The southern one imitates tent structures; the northern one imitates reed structures. The whole complex is arranged orthogonally, but not axially. Many surface features are used to articulate the forms. The use of dummy structures indicates the symbolic character of this complex. On an immediate level, it imitates urban and palace architecture.

## PYRAMIDS, GIZA (2680-2500 BCE)

In Egypt, art and architecture glorified the pharaohs, who personified divine power. These structures indicate a change in planning and design of tomb architecture. The tomb was no longer a residence, and the funerary complex no longer a stage for rituals. What mattered was not that the architectural forms were pretty, but that they were complete. The principal theme of pyramid tombs was that of a processional stage along a sacred way, defined by a succession of rooms, passages, courts, gates, and pillars. The procession ended in the tomb chamber.

These three pyramids represent the culmination of pyramid building in Egypt. Each of them is perfectly aligned toward the North Star and the axis of the sun perpendicular to this. As in most Egyptian architecture, simple stereometric shapes and strict geometric organization prevail. Overall form and its individual external planes are not linked in an organic manner.

The first constructed was that of Cheops (Khufu), the second pharaoh of the 4th dynasty. It is the largest, and has lost its original top layer. It contains a burial chamber almost exactly in the center of the pyramid's mass. The second was for Khufu's son, Chephren (Khafre), third pharaoh of the 4th dynasty. This one measured 707 feet square and 470 feet high. It still has some of the original limestone cover on top. The last was erected for Khafre's son, Mycerinus (Menkure). This is the smallest, measuring 356 feet square and 281 feet high.

The pyramids were approached through canals from the Nile. At their end stood a valley temple with auxiliary buildings. A causeway then led to the East side of the pyramids. At their foot was a mortuary temple and a necropolis. Entrances are on the northern sides.

Pyramids consist of an inner mound of local stone and an outer facing of limestone. In actual construction, the inner core, triangular in shape, was surrounded by masonry buttress walls, inclining inward at an angle of 75°. The exterior casing stones were laid slightly inclined toward the center. Tools used were of wood, stone, and copper. No wheeled vehicles were employed. The stone blocks (limestone) were pulled on sleds or rolled over logs. The building sites were leveled by means of trenches filled with water. The stones were most probably pulled along a circular ramp made of earth.

Construction took place during the period of inundation, when farming ceased and the water was at the level of the pyramids. Most probably, the construction workers were not slaves, but inhabitants of the kingdom. Securing the afterlife of the representative of God on earth, namely the pharaoh, also secured their own.

Egyptians seemed to have considered architecture to be monuments of visual art, not buildings. Their forms present material entities with planar exteriors that do not give any clue to the three-dimensional space inside. Even their temples, with their tapered walls, still refer to the pyramids, more so since they do not have windows. The external planes of many Egyptian buildings are decorated with non-tectonic scenes. Their spatial conception also emphasized the interior as a material entity. Hence, the interiors are either open to the top, or filled with supports, that is, with stone individuals inside a space individual.

As with most Egyptian buildings, the pyramids too are an architecture of great mass and monotonous regularity. They impress by their sheer size, and by the precision used in their construction. Articulation is abolished to strengthen the effect of the surfaces and masses.

The development from Saqqara to Giza is one of abandoning of pictographic motifs toward a greater systematization of space and increasing abstraction.

FIGURE 1–1. Stone Circle, Stonehenge. Shows the post-and-lintel construction of the outer circle and the taller trilithons of the horseshoe-shaped inner sanctuary. One post shows the tendon used to secure the horizontal lintels to the vertical posts.

FIGURE 1–2. Stonehenge, Detail

FIGURE 1–3. Mortuary complex of King Zoser, Saqqara View of the ruins showing the Stepped Pyramid and the Houses of the North and South.

**FIGURE 1–4.** Pyramids of Cheops (left) and Chephren.

**FIGURE 1–5.** Sphinx with the Pyramid of Chephren.

# Chapter 2

# Houses, Cities, and Gardens

A warming of the earth produced the Neolithic "revolution." The origins of the city are found in social organization and human behavior. Human beings have a disposition toward social life. Through communal engineering, they changed the environment. Freestanding buildings precede the organization of villages. Such buildings include those that satisfied the ceremonial concern for the dead, and natural shelters like caves. The practical benefits of an area, such as fertility of the land, availability of water, and protection through topography may also have led to the foundation of a city. In addition, there is the need to secure food provision for a large group.

## HOUSE, UR

Depending wholly on agriculture and increasing the skill of growing and producing food were the main reasons for the devel-opment of cities in southern Mesopotamia. There was obviously a long history before the third millennium BCE of living together in villages and small towns. But it was around this time that early civilizations formed cities. The fertility came from irrigation technology and was not natural to the area. Politically, Mesopotamia was based on city-states, which consisted of a capital city and surrounding villages. The city-states belonged to the gods, who had installed the kings as caretakers; their task being to bring peace and prosperity to the people.

Houses and palaces were generally laid out around a central courtyard. At this time, the typical courtyard house was formulated. Palaces had more than just one courtyard. Windows were only on inside walls, doorways were covered with a wood lintel, and flat roofs were constructed of tree trunks and reeds, and covered with earth and clay. The mud-bricks of the walls were laid on end, leaning diagonally against each other in alternate layers, forming a herringbone pattern. The cubical spaces and the courtyard plan point to a cell-like structure for houses. Larger houses simply contain *more* spaces, not larger ones.

## HOUSES, BANPO (3<sup>RD</sup> MILLENIUM BCE)

This agricultural village covered 2½ acres on a riverbank. It consisted of three distinct parts: a residential area, the pottery kiln, and necropolises. Four layers of houses were found in the residential district. The earliest houses were circular wattle-and-daub huts with reed roofs and plaster floors. A ditch for drainage and defense surrounded the entire residential area. A fire pit for heating and cooking was in the center. The form was most probably copied from earlier tents.

Subsequent houses were of square or rectangular plan, constructed of a timber frame with wooden planking, sunk several feet below ground, and accessible through stairs. They had southern exposure. The roofs of larger buildings were supported on rows of wooden supports.

## JERICHO

At Jericho (8000 BCE), the availability of water was the generating principle. This site provides detailed remains of a Neolithic city. It had ca. 2,000 inhabitants. Jericho is famous for a public work on a scale that presupposes community cooperation and division of labor: a wall. It was built of large boulders held in place without mortar. It is six feet thick at the bottom, and stands twelve feet tall. On the inside, it is supported by rubble and rock fill. Inside the wall is a tower measuring thirty feet in diameter. Many houses were built against its inner face. Outside this wall was a ditch carved into rock and measuring nine feet deep and twenty-seven feet wide. This wall is documented in the Old Testament. Genuine streets are missing from this city.

# ÇATAL HÜYÜK

At Çatal Hüyük (6000 BCE), trade with obsidian (best available material for cutting tools) provided the rationale for settlement. In addition, traces of metalworking were found. This city covered thirty-two acres and housed approximately 6000 people. The layout suggests a pre-existing master plan. There are no fortifications. The houses are in tight groupings without streets. Open courtyards were used as garbage dumps and public lavatories. Ashes from the house fires would be spread over the refuse to contain the smell and to prevent flies and mosquitoes from assembling. The entire appearance of this city demonstrates the existence of the social process of forming a community, that is, the interaction of people with one another to achieve communal goals. The characteristics of the domestic house were already established: entry and light from above, no detached houses. Shared walls are economical and efficient. Houses had one rectangular room with storage space to one side. Built-in platforms on two served as beds, one for the men, the other for the women and children. The construction consisted of a timber framework of posts and beams, which also provided the main wall division and elevation. Mud-brick infill was plastered over. The roofs rested on a timber frame, which supported a mat of river reeds that had been woven closely and prevented bits of the plaster from falling inside. On top of this were bundles of reeds tied together and laid in rows. On top of this was a thick layer of mud that was covered with plaster made from a local white clay. The roof had to prevent rain from entering the house, and had to be sturdy enough to serve as passage to and from the houses to the outside. It appears that the roofs were yearly renovated.

There were also shrines decorated with plaster reliefs and paintings dealing with a cult of the mother goddess. The bull represents the goddess's constant companion, and stylized heads of bulls function as cult objects. Offerings of the early harvest were made to the Fertility Goddess at the Leopard Shrine, decorated with two facing leopards in plaster relief. After the hunt, a feast was consumed in the Hunting Shrine, which was decorated with paintings of hunters and deer. The Vulture Shrine was used for burial. Dead people were left on racks for the vultures to pick the bones dry. Then the bones were buried in the sleeping platforms.

This village expresses a clear self-view as a city community. Çatal Hüyük presents a telescoped view of human history from the Stone Age hunter to the city dweller. It is one of man's first tries in the development of city life. The wildness of the horned beast is at home with agricultural technology, and hunter and farmer live side by side with the specialist in metalwork and the merchant.

# BABYLON (612 BCE)

Laid out in ca. 2000 BCE, Babylon enclosed roughly a rectangle of 2,500 x 1,500 m, divided by the Euphrates. It was rebuilt in 612 BCE, after the fall of the Assyrian Empire, and was among the largest cities in antiquity.

Babylonian city planning combined Sumerian and Assyrian features, namely the geometric order, central placing of religious building, and eccentric placing of palace. The rationality of the plan has its basis in the practice of the military state. Due to the rational, rectangular street layout, divisions between public and private buildings became less apparent; the city was consequently rather divided into different quarters, of which the innermost ones were only accessible to the kings and priests.

The inner city on a roughly rectangular plan was fortified with the perimeter wall measuring five miles. The city wall was doubled, with pairs of towers at sixty-five-foot intervals. The moat was navigable and connected to the river. There were six gates, the main one the Ishtar Gate (575 BCE), leading to the palace. The main buildings inside were the ziggurat with temple, and the palace of Nebuchadnezzar. This palace was behind the Ishtar Gate, and contained the Hanging Gardens, a system of garden terraces. Five yards are lined up in a chain. They were connected through porticoes.

## HANGING GARDENS, BABYLON

These were built by a prince who wanted to create an environment for his Persian bride that would remind her of home. A 400 feet square platform was supported on levels of arches. The garden wall had battlements and bulwarks. The platform was carried on stone beams and covered with reeds imbued with bitumen. Two layers of mortared tiles were laid on this, which was in turn covered by sheets of lead. Then, a layer of earth was laid on top and planted with trees. Irrigation water was pumped from the river Euphrates.

## Ishtar Gate (575 BCE)

This gate was associated with processional entry into Babylon with emphasis on ceremony. This consisted of four towers and a huge rectangular gatehouse. Its facades were faced with glazed bricks and reliefs of lions, bulls and mythical animals. Parts of the decoration, such as rosettes (imitating buttons?), were inspired by textile fabrics. The reliefs were constructed of individually cast bricks.

# MOHENJO DARO, INDUS VALLEY (3RD MILLENIUM BCE)

This site, meaning "Hill of the Dead," was discovered in 1922 under a 2nd-century Buddhist monastery. Since then, the main research question has been whether this culture was imported – from Mesopotamia – or originated locally.

This civilization had originally settled on higher altitudes. A population increase, combined with an enlarged economy, technological inventions in metallurgy, and an increase in trade, marked the beginning of a social hierarchization derived from the specialization in crafts. Consequently, cities were relocated to the flat land.

In Mohenjo Daro, architecture was composed of private houses, public buildings, and a water and sewage system. This was an urban civilization. It either centered on the two cities, Mohenjo Daro and Harappa, or consisted of four provinces. The social system is not yet totally clear. Either, it relied on a theocratic or imperial government, or was determined by a class or guild organization. Interestingly, neither temples, nor palaces, nor cemeteries were found, all building types which would support a class structure. Instead, the towns were full of houses. The variety of house types and their spatial distribution implies complex social structure. It seems clear that this suggests the beginning of urban planning. What counted was the city – a rigidly planned arrangement of standardized structures and works.

Mohenjo Daro's plan appears modern and rational, with a simple presence. Massive defensive walls surrounded the city. Usually to the west, there was a separate citadel/acropolis, seemingly the site for the town elite. This was built on higher ground. The lower city was to the east. Both were placed on manmade platforms (the one for the lower city was probably of clay). Cities were oriented along the cardinal points. North-south streets were the main thoroughfares, followed a straight line, and were laid out ca. every 170 m; east-west ones were bent and sometimes not continuous. Main streets were ca. ten m wide. Narrower alleys accessed the residential quarters. There were no cul-de-sacs, hence the streets did form an incomplete and irregular grid. All of this suggests that cities were planned with predetermined guidelines, and following a social hierarchy. Remains suggest that neighborhoods were separated according to the productive specialization of the inhabitants. The concept of the city was based on a collectivist utilitarianism and a planned functionalism. Monuments are lacking, as are variations in taste and conceptions. Public utilities existed, such as public baths, drainage canals, and a sewage system. Brick-lined open sewers ran along the streets. Occasional catch basins collected larger debris. House drains opened into an open gutter, which connected to the street sewer. Some houses had brick toilets.

The houses had central courtyards, on which doors and windows opened. Toward the street, they presented blank walls. Rooms were arranged around the courtyard. Five different plan types, differentiated according to the placement of entrance and courtyard, were found. Entrances led to side streets. Main roads were consequently flanked by solid walls. Buildings were constructed of air-dried, standardized bricks, which were formed in wooden molds, and with timber for the upper stories. This system may have brought the decline of the Indus Valley culture. It eventually produced an ecological change through the deforestation in the valley due to construction needs. This deforestation also increased the floods. The rectangularity of the building suggests that this civilization had instruments to determine horizontals and verticals.

To the West of the citadel was the Great Bath, one of the largest buildings. This was used as a public bathing facility and for ritual washings. In its center was a basin, thirty-nine feet long, twenty-five feet wide, and eight feet deep, accessible to the north and south by stairs. The basin is constructed of double brick walls with an inch-thick covering of asphalt under a layer of bricks set on edge into gypsum mortar. The floor sloped toward a drain. There are concentric ambulatories around this basin. On the north side are a series of smaller bathrooms. It is believed that bathing was considered a religious duty.

Further west from the great bath is a structure believed to have been used for grain storage. Hypothetical reconstructions have proposed that these were platforms, on which a wooden structure was placed. However, there is no evidence for this, as well as for the function of this structure.

A large number of cylindrical wells were also found in this city, suggesting that it had an independent water supply system. It appears that two fundamental factors influenced this settlement. On one hand, the platforms indicate the need to be protected from the floods of the Indus River; on the other, the wells suggest a provision to secure water even when the river dried out.

It is not clear why this culture ended. Various theories proposed include emigration to avoid the Aryan invasion, a flood of the River Indus, or the drying out of the river. The structure as it exists today was reconstructed in 1925-27. In 1967, this site was placed on the UNESCO list of world heritage sites.

# PANELS, NINEVEH (668-627 BCE)

The Tigris valley around Babylon was also the area of the first garden. This was probably the biblical Eden (=delight). Gardens evolved out of agriculture, and their development was fueled by powerful symbolism: Paradise and Garden of Eden.

Gardens could simply be places set apart. In Mesopotamia, parks were extensive walled places, with animals to be hunted: zoo. They had grass, woodlands, and animals, and were used for entertainment and relaxation (hunting), as well as to simply escape the city heat. The concept of the vacation may have been invented here. The animals and fruit trees were in accord with Genesis.

Gardens are reactions to environmental conditions. There is a contrast between garden and landscape. The land is wild; the garden is enclosed, fertile, and rich with vegetation. The land is dry and hot; the garden has water, is cool, and has shade. The land is vast; the garden is ordered and tranquil.

From this comes the concept of the Paradise garden: the term "paradise" means walled garden. Its main features are the division into four parts through the rivers of life, with a mountain at their intersection, and an enclosure. The paradise garden has religious meaning: For those who believe and do good work, there will be a garden of Eden (Koran). This has rivers of water, milk, and honey, fruits, and is used for relaxation.

# ADDITIONAL BUILDINGS AND MONUMENTS

## PERSEPOLIS (518-460 BCE)

Cyrus the Great conquered Babylon in 539 BCE and established the Persian dominance over Mesopotamia. In 518 BCE, Persepolis was made the capital by the emperor Darius. The building campaign was completed in 460 BC.

Persepolis was intended as the spiritual sanctuary of the Achaemenid Empire. Based on its decoration, it is believed that the Persian king had a cosmic kingship. The platform can be interpreted as a means to observe and record the movements of the heavens. The goals of this complex were to display the splendors and majesty of the world's first empire.

Here, the influence from Greece and other cultures is noticeable. Palaces were built on platforms, in imitation of earlier Mesopotamian traditions. The same influence accounts for the walls, which were of mud-bricks with glazing. Wooden columns were used, and wall openings framed in stone. The Greek influence is revealed above all in the relief sculpture, which became less schematic and more three-dimensional, as well as in the use of Ionian columns. These reliefs were used on the exterior walls of the terraces.

In spite of the long building campaign, this palace appears as a rationally planned ensemble. The design suggests that a master plan existed before construction began. Underground channels used to carry off water do not interfere with the main points and lines of load. The main axis of the complex runs north-south, along the longest dimension of the platform, and all the structures follow this axis.

The platform was established from a natural rock terrace, which projects 5800 feet from the rugged hillside. Natural level differences were exploited to make three surfaces at different heights. A limestone retaining wall was placed around the three projecting sides of the terrace. Mud-brick walls were raised along the edges of the platform. Eventually, the entire platform was filled with structures. There are corridors between the buildings, and staircases. Construction is in stone, although the technique is rather that of wood carpentry or sculpture. There is no standard stone size. However, the stones were dressed, so that joints are hardly visible. The ashlars are held together with iron clamps in lead beds.

One main stairway leads from the plain to the platform. This is a double reversing stairway in two flights.

Darius completed the platform, the main stairway, the triple portal, and his palace. He began the treasury and the apadama. Xerxes completed the apadana, the portico, his palace with the harem; he also began the throne hall. This was completed by Artaxerxes, together with a portico.

Upon reaching the platform, there is a Gateway to All Lands. Colossal figures of winged bulls are attached to piles of masonry. These structures are at either end of the gateway. This was a chamber eighty-two feet square. Its roof was supported by four columns.

Behind this was the apadana. This audience hall was raised eight feet above the gateway level. Two staircases gave access to the interior. On their walls are depicted representatives of the lands of the empire, shown paying tribute to the king. There are also processions. The walls of the stairway are made of stone slabs placed on the rock platform. The apadana consists of a hall with thirty-six columns and columnar porticoes. It measured 197 feet square, and was sixty-five feet high. In its articulation, it was not very functional for the purpose of an audience hall. The interior was rather dark.

The construction sequence was started with the columns and capitals. Then, portal and window jambs, as well as lintels, were placed. The spaces in between this framework were filled with mud-brick walls, seventeen feet thick. Then, the roof beams were fixed in a grid, onto which a secondary grid of smaller timbers was placed. The roof was made of a layer of planks and straw mats, onto which gravel and soil were placed. The exterior surfaces of mud-bricks were extensively decorated with glazed bricks. The throne hall was a hypostyle hall of 100 columns. It was accessed by a processional corridor from the main gate. The entrance was a central portico with eight columns in two rows, placed in antis. The hall is 225 feet square, and the thirty-seven feet high columns are arranged in ten rows of ten.

Behind the apadana was the Palace of Darius. Together with the other palaces, this was a maze-like arrangement of rooms. The various palaces are on the highest level of the platform. In addition, there was the triple portico, the Palace of Xerxes, and three unidentified structures.

Behind the throne hall was the Treasury. This consisted of a courtyard with columned buildings around. It appears to have been the first building constructed on the platform. It housed the treasure of the empire.

Between the treasury and the palace of Xerxes was the harem. In addition, there are four-columned storerooms, stables, and military quarters. There was also a settlement on the plain beneath the platform.

FIGURE 2–1. Ishtar Gate, Detail (Pergamon Museum, Berlin, Germany)

**FIGURE 2–2.** Persepolis, view of columns and the reliefs on the retaining wall of the palace platform.

# Chapter 3

# Egyptian Temples

## MORTUARY COMPLEX OF QUEEN HATSHEPSUT, SENMUT, DEIR-EL-BAHARI (15$^{TH}$ C. BCE)

After the First Intermediate Period, the power of the kings declined. The construction of pyramids was superseded by tombs and temples. A trabeated system of construction replaced the megalithic mass.

This monument served as a mortuary temple for Hatshepsut, her father, and her husband, as well as for the cults of Amon and other gods.

The whole complex, built of limestone, consists of three terraces, connected by ramps, which divide the whole into a northern and southern half. These terraces assume the role of the missing pyramid, and were carved into existing rock, with additional masonry support. Along an axis that connects it to the Amon temple at Karnak were laid out a valley temple and a causeway lined by sphinxes. The western wall of the lowest level of the mortuary complex has two narrow halls, each supported by eleven pairs of piers and sixteen-sided columns. A ramp leads to the next higher terrace, also featuring a double colonnade. The two halls are the birth hall and the hall of Punt. At their sides are temples dedicated to Hathor and Anubis. On the top level was originally an open peristyle court, flanked by temples of Amon and Ra, which were cut into the cliff face. Most of the flat wall surfaces are decorated with paintings of the queen's life.

Here, an important architectural transformation took place. Previous structures had simply been articulated on their surfaces in imitation of a post-and-lintel frame (e.g., Ziggurat and Zoser pyramid). Now, the architecture has become the actual structural formation. The previous decorative articulation has become the frame that supports the building. In addition, true axially and orthogonally organized space has been realized. Partly, the older practices can still be recognized, as the mountain now takes the place of the pyramid, and the pyramid's vertical emphasis is repeated in the ascending ramps. In general, there is a greater variety in the individual details. This monument is remarkable in being aesthetically adapted to its natural setting.

## TEMPLE COMPLEX, KARNAK (CA. 1991-670 BCE)

Temples were places of worship, but also centers of learning and administration. They were intended as a representation of the Egyptian cosmos. The pylons were almost literal repetitions of the hieroglyph for world, a section through a valley with the sky above and the transversely moving sun inscribed.

The temple district of Karnak encompasses the Amon temple, as well as temples dedicated to Rameses III, Amenophis II, and Khonsu.

### TEMPLE OF AMON

This temple had existed since the Old Kingdom and became a major site after the 10$^{th}$ Dynasty. During the 18$^{th}$ Dynasty new buildings were erected, and the complex was subsequently enlarged. At Karnak, temples dedicated to other gods were added.

This district is not built after a coherent master plan. It was aligned toward the mid-winter sunrise. This east-west alignment may also have been dictated by the north-south direction of the Nile. Although it is thus in itself axially aligned, it is not the building's own, but that of the universe.

The planning principle of the temple was based on the worship of the sun in open courts, guarded in front and back by pylons and obelisks. Temples consisted of the following parts. They were approached through an avenue lined by sphinxes or rams, and entered through an entrance pylon. These pylons probably resulted from a process of thickening and raising the front walls of large courts on either side of an entrance gate. The pylon consisted of two towers with battered walls on all sides, beaded fillets at the corners, and an encircling concave cornice at the top. In the front wall were recesses, which on the holy days contained masts with pennants. Wooden braces projecting from narrow windows on top stabilized the masts. Inside the towers were stairs leading to the upper floors and the roof. The pylon gave the temple a strong accent and monumentality. It also suggests a fortress, thus rendering the temple defensive against hostile powers. Accordingly, they were decorated with the king's victorious battles. Hieroglyphic inscriptions, reliefs, and decoration were essential elements of Egyptian architecture, allowing still today the identification of deities and kings to which they were dedicated. They serve to interpret the whole building. Having passed the pylon, one acceded into an open forecourt enclosed by colonnades. Next came the hypostyle hall, beyond which lay the sanctuary reserved for the priest, and containing a barge. As on the exteriors of other buildings, the columns in the hypostyle hall are not decorated with tectonic illustrations. Indeed, it is only the cavetto molding on the pylons that alludes to form and gives the forms some expression of movement. At right angle to the main axis were side chambers for diverse uses. At the rear was a chamber containing an image of the god. The deeper one gets into the building, the smaller the rooms become, similar to the path of life back toward the origin.

The Temple of Amon consists of a total of six pylons. The extension to the south has an additional three pylons. The oldest part of the temple is the sanctuary behind the sixth pylon. During the 16th c. BCE, a large courtyard with columned halls was built around this, closed by the fifth pylon in the west. This was followed by the fourth pylon with a wall around the entire complex, and two obelisks in front. The hypostyle hall between fourth and fifth pylons was altered in the 15th c. BCE, and the sixth pylon was added. Toward the end of the 15th c. BCE, the third pylon was added. In the late 14th c. BCE, the second pylon was built, and in the 13th c. BCE, the great hypostyle hall was constructed. 134 papyrus columns, arranged in rows of sixteen, carry the ceiling. The two rows in the middle are higher; they have open capitals, whereas all others have closed ones. The middle row is opened through clerestory windows with stone grilles. This is the first monumental basilica interior of Egyptian architecture, i.e., a tall central aisle with lower side aisles. The first pylon was constructed in the 10th c. BCE. The courtyard behind this is flanked by two loggias, and contains two smaller temples.

Sacred lakes were permanent features of temples. They were the source for the holy water used in the rituals, and the scenes of the excursions of the sacred barges.

To the north and south of the main axis are additional temples, one dedicated to Mut, the consort of Amon, the other to Khonsu, the Moon God and child of Amon and Mut.

# TEMPLE OF AMON (RAMESES II) AND TEMPLE OF HATHOR (NEFERTITI), ABU SIMBEL (1250 BCE)

These were carved directly into rock. By building his own temple, Rameses II completed the final step toward full equality between god and king. The entrance portal is oriented to the East, to the rising sun. On February 20, and October 20, the first morning rays of the sun reach to the god figures at the rear wall of the sanctuary.

A ramp led to the terrace in front of the temple. The front of the terrace is decorated with representatives of various peoples paying homage to the king. The balustrade is formed of alternating statues of hawks and the king. Within a trapezoidal area, four colossal statues of king Rameses II (builder of the temple) were carved in imitation of earlier pylons. These statues represent the god image of the king. They express stylized calm and harmony. Between their legs are smaller statues representing members of Rameses's family. The upper border of the entrance facade is formed by a row of baboons greeting the rising sun.

The interior consists of a pillared hall, which imitates the main courtyard of traditional temples. Two rows, of four square pillars each, divide this room into three aisles. Statues of the God King in his Osiris image face the main aisle. Pillar surfaces and walls are decorated with images of the king in a variety of activities. The pillared hall is flanked on both sides by side chambers, which served as treasury and storage rooms. A hypostyle hall follows the pillared hall. Then comes a transverse chamber, leading to the sanctuary, which is flanked by two smaller rooms.

The smaller temple is laid out along a north-west south-east direction. Originally, this temple was accessible directly from the Nile via a pier. The façade consists of six statues of the king and his wife. Small statues flanking them represent their children. Behind the entrance is a pillared hall. Behind this is a transverse hall, which leads to the sanctuary.

The temples were moved to protect them from the rising waters of Lake Nasser in 1964-68.

# CONSTRUCTION

In Ancient Egypt, this involved special motives, thorough planning, and elaborate preliminary ceremonies. The king led a festive procession to the temple site. During the night, he fixed the four corner points and the orientation of the temple, with the help of the stars. Then followed the actual marking of the building. An elaborate groundbreaking then took place.

# EXPRESSION

Like the pyramids, these temples also did not change over time. The goal of Egyptian culture was continuity and order. Egyptian society was one in which man and nature were bound into a fixed pattern. Order and constancy indicate the basic aim of Egyptian architecture.

Mass and weight are abstracted so as to become part of a system of symbolic orientation, as are also the preponderance of horizontal and vertical. This level of abstraction can be called the first integrated architectural symbol system in the history of mankind. The architecture indicates the wish to present an eternal order in symbolic form. In general, Egyptian buildings form a synthesis of four intentions: the enclosed "oasis," the durable mass, the orthogonal order, and the path or axis. There is the intention to articulate, especially with vertical supports and horizontal moldings. Plant motifs were used in decorations to give every aspect of life an absolute eternal form.

# EXCURSUS: WILHELM WORRINGER'S *ABSTRACTION AND EMPATHY* (1910)

Worringer (1881-1965) introduced an interesting interpretation of Egyptian Architecture in this book. For him, art and nature have different esthetics. For long periods, art consisted of the imitation of nature. In the early 20th century, abstraction became important. Naturalistic art is understood through empathy. Hence, esthetic pleasure is self-pleasure, experienced through feeling life into the art (and architectural object). Form is then informed through my own feelings and emotions. Beauty exists if my empathy corresponds to that of the architectural object.

Abstract art created the need for a different manner of perception and understanding. In general, art works stem from artistic volition, which derives from a psychological attitude. For Worringer, this volition produces the urge to abstract, which stems from an inner worry about the phenomena of the world. In abstract art, there is an urge to be delivered from the arbitrariness of organic existence. This existence generates a spiritual fear of space.

Through abstraction, the object is removed from its natural context. Art can extract the natural object from the willfulness of its context. It makes objects absolute and establishes a "bodily" unity among objects.

Abstraction creates in the plane and suppresses spatial representation, and reproduction of individual form. It excludes everything sensual and treats the cubical as planar. Hence, depth is revealed as planar relationships. Abstract art produces stable points in a disturbing and changing world. The goal of abstract art is to create a conceptualization of the world, not a representation.

Consequently, Egyptian architecture expressed a fear of space. Its forms attempted to suppress the 3rd dimension, either by making buildings massive on the outside, thus appearing flat, or by filling the interiors with columns.

FIGURE 3–1. Mortuary Complex of Queen Hatsepsut, view to the North showing the terraces faced with rows of square columns.

FIGURE 3–2. Temple of Amon, Karnak, view of the ruins.

FIGURE 3–3. Temple of Amon, view of the reconstruction.

# Chapter 4

# Non-Western Architecture

Philosopher Karl Jaspers said in his book *The Origin and Goal of History*:

> The unity of mankind is impressively evident in the fact that similar basic traits of religion, forms of thought, implements, and social forms recur all over the earth." "In history, that which is unrepeatable and irreplaceable comes to light in unique creations, break-throughs and realizations . . . these creative steps . . . are like revelations from some other source than the mere course of happenings . . . they lay the foundations of the humanity that comes after. From them man acquires his knowledge and volition, his prototypes and antitypes, his criteria, his thought-patterns and his symbols, his inner world.

Asian architecture began as a form of design and construction that was closely and physically tied to the earth, both in terms of materials and topography. These particular origins have preserved a respect for things earthly that has been kept up to modern times. The care for building materials and construction, as well as the place of architecture in the greater scheme of the universe, are still seen in contemporary buildings.

## INDIA

### VEDIC CULTURE

Ca. 1500 BCE, Indo-European immigrants moved into India from the North and settled in the Ganges valley. These Aryans evolved later into the Hindus. Most of our knowledge about this culture stems from the Vedas (= knowledge), as architectural remains are scarce.

The towns seem to have been walled, a custom that may have continued in the Stupa fences. Houses were built either in mud-brick or with wooden weavings covered by mud. The first ones were circular, and later ones rectangular. This information comes primarily from illustrations of Vedic architecture on the Stupa at Sanchi.

### CAVES, BARABAR MOUNTAINS (CA. 250 BCE)

At first, these remains consisted of rock-cut architecture. These exemplify the stone carving skills of this culture. Both Buddhist and Hinduist architecture are primarily carved.

There are two kinds of spaces, either circular, or elongated and rectangular. The circular space is for the altar, and the rectangular for the congregation. This is the prototype of the later Chaitya Hall.

This activity expressed the rapport that Indians feel exists between the sacred sphere and the bowels of the earth. This technique presents almost no static requirements, although forms tend to preserve the forms of traditional interiors. The lighting presents a number of problems. Rock-cut architecture in general imitates wood structures. A characteristic feature is the use of the horseshoe arch for openings and vaults.

An interesting basic characteristic of Indian architecture was that the making of a building was more beneficial and important than the finished product. Hence, Western aesthetic approaches hardly work for Indian architecture.

The caves represent the cosmic night, that is, the darkness before everything originated. Visitors find there a center in which they can experience a rebirth from the "mother-house." The concept of the cave as heart was later continued into the practice of freestanding buildings.

## AJANTA (2ND C. BCE)

This is a series of monasteries partly carved into rock. These are chaityas with small stupas at the end. Thier plans feature a semicircular apse, and false aisles.

The resident monks lived in cells, which were carved around a large central hall. Access to the cells was provided through a veranda.

## STUPAS, SANCHI (5TH C., 237-232 BCE)

This form began as a tomb monument in the form of an earth mound over the relics of a Buddhist saint. It is usually of earth inside with a cut stone surface. In the stupa, architecture acquires religious and symbolic function. The very act of building demanded a sacrifice from the earth. A relationship between architecture and nature existed, which was formulated on the basis of invisible forces.

The stupa is a construction lacking interior space. Its size can vary from miniature to mountain (e.g., Borobudur). The stupa is surrounded by a fence and gates at the cardinal points. These are assembled from posts and horizontal beams. These demonstrate that originally wood-carving techniques were used in the new material stone. On top of the stupa is a small belvedere through which the pole reaches, usually with a number of stone umbrellas.

The stupa is used in ritual processions that symbolize elementary cosmic events in imitation of the path of the sun. The stupa dates from before Buddhism, but was assimilated by this religion.

Relatively recent, it has been interpreted as the image of the Buddhist cosmos. The pole with the umbrella symbolizes the world axis. This world stands in water (= ground). Water and the umbrella (= abstract tree crown) are symbols of life. Their meaning comprises the magical center (axis of the world), a representation of the universe seen from outside, a tomb (marker), and a reminder of miraculous events. The form is a geometric expression of the perfection and infinity of the universe.

Indian architecture tends to be a means to facilitate meditation. The aim of meditation is to surpass the present physical world. The aim of life is to achieve spiritual purity to reach nirvana and escape the cycle of rebirths (reincarnations). Mostly, design is done through superimposition of circle and square.

The form of life in India is derived from the old myths, and architectural form is based on rituals meant to ensure human success.

The fundamental motif of Indian architecture is the representation of the center. Temples were axes of the world, where celestial, terrestrial and infernal spheres meet. The circular form likewise expressed the attempt to convert the magical forces of the soil into a basis of support for human construction.

The theoretical units of Indian architecture can be traced back to the altar (stupa), the pillar, the mountain, the cavern, and the door. The aesthetic base of Hindu sacred architecture is movement. Architectural creation is based on geometry and light, on the movement of masses and the real, slow movement of men.

## CHAITYA HALL, KARLI (1ST C. CE)

This is simply an enclosure for a stupa. The vault symbolizes heaven. The columns lean inward to counter the vault thrusts. There are three aisles and an apse. A small stupa serves as sacred object. Chaityas were halls for communal activities. The hall measures thirty-six meters long and thirteen meters high. Its entrance faces the direction of the setting sun, west. This is the time when the interior is visible in natural light. The forty-one columns divide the interior into three naves, and have figural capitals. The columns taper slightly toward the top, and are placed vertically.

## KANDARIYA MAHADEVA TEMPLE, KHAJURAHO (11TH C. CE)

Hindu temples deal primarily with places and paths. The centrally located temples constitute the places, which are considered houses for the gods, and serve as imitations of the world mountain. These identify the monumental sites of the gods, which are unintelligible to humans.

In the Hindu world, temples signify the places in which the Gods manifest themselves in daily and seasonal rituals. The worlds of humans and of the Gods touch there. In the temple, human liberation is signaled through the passing of the border between these worlds. Plan, section, orientation, and siting refer to the order of the universe. The temple represents the essence of the cosmos, and becomes this cosmos in the ritual. Temple towers are images of the mythical world mountain. On top of the towers is a water cup, which symbolizes luck, and the border where the worlds of the humans and Gods meet. The interior is dark and simple, and symbolizes movement from light to dark.

# INDONESIA AND CAMBODIA

## STUPA, BOROBUDUR (8ᵗʰ C., CA. 760-847 CE)

This is a colossal stupa built around and over a small hill 270 m above sea level, almost as if it were a roof over an invisible shrine, namely the mountain itself. This mountain is terraced, so that the stupa is just the last part of the steps. It was built out of volcanic rock. It measures roughly 400 x 380 ft and is ca. 98 ft tall. The sides align with the cardinal directions. Site choice and building form express a complex symbolism of center and mountain. The stupa proper rests on a hidden foundation (with decorations representing hell) and five approximately quadrangular terraces. These diminish gradually in size. On top are three circular platforms, symbolizing the celestial plane. Speculation has it that originally a giant stupa was to be placed on top of the square terraces. However, uncertainty about whether the substructure could withstand all the weight prevented this design. A story has it that when the disciples asked Buddha how he wanted to be buried, he folded his coat into a square, placed the bowl for his alms upside down onto it, and then stuck his pilgrim's staff into the bowl. Centrally placed and facing the cardinal points are four stairways. From the top, the whole looks like a mandala figure, which probably explains why Borobudur is square and not round. The square forms symbolize the earth, the circular ones the vaults of heaven. The square terraces are defined by two walls, the inner one serving as balustrade for the next upper level. The sculptural decorations depict saints, didactic stories, and scenes from the earthly life of Buddha. These are generally on the lower levels of the interior walls. The stories come from a number of books on the life of Buddha. The figures and scenes were probably painted originally. The walls are periodically surmounted by niches and small stupas. The three circular terraces are not decorated at all, because one has views of nature from that level. The intention of the relief decorations is to show the benefits of living according to Buddhist thought, and provide instruction as to what is necessary to arrive at enlightenment and perfect knowledge. The main stairways lead through gates from level to level. These gates symbolize the passage from one spiritual stage to the next. The circular terraces hold stupas that are pierced, to lighten their weight and offer views of the statues of Buddha inside.

This stupa may have served as a place of meditation and edification that was used by walking around and through it. Whoever ascends it will reach the metaphysical level of the supreme Buddha. The monument is experienced as a number of vertically stacked horizontal layers. Each one helps to shed one's worldly concerns more, until whatever is, is. It also represents the infernal, natural, and celestial spheres. Many other Buddhist and Hinduist religious monuments were built near its location. On the square levels, one is enclosed on both sides. Upon reaching the round terraces, the view opens up to nature and the cosmos that surround the monument.

Borobudur deals with three levels of symbolism. The first level represents the world of the senses: desires and passions. People are depicted as victims of their own desires, because they cannot see the essence of reality, but only what their senses tell them. This level is actually hidden underneath a plinth that was erected above the original monument. The scenes generally depict stories of cause and effect, showing the outcome of bad or good actions. The hidden base was discovered in 1885. The second level represents the world of form. This teaches the multiplicity of consciousness about the world. The third level represents the secret inner world, where being and nonbeing are one.

Here, the nature of the mountain and the cult building (the center) have been composed together, a design practice that seems to be concentrated in Indonesia.

There is also number symbolism in this monument. Among the numbers represented is 8, which has significance in Buddhism.

Borobudur was deserted ca. 860 CE. When it was discovered in the early 19ᵗʰ century, it was covered with earth and volcanic rock. It was restored in the early 20ᵗʰ century, and then again after the Second World War. In 1975, with the help of UNESCO, the Indonesian government undertook this task, finished in 1983. The entire monument was dismantled. A new waterproof foundation was laid; concentric rings of concrete support each level.

The meaning of the word "Borobudur" is not clear. Two readings seem to be favored. Either, it means "monastery of Buddha," or "mountain of the accumulation of virtues."

## TEMPLES AT ANGKOR (12-13<sup>th</sup> c. CE)

The basic architectural types used here were the tower sanctuary and the temple-mountain. The temple-mountain at Angkor Wat is bounded by a trench. An access road approaches the main, western facade. The complex is a pyramid with three superimposed terraces, each surrounded by a gallery interrupted by towers.

The temples were constructed of sandstone. The name Angkor Wat means "The Pagoda of the City," and this was a funerary monument. The architecture and layout were to represent the entire universe. The central tower symbolizes the sacred Mount Sumeru, which is situated at the center of the universe. The five towers make the symbolism consistent with the five peaks of Mount Sumeru. The outer wall represents the end of the world, and the surrounding moat represents the ocean that encircles the world. On the walls are carved bas-reliefs illustrating scenes from the *Ramayana* and the *Mahabharata*—epic poems that are also sacred Hindu texts. The monuments at Angkor integrate astronomy, the calendar, and religion since the priest-architects who constructed the temple conceived of all three as a unity. To the ancient Khmers, astronomy was known as the sacred science.

At Angkor Thom, the main sanctuary on top and in the center is circular and is also supported on a tiered pyramid.

The towers are pleated vertically and striated horizontally. The sharp edges were then softened with applied sculpture.

# JAPAN

## SHINTO SHRINES, ISE

Shinto is the native Japanese faith, and means "Way of the Gods." It is based on love of nature and of the family. It is concerned with nature as divinity manifest. The Japanese assigned gods to all natural phenomena. These sanctuaries were meant as dwellings for the gods. Originally constructed during the 3<sup>rd</sup> and 4<sup>th</sup> centuries CE, they are rebuilt every 20 years. The new shrine is constructed on an adjacent lot, and the existing building destroyed. The shrines are built on natural sites with an air of grandeur or mystery, as the gods were considered to live there.

They consist of two similar complexes, about four miles apart. The Inner Shrine is dedicated to the Sun Goddess. The second one is to the Goddess of Food. The Inner Shrine is enclosed by a fence, and the ground is covered with white gravel. The main building is the Shoden, containing the sacred mirror. There are also Honden, treasure houses. The Ise Shrines are built of cypress. The wooden parts are smoothed and left in their natural state. The roofs are of thatch, laid in layers of bundles that thin toward the ridge pole. The thatch is sheared smooth to create a gentle contour. Decorations evolved from structural features and consist of cross pieces and wooden weights on the ridge pole.

The entire building is a study in rhythmic form. The entire complex is an expression of purity and dignity. This is emphasized by the simplicity of precisely planned proportions, textures, and forms.

## HORYUJI MONASTERY, NARA (607 CE)

Buddhism arrived in the second half of the 6th century CE. The first temples followed closely the Chinese and Korean models. The main south-north axis had the main and secondary gates, the pagoda, the Buddha, and lecture halls in one line. Temples were monastic colleges intent on teaching the faith. Buddhism brought, above all, the concept of trabeated architecture from China.

This design is heavily influenced from China. It was most probably rebuilt after a fire in 670 CE. This temple has a five-tiered pagoda and the Kondo, the main – or Golden – hall. This is surrounded by the corridor, a covered loggia that surrounds the entire complex. There are also a lecture hall and a refectory. This complex marks a move away from axiality to asymmetry in plan. The main hall and pagoda are placed flanking the main axis.

The Golden Hall is a pillar hall. The pillars have a strong entasis and are topped by cloud-shaped brackets. The ceilings are coved, and have a horizontal lattice, or coffered pattern created by straight lengths of wood forming a grid. Small fields produce lattice, large ones, coffered ceilings. On top of the pillars are a series of brackets and beams. On the outside, one or more beams are divided by vertical struts, and bridge the gap created by the brackets.

The halls and pagoda are decorated with circular roof tiles with lotus flowers with multiple layers of petals around, as well as anthemias.

The roofs have broad eaves to signify solemnity.

Monks quarters were in buildings housing rows of cells.

FIGURE 4–1. Stupa, Borobudur, view of the entire monument.

FIGURE 4–2. Stupa, Borobudur, detail showing the passage around the stupa.

**FIGURE 4–3.** Temple of Angkor Wat, aerial view.

**FIGURE 4–4.** Temple of Angkor Wat.

**FIGURE 4–5.** View of the ruins showing how much nature has reoccupied this site.

# Chapter 5

# Minoan and Mycenean Architecture

## HISTORICAL AND CULTURAL BACKGROUND

The eastern Mediterranean was an area in which many cultures overlapped. Trade routes linked Egypt with the north-western extensions of Mesopotamia, which itself was linked with the Aegean world. This area – Greece – is shielded to the north, west and east by mountains, thus allowing the formulation of an inherent culture. This became the first European high culture.

## EARLY PALATIAL PERIOD (2000-1700 BCE)

At ca. 2000 BCE, a complex urban civilization, based in large measure on overseas commerce, began to institute itself on Crete and supplanted the existing Neolithic culture. Strong central authorities emerged, and the palaces of Phaistos, Knossos, and Malia were built. Linear script A appears, as well as pottery with spiral motifs.

## PALACE, KNOSSOS (1600-1400 BCE)

Knossos sits on a ridge; the southern and eastern parts drop down in stages. To clear the area for the foundation of the palace, they had to cut into the eastern side of a hill. The earlier palace had been destroyed ca. 1700 BCE.

An interesting feature of Minoan architecture is the rarity of temples. This certainly is a sign for the importance of mother earth, as the landscape features assumed the function of temples.

The siting, orientation, and design of the palace architecture of Bronze Age Crete made conscious use of the images found in Neolithic art and architecture. These palaces and their use of the site represent a late and full ritualization of the traditions of Stone Age culture. These traditions include: belief in the earth as a mother, especially that of the grass-eating animals upon whose continued presence human life depended, the magic purpose of paintings, and the labyrinthine passages within the Paleolithic caves, which were used for ritual processions.

Each palace makes use of the same landscape elements. These are: an enclosed valley in which the palace is set, a gently mounded or conical hill on axis with the palace to north or south, and a higher, double-peaked or cleft mountain some distance beyond the hill, but on the same axis. The cone was seen as the earth's motherly form, the horns as the symbol of its power. Such landscape properties were seen as manifestations of a natural order, and as personifications of various gods.

The formal articulation of the palaces emphasizes less tectonic logic than decorative effect. Rich and picturesque articulation, and especially the Minoan column order, support this interpretation. Columns tapered downward and were brightly colored. The abacus was supported on an emphatic cushion capital. Decorative patterns were not structurally organized.

The exterior form follows the rather haphazard plan, as if the palace had grown through addition by need. A multipart organism is assembled from differently sized rectangular volumes. This loose order is not dominated by axes, symmetries, or continuous façades. Characteristic motifs were the column orders, wide cornices, and balconies with balustrades. This articulation produced a facade with contrasts between openings and wall parts, as well as shaded and lit parts. The main orientation of the palace was toward the interior courtyards. Here, the division and articulation are more formal.

At Knossos, ceremonial entrances were on the north and south sides. From the west, a raised stone causeway, which forced visitors to walk in single file, split into two separate paths leading into the palace. On the northern entrance, one approached on the Royal Road, and entered through the double stairs of the theatral area. Entering thus took on characteristics of Stone Age rituals. The large complex was centered around a court oriented along a north-south axis, continued to the cone and cleft mountains to indicate that it was imposed by these natural features. The movement through the whole palace complex was labyrinthine, probably reflecting the labyrinths the Greeks remembered in their myths. Although the whole is organized by rectangles, it is fluid and moving. The entire arrangement is probably influenced by the Near East (labyrinths and courtyards) and Egypt (axial arrangement). The various building campaigns seemed to proceed from inside out. The rooms were grouped according to function: ceremonial, administrative, religious, or domestic. The rooms are arranged along two corridors. The first, along the north-south axis on the western side separates the official and ceremonial rooms from the storage spaces. The second, along the east-west axis on the Eastern side of the palace, separates the workshops of the palace crafts-men from the king's and queen's quarters. The royal apartments were on ground level, the ceremonial rooms were relegated to the upper floors, indicating the wish to establish close visual contact with the land. The palace had three stories; the stairwells were lit from above.

Within the palace, four types of enclosures were created: the labyrinthine passage, the open court, the columned pavilion, and the pillared cave.

The construction consists of a mixture of wood, rubble, and ashlar structures. Stone and wood were used in corners and wall openings, and for the foundation. Mural paintings of sea creatures indicate the dependence of this culture on the ocean.

## CITADEL, TIRYNS (1400-1200 BCE)

About 1400 BCE, Knossos and the other towns of Crete were devastated in a natural disaster (volcanic eruption). At this time, the Myceneans, who had ruled over the Greek mainland, extended their dominion over the island and replaced Minoan culture. Mycenean architecture introduced typological and structural changes to Minoan. Mycenean palaces were built on strategically located, defensible hills with a good supply of water. On the highest point was the palace of the king, with a common courtyard below, to be used by the people in time of danger as shelter.

At Tiryns, the site had been occupied since Neolithic times. The citadel is placed on a rather low hill, so as to respond adequately to the sacred landscape features. It served as the governmental center of an independent state, and consisted of the closed commons to the north, which occupied the greatest part of the citadel, and the ruler's palace. The citadel walls follow the contour of the land, and have protrusions and recesses to eliminate dead angles.

The palace proper was entered through a gate in the southwest wall. It occupies the higher south level, and was densely built. It comprised the residence of the king, the administrative spaces, and a lower enclosed courtyard. A propylon to the south gave access to the inner courtyard, which was framed by colonnades. To the north lay the palace buildings. They were dominated by the megaron, which determined its axis. It faced south and was entered through a front porch. First came a set of guard rooms, then the large hall. Its ceiling was pierced by a lantern supported on four columns. Below this were a hearth – surrounded by the four columns – and an offering table; the king's throne was along one of the longer sides. Walls were painted. The floor was stuccoed and laid out in squares, each painted with a different abstract pattern and color.

Secondary rooms around the main megarons are separated by corridors, a feature that may have been imitated from Minoan architecture. There are also traces of staircases which suggest the existence of upper stories. There is also a bathroom, with a floor of a single slab of limestone.

Cyclopean masonry of boulders – each weighing several tons – were piled up for the outer walls. These irregularly shaped blocks were packed with smaller stones, and clay. There is no precedent for this type of construction in Greece or Crete, which suggests that it was imported from central Asia Minor. Inside the walls are galleries with corbel vaults, which may have been an attempt to lighten the load of the walls by creating a hollow center. The palace was built of rubble, strengthened by a massive framework of horizontal and vertical timbers. Outside walls were faced with limestone.

## CITADEL, MYCENAE, WITH LION GATE (1250 BCE)

Mycenae was located away from the coast to guard against attacks from the sea. Its location allows its inhabitants to survey a large plain in front. In 1250 BCE, it was expanded greatly. Most walls were constructed in Cyclopean masonry. The circular walls of the cemetery are enclosed within the city wall. The palace and residential buildings were constructed of gypsum slabs covered by a layer of stucco. Residences may have had multiple floors. They were laid out axially in megarons. A drainage system removed wastewater from the citadel.

The Lion Gate is articulated as a megalithic structure. Four "menhirs" form a stone frame, supported by a relieving triangle. This is simply left open in the city wall by a corbelling technique.

In this case, the decoration expresses the structural system. The form is derived from the purpose (entrance), the material, and the structure. It also expresses a heroic attitude.

## TREASURY OF ATREUS (1300 BCE)

This is a tomb. It combines the circular form, the mound (tumulus), and the corbel vault. In form, this building combines earlier Near Eastern and North African types. Burials had been done originally in shaft tombs, similar to Egyptian practices. This was replaced by rock-cut tombs, which were finally superseded by tholos tombs, such as this treasury.

Formally and structurally, this is a typically Mycenean work. However, the decoration of the entrance gate clearly uses the delicate patterns of the earlier Minoan style. Two columns flank the entrance, totally covered with ornamentation. This ornamentation is completely atectonic. It is a symbolic representation of the entrance to a palace. Two large stone megaliths cover the entrance opening. They are topped by relieving triangles left open through corbelling.

Inside, a tomb shaft is cut horizontally into the wall. This is formed of a total of thirty-three rings. After laying the stones, they were smoothed to form a continuous curve.

FIGURE 5–1. Remains of the Northern Entrance, Palace of Knossos.

FIGURE 5–2. Palace of Knossos, view of the storage area.

# Chapter 6

# Greek Architecture

## URBAN AND LANDSCAPE DESIGN

Greek culture was influenced by geography and climate. Greece included, next to the main peninsula, also a multitude of islands in the Ionian and Aegean Seas. The Greek landscape is rough, with lots of mountain ridges. There is little flat land. However, there is ordered variety, clarity, and scale in the landscape, so that the human being is neither engulfed nor adrift in it. Greece is made up of three parts: Attica with Athens, the island of Euboae, and the peninsula of the Peloponnes. The preferred system of travel, due to the topography of the land, was by sea. The environment is quite hard, with rough weather and frequent earthquakes.

The political system in Greece was based on the city-state, the polis. This was a community of families related by common ancestors, by being born in the same place. Government systems included tyrannies, oligarchies, and democracies. One might say that the form of government in Ancient Greece was urban, in the sense that politics really came from the art of living in cities. However, there was one language and culture that united the ancient Greeks.

The Greek concept of the city has a number of distinct characteristics. It was a single, united entity in which there were no restricted parts. Dwellings were alike, differing only in size. There were three zones: the private one for dwelling, the sacred one for temples, and the public one for political meetings and other communal events. The city was basically an artificial organism inserted into the natural environment. It did, however, respect the natural lines and topography. While basically a living organism, the city was rather stable. Most Greek cities were self-contained agricultural communities.

### ATHENS

The city was the primary communal organization of Ancient Greece. The topography of Greece led naturally to city-states. Generally, there was an urban nucleus, which was surrounded by countryside and agricultural villages. The favorable climate fostered open-air cities.

Athens had begun in an area on higher ground that was used for protection, in a citadel. Ultimately, the city had two parts: the upper city – acropolis – and the lower one. This part was divided into administrative units. Its main part was the agora, where citizens listened to government decisions.

This city centered on a citadel in the late Bronze Age. By the late 8th c. BCE, Athens consolidated its control over outlying areas and villages, primarily due to an increase in its wealth. During the 6th c. BCE, the acropolis was redeveloped, but it gained its final form only after the end of the Persian Wars, in the late 5th c. BCE.

Rebuilding began with the temples on the Acropolis and in the city below. The agora was a public space where the Athenians paid respect to their ancestors and heroes and gathered for festivals, athletic events, and entertainment events. Most buildings constructed in the agora were intended to house the democratic and civic institutions that gradually began to determine the Greek political system. The **Stoa of Attalos** was a long building that formed one edge of the agora. It was two stories high and had a pitched roof whose main beam was supported by a row of columns dividing the interior into two naves. On one side, shops lined this interior. Other public buildings were constructed in the agora. The street layout does not seem to follow a predetermined plan, but rather followed natural lines of traffic. The houses generally have an open courtyard to which the rooms face. The houses had irregular plans. By the end of the 3rd c. BCE, Athens had lost its earlier importance.

In Greek cities, the population was controlled: whenever the number of inhabitants became too high, an expedition to set up a new colony was organized.

## MILETUS, HIPPODAMUS OF MILETUS (479 BCE)

This city had been destroyed by the Persians in 494 BCE. Rebuilding began after 479 BCE and was planned by Hippodamus of Miletus, the inventor of the division of cities into blocks. The site was a level peninsula. A strict orthogonal street grid was aligned with the general direction of the peninsula. This grid was simply laid out, except where topography, or public and religious structures, did not allow it. Urban accents were introduced exactly through these deviations from it. The grid plan was associated with a social system. The city was divided into three parts: sacred, public, and private; and the population into three classes: artisans, farmers, and warriors. Temples, markets, and government buildings were centrally located. Miletus had four harbors.

This city was a thriving center of learning, combining ideas from the West and the East. The town flourished into the Ottoman period, when it was reduced to a village.

## PRIENE (350 BCE)

This Greek city has distinct characteristics. It is a single, united entity without restricted parts. There are three zones: the private one for dwelling, the sacred one for temples, and the public one for political meetings and other communal events. The city was an artificial organism inserted into the natural environment. Its plan was systemic, with the components organized into an integrated urban entity.

Priene was oriented to cardinal points. It had four terraces: the acropolis was on top (fourth level), temple and theater were on the third level, the agora on the second, and gymnasium and stadium on the lowest one. East-west streets follow the contour of the land, north-south ones are stepped.

# SANCTUARY OF APOLLO, DELPHI (350 BCE)

Ancient Greek gardens evolved from paradisiacal origin. This is revealed initially in architecture that is composed to the natural landscape. Architectural forms are complementary to topography. The Greek myths are full of references to trees, flowers, sacred groves, parks, and gardens. The Ancient Greeks had a special capacity to select a site and fit individual buildings into it.

Delphi was the site of the most important oracle in Ancient Greek times. Here, a steep, rocky slope was translated into a dramatic, powerful setting that was deemed adequate to the status of this oracle. The site is terraced, and accessed through a zigzagging path. There was an attempt to express the genius loci, the spirit of this place.

A sacred way snaked its way up from the plain to the Sanctuary of Apollo. This consisted of a temple and a theater; a stadium, a gymnasium, and a tholos were nearby. Building this site happened in a piecemeal manner, which increased the overwhelming impression of the landscape. Close by is the Castalian spring, whose waters were used for purification before consulting the oracle. The overwhelming topography indicates that at first this was a sanctuary to the Mother Goddess Earth. The Greeks thought of Delphi as the center of the world. According to legend, Zeus released two eagles from the opposite ends of the earth, and they met in Delphi. Later, Apollo slaughtered the original serpent, and appropriated the oracle for himself. From then on, priestesses would be the medium through whom the oracle pronounced its decisions. These priestesses sat on chairs in a cave over a fissure in the ground, from which vapors rose that put the priestess in a trance and made her utter the decisions of the oracle. At first, the oracle was of the mother goddess earth. The oracle was consulted on questions of religion, guilty judgments and punishments, and decisions on problems in life and fate.

The first construction dates from the 7th and 6th centuries BCE. After the fire of 548/547 BCE the sanctuary was reconstructed with a bigger temple. There was also destruction after a rockslide in 373 BCE.

There was a wall around the sanctuary.

The Temple of Apollo dominates. This sits on an artificial terrace with retaining walls of polygonal masonry. The present ruins represent the sixth building on this site, beginning in 548 BCE. The eastern pediment shows Leto, Artemis, and Apollo among the muses. The western pediment shows Dionysius and the Thyiades. The peripteral colonnade numbers six by fifteen columns. The interior contained a cella with side aisles.

Additional buildings are placed in a haphazard manner. They are primarily oriented for viewing, to dominate, or according to landscape features. The entire complex emanates a complementary attitude of buildings towards land and nature.

## SIPHNIAN TREASURY (CA. 524 BCE)

Treasuries were chapel-like buildings with an anteroom and rich façade decoration. Most of the treasuries at Delphi were begun after the fire of 548/547 BCE.

This is one of the most lavish examples. A thirty meter long frieze depicting four myths encircled this building. The frieze measures sixty-three centimeters in height. On the eastern side, the Trojan War is shown; on the west the judgment of Paris (as the war's prehistory); on the north the battle between the Gods and the giants, and on the south most probably the rape of the Leukippides. The entrance lintel is supported by two caryatid columns. The eastern pediment sculpture depicted the struggle for the Delphic Tripod between Hercules and Apollo. The western one may have shown the punishment of Tityos (for his vehemence against Leto, the mother of Apollo and Artemis) by Apollo and Artemis. These subjects deal with Apollo's claim of the oracle, and general themes of fame and heroic deeds.

## TREASURY OF THE ATHENIANS (510-490 BCE)

This temple-like building was constructed to house the gifts to the oracle by the Athenians. Its exterior walls were decorated with inscriptions extolling Apollo. The metopes depicted the heroic exploits of Hercules and Theseus. The pediment on the entrance side showed a group of people facing toward the approaching visitor, flanked by two carriages. On the opposite, western, side was a battle scene.

The building that exists today was reconstructed from 1903 – 1906.

## THEATER (4$^{th}$ - 3$^{rd}$ C. BCE)

During the winter, Apollo was believed to have vacated the premises, and Dionysius took over. Performances and rituals were performed then in the theater. The seats were made from marble. Scenes of Hercules's deeds decorated the stage façade. The stage measures seven meters in diameter. An irrigation canal surrounded it. The spectator stands are supported by the land and by added earth slopes. The stands are divided into seven wedges.

## STADIUM AND GYMNASIUM

These were located above and outside of the sanctuary. The Pythian games, a combination of athletic and intellectual competitions, were held in the stadium. They were second only to the Olympic games. A gate with three arches serves as access to the stadium. Retaining walls protect the stadium against the mountain. These were widened to serve as spectator stands.

In addition to these buildings, there was also the Hall of the Athenians (against the foundation wall of the Temple), and a Banquet Hall (above the Temple). This latter one was decorated with mural paintings inside.

## SANCTUARY OF ATHENA PRONAIA AT MARMARIA

This lies east of the Sanctuary of Apollo, and took its name from the marble used for some buildings in the vicinity. It contained two large rectangular temple and a few treasuries, apart from the buildings listed below.

## THOLOS, THEODOROS OF PHOKAIA (380 BCE)

This was reconstructed in 1937. Its architect considered it an ideal building. Constructed of marble, it has twelve slender Doric columns. The metopes show battles between amazons and centaurs. The circular cella wall was articulated with engaged Corinthian columns.

The interior had a bench fixed to the circular wall.

# PUBLIC BUILDINGS

### THEATER, EPIDAURUS (350 BCE)

The small city of Epidaurus had a sanctuary of the healing god Asklepius, of which the theater was a part. It has been restored and is still used for performances of Ancient tragedies.

This theater consists of three basic parts: seating for the spectators, a circular stage, and a backdrop or scenery. Epidaurus had thirty-four rows of seats, later enlarged by another twenty-one. The total capacity was 14,000 spectators. The design is based on a rational geometrical figure, which begins with the circle of the orchestra. A polygon of twenty sides determines size and shape of the wedges of the seating. This seating is larger than a semicircle. The stage backdrop was formed as a hall, with engaged Ionic columns. It had three portals. The acoustic solution is perfect, although it still cannot be convincingly explained.

### CHORAGIC MONUMENT OF LYSICRATES, ATHENS (335 BCE)

This structure presents a synthesis of formal and iconographic elements from theater, architecture, and ritual. Formally, it refers to an altar and a tomb memorial. This monument was erected to display a prize tripod won by the poet Lysicrates at the Athenian festival of 335 BCE.

It sits on a square pedestal fashioned as an unornamented cubic mass that indicates its support function in a straightforward manner. The joints between the ashlars are emphasized through reveals. The monument is mainly articulated in the vertical direction, quite unusual for the pronounced horizontality of Greek architecture.

On top of this base sits the monument, composed of six Corinthian columns. The curved slabs connecting these columns may have been inserted for structural reasons. The eastern bay is slightly wider, and may have been open, revealing a statue of Bacchus. On the frieze is represented a scene involving Dionysius , thus identifying this monument with the theater of which Dionysius was patron. The circular arrangement may then refer to the Ancient theater chorus.

### MAUSOLEUM, HALLICARNASSOS (353 BCE)

This was the tomb for king Mausolus. It was included in the Seven Wonders of the World. A description of the monument is given by Pliny. The whole consisted of a high podium on which a hall with thirty-six peripteral columns stood. A pyramidal roof of twenty-four layers was on top, crowned by a quadriga.

A number of earlier building types were combined here, among them the Egyptian pyramid and the Greek peripteral temple. Recent studies have established the base as a rectangle.

# TEMPLES

This was the most important Greek building. It was placed in a sacred district, the temenos. The form of the temple is quite old, going back to crude wooden buildings with columns surrounding the central chamber. This theory of origin is influenced by positivism. They were mostly built on sites where altars had long been in use. As the older Minoan and Mycenean structures, temples were also laid out in a complementary position to the landscape. In addition to terrestrial orientation came now the orientation toward a new celestial orientation. Many of the new temples were laid out along an east-west axis. That this was not always the case indicates that the transition from the Mother Earth to the Olympian Gods took some time. Nevertheless, the introduction of the gable does indicate the change from the Mother Goddess Earth to the Olympian gods. The upward thrusting gable is an abstract, human approximation of the sacred mountain. The Greek temple also enclosed an image of the god or goddess. From the houses of chiefs that complemented the landscape, there are now just houses of the gods.

In these temples, the peripteral colonnade was introduced. This creates an ambiguous exterior, partly impressing the viewer as a piece of sculpture, partly as a solid wall, thus balanced between sculpture and shell. It serves mainly visual and practical purposes, namely to articulate the exterior so that it becomes a mid-element between inside and outside, helping to perceive both parts. Consequently, the corner-view is the intended view, not a frontal one. Interiors, in contrast, give the impression of being filled, not of being divided into clearly ordered elements. Thus, there is a contrast between interiors and exteriors: the main part is the exterior, and the interior is of secondary importance. The columns introduce a rhythm of individual units when seen from their base. Only at the top, through the pediment, is an order imposed on this front facade of the temple. If one goes by the number of columns, this impression is increased. Because usually an even number of columns is used at the front, a clear symmetry is established through the intercolumniations. On the side facades, however, there is more of a rhythm, because the uneven number of columns emphasizes a column, not an intercolumniation. The typical form chosen for the temple derived from the effort to design a building that could best satisfy the expressive requirements placed on it.

Interestingly, while the temples themselves were clearly organized individual bodies, their placing seems irregular and haphazard. The orthogonal structure of the temple may be interpreted as a symbol of man's organizing intelligence, in relation to the experience of the horizontal surface of the earth and the force of gravity. A similar ambiguity is introduced through the distinction between the mathematically/proportionally designed architecture and the pediment sculptures. While one is elegant and geometrical, the other depicts unruly violence. This creates two different meanings.

Temples were generally painted to more clearly articulate and separate each part from the other.

## CONSTRUCTION TECHNIQUE

The earliest temples had wood columns surrounding the cella. These were replaced by stone columns, probably influenced by public pride, which wanted to erect more durable structures. In the earliest temples, one finds a variety of capital articulations, suggesting that this process took a considerable amount of time. In addition, contact with Egypt, beginning in the 7th c. BCE, taught Greeks about stone architecture. The main problems at that time had to do with quarrying and transporting stones; construction techniques and structural soundness were of secondary interest. Columns were made of drums with holes into which pegs could be inserted. Fluting was added when all drums of a column had been stacked.

## OPTICAL REFINEMENTS

Entasis: Slight bulging of the shaft profile.

Corner problem (Doric order): If the placing of triglyph over column axis would be followed, there would be a short metope at the corner. Architectural symbolism required that a triglyph be placed at the edge of the entablature. To be flush with the corners, the last triglyph had thus to be displaced in relation to the corresponding capitals below. Since this move would have made the last metope unaesthetically wider, the last column bay was shortened. The Ionic and Corinthian orders, by excluding the triglyph/metope frieze, eliminated this problem. The Ionic capital introduced a different corner problem by its two articulations. In addition, the corner columns were slightly thicker, to make them stand out more clearly against the sky.

The terrace of the temple curved upward toward the middle of each side. The four corner columns leaned inward and back and were made thicker than the others.

## PROPORTIONS

The entire assembly of parts in the Doric order is guided by a clear order and division. Over each column bay are two triglyph bays and four mutuli.

The size of the stylobate dictated the number of columns used. Their spacing depended on two things: the choice of the diameter for the column, which dictated their height, and the disposition of the frieze, which determined whether the interstices between the corner columns would be smaller than those of the others. Thus, each element was proportionally generated and proportionally keyed to all others.

## ORDERS

Doric order: Capital consists of echinus and abacus. Columns support the architrave, which separates them from the crowning elements of the temple facade. Frieze consists of triglyphs and metopes, which repeat the rhythm of the columns below. The frieze was normally painted in gay colors. The frieze division is generally explained as the transposition of wood construction into stone. Triglyphs would be the ends of the ceiling beams. Since the actual ceiling, however, is above the frieze, this explanation is not totally convincing. This transposition is also held responsible for the creation of the corner problem, as the stone beams had to be thicker than the earlier wooden beams. The narrowing of the corner bays is, however, noted even in those temples for which a wooden colonnade is reported. Hence, it may as well have been that this division was purely decorative, and influenced by a long tradition that can be noticed in geometric vase painting. The corner problem then arose because the corners broke the continuity of the round vase circumference. This gains credibility when one considers that the earliest (wooden) temples sometimes had oval colonnades.

Ionic order: This capital introduces the division into a primary and secondary view, hence rendering the frontal view of the temple façades the dominant one. In its entablature, this order is more openly reminiscent of carpentry than the Doric.

## TEMPLE OF NEPTUNE, PAESTUM (450 BCE)

The colonial city of Poseidonia was established between 700-650 BCE. It was renamed Paestum when it came under Roman control in 273 BCE. This settlement was a rich agricultural community. The city is surrounded by a defensive wall. Paestum was a grid plan city. A strip of land for religious and civic buildings runs north-south through the city.

There are three Doric temple ruins in the temenos: two in the southern sanctuary–Basilica and Temple of Neptune–and one–Temple of Ceres–in the northern precinct.

The Temple of Neptune was dedicated to Hera. She was the wife of Zeus and, hence, the mother of the gods. Its construction may have celebrated the Olympic victory of a citizen of Paestum in 468 BCE. It is a pure application of the Doric order.

The cella with pronaos and opisthodomos is placed in the center of the peripteral hall of six times fourteen columns. All optical refinements are present. The cella is divided into three naves by two rows of double-story columns. It is set between a vestibule and a treasury. The emphasis is on the exterior impression of a sculptural body.

The temple was oriented toward a conical and cleft mountain peak. As all other temples, it is set on a three-stepped platform. The metopes and pediment were left bare.

As in early Greek art, architecture is also guided by a rigid pattern that is subordinated under a geometric system. Buildings and details are simple, and clearly arranged. Nothing unnecessary is found. Nevertheless, care was taken not to make the design appear clumsy. Through optical refinements, buildings were made to look almost elastic. Egyptian art was based on knowledge, Greek art on how the eyes perceived it.

# ACROPOLIS, ATHENS

The Acropolis is a defensible limestone mass rising out of the Attic plain. Already during the Mycenean period, it had been used as a citadel. Subsequently, it was changed into a sacred precinct. During the Persian Wars, it was briefly occupied and partly destroyed. The district was the end point of the processions to celebrate Athena's birthday.

After the Persian Wars, some topographical alterations were executed. The southern flank was enlarged, by building a new support wall and filling the resulting space with the debris from the destroyed buildings.

During the last quarter of the 6th c. BCE, a temple of Athena was constructed on this site.

## TEMPLE OF ATHENA NIKE (449/8, 427-424 BCE)

Built by Kallikrates, this temple sits on a bastion that projects from the extremity of the platform. It was placed on a traditional stylobate, and had four delicate Ionian columns at either end. The whole temple is so small, that the peripteral colonnade had to be left out. The cella is wider than it is long. The pronaos is fused together with the cella wall through the two pillars that form the door frame. This temple is constructed of marble.

## PROPYLAEA (437-432 BCE)

The present structure replaces one that was destroyed in the Persian attack of 480 BCE. It was an integral part of the new Acropolis and designed by Mnesicles. It was begun after the Parthenon was completed. The site had been the entrance already in Mycenean times.

This building consists of a forecourt flanked by two unequal wings. The north wing, a refreshment station for pilgrims, was decorated with paintings. The south wing is incomplete and gave access to the temple of Athena Nike. Both are in the shape of temples in antis, without pediment. The southern pavilion is only a façade; there is no space behind it except a shallow recess. In between was the entrance passage with a wide central opening, flanked by two narrower ones on each side. The passage is in the form of a hypostyle hall, as the wall, which would traditionally have been in the center between the eastern and western halves, is dissolved into pillars. The porticoes on either side had six Doric columns. Once inside, the ground rose steeply; the difference in level was mastered by stairs.

The axis of the Propylaea was oriented toward the Parthenon. Passing through the gates, one is offered a corner view of this temple.

This building marks a definite step in Greek architecture, where a stronger consideration of the mutual influence of interior and exterior aspects is felt. It is also a building with a message (entrance) and the intention to impress the approaching visitor.

## ERECHTHEION (421-405 BCE)

This was the most recent addition to the Acropolis. It was built on several layers, and housed a number of shrines. These various cult requirements and the difficult topography of the site may explain the unorthodox form of this building. On the northern side, a projecting porch sheltered the trident mark of Poseidon, left there when he struck the rock for water. There are also tombs of Athenian kings and heroes, such as Erechtheus and Cecrops, as well as the holy olive tree of Athena. Most probably, the architect was Kallikrates, or one from his workshop.

The core of the building was a rectangular space, to which six prostyle Ionic columns were added on its eastern front. The height of the entablature was continued around the whole façade; however, in the west the ground level was about ten feet lower. On the northern side, a curious hall is added, which does not correspond to the central part. This building houses the mark of the trident. On the southern side, the Porch of the Maidens balances this outbuilding. Its western end is flush with the wall of the central hall. The northern and southern additions have the same amount and placement of supports. The Caryatids exemplify the fusion of sculpture and architecture. Vitruvius wrote that the city of Caryae sided with the Persians against Greece. The Greeks defeated Caryae and carried the women away to slavery. They were not allowed to change their long robes, which identified them as married. These wives were then identified as a particular type of slave, burdened with their shame and atoning for their city. From there, they were transposed into carrying positions within architecture. (Vitruvius, Bk. 1, Ch. 1:5)

The sacred tree of Athena is enclosed in a western courtyard. The entire arrangement may simply exemplify the achievements of Greek design and the versatility of the Ionic order.

## PARTHENON (447-432 BCE)

After the Persian wars, a proto-Parthenon was begun. It was slightly longer than the Temple of Zeus at Olympia, and was constructed of marble. Cella and opisthodomos no longer had columns in antis, but prostyle ones.

The building that still exists today was begun under Pericles. It was to become a symbol of the new Athens. The proto-Parthenon was disassembled, and a new, broader structure begun. This building became the most famous of Greek temples, and was most lavishly decorated. The greatest artists of the time were employed and it was the largest marble structure on the Greek mainland. Its main axis was aligned towards Mount Hymettos.

The architects of the new temple were Iktinus and Kallikrates. It is an octastyle temple with seventeen columns down each side. This established a proportional system of 1 : 2 (+1), which can be found in other dimensions as well. Column drums from the earlier temple were reused, which dictated some dimensions of the new structure. The cella was broad, and had an interior colonnade around three sides, framing the statue of the goddess Athena. This was a ten-meters/high ivory and gold statue. For the first time, architecture took account of the interior function. The widening of the cella accommodated the huge statue better. The sculpture itself introduced vertical accents, which accorded with the interior colonnade along the narrow side. Hence, the interior dimensions were dictated by the size of the statue. The fronts of the cella consisted of six prostyle columns. In the east, behind the cella, is a hall with four columns. The stylobate curvature measures eleven centimeters on the longer, and six centimeters on the shorter sides. This curvature is carried through to the architrave. The peripteral columns incline seven centimeters toward the center. This complete subordination of the entire articulation under a dominating design idea is the most impressive feature of this building.

## SCULPTURAL DECORATION

This was mostly the work of Phidias, who was in charge of the whole building construction. On the west pediment, Athena and Poseidon fought in the presence of the other gods to determine who would rule over Attica. The metopes illustrate a different subject on each of the four sides. The main content of this sculptural program is the union of all forces to achieve victory. On the western face is the battle of Marathon (or a mythological prefiguration of the Persian wars), on the northern side the battle over Troy, on the eastern side, the gigantomachy (fight between the Olympian gods and the giants), and on the southern side the fight between the Greeks and the centaurs. All these battles were won by the party that could overcome superficial quarrels and unite for a higher good. Inside, along the outside of the cella wall ran the Panathenaic frieze, the depiction of the cult procession celebrating the birthday of Athena. On the east pediment, the birth of Athena from the head of Zeus was depicted. On each side, the various subjects bear some correspondence.

## MEANING, EXPRESSION

One should divide between the aesthetics and the meaning of the Greek temple.

Beginning with Greek architecture, design is no longer guided by nature or reality, but by an idea. This idea is truer and more beautiful that anything that can be achieved even by the best artist. These ideas form the paradigms for artists to follow. This elevates human artistic creation to the same level as natural creation, the products of nature. Greek architecture is thus human architecture, no longer an environmental one. Art is no longer imitation or copying, but becomes independent creation. The subject represented by art and architecture is an inner, mental idea, a concept. Art was appreciated for its own sake, not only for its religious or political function. Suddenly, various styles can be used side by side.

This development was influenced by contemporary formulations of philosophy. Greek mathematics do not just measure proceedings or give recipes; they instead form an intellectual system. The Greeks were aware of the fact that mathematical facts were different from real facts, because they can be proved and they are always correct.

Pythagoras (550-500 BCE) discovered proportional relationships, and established that they can be expressed through numbers. Hence, numbers seemed to be the first things in the whole of nature. And, knowledge of mathematics gave insight into the fundamental structure of the universe. The nature of the universe, for the Greeks, was fundamentally mathematical, in a geometric view of this discipline, not an algebraic one.

Plato (427-347 BCE) began to draw esthetic conclusions from these findings. He established the difference between Forms (= the above mentioned ideas) and Particulars (= objects in reality). Order, symmetry and proportion were established as the aesthetic measures of architecture. This simply means that architecture must follow rules in order to be beautiful.

**FIGURE 6–1.** Sanctuary of Apollo, Delphi, view from the theater to the Temple of Apollo.

**FIGURE 6–2.** Sanctuary of Apollo, Delphi, view to the Treasury of the Athenians.

**FIGURE 6–3.** Theater, Epidaurns

**FIGURE 6–4.** Temple of Neptune (also called 2nd Temple of Hera), Paestum

**FIGURE 6–5.** Acropolis with Parthenon and Erechtheum

**FIGURE 6–6.** Northern view of the Erechtheum with the Caryatid Porch.

# Chapter 7

# Roman Architecture

## INTRODUCTION

Among the particularities of the Roman arts was that it followed a highly articulate cultural achievement, that of the Ancient Greeks. Roman arts derived from Greek and did not, therefore, go through an evolutionary phase as the earlier culture. The Roman beginning was antiquarian, originating from the Hellenistic world through Etruscan and later mainland Greek prototypes. Throughout its history, Roman art had a composite appearance. During the Hellenistic period, the political systems were not stable. Culturally, however, Hellenism created a unifying force. When Rome asserted its power, it complemented the cultural unity with political unity and stability.

A further interesting aspect is the anonymity of Roman art. This was art in the service of the ruler, the artist being merely an employee who did not matter. What counted was the patron. Also, in contrast to Greek art, Roman was utterly secular.

In regard to architecture, the most outstanding Roman achievement was civil engineering on a large scale. Roman architecture is primarily, and in contrast to Greek building, an architecture of space, enclosed internal space and outdoor space on a grand scale. Many of their buildings were meant to contain large groups of people; they were public architecture. Romans developed new building types that enclosed space for the use of the public. These illuminate the fact that, for Romans, the world has ceased to be a collection of disjointed phenomena, expressed in the scattered city-state. Rather, it has become a coherent cosmos, expressed in the empire. Consequently, scope and size characterize architecture.

The Roman character was formed during the early Republic. In this effort, Romans developed a sense of ingrained discipline, patriotic responsibility, and serious purpose, in short, a sense of the importance of matters at hand. Romans were pragmatic and realistic. These traits also influenced architectural development. The aim of art was no longer harmony, beauty, or dramatic expression, but rather accurate, matter-of-fact rendering and clear-cut narratives. A large part of Roman architecture consists of engineering works: roads, bridges, and aqueducts.

Roman religion centered in the house. Each of them contained little shrines. The world of gods came to Romans from the Etruscans, and was similar to that of the Greeks.

Ancient Rome is divided into three phases: the rule of the early kings, the Republic, and the Empire. The earliest settlers on the site of Rome came from the Balkans, around 1,100 BCE. Ca. 300 years later, the Etruscans became dominant. In 509 BCE, the citizens of Rome rebelled against their rule, and substituted it with a republic governed by a senate of patricians, with two consuls being in charge of executive power. From then on, the major task was to secure their liberty. By 265 BCE, Rome was in control of the Italian peninsula. At the start of the first century BCE, the Roman Empire stretched all around the Mediterranean Sea. The Roman Empire ceased in the 4th century CE.

# SANCTUARY OF FORTUNA PRIMIGENIA, PALESTRINA [PRAENESTE] (80 BCE)

This sanctuary is situated on a hill slope above the forum. The topography of the site seems to present a cosmic scale, hence its dedication to Fortuna, fate. A circular temple of Fortuna Primigenia (= Firstborn) had been built there during the 3rd century BCE, and there was also a statue of Fortuna with Jupiter and Juno in her lap.

The architecture demonstrates how the Ancient Romans replaced earlier practices of exploiting the natural topography with artificial structures of geometric planning. At Praeneste, a specifically Roman monumental building was created, enabled by the new technology of concrete construction. It combines the regular sanctuary type (with the temple on a podium, the columned hall, and the stairways of Hellenistic times), with the new Roman type of buildings on a massive substructure.

The new sanctuary was laid out on axially disposed terraces. Shops are placed on the lower levels. The large square served for ritual meetings. The walls of the piazza are decorated in an early triumphal arch motif. Semicircular steps provided seating, behind which was a round Temple of Fortune. The top levels are arranged along a straight axis, somewhat softened by the curve and counter-curve motif of the colonnade and temple at the end. The traditional facade decoration of columns and entablature conceals concrete barrel vaults, thus combining these two different structural systems.

# MAISON CARRÉE, NÎMES (20 BCE)

Roman temples derived from Etruscan prototypes. They were similar to Greek temples, except for the rationale for siting them, the placing of them at the end of an open colonnaded courtyard, the provision of a high podium, the use of stairs only on the front, the use of a deep porch, and the merging of the cella with the peripteral colonnade.

The Roman world was always centered on the capital. When siting a building, Romans did not interpret the natural character of the existing landscape. Instead, the two main axes through the site were determined by an augur, and the division into left, right, front, and back was established. Compared with the sculptural Greek temple, the Roman one was two-dimensional; its rear was not important.

The Maison Carrée used the Corinthian order. The temple type is called pseudo-peripteral, as engaged columns are used. The porch is three bays deep. The frieze is of tendril patterns.

# TEMPLE OF VESTA, TIVOLI (LATE 1ST C. CE)

This is a round temple in the Corinthian order. Its frieze is of oxen heads connected by garlands. It has a dramatic setting to express the spiritual quality of landscape.

# PANTHEON, ROME (118-128 CE)

This structure best symbolizes the Roman enclosure of space. It is entirely built of concrete, and measures 142.5 feet across and in height. If the hemispherical dome would be allowed to continue, its apex would touch the floor. The only source of light is the 30-foot oculus in the center of the dome. On its interior surface, the dome has five rows of diminishing coffers. These remove material and, hence, lighten the total weight. The dome rests on cylindrical walls. Eight barrel vaults in the thickness of these walls support the weight of the dome. Under these vaults, between the piers of the structure, are deep niches, closed by columnar screens, intended for images of the planetary gods. On the piers were small tabernacles, or temple fronts. The second level consists of blind windows and triplets of decorated panels. The floor is paved with discs and squares of granite, marble, and porphyry to form a grid along the main north-south axis of the temple.

The Pantheon is a monumental building. The exterior form presents itself as a material individual, due to its geometric shape. It is perceived as a singular body in one view. Only its curvature refers to a development in depth. The central unity of its exterior form is a haptic one.

A particular inconsistency of the interior decoration is that solids and voids do not align from bottom to top. The three-part division is not aligned vertically. To place ribs over an opening is a mistake, as it is not structurally logical. There are also differences in scale among the three levels. These discrepancies are the result of the extreme size of the interior. This is so large that the interior elevation is treated as an exterior facade. The attic level hides the arches that span the openings of the exedrae. The windows bring light from the rotunda into the exedrae. The colonnade of the attic level is decorative, influenced by Hellenistic examples from public squares and triumphal arches. The twenty-eight ribs of the dome signify the moon's circle around the earth.

Each of the three interior levels must be read as an independent part. Only the shaft of light and the cornice below the springing of the dome unite this interior. The temple interior then displays cosmic motion. The statues of the gods in the exedrae are the spectators. The dissonances in scale are intended to eliminate the building's own impact on this impression. The dome must be seen as consisting of a grid, rather than of ribs. The attic level breaks the vertical continuity. Consequently, the dome appears to be of a different order than the lower parts, namely of the celestial order.

On the exterior, the Pantheon consists of an octastyle portico, backed against a tall, square attic block, which serves as connection between the cylindrical walls and this portico. These are a bit uncomfortable, as they present a disharmonious combination of parts. The attic block prevents one from seeing the dome behind it when close to the facade, thus making the entrance portico totally Greek. The exterior of the dome rather looks like a cone. Toward the bottom of the dome the wall thickens to contain the dome's thrust. The concrete of the upper parts contained stones that were lighter than those used farther down. The oculus on top of the dome acts as a keystone, as well.

A wall twenty feet feet thick really supports the weight of the dome. The relationship of load and support is not direct. The wall is not completely solid, but full of open chambers, which helped to quicken the drying of the concrete. There are also a series of transverse barrel vaults to distribute the weight onto the points of the eight pillars inside.

It was a temple to the seven planetary gods. The Romans imagined the earth as a disk covered by a heavenly dome, and the Pantheon symbolized this conception.

The Pantheon was among the first major monuments to be designed not just as an exterior. Nevertheless, the interior is still individualized, as even the side niches do not introduce a spatial division, that is, the interior is meant primarily to be viewed, not walked through. Even if there are partly separated rooms, these are totally subordinated to the absolute unity of the whole. The limits of this space are material and clearly visible. Hence, both inside and outside, the Pantheon presents absolutely closed individual unity.

# PONT DU GARD (14 CE)

The city of Rome was laid out in a hilly terrain, necessitating large-scale engineering and support structures. This may be among the reasons for the structural prowess of many Roman buildings.

This aqueduct was one of the monumental bridges used to bring fresh water into the city of Nîmes over a distance of 25 miles. The Pont du Gard consists of a triple arcade in perfect vertical proportion. This remaining section has a water channel 160 feet above ground that is covered with stone slabs. Huge blocks of stone were joined without mortar and strengthened with iron clamps to erect this giant "bridge." The few projecting stones were most probably used to support scaffolding during construction and later maintenance. In its simple and straightforward articulation, this structure presented engineering as an art form.

During the 18th century, the lowest piers were widened to support a road bed above.

# URBAN DESIGN

## POMPEII (7TH C. BCE-79 CE)

This was not so much a metropolitan, as rather a rural town. It was not Greek, but originated in the Greek manner on an elevated, defensible part with a grid plan and an open area in the center, with a temple dedicated to Apollo. From this beginning, the city expanded eastward in the 6th century BCE. The next expansion occurred toward the east and north in the 4th century BCE. The city was enclosed by a fortified wall.

The Forum was an oblong rectangle, dating from the 2nd century BCE. It was surrounded by colonnades, and had the Capitolium at the northern end. There was also a later version of the original Temple of Apollo, a basilica, a market building, some minor temples, and the comitium. A short distance apart were the theater, the public baths, and the gymnasium. A larger amphitheater was added later.

There are a number of cardos and decumanuses because of the various expansions of this town over its history.

## Forum, Rome (6ᵗʰ c. BCE-2ⁿᵈ c. CE)

At the heart of the Roman city was the forum, the civic open space lined with colonnades and civil buildings, including a temple dedicated to Jupiter, government structures, a basilica, and various other temples. The forum – the market place – was the center of business and social life. Generally, this was an oblong space enclosed by colonnades on three sides and by the basilica, or town-hall, on the fourth. Its articulation exhibits the Roman tendency to enclose public spaces.

In Rome, the layout of the forum began at the beginning of the 6ᵗʰ c. BCE in the area between the Quirinal and Capitol. Its ever-changing plan reflects the political changes over time. Several emperors began new fora to relieve the congestion of the original Forum Romanum. Julius Caesar started this development in 51 BCE with a reconstruction and enlargement. The largest structure he built was the **Basilica Julia** (55-44 BCE). This was a marble-faced building with a colonnade enclosing the central hall. The other main building was the **Temple to Venus Genetrix** (46 BCE). He was followed by Augustus, Nerva, and Trajan.

### Forum of Augustus

This was flanked by colonnades and had two apses. The main temple was dedicated to Mars Ultor (2 BCE). It had eight columns, and was placed on a podium reached by a single flight of steps.

### Forum of Trajan, Rome (106-113 CE)

The Forum of Trajan culminated the imperial fora in Rome. It was designed by Apollodorus of Damascus. It consisted of a broad stoalined forecourt measuring 660 by 390 feet, with two exedrae on each side. At the end of this space was the large Basilica Ulpia. Behind it were two libraries, Trajan's column, and a Temple to Trajan built by Hadrian. The column is decorated with a continuous spiral band containing a picture chronicle of the two Dacian (Romania today) campaigns of Trajan.

### Basilica Ulpia (98-117 CE)

Basilicas were designed to provide spaces for legal proceedings. Normally, they consisted of a long rectangular building placed next to a forum. Inside was a colonnade and one or two apses, where judges would sit.

The Basilica Ulpia measured 385 by 182 feet. It had two colonnades, separating the two aisles, and was covered by a timber truss roof.

### Trajan's Market (100-112 CE)

Beyond the northern exedra of the forum forecourt, on a hillside, were public markets in the form of a multilevel commercial facility. Three stories of shops made up the lower markets. All shops were barrel-vaulted spaces, and were fitted into a semicircular exedra. They were accessible from streets or corridors. The upper markets consisted again of three levels of shops and a large market hall. This hall is vaulted and has two levels of barrel-vaulted shops branching out from it.

## COLOSSEUM, ROME (72-80 CE)

Roman civilization was essentially urban, one reason for the further development of the building type of theater. While deriving from Greek models, Romans built them freestanding, in open space, much larger, and in the round, instituting the oval amphitheater. In contrast to Greek theaters, Roman ones were enclosed, not open and integrated into the landscape. This necessitated that the seats be ramped up on radiating and tilted concrete barrel vaults. Most theaters were erected over a semicircle, thus also changing the form of the stage from the Greek models.

The Colosseum stood on a concrete foundation. Piers supported the concrete vaults that served to support the rows of seating. It measured 615 by 510 feet; the arena alone was 280 by 175 feet. The seats rose to 159 feet. Spectators reached their seats by way of two annular corridors at ground level, and then by means of three stories of stairs to the different levels. The stage floor consisted of wooden planks over a series of subterranean chambers and passageways. The wooden floor could be removed and the area underneath flooded with water. The capacity was between 45,000 and 55,000 spectators. These entered through seventy-six entrances. The top floor was reserved for women and the poor, the third for slaves and foreigners, and the other two for the middle class and the wealthy. Senators and other distinguished Romans had ringside boxes.

The exterior is made up of four tiers of arcades, with piers and engaged columns. There are a total of eighty arches around. The orders used were Tuscan (similar to Doric) on the ground floor, Ionic and Corinthian on the second and third stories, and Corinthian pilasters on the fourth level. The material used is travertine. The form combines columnar structure with arched structure in a masterful solution. The pillars of the three arcades have to incorporate horizontal bands, which accommodate the interior vaulting. This break is optically smoothed over by the applied engaged columnar orders. The three orders have the same dimensions, and are only distinguished by their capitals, pointing to their purely decorative purpose. Provisions for an awning around the perimeter of the theater were added.

# BATHS OF CARACALLA, ROME (211-217 CE)

Baths were another of the Roman buildings for public use. They are also another example for their structural achievement in covering large spaces. Baths contained, next to "health club facilities," also libraries, shops, restaurants, exercise yards, and reading rooms. They replaced the Greek stoa, and also the forum as the place of public conversation area.

The Baths of Caracalla covered an area of thirty-three acres and were capable of accommodating ca. 1600 people. The whole complex measured 1152 by 1240 feet. Along the south side were shops, and the exedrae on either side housed libraries and lecture rooms. The remaining space within the walls was planted with groves of trees. The bath buildings (750 x 380 ft.) were on the northern half. They consisted of caldarium, tepidarium, frigidarium and swimming pool. The whole complex was built on a twenty-feet high platform that housed underground utilities and facilities.

The bath was primarily oriented toward the interior as a true spatial composition, consisting of individual rooms. There, the most lavish decoration was applied, not on the exterior. A succession of diverse interiors was reconciled in an overall harmony achieved by vaulted and colonnaded vistas.

# BASILICA OF MAXENTIUS, ROME (307-312 CE)

This is among the most impressing basilica fragments. The nave was made of three cross-vaulted bays, 114 ft high. Three transverse barrel-vaulted bays on each side eased the lateral thrust. At the western end was an apse, at the eastern an entrance lobby.

During Constantine's rule, the axis was changed to a north-south direction by adding an apse on the northern side, and an entrance on the southern. The main impression of this interior is of a coherent space.

# RESIDENTIAL AND LANDSCAPE DESIGN

## HOUSES AND VILLAS, POMPEII

The basic scheme consisted of an open courtyard surrounded by rooms. At Pompeii, rooms were grouped symmetrically around the atrium, which usually contained a tank for rainwater. The entrance door lined up with the main axis of the house. Through a short lobby, one enters the main room, the atrium, with the impluvium. Two wings flank the atrium, enclose the peristyle, and lead to the main rooms across the back. The central room there was the tablinium, the main reception room.

Interior walls were painted with murals. The interior aims to preserve itself as a spatial individual, with clear connections between rooms and a focus on the atrium.

## APARTMENT BUILDING, OSTIA

Due to the rise in urban population, accommodation had to be denser there. Buildings grew vertically, not horizontally. Tenement buildings of five to six stories were the result. Externally, they presented a functional expression. They were mostly built of brick with painting and the use of wood inside. Stairs led to the upper floors, either from the street or from an interior courtyard. Apartment plans were laid out along a corridor leading to the largest room.

### HADRIAN'S VILLA, TIVOLI (118-134 CE)

This is one of the most extravagant country palaces in Roman history. This villa is both imperial palace and summer residence. It stretches for a mile across the slopes of Tivoli. The remains cover ca. ½ of an acre. The rise of the terrain is ca. 150 feet toward the south, broken by wide terraces. It combines features expressing distant parts of the empire that had interested Hadrian during his travels. These included Athens, Thessaly, and Egypt. This makes it a private world of the emperor, who wanted to reproduce the landscapes and buildings of his empire. Names of four buildings in Athens are used: Lyceum, Academy, Prytaneum, and Stoa Poikile. These features are separated into building groups serving administrative, representative, or private-contemplative functions.

Four individual groups with separate orientations are integrated to the topography. The Great Palace contains the living quarters. This part existed before Hadrian began his enlargement. The Academy (or Little Palace) is on the other side of this complex, on a natural terrace. A viewing tower is added to this part. The Poikile is a garden laid out in the plan of a forum with a surrounding colonnade. Added to this garden is a building grouped around the stadium. Connected to this is the complex of baths. Connecting the palace with the poikile is a small island carrying a building (Hadrian's study), approached over bridges, also called the Teatro Marittimo. The largest feature is the Piazza d'Oro, an open colonnaded courtyard around which are apartments with diverse plans, including an octagonal room with alternate apsidal and rectangular bay, and one supported by eight columns connected by alternating convex and concave columns screens. The Piazza d'Oro has the same function as the peristyle garden. Curvilinearity has become the issue in this building. Other parts include the Canopus, a pond resembling the canal that connected Alexandria to the city of Canopus and the temple of Serapis in Egypt, the Prytaneum, the Valley of Tempe, which resembles the original in Thessaly, Greece, the Styx, and the Elysian Fields.

There is no dominant axis in this villa; rather, there are a number of them. The entire structure appears to be hinged around the Teatro Maritimo. The common denominator in this complex is curvilinearity, both in plan and elevation. The building shows a deviation from the conventions proposed by Vitruvius that creates an impression similar to Baroque architecture.

# AESTHETICS

There is still the Greek separation between idea and form. However, both are now given equal value. The form, or the artistic creation, is treated as a distinct element, thus giving artistic creation the power to give form to matter. In this way, the idea is treated as form-giving, and the act of forming is given greater value. This value comes out in the fact that form-giving can be done with varying skill, that is, one work can be judged as better than the other can. Beauty becomes consequently the measure of art's success, no longer truth, as in Greek times.

This attitude also expressed Roman self-confidence. It brought with it the possibility of changing the principles of the Greek orders. The rules of combining, for example, were altered when the three orders were stacked and superimposed onto the facade of the Colosseum.

Roman architecture visualized the order in the lives and affairs of its citizens in the urban spaces they shaped, which were framed by clearly ordered ranks of axially disposed and colonnaded buildings.

FIGURE 7–1. Maison Carrée, Nîmes

**FIGURE 7–2.** Pantheon, Rome

**FIGURE 7–3.** Pantheon, view of the interior with the shaft of light entering through the oculus.

**FIGURE 7–4.** Pont du Gard, Nîmes

FIGURE 7–5. Colosseum, Rome, exterior.

FIGURE 7–6. Colosseum, view of the interior arena.

# Chapter 8

# Sustainability and Ecology in Architecture

## INTRODUCTION

The term "style" was derived from "stylus" (= how it is shaped on the outside). It deals with how something looks. Style is conceived as part of a visual experience. In architecture, style has to do with form and surface treatment. It defines a group of characteristics that is constant, and recurring.

Why are we interested in questions of style? How something looks is related to the period during which it was done. Style teaches us about the people that produced a work of architecture. It also gives us clues relating to the evolution and the development of architecture. Objects created in the same age tend to look similar. It also serves well to organize the vast body of knowledge and information that constitutes architectural history.

Is this infatuation with style ill-advised? There are problems with this approach. It only orders and classifies, focuses on historical periods, taste, cultural values, belief systems, social organization, and symbolization/expression.

How does stylistic analysis shape our historical investigations into architectural design? Take for example the Italian Renaissance. There are formal similarities to Classical Antiquity. Research will find support for these similarities in theory, philosophy, culture, civilization, and the other arts. However, there is a suspicion that this may not explain convincingly the complete architectural scope of the Renaissance. Should architecture not be creative, imaginative, clever, and so forth?

Stylistic concern has created havoc in architecture since the 1960s. Postmodernism aimed to design buildings that the everyday person can understand. To achieve this, architects used the historian's approach. Designs such as the Piazza d'Italia and the Portland Building can be explained in this way. This led to an infatuation with surface quality in architecture.

It seems obvious that we need to look for other ways to evaluate and understand architecture. We need to find a different basis for the definition of architecture. Sustainability and ecology offer this. These approaches are mostly found in non-Western areas. There, we find architects who are not concerned with how something looks, but with how something works. They also show care for the existing environment. In architecture, this approach is mostly achieved through the exploitation of topography, materials, climate, and human needs.

Why is there a difference between the architecture of the Western – industrialized – world and that of the rest of the globe – the so-called developing world? These two areas had different paces of evolution. Europe and the Middle East were privileged areas for settlement, because of the abundance of water and fertile ground. Hence, civilization began there, and subsequently spread to other parts. This diffusion followed the East-West direction. In contrast, North-South migration was obstructed, and in some areas did not occur until sea transportation was possible. For instance, in Africa, a desert prevented North-South travel. Asian civilizations simply did not seem interested in exploring and colonizing the rest of the world. The Americas were separated from the rest of the world by oceans. In addition, European and Middle Eastern areas had more plants and animals that could be domesticated than the other areas of the world. Consequently, people who lived there were immune against everyday diseases earlier than people in other parts of the world.

Examples of sustainable and ecological architecture include many variations. Architecture can be determined by the manipulation of landscape and topography. Original cave dwellings ultimately lead to rock-carved architecture. Architecture can also be determined by materials. Locally available, found, ones produce stick-and-straw houses, so called "primitive huts," or stick-and-mud houses, wattle-and-daub construction. These primitive houses are quite capable of articulating the physical and social organization of a community. There are also snow houses, an approach that leads to tents and windbreaks. These are creative, pragmatic, and efficient satisfactions of needs. A particular life style is determined by land yields and climate.

In hot, but windy climates, we find wind towers, where material and form are adapted to generate the most benefits from the environment.

# AFRICA

African architecture can be divided into three major stylistic and cultural legacies: indigenous, Greek/Western, and Islamic. Remains and traces reach back to the 6th millenium BCE.

Paintings in rocks suggest that long-horned cattle was domesticated in Africa around the 7th millenium BCE. The area stretches from Ethiopia to Mauretania, and touches the Sahara. This evidence has been supported by excavation of animal bones. Earliest remains, after the cave dwellings, consist of tents and round huts. These eventually evolved into rectangular houses, a development that was most probably influenced by the architecture of Ancient Egypt. Pylons and obelisks are still visible in houses, as decorative features in a variety of forms.

## KENYA

### Kikuyu

The Kikuyu build villages that consist of unit houses belonging to members of the same ancestry. Houses are built by communal labor. Individual houses are constructed of a circle of timber poles, with conical roofs made of the same poles and covered by thatch.

## TOGO

### Taberma

Here is a tradition of anthropomorphism in architecture at work. The human body is seen as a (structural) paradigm for all sorts of spiritual bodies. The Taberma of northern Togo consider anthropomorphism "one of the most important concerns of building design, decoration, symbolism, and use." This belief makes their houses integral parts of the family, and helps maintain psychological and social stability.

The materials of the houses are compared to the human body: earthen core is the flesh, pebbles are the bones, and smooth clay surfaces are the skin. Thus, like the ancestors, who are said to model and shape each baby from sacred earth, the Taberma are shaping their houses. Like their care for their children, the Taberma also maintain their houses through a determined life cycle. Both form and plan of the house are seen as human, once in the upright, once in the lying position. Windows are eyes, doors mouths, grinding stones teeth, lintels tongues, and drain pipes penis or anus. The courtyard is the chest, women's bedroom vagina and womb, and the entrance room the legs.

This symbolism of the house also informs daily and ritual practices performed inside. A husband going to sleep with his wife is entering the womb, the "eyes" allow insiders to look out, the "mouth" receives the gifts. In initiation rites, the novices wait in this same bedroom, and emerge as if born again from the womb. Houses are dressed with markings or pieces of cloth hung over the walls, just as human beings are. The house's soul and the family's spiritual ancestors are symbolized through mounds and cones placed before the house.

## UGANDA

Indigenous architecture consists of beehive-shaped houses made from saplings, twigs, and reeds.

## NIGER

### Indigenous Architecture

West-African architecture is heavily determined by its choice construction technique: adobe. The above mosque reproduced the layout of traditional architecture, with houses set next to the exterior wall around a family compound, that encloses communal open space. The individual buildings tend to be either dome-shaped, or cubical with domed roofs.

## NIGERIA

### Urban Beginnings

Toward the end of the 1st millennium CE, ceremonial centers sprung up in the Yoruba territories. At the center of these communities was a palace precinct, housing the priest-king. There were also shrines to national deities there. This complex was built on a platform.

### Hausa Architecture

Rooms are arranged within or around a courtyard, and occupy the cardinal points. Eastern and southern points are masculine; western and northern are feminine. The center is the point for the vertical axis linking heaven and earth. The houses are built of adobe, and decorated in patterns that originate from the hand movements of the builder and imitate animals.

## GREAT ZIMBABWE, ZIMBABWE (1000-1500)

During the 4th century CE, farmers moved into this area, which had up to then served a hunting tradition. They probably lived in huts sheltered next to big boulders.

In the 9th or 10th centuries, there was a renewal of immigration from a different culture. Cattle played an important cultural and economic role for these people. During the late 12th century, this civilization changed. The old Iron Age cultures died out, and relationships with East Coast cultures were forged. The site declined in the later 15th century

This site lies on a platform 4000-5000 feet high. Zimbabwe means palace; the original meaning is "stone enclosure." At this site, there are two sets of ruins, the temple (or priest's house) on the hill, and the chief's house in the valley. This latter one is surrounded by other, smaller enclosures. The complex was enlarged during the 15th century. This culture created its wealth through gold mining and ivory collecting. There is no other parallel monument in the rest of Africa.

The walls were done in dry masonry of dressed granite blocks, with a rubble core. Both outside and inside faces taper toward the top, and there are buttresses on the inside face. These stones flaked off naturally from the surrounding hills in pieces between eight and eighteen cm thick. This exfoliation occurs due to the daily temperature changes. Construction seemed to begin with a small section built to its total height and then proceeded horizontally, thus eliminating the need for scaffolding. These walls are circular, but do not follow a pre-set plan. There were no roofs over these outer walls. There are doorways with arched tops in this wall.

In addition, there are mounds filled with rubble masonry, but faced with regular stone courses. Most probably, these represent the foundations for huts of a second occupation of this site. These structures were not sacred or ritual objects, but everyday dwellings. The forms imitated the shapes of the surrounding landscape. The surrounding walls served as protection from enemies, enclosure for outdoor living space and storage for food and livestock, house and garden wall, and simply the walls that separate the natural from the built environment.

The circular plan follows the concept of the kraal. Houses are a big part of the ancestor worship, as they provide a place for communion between them and us. Hence, daily living constantly partakes of religious practice.

### Chief's House (Elliptical Building)

This is an example of the hill style. The enclosing wall is 800 feet long, 17 ft thick, and 32 ft high. The maximum diameter is 292 feet. Along parts of it, there is a chevron pattern on top, which was made of thin granite plates.

Inside the wall were other walls forming a series of enclosures. There is also a conical tower, which is solid and believed to be a symbolic grain storage bin. It has been ruled out that this was a tomb. It could be a phallic symbol, or a symbol for the majesty of the king. However, it could just as easily be an imitation of the nearby hills. This seems to have been the major religious focus of the complex.

Several circular structures are placed inside the wall. Houses inside these walls were round, constructed in wattle-and-daub walls with thatched roofs. Interestingly, this is still the plan form of kraals of today.

### Hill Ruin

The Great Zimbabwe was most probably a religious center. The acropolis is on a granite outcropping 300 ft. above the valley. Its Western Temple has a wall with four cones on top. There are soapstone sculptures of birds on top, forming a balustrade. These were for protection from lightning.

## CHRISTIAN CHURCHES, LALIBELA (ETHIOPIA)

Christianity reached North Africa in its infancy, in the 4th century. It survived only partly after the Islamic conquest. These churches have a variety of plans. King Lalibela was given the command from God by angels to build ten churches. Construction is said to have taken twenty-four years. There is speculation that Egyptian or Indian stonecutters were employed. There is, however, also credible evidence that earlier construction techniques were carried over into these rock-carved churches. Sculptured doors with proper accessories are already found in obelisks of the Kingdom of Aksum (300 BCE-300 CE). The reliefs on the outsides also may refer to construction techniques of masonry walls with rubble infill. There, timbers were laid parallel and perpendicular to the walls for reinforcement. The amount of stone removed was five times bigger than that of Abu Simbel. The plan of most of these churches is a square.

### Amanuel Church

This imitates stone reinforced with wood, especially in the carving of doors and windows.

### Beta Madhane Alam (Church of the Redeemer)

This measures 33.7 x 23.7 m, and is 11.5 m high. The plan has five aisles, with the nave covered by a barrel vault and the aisles by flat ceilings.

### St. Beta Giyorgis (St. George Church)

This is essentially a tower in a deep pit. The wall surfaces alternate between projections and recesses, formed as if by interlocking wooden beams.

FIGURE 8–1. Potala Palace, Lhasa. This was the residence of the Dalai Lama.

# Chapter 9

# Early Christian and Byzantine Architecture

The temporal comforts and pleasures on which Roman life focused were replaced by a new religion. Concurrently with the political breakdown came a new focus from within, emphasizing spiritual concerns. As a result, new building needs arose. Architectural innovation shifted to these new building types to house communal groups of worshippers.

The new religion was appealing to Romans in the first century CE. A favorable ground existed for a humane and social religion of redemption in the lower classes. Jesus had studied Jewish scripture, and began a career as an itinerant teacher at age thirty. He preached brotherly love, charity, humility, and adherence to the spirit of Jewish law. In contrast to existing Jewish religious authorities, he forgave sins. He also criticized religious practices that, while adhering to the letter of Jewish law, were insensitive to human needs. In addition, he infuriated existing authorities because his followers believed him to be the promised Messiah. The most important factor in spreading Christian teaching was the work of Paul of Tarsus. The church developed a particular form of organization. Volunteer bishops supervised the congregations in a single city. Eventually, the bishop of Rome was accorded primacy among the bishops in the western half of the Empire. The bishop of Constantinople was accorded the same status for the eastern half, a division that developed into a permanent split. In 394 CE, Christianity was made the sole religion of the Empire.

The decline of Rome was precipitated not only by the spiritual crisis exposed by the new religion, but also by other factors. The disorderly successions of emperors ended the established one-man rule. The city of Rome itself became vulnerable, due to its large size and unstable government. Rome also received competition from other cities in the vast empire.

In 284, under the emperor Diocletian, the Roman Empire was divided into two halves. In 312, Constantine, fighting under the sign of the cross, defeated his co-emperor Maxentius. As a result, he issued an edict in which Christianity was given full equality with other religions. By 324, he was sole ruler of a once-more united Empire. In 330, Constantine moved the Roman capital to Constantinople. Other events contributed to the fall of Rome. More Germanic tribes, who fled the Huns, were allowed into the Empire.

## CHRISTIAN BUILDING, DURA EUROPOS (231)

From its beginning, Christianity needed a building type appropriate functionally and symbolically for public worship. In contrast to earlier practices, Christian services were held indoors. The temple belonged to all, and was not considered a privileged sanctum off limits to popular use. Thus, the old temples could clearly not be used. The requirements of this building were two: mass and baptism.

At first, residences were adapted to serve as public worship places. Here, a peristyle house was modified. Walls between rooms were eliminated to create a large meeting room. The eastern wing was raised to form a platform for the bishop's seat. Another room was set aside for the members that were yet not baptized, who nevertheless were allowed to hear mass. A small room with a tub was set apart for baptism. This oblong space has a niche in one of the narrow walls, into which a basin was placed. Murals fill the walls of this room. The niche has an illustration of Christ as the Good Shepherd, and of Adam and Eve holding fig leaves, in front of the tree of knowledge – a snake coils in front of this scene. On the sidewalls are murals of Jesus walking on the water, David and Goliath, the healing of the paralytic, the three Maries coming to the tomb of Christ, and the woman at the well. The baptistry room was reconstructed at Yale University in 1930.

Dura Europos, which had been founded by the followers of Alexander the Great, was a Roman garrison in Mesopotamia, on the river Euphrates. Dura means wall of fortress, and Europos was the name of the village in Macedonian times, probably indicating the origin of the ruler. The village was destroyed by the Persians in 256, and only discovered during World War I. It is situated on a plateau, ca. 100 feet above the river plain.

# CATACOMBS, ROME (4<sup>TH</sup> C.)

A second characteristic Christian building was the cemetery. Due to lack of space above ground, Christians followed other cults, and went beneath the ground. The Roman catacombs form irregular, maze-like underground streets. Walls were decorated with religious murals. Graves were cut into the two side walls in superimposed rows.

# OLD ST. PETER'S, ROME (319-329)

Once Christianity became the official religion, the buildings not only had to accommodate large numbers of converts, but also needed to facilitate hearing the spoken word and chanted psalms. The exciting aspect of early Christian architecture was that its forms were not prescribed by the faith. Thus, the new buildings were fresh innovations. The inspiration came from secular buildings, especially the Roman basilica for the congregation places, and centralized structures for shrines and baptisteries. The use of a miniature triumphal arch façade for this building denotes its use as an insignia of rule. Originality was not a creative issue. Copying was not thought of as imitation, but simply as using an older example that was venerable and had proven its usefulness.

This church was built over the grave of the apostle Peter. It was begun about 319-322. The atrium took until 390. The apostle Peter's grave became the focal point of this T-shaped building. It was a monumental structure; the nave measured 301 feet, the total width was 216 feet, and the ceiling height 104.5 feet. It is a double-aisled basilica. The transept measured 297 feet x 68.9 feet. Behind the transept was a semi-circular apse capped by a half-dome, rising over Peter's tomb. This apse distinguishes the building from the earlier converted meeting places.

Christian buildings at first discontinued Roman vaulting in favor of a more traditional system. This may have been intended to dissociate the new buildings from the old Roman secular ones. However, the open roof trusses united the interior into a dynamic whole, different from the Roman division into static vaulting bays. Stylistically, the origin was the stripped Classicism of the late Roman Empire. The nave arcade established a flat plane for the walls, which continued upward into the clerestory wall. With the painted decoration, these walls become devoid of substance. The interior impression relied on large spaces, clarity, and the use of large planes. The interior appears as an indeterminate space between two parallel walls. The timber rafters of the roof similarly seem not to seal off the space underneath completely. In fact, there seemed to be a deliberate effort to counteract any feature that might create a unified interior impression.

For St. Peter's, 100 ancient columns were reused. Christian architecture transformed the earlier capital into one from which the arched ribs spring. The capitals received a trapezoidal form, and the abacus was eliminated. While originating in the Roman basilica, certain modifications were added: narthex, colonnaded forecourt with fountain, and gate. The total length of the complex was 669 feet. A triumphal arch led from the nave into the transept. The hybrid forms and origins of the Christian basilica also point to the fact that at the beginning, the people were the architecture, not the building.

The exterior is merely an enclosure of the interior, and reflects the spatial sequences in a straightforward way. The principle of assembly is one of addition of volumes. In fact, the basilica is a building that is joined in a rather unwielding manner.

# S. APPOLLINARE IN CLASSE, RAVENNA (532-549)

This is a basilica-church without transept. The longitudinal direction toward the apse is reinforced by the articulation of the murals into strips. The apse is polygonal and flanked by smaller apses in the aisles. This basilica presents an exterior composed of individual masses, as secondary spaces protrude on all four sides from the main part, the nave. The incoherent building-block appearance of this volume is unified by the dominant articulation into planar and boxlike units, which continues even when a circular volume on the inside has to be enclosed.

Statues were not allowed in early Christian churches. There were two attitudes toward pictorial decoration. The West stated that paintings were needed so that the illiterate could understand the teachings of the Bible. Clarity and simplicity of storytelling were consequently more important than aesthetic skill.

# S. VITALE, RAVENNA (526-)

In the 5ᵗʰ and 6ᵗʰ centuries, experiments in Christian architecture were directed at fusing the congregational and occasional buildings. The question was, whether centralized buildings could be used to hold congregations, or whether the longitudinal liturgical axis could be combined with the vertical heavenly axis. In the eastern half of the empire, political and church administrations tended to merge. The eastern half achieved its pinnacle of cultural and political importance during the reign of Justinian (483-565), who acceded to the throne in 527. After 395, the western half of the Empire declined, as it was occupied by a succession of tribes from northern Europe, with the Ostrogoths under Theoderic ruling the area from Ravenna in 526. Each of these tribal warlords considered himself an ally of the Eastern Roman Emperor. During his reign, Justinian managed to reconquer much of the area of the former Roman Empire. Ravenna then became the western capital of Justinian's Empire.

San Vitale's plan is central, and derives from Ancient Roman palace reception-halls, such as the octagon in Nero's Domus Aurea. In these spaces, the emperor would hold court; hence they became symbolic of his dominion. The dome that covered this space would have emphasized the quasi-divine status of the emperor. Eight wedge-shaped piers, connected by arches, support the dome on a high drum. A second, lower octagon surrounds this core. The dominant vertical axis was complemented by a strong longitudinal accent, emphasized by an entrance atrium and a deep chapel. The chapel bay occupies one of the eight sides of the ambulatory. It is expressed outside by a higher gabled roof. Inside it is capped by a barrel vault. Two circular one-story buildings flank the main apse.

The ambulatory around the central circle is two stories high. The gallery was reserved for women. The ambulatory is separated from the center through triple-column screens, which curve into the ambulatory. Oblique views prevail, presenting a rich interlocking of primary and secondary spaces. Light enters directly through the windows of the drum and indirectly through gallery and ambulatory. The interior walls were covered with mosaics, resulting in an overwhelming layering of various light effects.

A narthex was added in the 16ᵗʰ century in a slight deviation from the main interior axis. It is an oblong room with apses. Two circular stair towers are inserted between this room and the octagon of the church. Originally, an open atrium would have allowed direct access into the ambulatory, offering a perspective view on the altar, framed by columns. Construction is of brick, with interlocked hollow terra-cotta tubes for the dome. The rough surface texture helps to increase the contrast with the mysterious, jewel-like interior. Radial walls and flying arches transmit the load of the dome to wall buttresses in the outer octagon.

# HAGIA SOPHIA (532-537)

In 532, there was a citizens' revolt in Constantinople, resulting in the destruction of large parts of the city. Immediately, plans for rebuilding started, among them the church of Hagia Sophia, which had existed since 360. Work on this drastically altering reconstruction was finished in 537. The new design appears to have been influenced by earlier central-plan churches and Ancient Roman buildings, such as the Pantheon, the Basilica of Maxentius, and the tepidaria of imperial baths, as well as the earlier Sts Sergius and Bacchus in Constantinople. Justinian engaged two philosophers to design the new church, known for their mathematical studies: Anthemios of Tralles and Isidorus of Miletus. Both were experts in theoretical physics and statics, academics, and were commissioned to design an ethereal, dematerialized building.

The new church was to be a double-shell building filling a rectangle measuring 230 x 250 feet. Inside, four massive piers, each 102 feet apart from the others, and pointed to the north and south, carried a dome on pendentives. The width of the nave is 30 m, the height of the dome is 56 m. It is therefore larger than a typical Gothic cathedral. This structural system creates a contrast between the east-west and north-south sides. At the eastern and western ends, semi-domes rise to the main dome and support it. At the north and south sides, heavy buttressing piers shore up the dome. Between them are the deep arches also seen on the inside. These arches are opened with two rows of small windows. The corners between the arches and the buttress piers are bracketed with diagonal niches. The western and eastern semi domes have different profiles. Hence, the exterior form swells out on east and west, and pushes in on south and north. All building parts are constructed of stone, bricks, and mortar; iron and timber are used for cramps and ties.

This central part was then surrounded by another, illuminated, spatial layer. On the outside, this layer is articulated through swelling and undulating walls and roofs. The plan provided a combination centralized/longitudinal building, as there were semicircular apses along the main axis and screen walls between nave and aisles. However, the boundaries of the longitudinal space are truly elusive. This is reinforced by the lack of correspondence between the lower and upper parts of the walls. The layout of a congregational basilica was married to a vaulted superstructure. This superstructure, with its geometric precision, and the various horizontal cornices are the features that help provide a unified impression of this interior. Most of the surfaces inside were pierced and covered with mosaics or marble veneer. In construction, the church is composed of masses and shells of brickwork laced with stone reinforcement. During construction, the buttress piers in the northeast and southwest aisles were built higher, to add more counterweight to the lateral thrust of the dome. The springing of the dome is at 120 feet and the apex at 180 feet. The inside appears in motion, with curving and intersecting surfaces, all bathed in light. At the base of the dome is a circular row of forty windows, making the dome appear to float like a Dome of Heavens. Roofs and tops of pillars are sheathed in lead. There is a difference in this church, between the sensuous decoration and the geometrical shapes of its construction. In the final appearance, individual parts are absorbed into a whole, creating a sublime environment. The scale is no longer human, but theocratic.

The original structure consists of the innermost, primary piers, spanned by arches and enclosing a square. Secondary piers support the barrel-vaulted passages between main nave and apses. A horizontal circle is supported by these arches, and in turn supports the dome. Pendentives bridge the curved areas between pier tops and dome ring. The north and south arches are closed with screen walls. The western and eastern arch are flanked by half-domes, again resting on an arch at the outer point. The half-domes are again flanked by two barrel vaults and a smaller half-dome on axis. On the northern and southern sides, barrel vaults form two aisles. Piers and arches were constructed of stone, the domes of brick.

Originally, there was an atrium before this church. The three western portals are inserted between flying buttresses supporting the roof of the gallery. On the western side, a large semicircular window is left in the upper wall. Like all other windows, this one has marble tracery. The windows are divided into three by vertical intermediate columns. This church has two narthexes. The outer one is covered by groin vaults; the inner one is sheathed in colored marble almost to the cornice level. It is accessible from a southwestern entrance with a mosaic depicting Justinian and Constantine presenting models of Hagia Sophia and the city of Constantinople to the Virgin Mary. The vaults of the inner narthex are covered with a golden mosaic ground, decorated with crosses, stars, and other geometrical motifs. It is lit from clerestory windows in the wall above the height of the outer narthex. From there, three groups of three doorways lead into the nave. The doors are sheathed in bronze and are decorated with crosses. The middle group is the Imperial doors, decorated more lavishly, also using marble panels. A lunette mosaic above the taller central doorway shows Christ enthroned on a lyre-backed throne, with the emperor kneeling before him. Flanking Christ are two medallions, depicting the Virgin and the archangel Gabriel. The doors between the two narthexes, apart from the central ones, do not line up, and the vaulting in the inner narthex does not correspond to the rhythm of the doors.

The apse semi-dome carries a mosaic depiction of the Virgin and Child. In the gallery north of the apse is a fragmented mosaic of the archangel Gabriel. In the pendentives are mosaics showing seraphim. Individual parts of the mosaics are glass, with color applied to the back. The walls between the stained glass windows are faced in marble. The apse is extended by a barrel-vaulted space. Flanking the apse are additional domed exedrae, angled to face the nave. They are bounded by colonnades, with different articulations in the two stories. The lower story has porphyry columns with an arcade decorated with fretted marble and disks; the upper colonnade is more colorful. Their capitals are bowl-shaped and decorated with undercut stylized acanthus and palm leaves enclosing monograms of the emperor. These colonnades continue westward, and form the nave walls between the inner piers. The difference between the two stories, and their separation with heavy cornices emphasizes the horizontal direction. The spandrels of the arcades continue the undercut leaf decoration of the capitals. On the upper level, these decorations are done in light marble inlay on dark marble. The three semi-domes of the eastern end in turn support a larger semi-dome terminating the nave. The semi-dome terminates in the arch spanning the two easternmost inner piers. In the lower parts of each of these semi-domes is a ring of windows. Along the sides of the nave are similar arches connecting the piers, enclosing tympana with two rows of windows over shallow niches. At the foot of the tympana are mosaic figures of standing bishops and other church fathers. The two eastern pendentives in between these arches are each decorated with a mosaic depiction of a seraph, with its face concealed by a star. The walls are covered with marble slabs of different dimensions and colors, bordered by white marble seams.

The innermost piers project into one's view, emphasizing the purpose of the central space as a nave. Large circular plaques fastened to these piers contain golden Arabic inscriptions on dark green ground. The aisles are separated by stylobates from the nave. At the western end, barrel-vaulted passages through the secondary piers also connect aisles with nave (at the eastern end, these passages are blocked by later barricades). The main piers connect to buttressing piers across the aisles and divide them into bays. These uneven bays are covered by groin vaults carried on columns. These bays are linked through barrel-vaulted passages to the adjoining spaces. Originally, the ceilings were decorated with mosaic crosses and other religious symbols on gold ground (These are now covered by later over-painting.). The walls are treated in the same manner as those in the nave. At the springing level of the vaults is a frieze using the same decorative technique as the capitals. Most of the light to the aisles comes now from the nave. The dome is not visible at first, but the light entering through the windows at its base eventually attracts the eye. Its ribs vanish toward the top. The top is covered by another plaque with Arabic inscriptions. It is a shallow dome, with the center of its curvature below the base cornice line. Access to the galleries is provided by ramps rising along spine walls in the four corners. The galleries are smaller than the lower levels. There is more natural light. The vaults are still groin vaults, but their section is more dome-like. The capitals are now of the Ionic order. All the upper columns lean outward, demonstrating the loads and forces at work in this building. Among the mosaics still preserved is a Deisis (Christ flanked by the Virgin and St. John), and a number of imperial portraits. These were added at various dates after the initial construction. The western gallery is a simple barrel-vaulted passage. Access to parts above the galleries is provided through staircases in the outer buttressing piers.

After an earthquake in 557, the original saucer dome collapsed in May 558. A new one, with a steeper profile, was built. Subsequent collapses of the dome occurred in 989 and 1346, after each of which it was reconstructed, finished in 994/5 and 1353 respectively. The present dome consists of northern and southern sections dating from 558, a western section from 989, and an eastern section from 1346. There are numerous deformations in the arches and supporting piers, demonstrating the forces of this structure. The meaning of the dome is that of an earthly analogue to heaven.

The basic themes of ecclesiastical architecture were formulated during the Early Christian period, namely those of center and path, as well as, of interiority. From the beginning, churches consisted of two major parts: the congregational nave and the chancel. Thus, the formerly secluded place for the clergy, while still only reserved for them, was opened, at least visually. There is also a contrast between the plain, neutral exterior and the richly decorated interior. The articulation of the interior is not anthropomorphic, such as in Greek architecture. Columns are used as emblematic motifs, and serve to emphasize the longitudinal movement. Walls appear as dematerialized. The center of the Christian world is something more than a concrete natural or man-made place. It is the abstract point where the meaning of life is revealed.

From Greece to Rome and ultimately into the Early Christian period, there appears to be a decline in artistic virtuosity and an increase in attempts to simply portray or represent the new faith.

# Chapter 10

# Romanesque Architecture

The Middle Ages, spanning the period from Ancient Rome to the Renaissance, are divided into three periods: Early (450-900), High (900-1200) and Late (1200-1450). Public building resumed only ca. 800, after a break since the fall of the Roman Empire. This resumption coincided with the appearance of Charlemagne. He aimed to recapture something of the intellectual achievement of Rome by improving education and establishing centers of learning. Building activity on a larger scale, involving above all churches, resumed after 1000, when political conditions became more settled. In general, the architecture is heavy and sturdy, for defensive reasons, and resembles the massive Roman structures, hence the name.

One cannot yet speak of national states in the Romanesque period. There was instead a profusion of large and small territories on one side, and the Empire on the other. It was, however, only at the end of the Romanesque period that the strongest parts of the Empire asserted itself, namely the crown lands in France, and the kingdom of England. This political division most probably accounts for the regionalism of the Romanesque architectural style. The small territories may be compared to a multitude of art centers, which are often sharply demarcated from each other.

## MEDIEVAL DESIGN THEORY AND PRINCIPLES

Ancient knowledge was scarce, due partly to the destruction of the library of Alexandria. Only a few fragments of Ancient philosophy survived. Beauty was defined in two ways. It was first the shining through of the idea in matter. This was specified by Dionysius Areopagite as the light metaphysic. Secondly, beauty was defined as an aesthetic quality based on numbers and proportions. In the Middle Ages, ideas were not objective, but were treated as God's thoughts. The artist and architect usually had a conception of the final form, before he began his creative activity. Art is not imitation of nature, but does similar things as nature, namely giving form to matter. Medieval man delighted in diagrams. Geometric systems of proportioning were the standard means of designing Gothic structures. Plans were drawn up and designed by means of transforming a basic module, which was either a square or a triangle. Similarly, in art one can see intricate patterns of interlocking ribbons, reflecting the diagrams and transformations of the architects. Medieval artists also expressed what they felt. In architecture, Romanesque church buildings express the idea of the church militant. The painted decoration of the Early Christian basilicas was replaced by sculptural decoration.

## PALATINE CHAPEL, ODO VON METZ, AACHEN (796-805)

Charlemagne is buried in this church. It stood at the southern end of a colonnade that connected it to the other buildings of the Royal Palace. This chapel was modeled on San Vitale in Ravenna. While built to resemble Roman or Early Christian models, it was rather crude compared to its prototypes. While the court was peripatetic, Aachen was established as the principal residence of the king. It was an octagonal structure built of cut stone with a stone vault. The cupola is decorated with a mosaic showing Christ adored by the twenty-four Elders of the Apocalypse. Surrounding this is an ambulatory of sixteen sides. This does not emphasize continuous space, but rather individual spaces around the central cylinder. Each bay of the ambulatory is covered with its own vault. The arched openings between central space and ambulatory are closed by columns screens. The Corinthian columns were salvaged from Ancient buildings in Italy. The drum is pierced by eight windows. This building was preceded by a rectangular atrium with two-story galleries on three sides. The fourth side had two flanking stair towers as high as the main cupola, thus forming a westwork. This part held the emperor's throne, on a balcony facing the choir. A conspicuous feature is the combination of massive enclosure and manifest verticality. Towers became formal elements of primary importance. The choir was added in 1353-1413.

# MONASTICISM

This institution arose in the East. In Egypt, towards the end of the 3rd century, a Christian named Anthony retreated into the desert as a way of conquering evil spirits, beginning the monastic movement. Groups of monks began to organize into communities. During the mid-4th c. an early form of monasticism was introduced to France by Martin of Tours. In the early 6th c., Benedict of Nursia laid down the basis of western monastic communal life. In 529, he founded the monastery on Monte Cassino. Among the major contribution of these monasteries was the preservation of Ancient literature, through copying and studying. Men and women coming to the monasteries sought to serve god, and pledged celibacy, poverty and obedience. They spent their lives in prayer and manual labor. Eventually, they functioned as the political, cultural, and agricultural centers of their surrounding regions.

## PLAN OF A MONASTERY, ST GALL (820)

At an important meeting of monastic officials, a model plan for a monastery was drawn up. On a rectangular sheet of parchment, 44" x 30", stitched together from smaller pieces, is a drawing for this plan. The principal building was the church, filled with multiple altars for the monks. It is double-ended and turreted. The interior is divided into compartments, each with an altar. This was to be the only stone building, and it divides the whole area into two parts. South of the church is the inner cloister. This courtyard is surrounded on the other three sides by economy buildings. On the northern side are the public buildings: guesthouses, school, and house of the abbot. To the east are the buildings for the novices. The quarters for the novices and the hospital replicate the cloister arrangement of the main buildings. Church and cloister are secluded from the other functions. Monks' dormitory, refectory, and pantry enclose the cloister. Monasteries served as hotels during the Middle Ages. The whole arrangement is grouped into various ensembles of buildings, each one with a particular function. The image is that of the city, including urban facilities and amenities. Particular aspects of this plan include the large size of the church. This was to serve the many pilgrims who would visit this monastery. Of concern also were the issue of comfort and the degree to which the monastery had to acknowledge the outside world. A primary objective of the plan was to clearly separate the daily activities of pilgrims and of the monks. St. Gall presents an ordered world for the pursuance of the blessed life. It shows a utopian monastic world fusing ideal order with perfection of utility.

## ST. MICHAEL, HILDESHEIM (1001-1022)

This was a monastic church. The monastery was founded by Bernward (933-1022), bishop of Hildesheim, in 996. Bernward was the tutor of the German Emperor Otto III, and received a splinter of the True Cross from the emperor as a token of their friendship. This splinter was enshrined in a monumental bronze cross, and the monastery took care of it. Later, Bernward endowed the monastery with his private possessions and built the church of St. Michael. It is dedicated to the archangel Michael, who will weigh the souls on the day of the Last Judgement. The original church was altered during the 17th and 18th centuries, and partly destroyed (by fire) during World War II. The existing church is a reconstruction. Everything except the walls of the building is modern.

The church is a basilica. However, it is double-ended. There are two transepts, the eastern one with three apses, the western one with one large and deep chancel. The transepts have three-storied galleries, reached by octagonal staircase towers. It is one of the earliest churches with a clearly defined (isolated) crossing. Square towers are placed over the crossings. The western apse is raised to make space for a crypt below, containing Bernward's sarcophagus. Interior spaces are simple, with undecorated, plain walls. Windows are simply cut into the walls.

St. Michael's has a multitude of altars. The many relics in the possession of the church needed separate altars, and clerics needed to read Mass daily.

The irregular grouping of volumes in this church goes back to the origin of the so-called "family of churches." This consisted of two basilicas and a baptistry, each fulfilling a special function. At Hildesheim, these functions are pushed together and combined in a single building. The westwork takes up functions of the centralized building. Volumes are clear-cut geometrical shapes. The walls are ca. five feet thick, which probably ensured their survival. They are of ashlar on the outsides, in between is a layer of rubble and mortar, and the inside face was plastered. These walls supported a wooden roof truss, hidden behind a flat, paneled ceiling fastened to it. The apses, crypt with ambulatory, staircase towers, and lower floors of galleries were vaulted.

St. Michael's offers a number of differences and developments from the Early Christian basilica. It has a greater variety of spaces, and more part spaces. It was among the earliest multi-towered churches of the Middle Ages. It is more massive and more decisively divided into its parts. The towers seemed to originate from the towers of a city wall. This adds the function of a refuge to the towered church, both symbolically and in actuality. The church thus becomes a sacred fortress. In this building, a visual unity is created, even though it is not put together in a simple, coherent way. As a result, whenever one is in this church, one sees similar things, as there is no clear axiality or other ordering structure that guides the layout and articulation. The building only comes together in the gaze of the viewer. The square of the crossing serves as basic module of the plan. Because it is demarcated by four arches, one immediately senses it to be a central bay of the interior. The 1:2 support rhythm in the nave arcade emphasizes this scheme. It is easy to overlook the modular plan, as the pillars rise at the corners of ground-plan squares. At St. Michael, two columns are flanked by a pair of pillars. The whole plan suggests order and balance. The beauty of the spatial effect is in large part a product of this abstract clarity of the plan. The east-west direction of churches was also based on a light symbolism. Evil was associated with darkness, salvation with light. Hence the eastern focus inside churches was also the light focus. In addition, representations of the Last Judgment were placed on the tympana over doors. One enters, thus, through death and judgment, to heaven.

## St-Sernin, Toulouse (1080-1120)

The two centuries after 1000 were marked by genuine piety and religious fervor. People lived for the afterlife. This fervor was paralleled by the increase of the cult of relics. The practice of traveling to churches that possessed powerful relics eventually developed into the pilgrimages. The most famous of them was the pilgrimage to Santiago de Compostela. Along the way, monasteries and churches set up a network of way stations. For pilgrimage churches, a particular plan was devised, so that the pilgrims and the monks did not interfere with one another. The church was given two spatial shells: a series of outer passages for the pilgrims, and the basilica for the monks. In addition, the apse was transformed into a choir. This was deeper than the apse and surrounded by an ambulatory with radiating chapels, which contained the relics. Moreover, the aisles continued around the transepts as well. Thus, such churches create an effect of simultaneous expansion and concentration. The plan of the pilgrimage church symbolizes a horizontal extension, to accommodate its function of serving as goal for pilgrims from all corners of the world. This is corroborated by elaborate entrances into the transepts. This church has two aisles on either side, the inner one with a gallery. The major source of light in the nave is the large rose window constructed over the western entrance. There are no clerestory windows so that the structural stability, as well as the height of the nave, could be increased. The interior is refined and slender, the exterior richly articulated. The design is based on the module of the crossing in a system of square schematism.

## Cathedral, Pisa (1063-13ᵀᴴ c.)

The historical contribution of Italian Romanesque architecture consisted of the continuation of Antique traditions. Italy had strong Classical traditions and was not very receptive to Gothic. The whole complex comprises the cathedral (begun 1063), baptistry (1153-1265), and tower (1174-1271). This is still a church in the type of "family of churches" with individual buildings for special purposes. It is the largest Romanesque church in Tuscany. It was situated at the edge of the old city. Pisa was the leading power in the western Mediterranean for about a century after they defeated the Saracens in a sea battle off Palermo in 1063. The cathedral testifies to this greatness.

Here, the decorative leitmotif is the arcade. The whole is a lacy marble specter. The entrance façade of the cathedral has a frieze of blind arcades on the ground-floor level, into which are placed the three entrance doors. Above are four rows of arcaded galleries. Behind this layer is a polychrome marble facade. The arcade decoration is continued in the tower, and turned into cylindrical form. The interior is strikingly Early Christian, with a flat timber ceiling (16ᵗʰ-century addition). It is a colonnaded basilica. It is monumental and spatially rich, providing vistas through column screens. The nave is flanked by two aisles on each side. This is an indication of a high claim to importance on the part of the church. The transept arms are similar to small basilicas, three-aisled and with their own apses. There is a deep choir. Galleries with alternating supports surround the whole interior. The clerestory zone deviates from the lower wall articulation. The crossing is rather complex, with the nave aisles continuing uninterrupted, cutting through the transept arms. Four strong pillars support the large cupola. The massing of the cathedral suggests expanding volumes. An oval dome serves as crossing tower.

## S. Miniato al Monte, Florence (1062-1200)

This church is a polished, elegant marble structure in a Classicizing, proto-Renaissance design. Marble was plentiful in Italy, which is probably responsible for the polychrome design. The exterior is assembled of taut, angular volumes. The articulation is rational and disciplined, with sharp detail. The decorative leitmotif is the rectangle. The main facade repeats the interior articulation, with a horizontal arcade supporting a vertical superstructure.

The interior is not vaulted, pointing to the impact of Early Christian architecture. The upper parts of the walls are decoratively articulated. The nave is divided by piers, with diaphragm arches. The eastern bay is split-leveled, with a crypt beneath the choir.

### CATHEDRAL, DURHAM (1093-1133)

English churches typically combined massiveness and decoration, and had sprawling and piecemeal plans. Durham Cathedral is of enormous scale and consists of overpowering forms. It has a twin-towered west facade and a large square crossing tower. It was among the earliest buildings with rib vaulting. The ribbing continues the shafts of the nave supports. Inside, a double-bay scheme is used. The proportioning of bays between nave and aisles is not modular, as nave bays are elongated transversally. The wall openings are much enlarged. The structure is rather heavy, consisting of three-layer piers and masonry cylinders. These heavy masses are all decorated in delicate, incised patterns. There is a wall change into a mass-dissolving double shell. All is gathered into linear columnar elements, which are extended into the vaults.

Already here, a feature that will distinguish English from French Early Gothic architecture is found. The English did not favor continuous nave shafts that connect the walls with the vaults. English vault shafts tended to begin above the nave arcade. This allowed them to increase the complexity of their interiors. In England, the pier system and its variations took precedent over the overall spatial-structural unity favored in France. Therefore, the English rejected the organic French system in favor of one that emphasizes parts.

# STRUCTURAL SYSTEMS

There was a need to replace timber roofs with stone ones, which would be more stable and fireproof. During the 11th and 12th centuries, there was a conscious attempt to match Roman vaulting technology. This happened through experimentation. During the Gothic period, structural science advanced through daring experimentation by the master masons. In contrast to Classical architecture, medieval architecture is characterized by its verticalism. The form of medieval architecture did not arise from a combination of supporting and supported parts, but from the constructive requirements of the stone envelope that enclosed its space. The vaults do not appear as carried, but rather as the merging of the walls. This quality is corroborated by the fact that these walls are arcaded on the ground floor, making the columns or pillars not appear as supporting features, but as left-over parts of the wall. The capitals appear less as part of the column than as part of the wall. Even the decoration follows this pattern, by articulating the continuous line of the nave arches, the transverse arches, and even the ribs. Hence, what appears to be structural articulation turns out to be on closer inspection an articulation of the wall character of these buildings.

# MEANING

The basic properties of Romanesque architecture stem from a combination of the Early Christian basilica with the protective and aspiring motif of the tower. The towered façades of medieval churches became symbols of protection and transcendental aspiration, as they imitate earlier city walls and palatial entrance gates. The addition of towers caused problems of formal coordination. The Romanesque church is an articulate, modular organism. This is manifest in the progressive subdivision and plastic articulation of interior and exterior walls (arcades with emphasized piers, pilaster strips, and corbel tables). Furthermore, the articulation of the nave by the rhythmic succession of columns served to relate the longitudinal axis more directly to man's movements.

FIGURE 10–1.  Palatine Chapel, Aachen

# Chapter 11

# Pre-Columbian Architecture

Ancestors of American Indians came as early as 40,000 BCE from Siberia. A second wave of immigration took place around 20,000 to 15,000 BCE. By ca. 12,000 BCE, a hunting tradition was established in the mid-continental valley, and a desert tradition in the great basin and the Southwest by about 8000 BCE. The central culture also branched out into the East, beginning in about 8000 BCE. By about 4000 BCE, the food plant maize had been domesticated, marking the point in time when these civilizations became sedentary.

## SERPENT MOUND, LOCUST GROVE, OHIO (ca. 1000)

There was a woodland tradition in the American East, lasting from about 1000 BCE to 1000 CE. This culture was technologically simple, using tools of chipped flint, polished stone, and beaten copper. A complex ceremonial life centered around a cult of the dead. There are remains of thousands of burial mounds, effigy mounds, and ceremonial enclosures. These are monuments, not intended to provide shelter. Rather, they serve to distinguish a space, or mark a space. The earthworks were built of basketfuls of earth carried by hand.

The serpent mound is an example of the universal prehistoric practice of creating visually impressive settings for ceremonial purposes. It is in the form of a snake, placed on a crescent-shaped promontory. The monument measures 1348 feet long and 20 feet wide. The height of the mound is between 2 and 6 feet. At the head of the snake is an oval enclosure, which has been interpreted as an egg being swallowed by the snake or being ejected from a leaping frog, or as the sun being swallowed by the snake. Many of these earth sculptures are oriented toward summer solstice, reminiscent of Stonehenge. Later cultures built rectangular mounds, and constructed temples and other sacred buildings on top. Mound building declined after about 1000 CE.

## NATIVE AMERICAN ARCHITECTURE

### SOUTHWEST

Around 9500 BCE, there was more moisture, and the temperature was colder in this area. Big game (mammoth, horse) brought hunters from the mid-western prairies. In ca. 8500 BCE, environmental conditions worsened, and only the bison survived. Bison died out ca. 6000-5000 BCE. Then, buffalo hunters from Colorado ventured south. Ca. 6000 BCE foragers began to occupy this area, moving in from the west, north, and south. At that time, there were probably rudimentary shelters in the form of stone walls that created sleeping circles, huts, and windbreaks (shallow depressions suggest this). Most were made of a framework of poles, with brush, grass, or hides as cover. There were also storage pits.

Beginning in 2000 BCE, agricultural traditions begin, with corn as the staple crop, accompanied by squash and beans. Villages were laid out in the form of camps. By 500 BCE, a "revolution" occurred, most probably through immigration from Mexico. The increased dependence on agriculture brought communal organization and permanent dwellings. Non-food production skills began. General architectural features appeared, beginning with pit houses. Distinctive cultures and areas resulted from this change. People became more attached to their places.

## HOHOKAM

This civilization occupied Arizona. Architectural features resembled Central American cultures. There were platform mounds and ball courts, and irrigation systems with canals. Villages had houses laid out around plazas. The Southwest traditions can be considered provincial, watered down versions of Mesoamerican cultures. Both domestic crops and agricultural methods came from there.

### *Casa Grande Ruins, Arizona (1300-1450)*

Between 1100 and 1450, there were villages with houses of solid clay walls with entrance from above. Casa Grande is a multistory example constructed of sun-dried mud, formed by hand, and timber beams. It is a Great House, either used for habitation, or special purposes.

## ANASAZI

### *Cliff Dwellings, Mesa Verde, Colorado (1100)*

Spanish conquerors began to move into New Mexico in 1539, and discovered there the Anasazi culture, a people of basket makers and potters. Of all American Indian peoples, they were the most attached to their place. Their architecture originated from the partly underground round houses their ancestors had built in Siberia. These structures were built around 1100. Originally, they were built into cliffs, but had to be moved to the flat land later because of a water shortage, as shown in the Pueblo Bonito. There, the original form was preserved – pueblos on flat land mostly in the shape of a D, with multiple stories on the curved side. They were built in masonry construction. Later development: a number of round houses were pushed together, and houses became consequently square. They were built in adobe construction. The original wall was made of sun-dried mud-brick, and each year a new layer of adobe was applied. Living quarters were on top; the bottom was used for storage. The roofs were made of logs, covered with branches, grass, mud and a layer of adobe. The buildings were massive, but energy-efficient. The round form of the ancestral Siberian huts were preserved in the kivas, underground circular chambers used for ceremonial purposes. Most Indian architecture can be traced back to the original round hut.

### *Pueblo Bonito, Chaco Canyon, New Mexico (1100)*

Due to water shortage, these civilizations moved down into the valleys. The Spanish conquerors called these "pueblos." The earliest settlements were assemblies of pit houses with pole, brush, or mud constructions above ground. Then, they changed to large apartment buildings, which could be up to five stories high. The central form was also important in the American Indian cultures. This indicates the primacy of the circle at the beginning. Here this form is used for kivas, subterranean or partly subterranean ceremonial chambers. They were religious and social centers for families or clans. A bench circled around, and there were posts for roof support. A small hole in the ground symbolized the entrance to the spirit world below. A roof opening served for access and ventilation. This pueblo had a unified plan in the shape of the letter D. Individual rooms adjoin one another with kivas and open space.

At one time, Chaco Canyon was a flourishing cultural area, known as the "Chaco Phenomenon." There was an increase in population achieved through impressive harnessing of runoff water. This enabled a network of villages and towns, connected by roads and signaling outposts for communication. The whole complex consisted of about 2000 sites, ranging from camps, to pit houses, to pueblos, to Navajo remains. This civilization most probably used celestial observation to make calendars, which determined ritual and farming cycles.

# SOUTH AMERICAN AND CENTRAL AMERICAN CULTURES

Among the burning questions asked of these cultures is where they originate from: Siberia, as the Northern American Indians, Egypt, or independent of external influences.

## OLMEC (2000-200 BCE)

This seems to have been the originary civilization in this area. However, it came into existence suddenly, without any evolutionary phase. Characteristic are the large sculptures (10 ft. tall) of the heads of rulers.

## *La Venta (900-400 BCE)*

An earthen platform that was ribbed on the outside so that it looks like a volcano, with basalt columns, marked the ceremonial center. Four huge sculptures of heads face out from this courtyard.

## Aztec

This was primarily a warrior people, settling on the high central plateau of Mexico. They had conquered the Toltec culture existing there. Only scarce remains survive of this culture. The capital, Tenochtilán (1325-1521), was destroyed by the Spanish in 1521.

### *Teotihuacán*

This "Place of the Gods" had three pyramid temples. It was destroyed by fire in the 7th century. It was the largest Pre-Columbian city. At its peak it covered 20 square kilometers and housed 125,000 inhabitants.

Its three temples were grouped symmetrically, flanking a broad street, the Avenue of the Dead, which measured 2 kilometers and is between 40 and 95 meters wide. This street was lined on both sides by apartment complexes. The Pyramid of the Sun measured 215 meters square at the bottom and was about 63 meters high. It had five platforms, and one stair. A cave used for rituals was underneath this pyramid. The Pyramid of the Moon was situated at the northern end of the Avenue of the Dead. Called Moon Plaza, this contains additional structures. The Temple of Quetzalcóatl, the Feathered Serpent, was in the center of a quadrangle measuring 400 meters square, bounded by terraced mounds. The North and South palaces are also part of this citadel complex. This pyramid had six tiers.

## Maya

Remains of this culture are found mostly on the Yucatan, Guatemala, and Honduras. It reached its peak during the early Christian era, its classic culture lasting from 250-600. Priests and nobles are thought to have constituted a theocratic government. The central and South American Pre-Columbian cultures did not know the arch. They knew how to build long, but not high. The only way to build high was the massive technique resulting in pyramids.

### *Chichén Itzá*

This city was the power center in the Yucatan.

### El Castillo (late 12th century)

Stairways rise to the top on all four sides of this stepped pyramid. On top is a temple dedicated to Quetzalcoatl (the plumed serpent-god). The serpent motif is used on the stair balustrades and the columns of the temple. The temple facade is carved with figures representing Tula warriors.

### Tikal (100 BCE - 9th c. CE)

The pyramids here are steep, and measure up to 200 feet. The temples on top had stone crests. The Great Plaza formed the center of this city. The main temple/pyramids around it were the Temple of the Giant Jaguar and the Temple of the Masks.

## Inca

This culture settled in the Andes mountains of Peru. It began a course of expansion in 1438 and consequently dominated the area from Ecuador to Chile. Their architecture is one of craft, not art. They were highly accomplished stonemasons.

### *Saqsaywaman Fortress, Cuzco (1400)*

The built structures of this fortress and shrine include towers and storerooms, as well as huge zigzag walls separating a ceremonial platform from the fort proper. The fortress contained a garrison, a religious sector, and a reservoir. It is about 760 ft higher than Cuzco, and was well visible. Most probably, it was meant to symbolize the power of the Inca and their hold over the region around it. The fortress is surrounded on three sides by high mountains. The architecture is integrated into existing natural features, that is, rocks that were on the site were integrated into the walls.

## *Machu Picchu (1450–1540)*

This was the royal estate of Emperor Pachacuti. It housed ca. 1000 people. The whole site is terraced to prevent erosion. The city is built on a saddle between two mountains at an altitude of 2,000 feet. It has multiple levels and comprises palaces, temples, houses, and agricultural terraces. The buildings are constructed of huge granite stones, which are fitted together without mortar.

The central great plaza is surrounded by the houses of the nobles, while the lower levels contain the houses of the peasants.

One building is called the "tower." Here, on winter solstice, the sun shining through a window lights a carved stone. At another place is the "hitching post of the sun," a carved stone.

**FIGURE 11–1.** Serpent Mound, nr. Locust Grove, OH, view of the linear mound forming the snake's body.

**FIGURE 11–2.** Mesa Verde, CO, view of the ruins.

**FIGURE 11–3.** Chichen Itza, EI Castillo (Pyramid of Kukulcan).

**FIGURE 11–4.** Machu Picchu, view of the ruins.

# Chapter 12

# Gothic Architecture

## ORIGINS

Gothic architecture should be seen as a contrast to Romanesque. It transformed Romanesque elements. Neither structural features nor an increase in height are the main characteristics of Gothic architecture. However, without precedent is the concept and accommodation of light in churches, and the relationship of tectonic structure and appearance. From the Romanesque emphasis on distinct light sources, Gothic architecture proceeds to the dissolution of massive walls. It is diaphanous architecture. The wall as plane and body is reinterpreted in linear forms. Everything inside churches was subordinated to the structural system, which determines the aesthetic impression. Concurrently, the structural articulation becomes refined and precise. The development of Gothic architecture was supported by a greater political (nation states were created) and economic (new class of bourgeois comes into being) stability. Gothic architecture is largely an urban architecture.

## EARLY GOTHIC ARCHITECTURE

### ABBEY CHURCH, ST.-DENIS (1130-1144)

This church is among first examples of opening up walls for stained glass windows. St. Denis (living in the 3rd century) converted France to Christianity, was the first bishop of Paris, and became France's patron saint. His relics were kept here. The abbey of St. Denis was the burial place for the French kings, and the actual crown was kept there. Consequently, this church was tightly connected to, and represented, the French crown.

Suger (1081-1151) became abbot in 1122. He embarked on a program of restoration and enlargement of the church that had existed since before the time of Charlemagne (755). This had been a typical double-apsed building, but needed to be renovated. The renovation was intended to reflect the status of the abbey, but was necessitated mostly by an increase in pilgrims. Suger began with a new west facade (1130-40), consisting of double towers with three portals. The facade was distinguished by three innovations: a clear geometrical compositional scheme, the rose window, and the door recesses filled by jambs and archivolts. This is not yet the dissolved facade, but rather closed and cubical, with a few dissolving members. Behind it was a three-aisled narthex of two bays, with three chapels above. The whole facade serves symbolically as a Gateway to Heaven. This meaning comes out of the sculptural decoration of the gates. The central tympanum has an illustration of the Last Judgment. Christ is in the center, surrounded by the apostles, angels, and the resurrected. This is a clear and simple representation, finished in a calm, majestic composition. In the lower corners are illustrations of the smart and foolish maidens, one group being allowed to enter heaven, the other being refused entry. In its articulation, it was derived partly from Roman city gates. The towers are not dominating; the facade rectangle is the important motif.

The next part built was a new choir (1140-44). Here, the main intention was to exploit natural light as a symbol for the existence of God as Divine Light. By using stained glass, natural light was transformed into a mysterious medium, which seemed to prove the immediate presence of God. This philosophy goes back to a 5th-century Eastern mystic, Pseudo-Dionysius, who had mixed Neo-Platonic philosophy with Christian theology. Centerpiece was the Gospel of John, in which the doctrine of Christ as the true light illuminating the world was espoused. Shiny objects are intended to illuminate the spirit, not the eyes. The Gothic style can then be explained as the combination of

Dionysian light metaphysics and Gothic "light filling." The new choir was built over the existing crypt, which received new vaults. It had two ambulatories and seven radiating chapels. These are only large enough to contain an altar; otherwise they are part of the ambulatory. This arrangement allowed light to enter freely. The ambulatories were covered with rib vaults of pointed arches. All parts actually merge and all supports are radially aligned from the center of the apse. The stained glass windows show scenes from the Old Testament. The additive principle of the Romanesque style was here replaced by a system of division, in which each part depends on the whole. This division allows light to enter freely into the choir. Mass and surface of the architecture are reduced solely for this purpose. Suger's choir was replaced in 1231. Suger already envisioned a new nave in 1149, but nothing came of this building campaign. The nave was finally begun in 1231.

## STRUCTURE

Walls were not immediately opened up; cathedrals rather became gradually larger and lighter. One result of this change was that clerestory and gallery windows were enlarged. This change called for a reduction of the thrusts of vaults. It was found that pointed arches thrust out less than circular ones. This form also had esthetic consequences to the liking of Gothic architects (heavenward impression). In addition, it can better cover rectangular bays. However, the thin vertical supports provided inside were not enough to support all the weight; hence, flying buttresses on the outside were introduced. These were used first as internal buttresses, arches connecting nave piers to those of the aisles. However, as the buttresses not only had to transmit the outward thrust of the vaults, but also the wind loads, flying buttresses were used.

## PARTS

The Gothic cathedral was quickly standardized, with regional variations. The plan derived from Romanesque pilgrimage churches with nave, side aisles, transept, crossing, and chevet. Choirs were generally larger, since this was the only part belonging to the clergy, all other elements being financed by the city or the guilds. Elaborate entrances were devised on the western facade. The interior elevation consisted of nave arcade, triforium gallery, and clerestory windows. The structural system was articulated by clustered colonnettes. These two systems determine the interior wall elevations. The Romanesque towers were absorbed by a general verticalism. The exterior was characterized by wall and flying buttresses.

## SPATIAL SYSTEM

The individual bays – both nave and aisles – of the Gothic church are lined up as a pure series of parts. This spatial arrangement draws the viewer to a distant goal, namely the choir and beyond. Thus, the effect of such churches with polygonal apses depends upon this magnetic longitudinal axis. The path forward pulls him/her to an unattainable goal in infinity. If an ambulatory closes off the apse, the spatial experience is one of an endless whirl.

## CATHEDRAL, LAON (1160-1225)

The building campaign began in 1160 in the south transept. By 1170, choir and transepts were finished; by 1178 the two easternmost bays of the nave were finished. Between 1190 and 1215, the rest of the nave and the west facade were constructed. Only one of the towers was completed. In 1205, a new choir, longer and with a square end, was begun. Side chapels were added between the flying buttresses in the latter part of the 13th century. The building was massively restored in 1845. This church is superbly sited on a hill 300 feet high. Above the west facade, the towers rise as skeletal structures. The entire west facade is an articulation of solids and voids, creating a deeply undercut surface. The facade is divided into three parts, echoing the interior wall articulation. There are several planes in space: porches, pinnacles, walls, and window reveals. The central portal is divided by a statue of the Virgin Mary. The tympanum shows the Adoration, the surrounding arches have Old Testament subjects, virtues overcoming vices, and angels. The southern portal depicts the Last Judgment. Above the portal zone, the arches of the two lancet windows flanking the central rose window depict the Liberal Arts on the North and the Creation on the South. In most other parts of this building, thick walls provide the main support. The massing of this church is rather complex.

Inside, a soaring vertical effect is created. The wall elevation consists of four parts: the nave arcade with round pillars, the gallery with a double arcade, triforium, and clerestory windows. Two of these vertical fields are combined in the sixpartite vaults. Alternating 5- and 3-part shafts and differences in the capitals acknowledge this change in rhythm. Structural logic has here turned into a play for visual stimulus. Direct light enters through the clerestory windows, indirect light through galleries and aisles. Aisles, gallery, and triforium allow the complete circumnavigation of the nave on three levels. A great spatial continuity is the result.

## CATHEDRAL OF NOTRE-DAME, PARIS (1163-1250)

Begun by bishop Maurice de Sully, most of this building was completed in Sully's lifetime; the façade was built in the first half of the 13th century. The cathedral chapter owned over half of the land on the Ile de la Cité, which together with other possessions ensured the continuous flow of building funds. An existing Carolingian church was demolished to make room for this building. The altar was consecrated in May, 1182, indicating the completion of the choir. The nave, except for the westernmost bay, was constructed from 1178-1196. In 1225, the clerestory windows were enlarged, and the triforium (an oculus between gallery and clerestory) eliminated. In the 1230s, chapels were added between nave buttresses; in the 1270s, between the choir buttresses. The transepts were elongated in the 1240s and 50s. When the clerestory was changed, flying buttresses were altered as well. Viollet-le-Duc added some flying buttresses during the 19th-century restoration, and changed the bays around the crossing back to their original state. The cathedral was originally planned as a double-aisled basilica.

The interior is 108 feet high, rather large for an early Gothic cathedral. Excavations have revealed the foundations to be 30 feet deep, thus reflecting the intention to build a tall church from the beginning. Originally, the choir of Notre-Dame had relied on thick walls and concealed (under the roofs) flying buttresses to equalize the thrust of the vaults. When flying buttresses came into fashion during the 1180s, a complicated system of them was used at Paris, making it one of the earliest buildings with them. Sections of thick wall between clerestory windows and double flying buttresses now began to take up the vaults' thrust. The single-arch buttresses over two aisles are a result of the 19th-century restoration.

The façade proclaims the militant attitude of the French kingdom at the time. It is of a rather mural quality. Its three divisions do not reflect the five-part plan. Massive vertical and horizontal features are combined into a subtle equilibrium. It has a geometric logic. The lower part forms a square, and with the towers added, this becomes a square and a half. The rose window is integrated into the articulation and serves as a giant halo for the Virgin and Child sculpture at its base. Over the entrances is the kings' gallery, depicting the kings of Israel as a Tree of Jesse. To counter a possible visual dominance of horizontal features, the rose window and the central portal are slightly higher and larger than their flanking counterparts. The main portal of this cathedral depicts the Last Judgment; the northern one is dedicated to the Virgin Mary and the southern to St. Anne. The central pillar shows a sculpture of Mary with her Child. The tympanum depicts Mary's death and her Ascension. The jambs are decorated with the smart and foolish maidens.

The ambulatory is rather squat and dark. Its trapezoidal bays are covered by three-part vaults, with extra columns between the main supports. This creates a diagonal line of thrust from the center outward. The axis of the nave shifts slightly from that of the choir. Western crossing piers are different from the eastern ones. The nave arcade consists of cylindrical piers. There is no alternation into major and minor supports. Only in the fourth bay from the crossing, colonnettes are added to the cylindrical nave column. An alternation is only visible in the supports separating the aisles.

## CATHEDRAL, CHARTRES (1194-1220)

A wood-roofed Romanesque church existed on the site. In the 1130s, a campaign of extension and modernization was launched. First part was a new double-tower west facade (1134-1165). The northern tower suggests the Romanesque in its massiveness and mural presence; the more undercut surfaces of the southern suggest early Gothic. These frame a three-part simplified version of the facade of St. Denis. The northern spire was destroyed and rebuilt in the 16th century. This facade was half finished, including the royal portal, when in 1194, a fire destroyed all but the western façade of the existing church. Almost immediately, rebuilding started, and the church was consecrated in 1260. The new cathedral was – while commissioned by bishop and clergy – the city's building, with even a wider patronage. The French king and the local count contributed, as did the local merchants. the stained glass windows are especially the proof of the wide support for rebuilding this church.

Due to the miraculous recovery of the virgin's tunic (the chemise worn at the Annunciation), it was intended to make the new building the jewel of Gothic cathedrals. It was built on the foundations of the one that had just been burnt. The plan was based on St. Denis. There is a double ambulatory covered with cross vaults, surrounded by three large and four smaller chapels. Exterior walls are of windows, except for supports. The nave is flanked by three aisles, all covered by four-part vaults. Nave span and height were unprecedented. The plan also includes aisled transepts. The interior elevation established the Gothic system with nave arcade, triforium, and clerestory. Clerestory and nave arcade are of the same height. This greater dissolution of the wall creates an effect of diaphanous appearance. The nave appears like a figure on ground. Supports are of a core around which four shafts rise. There is an alternation of supports in the nave arcade. Above the nave piers, bundles of five shafts reach to the vaults. Every part of this structural system is equally formed. There is a clarity in the interrelation between pier and colonettes and ribs, as well as a balance between clerestory and nave arcade, that creates a harmonious interior.

Outside, a system of flying buttresses, at right angle to the nave wall, support the interior vaults. The flying buttresses consist of two arches, connected by radially arranged supports. An interesting phenomenon is the lack of many towers. As the trends proceeded along greater heights for the nave, this assumed the function of the earlier towers. Transept entrances were articulated in the same three-part, double tower manner as the main entrance. Chartres inaugurated the High Gothic in plan, interior elevation, structural articulation, and the streamlining of the flying buttresses.

The sculptural decoration of the main facade is a statement of theology. The theme was the ultimate unity of all knowledge, spiritual, philosophical, and scientific, under Theology. The western entrance consists of the royal portals. The right tympanum depicts the incarnation of Christ. On the lower lintel are Annunciation, Visitation, Nativity, and Annunciation to the Shepherds. On the upper lintel is the Presentation of Christ in the Temple. On the tympanum, Mary and Child are surrounded by angels. These events are depicted in a simple manner, to ensure their easy understanding. A vertical axis connects all three scenes. They combine the divine (He is always shown on an altar) and human nature of Christ. The newborn Child lying on the altar-like manger alludes to the Eucharist. This is reinforced by depictions of Christ's passion on the capitals immediately to the left. Christ enthroned can also be read as representing wisdom. This is supported by the representation of the Seven Liberal Arts in the archivolts, which present the instruments of human wisdom. These comprise grammar, rhetoric, logic, arithmetic, music, geometry, and astronomy. Underneath each of them is an author whose work is characteristic for the art. Six of the liberal arts are represented on the outer archivolt. Grammar, with two pupils, begins at the lower right, followed clockwise at the lower left with dialectic, rhetoric, geometry, arithmetic, astronomy, and music, which is on the lower right of the inner archivolt. The authors chosen are Priscian/grammar, Cicero/rhetoric, Aristotle/dialectic, Boethius/arithmetic, Ptolemy/astronomy, Euclid/geometry, and Pythagoras/music. The figures for the arts practice their methods: Grammar teaches two boys, rhetoric speaks, geometry traces, astronomy contemplates the sky, and music plays instruments. Arithmetic's attributes no longer exist. The authors are writing or meditating. The lower lintel, in addition, depicts various scenes of revelation. Seen together, this tympanum represents the dependence of human knowledge on divine wisdom. The remainder of the inner archivolt is occupied by angels.

Christ's ascension is shown on the left tympanum. Christ is received by a cloud. On the upper lintel, four angels predict His return to the apostles on the lower lintel. These scenes are framed by the signs of the Zodiac (with the exception of Gemini and Pisces, which are on the right portal) and the labors of the months. The archivolts therefore introduce the concept of time. The two flanking portals thus appeal to the scholar and the agricultural laborer.

The second coming of Christ is represented on the central tympanum. Here, tympanum, archivolts, and lintel are closely connected. On the lintel are the twelve apostles with two flanking figures. In the archivolts are angels and the twenty-four elders. Christ is enclosed in a mandorla and surrounded by the creatures of the apocalypse.

The figurative capitals connect the three portals horizontally. This frieze is connected to the tympana above. They depict scenes from the lives of Christ and Mary. The scenes begin in the center, and spread out to either side. The three portals are connected by twenty-four statues, which function both as columns and statues. They depict figures from the Old Testament: patriarchs, kings, and prophets. Their meaning is to unite the secular and priestly powers under divine control. In addition, they allude to the foundation provided by the Old Testament for the New Testament scenes praising Christ.

The North transept portals show the triumph of the Virgin in heaven, with scenes of her death and resurrection on the lintel. The tympanum shows her enthroned with Christ. On the lintel, apostles surround her as she is dying, while angels lift her body to heaven. The innermost archivolt contains angels; the others depict Christ's ancestors. Here, Mary is glorified and typifies the church as the bride of Christ. The statues flanking this portal depict from left to right: Elisha, Melchizedek, Abraham, Moses, Samuel, and David, and on the right side of the door: Isaiah, Jeremiah, Simeon, John the Baptist, St. Peter, and Elijah. These statues are more realistic in comparison with those on the main entrance. On the trumeau is St. Anne holding the infant Mary. These statues relate Christ to the history of the church. On the portal to the left of this central one is depicted the Nativity of Christ and the Annunciation to the Shepherds (lintel) and the Adoration of the Magi (tympanum). The jamb statues represent the scenes of Annunciation and Visitation, plus Isaiah and Daniel. The second and lower part of the third archivolt contain the wise and foolish maidens. The right portal shows on the tympanum Job being tortured by the devil, and on the lintel, the judgment of Solomon. The archivolts contain the stories of biblical characters. This portal serves to prefigure the hardships of Christ, as well as of the church. Together, the North transept celebrates Mary as the instrument of His incarnation, and as the bride of Christ, the church as His body. Beginning in 1220, a porch was added in front of the north transept portals.

The South transept façade depicts the theme of the Christian church on earth and in heaven, as well as the Last Judgment. The statues flanking the central portal depict the twelve apostles, those on the left the martyrs of the church, on the right the confessors. The central tympanum depicts the Last Judgment. He is depicted surrounded by angels holding the instruments of His passion. On the lintel, St. Michael divides the blessed and the damned. The archivolts show the hierarchy of angels. The left tympanum shows the martyrdom of St. Stephen. On the lintel, he is led out of Jerusalem, and upon seeing Him in a vision, asks for forgiveness for his executioners. The right tympanum shows scenes from the lives of two confessors, St. Nicholas (gives money to the impoverished) and St. Martin (cut his coat in half and gave it to a beggar). In the tympanum, the saints perform good deeds even after death. Here, sacrifice and good deeds one must do for the church are depicted.

The stained glass windows were a gift to the cathedral. They came from clergy, the royal and noble families of France, and the trade guilds of Chartres. The guilds signed their windows with small scenes of their activities at the bottom of the plate. The transept rose windows have a coherent iconography. In the north transept, Solomon is shown in center, in the south the risen Christ. Below this are stained glass windows showing the four evangelists supported by four prophets.

# HIGH GOTHIC ARCHITECTURE

## REIMS CATHEDRAL, JEAN D'ORBAIS (1211-1287)

This cathedral was first built during the 5th c. Successive rebuildings took place in 862, the 10th and 12th centuries, before the High Gothic version was completed.

The interior presents a balance between soaring verticality of shafts and pointed arched windows, and a series of horizontal lines, first through the capitals of the nave supports, then the stringcourse below the triforium. The elevation is of three parts. The continuity between nave piers and shafts above is much improved. The arches of the nave arcade are more pointed, and the multiplicity of their moldings, added to the shafts, makes for a smoother transition of these to the capitals and piers below. The clerestory windows are less cut-out, as at Chartres, but consist completely of tracery, thus allowing for more glass. This is an innovative aspect of Reims. There is only one ambulatory with five radiating chapels.

The western facade was begun in 1235 and designed by Jean le Loup. It shows a shift to steep pinnacles and multiple gables, and is already part of a new stylistic development. It is a direct reflection of the interior disposition. The central portal repeats the form of the nave arcade. The triforium is continued on the west façade, and is visible beside the gable over the central portal. The rose window reflects the clerestory. Two open lancet windows to either side allow the view to the nave buttresses, and the pinnacles over these buttresses are continued around the west facade. The central portal glorifies the Virgin; on the right are scenes from the Apocalypse and the Last Judgement, on the left, saints and martyrs.

## AMIENS CATHEDRAL, ROBERT DE LUZARCHES, THOMAS DE CORMONT, RENAUD DE CORMONT (1220-88)

The façade of this church is a riot of verticals and horizontals, and reflects the interior elevation. The façade consists of a number of layers in a system of multiple planes in space. There is a contrast between the front and the other exterior façades. The main entrance wall acts as a propaganda screen; the other walls are articulated as structural and masonry systems. Nevertheless, the decorative layer is too heavy for the light structure behind it. The later rose window is squeezed inside the facade. Amiens is devoid of heavy walls. The buttressing system is hidden in the boundaries of its spatial layout, with chapels, aisles, and nave in the eastern end.

Inside, the push for verticality is further increased. The nave arcade is now the same height as triforium and clerestory combined. A floral stringcourse separates arcade from triforium and clerestory.

In contrast to Ancient support-and-load structure, Gothic architecture tries to hide gravitational forces. The building mass is divided into ascending lines of force. Pillar and vault are connected. Pillars become arcade pillars with thin cores and attached colonnettes, which continue into ribs.

## STE-CHAPELLE, THOMAS DE CORMONT, PARIS (1241-1248)

This small church achieved the elimination of the wall as a structural support by making the building frame a true skeleton. This chapel was built to house the king's collection of relics, which were amassed by St. Louis, the most famous of which was the Crown of Thorns.

The chapel was connected to the palace by a two-storied porch. Inside are two chapels, a lower one for the court, and a tall upper one for the king. The lower chapel has narrow aisles and an ambulatory. Across the ambulatory are flying buttresses, reinforcing the transverse ribs of the main aisle. The upper chapel has four-part vaults covering the entire width of the interior. The interior is an intimate, sparkling, jewel-like space. The vaults were painted deep blue with gold fleur-de-lis stars, in imitation of the heavenly sky. The whole looks rather like an oversized reliquary. The interior elevation consists of low arches underneath large windows.

Here, the structure consists of a few buttresses, in between which were large stained glass windows. Inside, the structure appears as bundled colonnettes and tracery. The design demonstrates the tension between the logical Gothic structural order and the mystical intentions that were at the heart of medieval Christianity.

This design may illustrate the later development of the Gothic style, namely a movement away from structural directness in favor of ornamental extravagance.

This building was restored in 1838-67.

## CATHEDRAL OF STE-CÉCILE, ALBI (1276-1397)

This is an example of a hall church. It was built as a fortified center with the bishop's palace and a jail. The consecration took place in 1480. At the end of the 15th c., galleries were inserted above the chapels between the buttresses.

The exterior is characterized by the fortified look. The wall buttresses inside are expresses as cylindrical piers outside.

Inside is a wide space flanked by compartmented chapels. Choir and nave form a unity. Five-sided chapels surround the apse. Width, including chapels, and height of the interior are equal.

The south porch is a Flamboyant design and dates from 1519-35. Here, round arches are filled with flame like tracery.

## CATHEDRAL, SALISBURY (1220-1260)

This is a stylistically unified church. In plan it is a double-transept building. Unlike French Gothic churches, here the exterior seems to be the primary façade. The west façade is a giant screen, wider and taller than the nave behind.

The nave wall consists of three layers.

## ST. ELISABETH, MARBURG (1235-83)

This church was built over the tomb of St. Elisabeth and became an important pilgrimage center. Elisabeth (1207-31) was the daughter of the Hungarian king. She followed Francis of Assisi's example, and worked for the poor, primarily in a hospital in Marburg. Shortly after her death, pilgrimages to her tomb began, and in 1235 she was sainted. The towers of the church were finished in 1340.

St. Elisabeth is one of the earliest fully Gothic churches in Germany. Departing from French prototypes, here a hall church was developed. The exterior is characterized by the buttressing piers alternating with windows. The eastern end consists of three equal semi-circular choirs, of which the lateral ones are dedicated to Elisabeth and the Dukes of Hesse. The western façade has a central entrance flanked by two towers. The number 3 is used throughout, even in the window tracery and the three stories of the western facade. The portal tympanum shows the Christ child as ruler of the world, holding the sphere of the world. Behind Him are birds in vines, as a reference to the sacrificial death of Christ, and roses as a symbol for Mary.

The basic module for the plan is the crossing square. Doubling its side results in the height of the vaults.

In the sacristy is a golden shrine (1240) containing the remains of Elisabeth. It is decorated with scenes from her life and works. It is made of wood and covered with gilded copper.

## SANTA MARIA DELLA FIORA, ARNOLFO DI CAMBIO, FLORENCE (1296-)

In 1292, Arnolfo di Cambio was hired to build foundations for enlarging a church that had existed since the 7th century. A cupola was planned for the eastern end. The main problem of this rebuilding was introduced through the choice between either the Romanesque or the Gothic style. This obviously had repercussions on the support structures needed. Eventually, a solution against a purely Gothic system was proposed. Nave clerestory windows were round, and interior tie rods countered the lateral thrust of the nave vaults.

An unsolvable problem arose with the dome at the eastern end. As there was no outside buttressing, questions of support and stability needed to be dealt with. In 1357, the decision to enlarge the church was made. During the 1390s, the octagonal substructure of the dome was begun. Around 1400, the piers for the dome were finished. In the early 15th century, still another architect was employed, who favored a return to the Gothic style. Again, the decision against this came. In 1410, it was decided that a tambour should be added on top of the existing octagon of the choir. A decision was also made to eliminate buttresses, and to design the structure so that the resulting forces would be absorbed in the parts. Brunelleschi probably had something to do with this decision.

This church has a barn-like interior consisting of four walls and a roof. This is meant to hold the congregation in a preaching barn. It is an open and muraled interior. The nave has triple aisles and is divided into four gigantic bays. It is closer to Ancient Roman public architecture than to French Gothic.

The campanile was constructed by Giotto in 1334-57, and finished after Giotto's death, by Andrea Pisano and Francesco Talenti.

The marble facing of the west facade was added in 1875-87.

# MEANING

The church is an image of heaven. The building is seen as a vision of the celestial city. This aspect is made visible through structure and geometry. Geometry was declared, by Gothic architects, the basis of their designs. Their drawings consist mostly of geometrical, linear configurations. A basic unit (mostly the square) was all the architect needed to work out the entire three-dimensional form.

The Gothic cathedral is a hierarchical organization of related parts representing a balance of structural forces that corresponds to the reconciliation of classical logic and Christian faith. They were covered from top to bottom with sculptural representation of Biblical stories. As well, walls virtually disappeared and were replaced by glass windows depicting stories from the scriptures. Thus, the whole building became a Bible for the illiterate. Here he was taught the history of the world from the creation, the dogmas of religion, the examples of the saints, the hierarchy of the virtues, and the range of the sciences, arts and crafts. Hence, the cathedral was a mirror of the world.

The driving force behind the structural innovations was a new interpretation of the meaning of light. Optical dematerialization (Romanesque) was replaced by a real dissolution of the wall. These intentions result in the fact that the exterior of the cathedral is determined by the interior. The diagonal rib helped in creating a greater integration of the bays of the nave.

Gothic architecture concludes the age of faith. Ecclesiastical architecture was of primary importance during this age.

FIGURE 12–1. Abbey Church,
St. Denis, view of western façade.

**FIGURE 12–2.** Cathedral of Notre Dame, Paris, western façade.

**FIGURE 12–3.** Cathedral of Notre Dame, Paris, view of the flying buttresses.

**FIGURE 12–4.** Cathedral of Notre Dame, Chartres

**FIGURE 12–5.** Cathedral of
Notre-Dame, Reims, West Façade.

FIGURE 12–6. Sainte Chapelle, Paris, View of the side buttresses.

FIGURE 12–7. St. Elisabeth, Marburg, side façade.

FIGURE 12–8. St. Elisabeth, Marburg, Interior view into vaults.

**FIGURE 12–9.** Santa Maria della Fiore, Florence, distant view of cupola.

**FIGURE 12–10.** Santa Maria della Fiore, West Façade.

# Chapter 13

# Islamic Architecture

## BACKGROUND

The Islamic religion began in the first half of the 7th century. It was the result of a literate, cosmopolitan environment, focused in the cities of Medina and Mecca, and presented an alternative to the older monotheistic religions, Judaism and Christianity. Its system was codified in the Koran.

The founder of this religion was Muhammed (570-632 CE). During his mature years, he attempted to convince his countrymen in Arabia that he was the last prophet of the Lord, and that he and his holy book presented the only remaining hopes for salvation. He embraced the pagan pilgrimage to Mecca – centering around the Kaaba and its black stone – and made it an obligatory observance of Islam.

Two years after his death, the Islamic conquest began. Surrounding areas were conquered and organized along the lines of its religion and view of life. By 636 they controlled Byzantium and Syria; Jerusalem fell in 637, followed by Persia, Egypt (641), Tunisia (670) and Spain. By 711, Islam controlled an empire that spread across the entire southern Mediterranean, reaching from Persia to the Atlantic.

## GENERAL CHARACTERISTICS

The oldest Islamic building is the house of Muhammed. After his death, he was buried there and the building was transformed into a public praying hall. The origin of this mosque in a domestic building had deep impact on Islamic architecture. The concept of court-yard architecture, and the use of solid façades without windows, became dominant principles.

Antique principles survived in a fundamental way in Islamic architecture. Sources came from the Ancient Greek and Roman areas in the eastern Mediterranean and northern Africa, as well as Mesopotamia.

Particular features include the plan of the paradise garden, the Persian hypostyle hall (which, together with the Roman forum, served as model for the mosque) and the technique of decorating walls with glazed tiles.

Islam forbids the making of images. Artists countered this restriction be creating arabesques, imaginative plays with patterns and forms.

### DOME OF THE ROCK, JERUSALEM (691-692)

At first, Islamic architecture adapted existing structures. This building was the first genuine monument of the new faith. It was built on the grounds of a Jewish temple and over the rock of Mount Moriah. This had been identified as the place of Adam's creation and death, and of Isaac's sacrifice. Arabs consider themselves as descendants of Isaac. The rock was also the beginning place of Muhammed's night journey to Heaven.

The building is a close copy of the rotunda of the Holy Sepulchre. The ritual performed inside this building is based on ambulation. The building has an inner and outer ambulatory. The decorative setting of this building stems in part from the attempt to match religious buildings of the other faiths. The exterior is of marble, up to the window line. Above this were originally glass mosaics, which were replaced in 1554 by tiles. Representations included trees, flowering plants, and buildings, in short, symbolizations of Paradise. The dome (reconstructed in the 11th century) is of wood with a painted inner shell and a gold-leafed outer one. The drum is articulated with four piers and eight columns, and a series of arched windows. Four portals face the cardinal points. The outer ambulatory emphasizes the horizontal direction with an entablature of eight piers with triple arches in between. Above the arches is an Islamic inscription. The inner ambulatory is divided from the center by a columnar screen of six piers and sixteen arched columns. These support the drum and dome. The plan is based on the turning of two squares on 45 degrees.

The interior mosaic decoration remains in its original state. Below the dome is a band of polychrome naturalistic and geometric curvilinear patterns. The inside of the dome is painted with arabesques. A frieze at its base is in Islamic calligraphy, reproducing a Sura of the Koran. Capitals are of Corinthian or Composite type.

## GREAT MOSQUE, CORDOBA (786-987)

The mosque was not just the religious center of the Islamic city, but it also assumed functions fulfilled by the earlier Roman forum-basilica complex. The term "mosque" (= masjid) comes from the verb "to throw oneself down." Primarily, mosques were prayer halls. The earliest ones were appropriated; Christian basilicas were used across, as the orientation was toward the south.

The mosque was without precedent. In contrast to Christian services, Muslim liturgy was not dramatically elaborated. The faith was based on strict monotheism without a cult of relics or saintly hierarchies. Initially, it was free of metaphysical arguments and of a priestly oligarchy intervening between the believer and god. Hence, the mosque had no need of a complicated architectural setting. It had a simple program: a large space laterally arranged for rows of believers, oriented towards Mecca, an open courtyard with a fountain for the ablutions. Usually, there is an enclosing wall around a congregational space and a courtyard lined with colonnades. The rectilinear, forum-like enclosure is oriented in the direction of Mecca. It contains a columnar hall, derived from the Persian apadana or the Greek stoa. The prayer hall is covered with a flat roof on columns, which divide it into multiple aisles. Unlike the Christian church, the mosque does not emphasize sight lines. The central aisles and the one facing the courtyard form a T. An additional part of the interior is also the mihrab niche. The other component of a mosque is the minaret, from which the call to prayer originated.

This mosque was constructed on the site of a Christian church, San Vicente, and had also contained a Temple to Janus in Roman times.

The main entrance is through the Gate of Penitence in the north. There are a number of doors in the wall surrounding the compound. All use either the horseshoe arch or pointed arches.

One first enters the Courtyard of the Oranges. This contains the fountains for the ritual washing. Originally, the mosque was open toward this courtyard. The courtyard has arcades.

The prayer hall comprised eleven arcades at right angles to the qibla wall. Inside, arcades have horseshoe-shaped arches below round ones. These create an impression of interminable space. The arches support a flat wooden ceiling. The structural system and masonry technique seem to have been derived from Roman sources, such as aqueducts. There are a total of approximately 800 columns inside. Most of them were taken from Roman buildings. These columns are each different from the others, both in height and surface, so that it can be assumed that they were not specifically constructed for this building. Some are sunk into the ground; others are placed on bases. Most have Corinthian capitals. The column grid creates a spatial complexity, which alludes to Arabic thought. This is determined by the infinity of the desert and infinitesimal calculus (as opposed to the geometric thinking of the Ancient Greeks). The system of arches allowed the interior to be higher than these columns would have allowed. The arches are striped, since they were constructed of sandstone and brick. Originally, thick carpets would have covered the floor. On the exterior, parallel gables mark these aisles. The exterior walls had buttresses. The courtyard has no arcades.

The first building campaign of this mosque comprised ten rows of columns, and was probably finished by the end of the 8th century. It was enlarged several times during the 9th and 10th centuries. In 832-48, the prayer hall was enlarged by eight bays, and an arcade was added to the courtyard. In 951, the courtyard was enlarged and a minaret was added. The yard was enclosed with porticoes. In 962, the prayer hall received an additional twelve bays and a double prayer wall. Four stone vaults over particular bays were added. Most of them serve as skylights and are of arch structures supporting roofs. The mihrab is an octagonal room covered by a shell-like ceiling made of a single marble block. This is supported by blind arches. There is a small chamber in front. Finally, in 987, there was a last addition to the west of eight new arcades. Here, all arches are in the horseshoe form and are painted, rather than made of different stones.

The interior is decorated with mosaics of calligraphy, floral patterns, and arabesques.

After the retreat of the Arabs, one of the four domes became the main chapel of a Christian church inside this mosque.

## ALHAMBRA, GRANADA (1238-)

Palaces were centers of large agricultural estates and meeting places for the ruler and tribal chieftains. Their forms symbolized fortifications.

They contained two stories of rooms around a central court. Rooms included a throne room and a mosque, but no kitchen.

Outside the building were guest houses, a wild game preserve, and baths. The bath building had functions similar to its Roman origin. It contained a state room, and was decorated with murals showing dancers, musicians, athletes, and personifications of the arts.

In 1231, the kingdom of Granada was established, and construction of the citadel, the Alhambra, begun. It consists of the citadel proper, the royal palace, and the royal city. The citadel is the oldest part, and consists of a number of towers. The external walls are of red earth and stone. The red color led to the name Alhambra, derived from the Arabic for "red." These walls enclosed a self-contained town of twenty-three towers and four gates. The more ordinary parts have since disappeared.

One enters the remaining royal palace through an audience hall into the rectangular Patio del Cuarto Dorado, which fronts the tower housing the Hall of the Ambassadors, the throne hall.

## COURT OF MYRTLES

This court is reached from the Cuarto Dorado, and is named for the rows of myrtle hedges flanking the long sides of the pool. The courtyard is surrounded by marble arcades. On its northern sides is the Sala de Barca, which was used as throne hall during the winters. This is a transverse barrel-vaulted hallway. Behind this is the Torre de Comares, named for its crystal-colored windows. On the ground floor is the Throne Room, the Hall of the Ambassadors. This is cubical with an elaborate cupola. Its decoration provides a symbolic representation of the creation of Allah, which resembles an earthly paradise. The square plan covered by a cupola refers to the squaring of the circle; there are references to the numbers seven and five, and the four elements air, water, fire, and earth are essential constituents of this building. A transverse barrel-vaulted hallway separates it from the pool. From this hall, one has access to the Patio de la Reja with a number of utilitarian spaces, such as the baths. In the corner between the two main courtyards were the quarters for the harem. The Patio de Lindaraja housed the private rooms for the preferred wife of the sultan.

This courtyard was used to receive distinguished visitors of state. Overall the architecture of the Alhambra expresses charm rather than intimidation. The floor of the patio is of marble, and there are also orange trees. The pond contains gold fish.

Through an ante-room, one can proceed into the Court of Lions. In the corner between these two courtyards were the quarters for the harem.

## COURT OF LIONS (1378-)

This consists of the court and four surrounding halls containing paved colonnades. The yard is laid out as a paradise garden. This was constructed later and constitutes a separate palace. Arcades surround this courtyard.

The fountain is among the few parts still surviving from the first building. It has twelve lions standing on a twelve-sided stone base. The lions signify princely power, and may also symbolize a luxurious setting associated with Solomon.

Marble, carved and painted stucco, tile mosaic, carved and gilded wood, and water all combine to form a metaphor for the Koranic paradise, there described as "pavilions beneath which water flows." On the longer, east-west axis, projecting pavilions at the end shelter fountains whose overflow drains through channels to the central fountain, to form two rivers of paradise. Transverse halls behind these pavilions served court functions. The Sala de los Abencerrajes housed on top harem quarters. On other sides are the Sala de los Hermanos, and Sala de los Reyes. A similar arrangement is used along the other two sides. The interiors have a magical quality. Structurally, marble columns (some clustered) hold up a timber roof, from which everything is suspended. The buildings around the Court of the Lions contained the royal apartments. Here, natural forms are merged into the architectural forms.

In plan, the whole is a succession of individual spaces. One does not really get ever a view of the whole. They were designed for experience in a sitting position, which may explain that apart from the central fountains, everything is flush with the floors, even the originally lowered flower beds. Windows too were set low so that one got a view even when sitting down.

## FRIDAY MOSQUE, ISFAHAN

This is an example of Seljuk architecture. Isfahan became capital of the Empire in 1063. The city was laid out around the square at the entrance of the original mosque. Originally, this mosque consisted of a columned prayer hall in the typical arrangement. Several additions took place, among them the one of the North Dome Chamber. Here, brick architecture attained a seldom-reached perfection. Brick alone generates the ornament; there is no glazed tile encrustation. By using structural or structurally symbolic devices, Seljuks sucessfully articulated interior spaces.

## TOMB, MOSQUE, AND MADRASA OF SULTAN HASAN, CAIRO (1356)

An example of Mamluk architecture,the mosque measures 150 x 68 meters. The madrasa is an endowed theological school. This was arranged around a central courtyard with a fountain, with individual buildings for each of the four branches of Sunni law. Four barrel-vaulted extensions open to the courtyard.

## MOSQUE, QAYRAWAN

This represents an Islamic import to Africa. The city plan is Roman inside the wall, and French outside the wall.

FIGURE 13–1. Dome of the Rock, Jerusalem

FIGURE 13–2. Great Mosque, Cordoba, distant view with Christian church protruding from the roof.

**FIGURE 13–3.** Great Mosque, Cordoba, interior.

**FIGURE 13–4.** Alhambra, Granada, view to citadel
and Palace of Charles v.

**FIGURE 13–5.** Alhambra, Court of Lions

# Chapter 14

# Early Renaissance Architecture

## BACKGROUND

Italians of the Renaissance desired an architecture no longer based in the traditions of the church, but expressing the mathematical clarity and rationality they perceived in the Divine order of the universe. Around 1400, Italy was divided into small political entities. During the 13th and 14th centuries, Florentine businessmen and bankers began to dominate others in Italy. Artistic patronage also changed. The church lost its dominance to bankers, merchants, and individual members of the church. A case in point is the Medici family in Florence.

In architecture, the Renaissance is characterized by a renewal of Classical architecture. This interest in antiquity began in literature, where scholars were not interested in using old text to corroborate church dogma, but in using them to further their knowledge and satisfy their curiosity. Renaissance inquiry begins as book-learning, especially of the Latin texts of the Ancients. This new philosophy, Humanism, was characterized by the importance of human values and achievement as distinct from religious dogma. It stressed inquiry guided by reason. The city of Florence was promoted as the new Athens. Consequently, it needed an academy to promote the new learning.

Harmony became an important aspect of the new Renaissance culture. The ideal person was the harmonious integration of everything humanly possible. Harmony also governed architecture. It was based on numerical relationships that were inspired by musical analogy. The visual arts were appreciated as ends in themselves.

### Filippo Brunelleschi (1377-1446)

Brunelleschi became known in his own day as the man who renewed Roman masonry work. This renewal was appreciated because it created harmonious proportions, and was economical, as it was able to erect a vault without armature.

He also developed a rational mathematical scheme for accurately depicting on a two-dimensional surface the arrangement of objects in real, three-dimensional space, that is, mathematical perspective.

### *Baptistry Door Competition (1401-2)*

The outcome of this competition between Ghiberti and Brunelleschi brought out the ideals of the Renaissance.

Brunelleschi's design for the scene of the "Sacrifice of Isaac" is traditional. It is full of emotional agitation. Abraham, summoning up the dreadful courage needed to kill his son, lunges forward, draperies flying, violently exposing Isaac's throat. Matching this energy, the saving angel darts in from the other side, arresting Abraham's stroke. The whole composition is too busy, and the two auxiliary figures are not sufficiently subordinated to the main action.

Comparing this entry to Ghiberti's submission, one detects that the vigor and strength of the content are subordinated to grace and smoothness. Abraham sways elegantly in the Gothic S-curve and seems to fake his deadly stroke. The figure of Isaac recalls Classical statues. The scenery is intended to create a spatial illusion, underlined also by the foreshortened angel. Ghiberti's composition is less daring, but more cohesive and unified.

## DOME OF CATHEDRAL, FLORENCE (1418-1436)

In 1292, Arnolfo di Cambio had been hired to build foundations for enlarging a church that had existed since the 7ᵗʰ century. A cupola was planned for the eastern end. Construction began in 1296. The main problem of this rebuilding was introduced through the choice between either the Romanesque or the Gothic style. This obviously had repercussions on the support structures needed. Eventually, a solution against a purely Gothic system was proposed. Nave clerestory windows were round, and interior tie rods countered the lateral thrust of the nave vaults.

An unsolvable problem arose with the dome at the eastern end of Florence Cathedral. As there was no exterior buttressing, questions of support and stability of the dome needed to be dealt with. During the 1390s, the octagonal substructure of the dome was begun. Brunelleschi was aware of the problems with the vaulting, and decided to study the manner in which the Ancients had built their cupolas. Around 1400, the piers for the dome were finished. In the early 15ᵗʰ century, still another architect was employed, who favored a return to the Gothic style. In 1410, it was decided that a tambour should be added on top of the existing octagon of the choir. A decision was also made to eliminate buttresses and design the structure so that the resulting forces would be absorbed in the parts. Brunelleschi probably had something to do with this decision.

At about this time, Brunelleschi proposed that he could finish the dome over the crossing without the use of armatures needed to hold up the centering. This was something nobody had dared before. In addition, he would eliminate the Gothic buttresses. Brunelleschi's solution consisted of the replacement of traditional centering with scaffolding. The masonry was then placed in a freehand manner, not on supporting boards. He proved the feasibility of his method by constructing a small masonry model of his proposed cupola, with a clear inside diameter of about twelve feet.

The cupola was intended to consist of an inner and outer shell with different curvatures. The inner shell was to be 7 feet thick at bottom, 5 feet at top; the outer 2.5 feet at bottom, 1.25 feet at top. The empty space between the cupolas was to be 4 feet wide. There were to be 8 corner ribs and 16 intermediate ribs. The corner ribs were 14 feet, the side ribs 8 feet thick. On them, the cupolas are fixed. The inner one was built of brick, laid in herringbone pattern. There were to be 6 circles of sandstone blocks, linked by iron brackets. In addition, there were iron chains. Between the ribs were barrel-vaulted connections. On top was an oculus, covered by a lantern.

This construction incorporated both Gothic and Classical elements, namely the ribs as a form of Gothic buttresses and the tie rings which imitated Classical examples. The first ring is a wooden chain a short distance above the tambour. This was most probably intended as a testing device, to see if distortions of the dome were occurring.

## FOUNDLING HOSPITAL, FLORENCE (1419-24)

The loggia in front of this building serves as a transitional layer of space between exterior and interior. Each of its bays is a separate compartment covered by a pendentive dome, to express its isolation from its adjoining spaces.

## SANTO SPIRITO, FLORENCE (1436-82)

Here, Brunelleschi attempted to duplicate the objective perspectival order he had invented in a work of architecture. The traditional basilica plan has been reinterpreted in terms of elementary geometrical units.

The plan is generated by the bay of the crossing. Choir, transept, and nave are multiples of this unit. Aisles are ¼ of the basic module. Originally, they would have been terminated by semicircular chapels. The same relationship of parts was used for the heights. Thus, beginning with the aisle chapels, one would have gotten units increasing in a proportional progression of 1:2:3:4:5. This would represent a fully constructed three-dimensional perspective, in which each element was assigned a precise position within a rationally ordered scheme. Perspective is here used as a means to describe space. Except for the longer nave ized, the plan is perfectly symmetrical around the crossing, making it thus an elongated centralized building.

## LEONE BATTISTA ALBERTI (1404-1472)

The different façade articulations of Alberti's buildings indicate that the Renaissance was not the unified style its reuse of Classical sources would suggest. Rather, it was a style based simultaneously on universal order and individual responses to context, expressive requirements, and individual taste. The universal components of this style seem to be the reliance on numbers and proportional relationships in façade divisions. The individual details used to articulate these divisions were derived from the architect's interpretation of the local particularities. The universal components then pointed to the relationship between music and architecture, or conversely symbolized the correspondence between the human microcosm and the Divine macrocosm.

For Alberti, beauty was the harmony and concord of all parts, such that nothing can be removed lest the whole become worse. The principal ornament in architecture is the column. Alberti's religious works stress the use of pierced walls in the manner of Ancient Roman arcades.

## PALAZZO RUCELLAI, FLORENCE (1455-1470)

Giovanni di Paolo Rucellai (1403-81) was one of the wealthiest men in Florence, deriving his riches from wool. In 1448, he began to build, considering procreation and building the main tasks of men in life.

This palace was rebuilt from eight existing houses on the site. These had been combined during the 1450s into one big house with rooms arranged around a courtyard carved into the existing buildings. Alberti designed a new sandstone façade for this palace. This elegant rendition of a typical Renaissance façade established a standard of harmonious architectural sophistication that well expressed the ambitions of the new ruling class.

Although, technically speaking, this façade composition uses an additive principle, we perceive it as presenting a hierarchical order because of the superimposition of the Doric, Ionic, and Corinthian orders. Alberti may have designed this façade pictorially, to deal with the narrow site and the views it allowed onto the façade. The height and width of the pilasters are proportionally exaggerated, since the façade can mostly only be viewed from an acute angle.

This palazzo articulates clearly one of the main differences between the Renaissance and the Gothic periods. At this palazzo, the wall is no longer considered a continuous surface. The facade here is controlled by the axes of the window openings and a heavy cornice on top.

The doorway in the third bay leads through a barrel-vaulted passage into the courtyard; the other door was most probably just decorative. It seems that the façade was first designed to have five bays with a central doorway. Then, adjacent buildings were purchased, and two additional bays with a second doorway added.

A little later, a loggia was constructed across from the Palazzo. This may have been designed by Alberti. The first one built had columns with entablature, and was finished before 1464. After this date, a second version with columns and arches was built. It was set back from the site of the first one, to accommodate the longer palazzo façade. The palazzo and the loggia would then have articulated the two shorter sides of a triangular square.

## SANT'ANDREA, MANTOVA (1472-1493 [NAVE AND WESTERN ENTRANCE])

This building was designed in 1470, and was built by Luca Fancelli after Alberti's death. Prior to construction, the existing church, dating from the 11th century, was demolished. In 1460, public veneration of the church's relics – two vases containing the blood of the crucifixion – had become so popular that a rebuilding was indicated. The eastern parts of this church were finished by 1600, and from 1733-85, a dome designed by Filippo Juvarra was added.

Alberti had to fit his façade to the existing Late Gothic bell tower. This forced him to make the portico narrower than the church width. He kept the dimensions of the nave arcade and the west façade the same. He was also faced with the challenge to combine a centralized plan with a longitudinal plan. These two conceptions guided the plans of the crossing and nave, respectively. The crossing cube extends in barrel-vaulted bays to the choir and transept arms. The nave is longer. Individual forms are based on massive Roman bath architecture with coffering. The three chapels off the nave also make the Basilica of Maxentius a source. Both inside and outside, the Ancient triumphal arch motif is used. The model is the single-passage one of the Arch of Titus in Rome. The pilasters of the temple front, which are superimposed on this arch, are placed so that they become ingredients of both motifs. The whole facade fits perfectly into a square.

The round, shrine-like roof above the pediment encloses the rose window. It also serves to keep rain from affecting the areas below. The two windows in the upper halves of the side bays bring light to two rooms. On festive days, the "Blood of Christ" would have been moved from the crypt to this place above the pediment. Then, the barrel roof would have served as a baldachin.

# SPATIAL SYSTEM

Church space in the Renaissance is built up from serially arranged or added individual parts or grouped parts. In their purest states, series and groups are incompatible. The church is formed by juxtaposing such separate centers. This prevents the viewer from aesthetically perceiving a unity, thus leading him/her to become aware of the church's real inhabitant, God. These interiors form wholes marked by tension and release. In a longitudinal church, the serially arranged nave draws us to the centrally grouped eastern end. Since each view gives the viewer a distinct experience, it is not possible to see the church as representing the superhuman Divine force. Instead, the interior is a humanly understandable place, giving the viewer a retreat of absolute freedom that he/she can visit.

# EARLY RENAISSANCE OUTSIDE ITALY

The rest of Europe imported the Italian Renaissance achievements. Attention in this activity focused on the results, the surface look, and the conventions established in Italy.

The decorative systems were among the first aspects to be used outside Italy, above all in window frames and classical details. In reality, the motifs of the Italian Renaissance were more immediately taken up outside Italy than the design principles. The new building types were imported: urban palace, country villa with formal garden or with bastioned defenses. Naturally, the new principles were also imported, such as symmetry and proportional harmony.

## FRANCE

### Castle, Domenico da Cortona, Chambord (1519-1550)

As these castles are the successors of the medieval fortresses, their shapes are a combination of old and new features. In the renovations of existing castles and new constructions, a typically French Renaissance style was introduced. At first, the new style was imported by hiring Italian architects.

Chambord combines the layout of a Roman fort with the medieval donjon into a moated castle. Traditional attributes of fortification are adapted to new requirements. The walls are thick, so that the interiors appear as if carved from rock. The plan is centralized and axial. The donjon is placed next to the northern enclosing wings. It forms a Greek cross within a square. It comprises a number of floors of living spaces, which are contained in the circular corner towers, each measuring 18 m in diameter. Three quarters of the circumference of these towers projects outward. The rooms are grouped into apartments: a large bedroom, two small rooms, and a closet. A cross-shaped central hall is in the square space in between. Thus, the four apartments are separated by the corridors of the cross arms. In its center is a spiral staircase with two flights. The king's apartment was in the northeastern corner tower of the enclosing wing; a chapel was in the southeastern tower.

The regularity of the plan, as well as the ingenuity of the double-spiral staircase, strongly support an Italian designer for this castle. However, there are some subtle asymmetries in the exterior façades, especially as regards the number of bays in the connecting wings.

The exterior is strongly influenced by medieval French forms. Outside, the medieval riot of chimneys, pinnacles, and dormers on the roof were combined with the classically articulated façades. The roofs create the impression of an overcrowded chessboard. The floor divisions present a horizontal accent. Windows are placed exactly above one another.

### Castle, Blois (1498-1638)

The west wing of this castle had existed since the 13th century. From 1498-1504, the east wing, incorporating the 13th-century Salle des États, was built by Louis XII. A statue of the king on horseback is placed above the entrance. The Salle consistes of a double nave, divided by an arcade. This wing was constructed of brick with stone trimmings in flamboyant Gothic style, with a profusion of gables and pinnacles. This entire wing was flanked by two towers. Between 1514-1524, the François I wing, and from 1635-1638 the Gaston d'Orléans wing were completed.

The François I wing presents a sharp juxtaposition of medieval and Renaissance features. The fortress-like appearance of the existing wing was abolished. At first, merely a Renaissance decor was applied to the facade features. The verticalism, pitched roof, and irregular contours show the Gothic style, whereas the pier system of the courtyard spiral staircase expresses an understanding of the weight and monumentality of Classical architecture. The cross-mullioned windows and the pilaster strips are also Renaissance features. This wing was enlarged to the outside and finished with the Façade des Loges, offering views toward the city.

The Orléans wing was designed by Francois Mansart, but was only partly built. Parts of the François I wing were torn down for this.

All the wings enclose a nearly square courtyard.

## Square Court, Louvre, P. Lescot, Paris (1546-)

This building replaced and enlarged the already existing medieval building and transformed a fortress into a palace. Lescot had to replace the medieval west wing of the Louvre. The original fortress had been built in 1190. It stood four-square, with a tower at each corner. On two sides, twin towers guarded entrances; the other two façades had single towers in their centers. Inside its courtyard was the donjon. The illustration in the *Très Rich Heures du Duc de Berry* depicts its state in 1370. The south and east façades are shown, each centering on a twin-towered gate house. The central keep was demolished and the ranges were redone in the domesticizing version of the Italian Renaissance demonstrated at Chambord, to change it into a purely palatial structure.

At the Louvre, a far-reaching synthesis of French and Italian traditions took place. The façades are essentially decorative. The orders are used in a classical manner, but the richness of the decoration is typically French and medievalist. Distinctive details like the pairing and stacking of columns, use of decorative sculpture, segmental pediments, and sloping hip roofs broken by dormers point out this style. Lescot preserved the five-part organization typical for French castles. The French prevalence for a dominant tract and end pavilions connected by recessed wings is used. The exterior expresses a Renaissance vocabulary. The pavilions only protrude slightly from the rest of the façade, and they are rectangular, not cylindrical. Their decoration is of Classical details. The pavilions have engaged columns, the connecting wings pilasters. The proportions are still expressing Gothic verticality. The niche flanked by paired columns is a characteristic French feature.

By the end of the 16th century, the west and south range on the river side were completed.

## SPAIN

### History

In 1492, Islamic control over Spain ended. Immediately, an exorcism of Muslim monuments was instigated.

## PALACE OF CHARLES V, PEDRO MACHUCA, ALHAMBRA, GRANADA (1527-1633)

Changes were also done to the Alhambra, where King Charles V odered the addition of a palace. This was added to the south of the patios and vaulted halls of the existing structure. It communicated with the Alhambra at one corner of the Court of the Myrtles.

The forms of the palace are severely Classicist, some what surprising for Spain. This addition was intended for large-scale ceremonies. A circular courtyard with a two-storied portico is placed within a square building containing rooms. Tuscan columns on the ground floor take up the thrust of an annular vault behind. Above this is an Ionic order. On the northeast corner is an octagonal chapel. No extraneous element diverts attention from the steady rhythm of the colonnade.

The exterior façades follow the typical Renaissance scheme of rusticated ground floor below orders and pedimented windows. The central parts have half-columns. The south and west façades are the main ones.

This palace contains two museums.

## ENGLAND

### Longleat House, Smythson, Wiltshire (1572-80)

Much of Elizabethan architecture is the expression of a cult of sovereignty; the houses were specifically built as places in which the queen could be received, as a tribute of loyalty.

Longleat was a group of monastery buildings before the 16th-century renovations and enlargements. One of the courtyards on the eastern side of the new building was most probably a cloister. Between 1547 and 1553, these buildings were adapted to residential purposes. Beginning in 1553, some additions were done to this core, finished by 1567. This state of affairs left Longleat a medley of degenerate Gothic with a few Classical parts.

In 1567, the second Longleat was destroyed by fire. In March 1568, Smythson arrived to work on the third Longleat. He did not design the building. Most of this campaign remains visible only on the interior courtyards. In 1572, work on the fourth Longlead began, principally a façade that wrapped around the interior stemming from the third campaign. This is a cubical block, symmetrical along the narrow sides. The dominating orientation is toward the exterior. Nearly all of the exterior is window. Among them are thirteen large bay windows set into a pilastered framework of Doric, Ionic, and Corinthian orders and reaching vertically over the entire height of the façades. The decoration is restrained, but refined. Chimneys and staircases rise from the interior courtyards.

Longleat House has a basement containing cellars, offices, and parts of the kitchen. This was a new feature for English manor houses. Inside the upper floors are a state suite, consisting of a great chamber, a withdrawing-chamber, and a bedchamber, as well as parlors. At Longleat, the state suite was on the second floor, the parlors on the ground floor.

The building was completed and renovated by Wyatville in 1801.

### Wollaton Hall, Smythson, Nottinghamshire (1580-88)

Located on a prominent site, this is a pretentious palace. It is Smythson's chief design. The house looks outward and lacks an interior courtyard. Inside, a lofty central hall overtops the surrounding apartments. The layout is a rectangle with four square towers in the corners, almost forming an H. The central hall sticks out to catch light. On top of this hall is an additional chamber with corner towers. The central hall is flanked on either side of the ground floor by great chambers. On the garden side was a long gallery.

The exterior has banded pilaster strips, strap work gables, columns, and some Gothic lancet windows. The square corner turrets are articulated by pilasters framing niches. The walls are glazed generously.

The building is a pastiche, fitting together ideas and features from several sources. A Renaissance plan rises into a fantastic castle. The design is influenced by existing architectural treatises and pattern books. The owner was one of the earliest industrialists, making his wealth through coal and mining. The interior was damaged in the 17th century, and again restored in the 19th century.

### Hardwick Hall, Smythson, Derbyshire (1590-96)

Enlargement of old Hardwick Hall occured between 1587 and 1590. In 1590, a new buildings to the side of this one was begun.

Here, there is an emphasis on the towers, six of them total. Along the ground floor of the longer façades are freestanding colonnades between these towers. Simple columns support a horizontal entablature. The massing is varied as one walks around the house. The building is biaxially symmetrical. The elevations use the same elements on all sides. Entablatures separate the floors, and a balustrade terminates the walls.

There is an inordinate amount of window area in this façade, most probably the emphasize the magnificent views from the house. The windows sit on wall brackets. The towers are topped by Flemish ornament. The initials "BS" stand for the owner, Bess of Shrewesbury.

Inside, the main two-story hall is across the central axis. The High Great Chamber with its adjoining bedroom is on the 3rd floor, with a long gallery taking up the other half of this floor. The owner's lodgings were on the 2nd floor, and utilitarian spaces are on the 1st floor. The floor division was not rigid, as some rooms and spaces reach over two stories.

**FIGURE 14–1.** Santa Maria del Fiore, Florence, distant view with tower and dome.

FIGURE 14–2. Foundling Hosptial, Florence, exterior.

FIGURE 14–3. Foundling Hospital, inside of loggia.

**FIGURE 14–4.** Sant'Andrea, Mantua

**FIGURE 14–5.** Castle, Chambord

# Chapter 15

# Far-Eastern Architecture

## IMPERIAL PALACE (FORBIDDEN CITY), BEIJING (1403 BEGUN)

The city of Beijing was laid out by Kublai during the 13th century on a rectangular plan with a south-facing entrance. The palace was situated in the center, copying pre-Han planning practices. The palace, or Forbidden City, was walled and moated and is situated within the Imperial City. This was again walled and moated and constituted the inner city. The Forbidden City is the only part that still survives today. During the Ming and Qing Dynasties, the Palace was divided into an outer court for the administration, and an inner one for the emperor's dwellings.

The Meridian Gateway served as the main entrance. It is horseshoe-shaped in plan, with the entrance at the apex of the arch.

The outer court contains three great halls, as does the inner one. Behind the inner halls were the imperial gardens. The palace was laid out according to functionally separate halls.

In the first enclosed courtyard is a meandering moat, crossed by five marble bridges, symbolizing the five virtues. At the end of this court is the Gate of Great Peace. This serves as entrance pavilion to the main precinct. Behind it, on a three-stepped marble platform, is the most important building of the complex, the Palace of Great Peace. Here, the emperor held audience. The platform encloses this palace and auxiliary structures behind. Then follow the private quarters of the emperor, and the gardens.

## GOLDEN PAVILION, KYOTO (END 14TH C.)

This was a retirement villa/temple of a Shogun. It marks a period of artistic resurgence. It is situated at a lake, which shows its reflection. The upper floor is a Zen chapel used for meditation.

FIGURE 15–1. Imperial Palace (Forbidden city), Beijing

**FIGURE 15–2.** Imperial Palace, 1st courtyard

**FIGURE 15–3.** Garden of Ryoan-ji, Kyoto

# Chapter 16

# High Renaissance

## HISTORICAL BACKGROUND

At the beginning of the 16th century, the Central and South American cultures were conquered by Spain and Portugal. The Ottoman Turks captured present-day Yugoslavia and Hungary. Thus, Europe had reached the shores of the Pacific, and Asia bordered on Austria.

## ARTISTIC CHARACTERISTICS

The major architects of the High Renaissance began as painters. Both Bramante and Michelangelo thus learned firsthand the new laws of perspective and the (humanist) study of nature as the basis of painterly representation.

## TEMPIETTO, DONATO BRAMANTE, ROME (1502-04)

This building was constructed over the spot of St. Peter's crucifixion. It fulfills Alberti's requirements of a church: it was placed in the center of a square, is free on all sides, and stands isolated on a platform. In addition, the church is a pure manifestation of Classical principles. This design contains three important properties: the reintroduction of anthropomorphic Classical members, the exclusive use of elementary geometrical relationships, and a strong emphasis on spatial centralization.

Yet, the building is in a basic sense only a monument, that is, it is primarily meant to be looked at. It is conceived in terms of the thick wall, although this is here translated into the relief of the surrounding colonnade. Hence, the interior has hardly any practical use. The cylindrical wall is divided by means of pilasters into circular and rectangular niches. This shows the progression from the flat, space-defining 15th century walls (with applied orders as relief sculpture) to a conception of the wall in three dimensions, as a piece of sculpture. The ambulatory around this building isolates it from its environment. The circular colonnade creates its own world.

The Tempietto combines the Ancient round temples with a Renaissance cupola. All contours are developed from the circle. The interior proportion is much steeper than the Ancient ones (e.g., the Pantheon). The circle of the plan can be superimposed two times to fill the interior. The dome springs from an intermediary drum.

The circle is here used as a highly evocative religious symbol of the perfection of Divinity. It demonstrates the unity, infinite essence, uniformity, and justice of god.

The design is an attempt to reconcile Christian and humanist ideals. Its form is that of the Early Christian martyrium, but here it serves no actual physical function, beyond that of a monument. It is given the gravity and poise of an Ancient building. The metopes are decorated with liturgical instruments and the keys of St. Peter.

## St. Peter's, Rome (1504-1590)

The rebuilding of this church was begun seriously in 1503. Pope Julius II ordered the demolition of the eastern end of the Early Christian basilica, and commissioned Bramante to design a central building on this site. This choice surprises, as central plans have liturgical disadvantages. The choice reinforced the formal and symbolic preferences of the humanist Renaissance. The new church also became a memorial over the tomb of St. Peter, hence reinforcing the central position of the Pope within the Catholic Church.

For the rebuilding of St. Peter's, Bramante proposed a Greek cross. This cross plan is repeated in the corners of the main cross. The plan thus is symmetrical along both the main axes and the diagonals. At the end of the diagonals are four niched octagons, enclosed on the exterior by square volumes.

The semispherical dome was to rest inside and outside on colonnades, and was to be capped by a lantern. The façades were intended to be two stories high, with pediments terminating the cross arms. Two towers were planned for the eastern end.

By 1510, the four crossing piers were finished, thus determining partly the continuation of this design. At Bramante's death in 1514, the building was still in an experimental stage and could be altered, which is what happened to it.

Many important 16th-century architects were employed on this design. After Bramante's death, Raphael was put in charge, followed in 1520 by B. Peruzzi. In 1539, Sangallo took over as architect.

In 1547, after Sangallo's death, Michelangelo was commissioned to complete this church. He prepared a new plan. He corrected some of Bramante's shortcomings, especially the inadequate support structure. That Bramante's pillars were too thin had already been noticed by Sangallo. Michelangelo changed the existing plans by slightly enlarging Sangallo's crossing piers and eliminating the planned ambulatory, to gain a more brightly lit interior. The main change was to alter the relationship between structural parts and enclosed space. He replaced the diverse spatial picture and the complicated structure of the secondary spaces by a simpler spatial distribution into central and ambulatory space. He redesigned interior and exterior wall articulation to achieve a more coherent appearance of the whole building. By 1552, the cornice below the dome was finished. Michelangelo had intended a hemispherical dome. Work was not finished when Michelangelo died in 1564. At this time, the drum was nearly completed.

G. della Porta took over finishing the dome in 1588. He raised the top of the dome, making it pointed. This was finished in 1590. The ribs are supported inside and out by coupled columns or pilasters. The ribs continue into the supports of the lantern. This is another of the multi-shell rib domes of the Renaissance and Baroque. The ribs form the structural frame; which supports an inner and outer shell, to lighten the mass and weight of the dome. In addition, both shells can be formed independently according to their function, the exterior to protect from the elements, the interior to articulate the spatial impression. Two chain rings add lateral support to the dome.

Between 1607 and 1623, Carlo Maderno added a nave to Michelangelo's central church. Michelangelo's plan had eliminated a nave, so that his dome would be completely visible. He had envisioned simply continuing the exterior wall around the front façade. Before this would have been placed a columnar porch with a pediment.

## Palazzo Farnese, Rome (1515- )

This began as a remodeling planned originally by Antonio Sangallo the Younger. At his death in 1546, it was unfinished. It is a huge structure, but without character. The whole constitutes a large island block. The façade was thirteen bays wide, each one exactly alike. A larger central window was on the main floor. The vestibule was coffered, and the courtyard was derived from Roman theater design, with tiers of arches and an ornamentation of applied orders.

Michelangelo won the competition held for a design to finish the palace. He raised the partly finished top story to compensate visually for the massively overhanging cornice and roof top. Also added were the second-story recessed window with the coat of arms. The courtyard windows show his characteristic decorative treatment of inventive handling of classical forms. The pediments are separated from the window framing, and the frieze of the entablature above is a row of little grotesque masks. Michelangelo gave this building a sculptural potency that Sangallo's design lacked. Sangallo's facade articulation was the same as that used during the early Renaissance; it lacks vertical elements.

The first floor gallery contains frescos painted by the Carracci brothers of mythological subjects from Ovid's *Metamorphoses*.

## VENICE

Italy was situated between two powerful empires: the kingdom of France and that of the Ottoman Turks, who had curtailed the Venetian trade with the Far East. Venice had been an independent power in Italy, outside the Roman sway. Architectural inspiration was drawn from Byzantium, Islam, and Gothic Europe.

It achieved the zenith of its urban form exactly at this moment, the beginning of its decline. The completion of the Piazza San Marco is the example that marks this point.

### LIBRARY OF SAN MARCO, SANSOVINO, VENICE (1536-)

Sansovino imported the Italian style to Venice, after leaving Rome in 1527. Beginning in 1537, the Piazza San Marco was tailored in the Renaissance style. By ca. 1400, the broad outlines of this square had been established. The church of San Marco was the main public building of the Piazza proper. In front of it was an elongated space, lined with buildings on three sides. Loggias lined these houses and made the whole look like a forum. The Doges' Palace was along a small extension of this square, the Piazetta.

Sansovino's task was to clarify these two plazas and freshen up the look of the existing conglomeration of buildings.

Originally, this structure was not intended as a library. In 1537, its purpose was changed to housing a collection of Greek and Latin manuscripts.

This building was situated across from the Doges' Palace, and had to acknowledge it. The new library had a unified two-story façade with a horizontal emphasis. The ground floor was designed as a portico; the upper floor contained reading rooms and stacks. While clearly Renaissance, this façade is obviously meant to echo the palace's articulation. Up close, the façade reads as a system of arches with engaged columns. Between the two stories are flat strips.

The exterior has the sculptural quality inspired by Roman theater buildings. It shows a combination of Classical forms and High Renaissance language.

This was one of the earliest times that a building dedicated to the practice of science and education was placed on a preferred site.

# SPAIN

## ESCORIAL, TOLEDO (D. 1567) & HERRERA, NR. MADRID (1562-84)

Burial vaults, ministers' houses, and the north staircase in the court palace were added in the 17th and 18th centuries.

This was an enormous rectangular precinct enclosing a royal palace, a monastery, and a church. The layout is rigidly rectangular and the façades unadorned. It was oriented along an east-west axis. Square towers mark the four corners of the building. The courtyards are surrounded by arcades resting on piers. This layout resembles Diocletian's palace at Spalato. The overall plan resembles the grid-iron upon which Saint Lawrence was martyred. The severity of the whole came from King Philip II, who ordered Herrera to "not forget what I told you – simplicity of form, severity in the whole, nobility without arrogance, majesty without ostentation." Resulting was a product with the severity of the Doric order. It reflects the introspective, isolationist, and austere personality of the king.

The long sweep of the main facade is broken only by three entrances. The main one consists of a two-story, pedimented portico. The church is a domed cross church. Its two flanking towers are slightly separated from the central section with pediment. The church is contained in a rectangle, thus articulating its centralized focus. Four massive corner piers support the crossing dome on pendentives.

The layout is a literal reflection of the Royal order and its relationship to government and church. All buildings are subordinated under a rectangular grid. Only the royal apartments break the strict rectangular circumference of the complex. The sober façade elevations continue this clarity. They are plain, punctuated by rows of tiny windows. The only ornament is stone and its outline. The façades are built of local pale grey granite. The whole is the abode of a fanatic ascetic who never alters his daily routine. The church is in the central axis. Behind a forecourt, it is the symbolic center of this complex. It is a monastery church, symbol of the state, as well as royal oratory and tomb church. It has forty-five altars. Around the choir are the royal apartments (including the picture galleries and the throne room), to the south is the monastery, and to the north is a later palace.

The library contains 45,000 printed works from the 15th and 16th century. On the ceiling are frescoes relating to the sciences and learning.

The gardens were an integral part of the design. Among them is a monks' garden.

# GERMANY

The shift of economy and banking to cities in southern Germany, the Netherlands, and England was responsible for their flourishing. During the 2nd half of the 16th century, formal details are developed there, which incorporate regional traditions.

## ST. MICHAEL'S, SUSTRIS, MUNICH (1583-97)

This was a church of the Jesuits, and is an expression of the counter-reformation in the countries north of the Alps.

The western façade looks rather secular in its flatness and its pilastered floors. It looks like the house of a burgher. It serves an iconographic purpose with its many statues. All figures symbolize the fight of the church for its existence in the world. On the ground floor level, in between the two entrances, a bronze statue of St. Michael dominates Satan. On the upper levels are kings and noblemen who have excelled in war and religion. They all stand guard in front of the church. The gable holds Christ as the savior of the world. The modeling of the façade is rather crude.

The interior is in the form of a wall-pillar hall. The pillars flank semicircular chapels on the ground floor, with gallery niches above. The supports continue into the barrel vault of the nave. This vault serves to unify the whole interior. Large windows let plenty of light inside, and everything is kept in white. The transepts do not project. A great arch, resembling a triumphal arch, gives access to the choir. The interior is partly influenced by the Basilica of Maxentius.

## ANDREA PALLADIO (1508-80)

He was born Andrea di Pietro in 1508 in Padua. In 1524, he was a member of the guild of bricklayers and stonemasons in Vicenza. For about ten years he was mostly engaged in sculptural work. Around 1536/7, he was discovered by Giangiorgio Trissino, who changed his outlook and profession. Trissino introduced Palladio to Vitruvius and took him on travels to Rome. In addition, Palladio received a humanist training in the Classical tradition. Among his literary output are two books on Antique architecture in Rome, which show his scholarship in measuring Ancient ruins and incorporating the writings of Ancient authors. In 1570, his *Four Books of Architecture* were published. These contained his survey of architecture including (1) orders and elementary problems, (2) domestic buildings, (3) public buildings and town planning, and (4) temples.

Palladio was a native architect of the Venetian region; he invented the Venetian variant of the Renaissance: eclectic, functional, and adaptable.

## SAN GIORGIO MAGGIORE, VENICE (1559-1610)

In general, Renaissance architects faced a problem when attempting to apply Classical articulations to their church façades. The Christian church has a stepped section, totally unlike the Ancient Roman halls and the rules of the Ancient orders.

This was part of a monastery on an island in the basin of San Marco. Due to its increased economic and political importance, a renovation of the existing buildings was necessary from the 15th c. onward. Palladio built the refectory in 1560-62. Commissioned to design the new church in 1565, he laid the foundation stone in 1566. In 1576, the building had reached the level of the dome; by 1591 the monks' choir was finished; the facade was added between 1597 and 1610. The campanile dates from the 18th c.

For the main façade, Palladio superimposed a tall, narrow temple front over a split, wide one. This articulation reflects the interior arrangement, and gives an illusion of three-dimensional depth, increased by the shadows cast by the engaged ¾ columns of the central portico. Italy had always favored this cross-section façade over the Northern European westwork. Building materials were white stone and red brick. Externally, the shapes suggest a cruciform basilica. The plan shows a rectangular main building with semicircular additions. The length is the same as that of the cross arm. The side aisles are half the width of the nave. The choir consists of a square presbytery (reserved for officiating clergy) and a long monks' choir.

The interior is flooded with light. The walls are crisply and correctly decorated with Classical details. The nave is divided by colossal composite columns. While using the basilica plan, the eastern parts of the interior give the impression of extension. The rounded terminations of the transept arms and the cupola are responsible for this. Each bay is experienced as a complete transverse section. The choir is separated from the nave by a circular arcade.

This church structures the whole and its parts in a voluminous manner. Plastic elements are developed from the walls, and do not strike the viewer as parts of an applied ornamentation. The building consequently becomes a shell.

## Il Redentore, Palladio, Venice (1577-1592)

In his churches, Palladio aimed to surpass the Ancients in the creation of a modern civic temple. This presents a new viewpoint, replacing the earlier ambition to just match the Ancients.

At the Redentore, Palladio achieved the successful projection of the Classical temple front onto the church facade. The nave wall is combined with the pediment of the Ancient temple, including platform and stairs. Into this is set the entrance aedicula. The temple front motif is repeated for the aisles and flanks the central front. A continuous cornice unites these two different fronts. Behind and above this façade appears the roof of the nave as an attic story. This roof is flanked by screen walls hiding the buttresses. Through this repetition, the temple motif is reinforced, and a transition toward the higher level of the dome achieved. This detail made the façade part of the street; it became a civic monument. The articulation was also a metaphor of space. This solution achieves the union between building volume and façade.

Inside, the nave is flanked by arches on piers. The nave is covered by a barrel-vault, lit through thermal windows. The side chapels are joined by open passages, suggesting partly aisles. The crossing piers are placed so as to continue the nave wall. The transept does not project far. The interior gives the impression of a Roman bath building.

This church had to fulfill three functions: monastic in the choir, votive in the transept and crossing of tribune, and congregational in the nave. The crossing is separated physically – but not visually and acoustically – from the choir and nave.

The structure is Roman, consisting of moldable wall masses that support the vaults. Niches penetrate these masses, and the columns on the surfaces are purely decorative.

## Villa Barbaro, Maser (1549-57)

Palladio's villas must generally be seen as realizations of the "dream of the country." They can be explained as being at the intersection of two streams, (1) the cultural ideal of the Classical renewal and (2) the economic transformation of Venice in the 16th century. In 1453, Venice lost Constantinople to the Turks, who eventually took over the whole eastern Mediterranean. Together with the discovery of sea routes to India and the Far East (by the Portuguese Vasco da Gama in 1497-98), this eliminated Venice from the profitable trade with products from these regions. During the 15th c., most inhabitants of Venice were connected to maritime trade. By 1522, however, Venice lost its reputation as the wealthiest Italian city, to Genova and Rome. This decline in economic power made it necessary for the city to become self-supporting. This led to the re-colonization and reclaiming of the Venetian possessions on the Italian mainland. The wealthy merchants now bought up land there, and became the new lords, replacing the old feudal authorities. These real systems of suppression were hidden behind ideological falsifications, through establishing relationships of agricultural activity to ancient philosophy and religion. The concept of agriculture was placed on a metaphysical level. It took on a sacral character. The agricultural estate was seen as an altar to god. Cultivating the terra firma was a holy mission.

There is no typical Palladian villa, although they form a style apart from others. Their common characteristic within a variety is a particular conception of architectural harmony and composition. Inside, one finds a plan composed of harmonious rooms added to each other. In this, Palladio's villas are not derived from the whims of the designer or client, but follow the absolute truth of mathematics. The villas are generally not integrated to their environment, but are placed on choice sites as an ideal architecture.

This is a villa in the country, serving as main residence of its builder. It is among the most complete villas, including main residence, a spring, farm facilities, and a particular siting. It is on a raised site, offering views across the fields and orchards of the estate. It is open to the outdoors. The main façade of the residence has a vertical arrangement in alternating triangular and segmental window gables. The flanking arcades were used to keep farm machinery and animals. They are terminated by dovecotes. Sundials with astrological symbols decorate their upper portions. The Villa Barbaro functions as a farm.

Behind the main block of the house is an enclosed court with a nymphaeum, fed by a natural spring. The water is then used for various purposes in the house and gardens. This gives the entire complex a sacred character, mediating between earthly and heavenly elements. The building is set into a sloping hillside. Toward the back, the ground floor is built into the hill, giving direct access to the outside from the piano nobile.

The main building is decorated by four Ionic columns, a motif which has its source in Ancient temples. Here, the gable serves as a marker for the entrance. It is filled with the Barbaro coat of arms. The stuccoed surfaces are scored in imitation of ashlar masonry. Façade openings are heavily framed and decorated.

With circular and arched forms, a rhythm culminating in the central temple front is created.

Inside, the main space has a cruciform shape. The frescoes, by Paolo Veronese, were painted in 1560-61. They connect everyday motifs with sacred ones. The paintings are masterworks of illusionistic depiction. Painted windows offer views on Arcadian landscapes with Ancient ruins, giving viewers the impression of looking through windows. Musicians are painted in front of illusionistic niches. The vault over the main room shows Olympus.

This villa represents a combination of the farmer's and the gentleman's world.

## VILLA ROTONDA, PALLADIO, VICENZA (1566-70)

For the planning of his villas, Palladio followed certain unchanging rules. He demanded a hall in the central axis, flanked by symmetrical rooms on either side. This articulation is axially symmetrical and centralized at the same time. This systematization of the plan was one of the changes brought by Palladio to existing villa architecture, and became a distinguishing attribute of his designs. His ground-floor plans consist of loggia and central hall, with living spaces on both sides, and spare rooms and stairs in between. The room sizes are always based on harmonic proportions.

Palladio conceived of his exteriors in terms of a solid, three-dimensional block. This led to an easily perceptible ratio between length, height, and depth of a building. To give these blocks a façade, Palladio used the Ancient temple front. He believed this to have been the form given façades in Ancient times. This was based on a fallacy, namely the belief that Ancient temples had derived from domestic architecture. A novel feature used by Palladio was also the central dome, which previously had been reserved for church buildings.

The Villa Rotonda is the most perfect realization of this plan. It seems to grow out of the landscape. It is set and detailed (re: four loggias) according to a functional response to the environment, namely to provide pleasing views of the surrounding countryside. The porticoes derive from the Roman platform temple. Seen from the side, the arcades project out at right angle, terminated by a freestanding column. The central intercolumniation is wider, leading to the pedimented entrance doors. Inside, the combination of rotunda and cupola presents another realization of a main plan type used in Renaissance church architecture. The individual parts are unified through stringcourses and formal similarities, such as pediments over façade openings.

Barrel-vaulted passages lead to the central rotunda. Four salons are set into the corners of the square. Frescoes and sculptures were partly later additions. The paintings are framed by illusionistic architectural parts, and depict Roman gods.

Palladio's designs use proportional relationships to govern the dimensions and volumes of his villas. This elevated them to the level of divine creation. This elevation also rubbed off on its owner. Palladio combined three goals in his villas: (1) representation of status, (2) living for the owner, and (3) agricultural facilities. While combined, care was taken not to bring the economical structures too close to the living ones. Palladio's merit is to have combined these two opposing types, namely the urban palace and the rural farmhouse.

**FIGURE 16–1.** St. Peter's Cathedral, Rome

**FIGURE 16–2.** Library of San Marco, Venice, main façade

FIGURE 16–3. Escorial, main entrance façade.

FIGURE 16–4. Escorial, interior study room.

**FIGURE 16–5.** San Giorgio
Maggiore, Venice, western façade.

**FIGURE 16–6.** San Giorgio
Maggiore, interior.

FIGURE 16–7.  Villa Barbaro, Maser

FIGURE 16–8.  Villa Rotonda, Vicenza

# Chapter 17

# Mannerism

In the 16th century, Renaissance architectural design had reached a perfect level of clarity of form and precision in the adaptation of Classical details, and had achieved pure design, absolute balance, and rational order. At the turn from the 15th to the 16th centuries a summation of the researches undertaken by Brunelleschi and Alberti took place. Architects moved toward an abstract, ideal perfection, conceiving equilibrated worlds of permanence and poise.

This set of rules was subsequently modified. About 1530, Renaissance style was replaced by a subtle tension and willful playfulness in design, known as Mannerism. Harmony and order were replaced by conflict and experiment. Space was transformed into a dynamic occupation of the environment. An animating play of forces and energies is depicted in these buildings. Plasticity, expression, force, movement, and subjective combination of parts replaced rational and objective order. Articulation became a means to express character. Art became an object of emotional experience. Nevertheless, Mannerism should be treated as relating primarily to stylistic matters, because artists and architects stylized the forms and details of the Renaissance. These artists simply saw the achievements of the Renaissance as dry. For them, there was no place for license in the rules, for invention in the order, for fluidity in creative skill, and for delicacy in style. They also saw no place for bizarre inventions or creativity in color in the rules of Renaissance art. Mannerist artists expressed and demonstrated personal skill, sometime in contrast to esthetic rules or ideals. This comes out as mastery in depicting the (actual) human form, as contrasted to a subordination of this depiction under pre-established rules.

There are two competing explanations of Mannerism. The first reads the intentional deformity of Mannerist architecture – if compared to the stability expressed by the Renaissance as intending, seemingly, to make the viewer uneasy, by projecting pain or malaise. Violation of accepted rules became an expressive tool of psychological tension. The interpretations of this style as portraying tension, conflict, and crisis, as well as, expressing a spiritual malaise originated in the 1920s and betray mostly that period's spiritual attitude. The second reading accepts that Mannerism could also have had a lighter purpose, viz. humor, playfulness, and invention for its own sake. The 16th century saw itself rather as a complex civilization with refined taste, high cultural achievement, and exquisite artistic skills. Artists began introducing variety in their works so as to facilitate critical appreciation of their talents by connoisseurs. This was seen as engendering visual delight and esthetic satisfaction in the viewer, as well as, demonstrating an attitude that sees their own age as more cultured than the past and themselves as more refined in their own skills and abilities.

## CAPITOL SQUARE (CAMPIDOGLIO), ROME, MICHELANGELO (1538-1664)

This square introduced a novel type into urban design. It is not closed in like the Roman Forum and medieval squares, but opens up to become full of incoming and outgoing movement.

Before Michelangelo's systematizing intervention, the Senators' and Conservators' (= town hall) Palaces stood on the square, enclosing an acute angle.

Apart from renovating the existing buildings (clothing them in Renaissance envelopes), Michelangelo added a new Palace of the Capitol facing the Conservators' Palace. He created the designs for all these buildings, which were executed by G. della Porta after his death.

The first action had been to place the statue of Marcus Aurelius in the center of the square in 1538. The Senators' Palace was raised on a blind basement. In front of the triangular block of the staircase was a statue of Minerva (touched up to look like the goddess Rome), which was flanked by reclining river gods personifying Nile and Tiber. A baldachin was placed over the landing of the new stair. The clock tower was added by Martino Longhi the Elder in ca. 1580.

The Conservators' Palace received a new facade. The new building (today the Capitoline Museum) was merely a screen, since there was not much room before the monastery of Aracoeli. This building was not constructed until the 17th century. The palace façades are all articulated in the same system. The use of a giant order was here invented by Michelangelo, a detail that was widely imitated, beginning with Palladio.

These buildings resulted in a symmetrical, trapezoidal square. The central axis is articulated through the staircase leading up to the square, differences in building height, tower and placing of statues. A circular element is introduced through the floor decoration of travertine bands, partly executed in relief. The surface of the square is slightly convex. Statues of Castor and Pollux frame the narrow entrance to the square. The restful, balanced visual order was here upset in a Mannerist design. The dramatic siting, the compulsive but thwarted axis, the constrictions and releases along the entry into and through the square – all combine with the architecture to a complete spatial and urbanistic event.

## LAURENTIAN LIBRARY, FLORENCE, MICHELANGELO (1524-1534; FINISHED BY VASARI IN 1559)

Michelangelo's later architecture is built up of ambiguous and complex forms. The Laurentian Library was commissioned by Pope Clement VII, a member of the Medici family. He returned the Medici collection of manuscripts to Florence in 1523, and donated it to the monastery of San Lorenzo.

The addition is situated above a monks' dormitory. It is vaulted above and below, for fire- and flood-proofing. This created structural problems, as the floor had to support the weight of the manuscripts. Michelangelo's solution consisted of a pilaster and buttress system.

As it could only be reached by means of a separate vestibule on the lower floor, Michelangelo filled this whole room with the stair. The staircase is an integral part of the entire complex. The stair organically flows out of, or into, the central division of the reading room. There were also lighting problems in this narrow space, which were only finally solved in 1900. The ceiling height of the stairwell is higher than that of the reading room simply because of lighting requirements; originally the two rooms were to have the same height. Originally, two stairs were planned. Then, Michelangelo decided on one stair with triple flights. These terminate in a landing, from where a single flight leads to the entrance. The side flights have different steps and profile. Because of their rounded steps, the stairs appear to burst forth from far back in the room. However, they are also laid out perfectly symmetrically, probably to reinforce the viewer that he can trust them.

The most striking feature of this vestibule is, however, the wall articulation. On first sight, it is still based on traditional structural systems where wall and support parts are clearly separated. However, Michelangelo created a wholly new effect with these elements. He fitted pairs of muscular Tuscan Doric columns into recessed wall niches. The wall in between seems to spill into the interior. These columns appear to be supported by light curved scroll brackets attached to the wall. All these elements are used here in defiance of the Classical rules. Michelangelo was manipulating them as elements in a gigantic sculpture. Even the stairs are formed in imitation of cascades, thus pushing the user back. Michelangelo departed from the kind of architecture regulated by proportion, order, and rule. The vestibule was an attempt to bring life into this library, to indicate that this library contained secular, not divine, manuscripts. The wall articulation is meant to trick the viewer into perceiving a perspectively receding space, so as to reinforce his sensation.

It is only in the library room that the ordered, calm articulation was again used. There, the architectural features appear as if they were drawn with grey stone on a white stucco ground.

In Mannerism, styles are liberally mixed, e.g., between Classicism and vernacular architecture. In architecture, one also finds the surpassing of the Ancient norms, mastered in High Renaissance, toward a refined and complex elegance. This is seen in Michelangelo's Laurentian Library lobby, where all Classical details are shaped with artistic license. The interior wall elevation looks like an exterior turned outside in. The structural parts are squeezed into the wall plan so that it seems as if the wall has come alive and moved forward. Hence, Michelangelo imposed his artistic will on the Classical forms and details.

Work on this library was stopped in 1527, at the sack of Rome. While Michelangelo moved to Rome in 1534, work on the vestibule was taken up again in 1534-1536. The library was finally opened in 1571.

## PALAZZO DEL TE, MANTUA, ROMANO (1527-34)

This building began as a small retreat next to existing stables. The first part built was one wing with two apartments beside an entrance loggia placed off-center. The windows in each of the rooms were arranged with regard to their function to light the respective interiors. This was the northern wing, constructed in 1525-26.

The result was so wonderful that Romano was commissioned to enlarge it, probably in 1527. The most probable reason for this undertaking was the Duke's desire to have a modern palace adequate to his standing. Whereas the original wing was a local work of architecture, the enlargement drew from the palaces of Rome. The western entrance loggia was modeled after the entrance to the Palazzo Farnese, and the Loggia di Davide after the Villa Madama. This was to make the new building the sum of the best palaces and villas being constructed at the same time in Rome. Until 1528, the north-eastern corner room and the two adjacent rooms of the eastern wing were completed.

This enlargement was the result of several logical planning steps. The dimensions of the additional three wings were determined by the first one, as well as by existing stables to the south and west. The enclosed courtyard was consequently square. The loggias were also continued. The main entrance was placed on the new western wing, making the eastern wing face the garden. In addition, the exterior was to be decorated with a giant order, appropriate to a palace for a nobleman of the Duke of Mantova's standing.

The façades have different forms of balance and unexpected juxtapositions of Classical details and surface textures. Similarly, the interior rooms are individualized and not arranged in a unified artistic or content program. Thus, they provide numerous diversions.

Due to the piecemeal enlargement (especially the corner rooms that had to be added to complete the square building), the need for a uniform system of palatial façades presented problems. On the northern façade, which incorporated the first building part, the existing wall openings had to be accommodated to the new façade requirements. Here, architectural norms are used in a contradictory manner. Windows are located eccentrically between pilasters, bays are of different width, paired pilasters are of differing distances, and the corners are of different distance from the loggia. Romano created a pictorial semblance of a canonic order. Inside the courtyard, each façade is treated differently, continuing the schemes used on the outside walls. At first glance, this system appears orderly. Careful examination is necessary to appreciate the differences. Romano thus exploited limitations in a creative manner. The original stucco rustication was more restrained than what exists today. A Doric order combines with rusticated frames for wall openings to form the exterior façades.

The garden façade was added as the third building campaign by Romano. The smooth garden façade contrasts with the rough texture of the main façade facing the city. It consists of the rusticated basement facing fishponds, which holds up the loggia of three arches and flanking bays using the Palladian motif. Reading from the corners toward the center, the architectural forms gain in volume, size, and importance. This façade stands a short distance away from the original wall, giving the illusion of a covered passageway. This façade may have been constructed from 1527 to 1531. Its marked difference from the other façades can be explained by the intended regal elegance. It reproduces a building illustrated in the mosaics of Sant'Appollinare Nuovo in Ravenna. This makes the building into a palatium, referring back to imperial Roman villas on the Palatine. In addition, the façade gives a Byzantine impression inspired by Venice. Its main reason for being was that it needed to express the new-found power given to the Duke of Mantova.

The interior courtyard is treated in the fashion of an urban square. No two façades are exactly alike. The frieze on the north and south facades is intact, while on the east and west façades the central triglyph within each bay drops. Here, either windows, or protruding rusticated blocks support the dropped triglyphs. The main windows are treated equally in all four façades. Their pediments are kept in their triangular shape by oversized keystones. Hence, these four façades should be seen as forming a unit. Most stones on these façades are smooth. Together with the intact friezes they constitute the correct appearance of the building. Therefore, all rusticated parts must be seen as unfinished. The impression is invoked that these pieces were hastily put into the facades to complete the building, before these elements could be finished properly. The triglyphs do not fall down because they symbolize unrest, but because they were not measured properly. These details can be understood as Romano's humorous allusion to the working conditions he was put under by the Duke, who wished this palace to be completed quickly. There is a contrast between the refined architectural details and the rustica of the walls. This may symbolize the contrast between artifice and nature, and between reason and libido.

The interior decoration deals with the topics of love and politics. The northern entrance is through the Loggia of the Muses. The Sala di Psiche is devoted to the celebration of love and happiness. The Sala dei Venti is decorated with a horoscopelike design. Political topics depicted e.g. in the Sala delle Aquile deal with the justification for Gonzaga's rule and the territorial claims of Mantova. The Sala dei Cavalli has an architecturally divided decoration depicting Greek gods and horses in front of landscapes.

The Loggia di Davide was laid out in 1527, the year of the Sack of Rome. Original plans called for it to be decorated with Antique statues. Next, it was to be adorned with statues of famous military commanders. Ultimately, scenes from the life of David were chosen, in an effort to link the Duke's experiences to the deeds of the Biblical hero.

Subsequent rooms and parts replaced erotic motifs with historical and mythological events celebrating the Duke's greatness. In the Hall of Giants, the decoration is a tour de force of illusionist painting, and is disquieting and bizarre. A huge circular temple floats in the ceiling, containing an assembly of gods, among them a lightning-throwing Jupiter. They fight a rebellion by the giants, who are depicted being crushed by falling boulders and crumbling buildings. Painted without framing devices, the whole room seems to crush down on the viewer. The room was also a masterpiece of acoustics, offering a complete experience of the theme depicted.

The east garden appears to have been an integral part of Romano's design. The exedra dates from the 17th century. The barn-like buildings to the south were changed into stables in the 18th century. During the 18th century, the palace belonged to the Academy, which used is as an educational facility, and renovated it. The original attic story of the palace was removed. In addition, a thick layer of cement was applied over the entire exterior of the building.

Upon its completion, the Palazzo del Te was widely admired. Verheyen rejects the psychological interpretation of the architecture and interpretation as a result of the attitude of the fear-ridden 1970s. He proposes instead the interpretation of this building as a rational balancing act of the architect between contrasting demands, above all the request to combine both the decorum of a palace and the license of a country villa.

**FIGURE 17–1.** Palazzo del Té, Mantua, showing courtyard façades

**FIGURE 17–2.** Palazzo del Té, Interior of Sala dei Giganti

# Chapter 18

# Baroque Architecture in Rome

Architects of the 17th century made something different of the forms and principles instituted by Brunelleschi and Alberti. Baroque architecture emphasizes complexity, ambiguity, variety, contrast, plasticity, and spatial depth. The Renaissance had defined beauty as order, whereas Baroque emphasized beauty as dynamism. It created a sense of mystery, an emotional impact, and was above all concerned with the shaping of space at the expense of structural expression. The effect of a form on the eye gained as much importance as the blind obedience to the Ancient rules. Baroque architecture is also characterized by a great jump in scale to vast complexes that surpass the limits of human visual perception.

There are a number of reasons for this change. As in any period of human artistic creativity in which the aim is to achieve absolute balanced order, once this stage is reached a reaction sets in. There was also a religious aspect to this change. This was brought about by the Counter-Reformation. Veneration of the saints was reasserted by the Catholic Church, and music, painting, sculpture, and architecture were seen as among the most powerful instruments enhancing religious devotion. Thus, the creation of a mystical atmosphere for worship in churches was strongly recommended.

In architectural terms, the Baroque period emphasized sculptural plasticity. In addition, it stressed the facilitation of prayer by requesting the planning of longitudinal churches. It marks the point in history where literal imitation of Classical forms ceased, because architects realized that the historical forms were no longer adequate for their own time. Instead, the historical models had to be understood, and transformed into structures that had relevance for the present.

Spatially, Baroque architecture is one of division. The individual components of an interior are fractions of a pre-existing whole. Space is one unit divided into parts, which are incapable of independent existence. In turn, the whole also appears as a fraction, namely of universal space. The perimeter of the interior is uninteresting, and the space has the effect of something incomplete, being in a state of becoming.

The term baroque was taken over from goldsmithing.

## COMPLETION OF ST. PETER'S, BERNINI, ROME (1624-1667)

Carlo Maderno won the competition held in 1607 for designs to add a nave to Michelangelo's building. Maderno's design consisted of three bays with flanking, communicating chapels. A vestibule ran along the front. For the façade, Michelangelo's giant order was preserved and fused with a temple front. The axis of the nave aligned with an obelisk in front that had been placed earlier as a result of Pope Sixtus V urban designs for Rome. This part was finished in 1615. At that time, the façade was to be framed by two towers, which necessitated the addition of two bays to either side. Eventually, these proved incapable of supporting the load, but the bays were left nevertheless, resulting in an inflated façade.

Subsequently, Bernini took over. He worked first on the interior, adding the canopy over St. Peter's tomb in the crossing and the Cathedra Petri. In 1656, Bernini was given the task to create an urban concourse in front of the church. This required enough space to hold the international crowds gathering there on feast days. Immediately in front of the church was an entrance square, followed by a wide oval and a small extension of this, which was never built. A colonnade of four columns across bound these parts. For the proportions, the giant order of the façade was followed. The colonnade was merely a covered corridor, and helps to enclose the observer in a kind of open-air antechamber. The colonnades end in temple fronts. The pavement sloped toward the center of the oval with the obelisk, and radial lines reinforced this emphasis. The rows of the columns were arranged around the radial lines of the half-circles through which they were formed.

Bernini's design has a symbolic aim, namely to express this church as the mother of all others. The colonnades are, thus, like outstretched arms, encompassing Catholics, heretics, and infidels. The oval form makes the square simultaneously closed and open (through the formal tension). This makes it communicate with the world beyond, a fact also emphasized by the transparent colonnades.

## SANT'ANDREA AL QUIRINALE, BERNINI, ROME (1658-70)

For smaller chapels, the old centralized plan could still be used. In Baroque churches, the oval was frequently used as a means to combine centralized and longitudinal plans. Through its deviation from the circle, the oval conveys an element of dynamic tension. This is increased by the biaxial duality of the oval. Bernini originally worked with two different plans: the oval and a pentagram. The Jesuits, who commissioned this church, wanted five altars.

In Sant'Andrea, the fact that its plan consists of an oval can be seen in the curved façade of the upper walls. Similarly, the half-oval walls flanking the small courtyard in front of the church allude to this geometric figure. There are a few contrasting curves in the entrance façade. Toward the center of the façade, plastic intensity increases. The colossal entrance, capped by a pediment, gives this entrance a new dimension. Although the façade is put together from separate pieces, it impresses as a unified composition. The bent Colossal piers mediate between the flat entrance façade and the oval space inside.

Inside, the oval is turned, with the main axis along the shorter diameter. A total of ten wall niches are arranged around the circumference, four of which are chapels in the diagonals between the two main axes. The main additional spaces have parallel sides; only the secondary ones adhere to the oval of the main space. This plan subordinated the ring of piers around the main oval, so that they turn in multiple turns around the corners. The altar uses an artificial light effect. The architectural details are altered in parts to accommodate the sculptural decoration. An oval dome covers this church. All these features partly stemmed from Bernini's training as a sculptor. Unification and dynamism are achieved through features of articulation. In Bernini's work, perspectival tricks and a fusing of architectural articulation with sculpture serve the spatial and dynamic expression.

Bernini presented his design in September, 1658, and in November 1659, the masonry shell was complete.

The sculptural decoration was added from 1660 to 1672, and consists of fishermen over the windows, putti, St. Andrew's soul in the pediment, and the lantern, which depicts heaven. The fishermen and putti watch St. Andrew's ascent to heaven. The altarpiece depicts the crucifixion of St. Andrew. The soul of the saint – being immaterial now – has passed through the marble cornice on his ascent. The Corinthian order is used throughout, except for the two columns flanking the entrance door.

## SAN CARLO ALLE QUATTRO FONTANE, BORROMINI, ROME (1638-39, 1665-67)

Borromini exemplifies the personal inventiveness of the Baroque. He was even more adept than Bernini at manipulating space and the classical orders in sculptural terms. San Carlo was a monastery complex, consisting of a monks' dormitory (1634- ), a church, and a monastery (1665). The plan and proportions of San Carlo were derived from geometrical computations, based on the module of an equilateral triangle, complemented by circles. Thus, the geometrical figures used for church plans were changed. Two such triangles, joined at one of their bases and inserted into an oval, form the ground plan. This is an interior of interacting spatial elements, modeled according to outer and inner forces, not a construction of plastic members. The new idea playing here was that space does not surround architecture, but is created by it. Nevertheless, Borromini's basic ideas center on uniform spaces. He produced unity and dynamism immediately through the spatial form.

Enclosing the ground floor walls are spaced pairs of columns carrying an undulating cornice. This form may have been suggested by the Piazza d'Oro of Hadrian's Villa. This articulation shows that framework is more important than the solid wall. Above this is an oval dome carried on four pendentives. The twisted and spiral forms of some supports point to the effort of reconciling horizontal and vertical emphasis. The dome is deeply coffered, and surmounted by a lantern. The coffers are in the form of crosses, hexagons, and octagons. The crosses were the symbol of the monastic order of this building. Everything inside is designed so that the resulting space is unified and integrated. Every detail connects with others to form a firm system.

The façade was added later. It undulates like rolling waves. The curved entablatures and the surfaces packed with architectural and sculptural ornament prepare the visitor for the interior. The undulating wall, among the most important developments of the Baroque style, appears to result from the interaction of interior and exterior forces. No longer is the façade simply an addition, but it encloses as a skin the interior spatial arrangement, and expresses the dynamism of the plan. The basic rhythm is based on a curve and counter-curve scheme. The middle element echoes the central focus by a curved pedimental addition. The tower on the left appears completely dissociated from the façade scheme. The whole façade appears as a reflection of the forces that shaped the space. While the upper half is rather dry, the lower one is soft.

# SANT'IVO DELLA SAPIENZA, BORROMINI, ROME (1643-48)

This was the church of the university. It is placed into a narrow end of the square around which the university buildings are grouped. This setting is reminiscent of Early Christian churches, such as Old St. Peter's. It is an interpretation of the Temple of Solomon, or Temple of Divine Wisdom. Palms, Cherubim, royal crowns, oak wreaths, six- and eight-pointed stars, and open flowers in the decoration articulate this meaning. The white interior symbolizes the jewels and crystal-like pillars in Solomon's Temple.

Its plan is generated from two equilateral triangles superimposed over one another to form a hexagon. Semicircular and triangular, with convex ends, chapels surround the central space. Four separate rooms in the corners are connected to this space as well. Actually, the interior consists of a triangle whose sides are open by semi-elliptical apses. The convex parts of the interior suggest universal space pushing in from the outside. Another source for the plan is the Barberini family's heraldic bee. In addition, the plan refers to the hexagonal Seal of Solomon.

The space inside is quite lively, due to the contrast between distinct forms. Here, Borromini energized the whole interior into a pulsating unification of the various spatial zones. This is continued vertically, as the ground plan articulation is continued through vertical lines into the cupola. The dome consists of six segments. Spatial form and articulation are the same. However, the equal segments of the cupola are different from the plan, thus making the comprehension of the interior difficult. The Corinthian pilasters and entablature add some unity to the interior. Once more, however, the use of the same dividing feature in differently shaped spaces adds confusion. Ultimately, the actual experience of this space and its rational plan do not immediately correspond to one another.

The decoration alludes to the papacy and the idea of knowledge and wisdom. The stars are taken from the coat of arms of the contemporary Pope Alexander VII. Palms are used as symbols of wisdom. The pouring of holy wisdom is also represented with the Dove of the Holy Ghost. This refers to the same act at Pentecost as described in the Bible.

The altarpiece was begun by da Cortona in 1661, and completed by G.V. Borghesi after 1674.

The lantern is unusual, and has led to numerous interpretations. It consists of the lantern proper, a spiral finial, a wreath, crown of fire, cusp of wrought iron, a globe, a dove, and a cross. The finial has four turns and is decorated with jewels.

The church was dedicated by the Papal lawyers to their patron, St. Ives of Chartres, a lawyer who pleaded the cases of the poor.

# CHAPEL OF SS. SINDONE, TURIN CATHEDRAL, GUARINI (1667-90)

Outside Rome, the diffusion of Baroque was spotty and slow. Venice and Florence continued their respective High Renaissance traditions. Only in Piedmont was a style developed that derived from Borromini and advanced beyond it. Aspects of Borromini's architecture were reminiscent of Gothic architecture. This may have been one reason why they were favored in the north of Italy.

Guarini's spatial ideas focused on the spontaneous action of contraction and extension, which according to him governed the whole living world. He formulated an organic theory of design, in which individual spaces are designed as groups or chains of cells. The plans are complex, and build up to high skeletal domes. These are usually constructed on an armature of interlaced arch-ribs.

Guarini's passion for intricate geometric calculations was applied to his dome designs, and altered the traditional idea of a dome as a clearly defined space bubble. The dome consists of ribs, or lunettes, which taper round and round above one another and are weaved syncopically into a transparent skeleton. This cupola has a pointed profile.

It is formed of three levels: a high drum with large windows to make the interior bright, a level of buttresses with zig-zagging hexagonal ribs, surmounted by a pagoda-like lantern over another layer of windows.

# SANTA MARIA DELLA SALUTE, B. LONGHENA, VENICE (1631-32)

This is one of the only native Baroque buildings of Venice. Majestically sited at the entrance of the Grand Canal, it is a distinctive element of Venice's skyline. The plan is an octagon with ambulatory based on Byzantine prototypes, such as S. Vitale. An ambulatory encircles this central space. The radial effect of the central space is played off against the peripheral movement of the ambulatory. The main bays of the ambulatory are covered with cross vaults, thus articulating their ambiguous movement nature. The entrance to this centrally planned, domed church is on a stepped hexagonal platform. The architecture is influenced by Palladio's colossal order and use of Roman bath windows. The entrance to this centrally planned, domed church is on a stepped hexagonal platform. The exterior is articulated by statuary and huge buttressing volutes. The geometry of the interior is rather complex. The exterior looks like an overscaled lantern. Being dedicated to the Virgin, Longhena intended the church to look like a crown for the Queen of Heaven.

# CASTLE, VAUX-LE-VICOMTE, LE VAU (1657-61)

The 17th century was the century of France. The royal house had assumed so much power, that it could be considered the social and political fulcrum of Europe. While not an economic superpower, it was the largest European nation and filled a vacuum caused by the decline of central power in Spain, Germany and England.

In 1666, the Academy of Architecture was founded by J.-B. Colbert, finance minister of Louis XIV.

The state ran an extensive program of public works, comprising royal residences, defense and urban interventions. In this last category, 17th century France instituted three enduring ideas of city planning: the square, the tree-lined boulevard, and the avenue radiating from a central point.

This is a pleasure castle built for Louis XIV's finance minister. Basically, this is a building consisting of one wing. It contains two apartments connected by a large central part. The entrance is through a square vestibule into an oval salon. The two apartments are almost perfectly symmetrical.

The exterior shows the traditional articulation, but is more dynamic and coherent than earlier schemes. The concave indentation of the central part echoes contemporary Baroque façades, although here a sense of life and lightness has entered. The castle is of stone, with brick used for the outer buildings.

In the garden façade, the central hall marks the focus of the various axes of the entire complex. One reaches this oval salon through a square entrance hall. The salon is surrounded by sixteen bays. These are topped by a drum of square windows with caryatids representing the signs of the zodiac and the four seasons.

The entire complex provides a setting where dimensions, proportions, and decor are in harmony and surrounded by a garden. The use of space and water are central to this complex. There is a progression from the wild forest, via the ordering of nature under man, to the triumph of man in stone and artistry. The moat serves ornamental purposes, as it reflects the building.

Le Vau was responsible for the buildings, Le Brun did the decorations, Le Nôtre the gardens.

The roof forms of the flanking apartments are repeated in the roofs of the adjoining service buildings, thus creating a roof rhythm of tall roofs connected by lower buildings. The castle is of stone, with brick used for the outer buildings.

# CASTLE, LE VAU, HARDOUIN-MANSART, ET. AL., VERSAILLES (1661-1750)

The decision to move the court to Versailles necessitated the enlargement of this castle. Lemercier had built the first castle as a hunting lodge in 1623 for Louis XIII. This consisted of a court surrounded on three sides by brick and stone buildings.

The first garden was laid out in 1638 by Jacques Boyceau. The "Plan de Bus" (1661) shows this to comprise the Petit Parc, which reached to the Fountain of Apollo. The gardens were divided into a number of square parterres.

In the early 1660s, Le Vau added a new and larger outside to this hunting lodge, and Le Nôtre laid out the gardens. This building can be called an envelope around the existing hunting lodge. The new garden front was twenty-five bays wide, with a flat roof behind a top balustrade. A deep setback terrace was left in the center of the second story. The northern wing contained the Grand Apartment, the southern one the Apartment of the Queen. A rusticated ground floor supported a first floor of the Ionic order, topped by a balustrade crowned with urns and trophies. By 1668, recorded in a painting by Pierre Patel, a U-shaped extension was completed. In the garden, the Grand Parc was added to the Petit Parc, and a large hunting estate extended the garden into the distance. This entire area was enclosed by a wall forty-three kilometers long.

In 1674, the court moved into this castle. In 1678, the next extension by Hardouin-Mansart was begun. The central protruding part of the garden façade was later filled in by Hardouin-Mansart with the Hall of Mirrors. Mansart also added new north and south wings to the main square palace, and partly revised the façade elevations of the first floor.

The Grand Trianon was built in 1687. The chapel was added in 1699.

The whole involved also the building of a town, with three major roads meeting in front of the new building. Enclosed between these were horseshoe-shaped stables.

The new palace became the focal point of both gardens and the city. The main room inside, the king's bedroom, was placed in the center of the main façade after 1701. Thus, this entire complex was an expression of the role and status of the French monarchy. The entire setting provided a vast theater for a continuous pageant of royalty.

The garden layout introduced the concept of the flat and far spread of the garden, as a change to the emphasis on height in the Italian Renaissance (hill) gardens. The plans are no longer based on harmony and unity, but could be expanded piecemeal. Le Nôtre's plans are organized along a dominant central axis, usually terminating in a pond or lake, with rectangular compartments on either side. The garden layout introduced a new world and state order, a new spatial order that would symbolize the principle of state power; and instituted the reference of Louis XIV to the god Apollo, who was the ancient leader of the Muses and the guarantor of universal harmony. Louis XIV wanted this to symbolize his intention to become the new head of a Christian world he attempted to dominate and pacify. The main theme of the garden layout was the sun, represented through numerous allusions to the Greek sun god Apollo.

Louis XIV had laid out a path through the gardens, which illustrated his view of the world. It began immediately behind the castle, after one had crossed the Hall of Mirrors. There, on the Parterre d'Eau one could have a view into the distance that seemingly united earth and sky in the reflective surfaces of the water canals. The world appears as an ordered space. Passing a copy of an Ancient statue of Apollo, one encounters the Orangerie, and continues to a labyrinthine garden with animal fountains. This parcours led one to twenty-five stations where one would experience the world of the mind and nature in mythological sculptures, panoramas, and actual nature.

The Bath of Apollo is the most dominant sculptural group in the gardens. Nymphs are bathing the god, and the horses are led to drink in a nearby sculptural group. There are also four fountains of the seasons: Spring-Flora, Summer-Ceres, Fall-Bacchus, Winter-Saturn. In addition, there are many allegorical statues.

The Apollo Fountain, by Jean-Baptiste Tuby, dates from 1668-1670.

A pumping station powered by horses brought water to the garden. During the 1680s, windmills provided the power, and water towers were built next to the basins. Ultimately, even water from the river Seine was deviated through aqueducts to Versailles.

Antoine Coyevox did the relief of Louis XIV on horseback in the Hall of War (1678).

Then followed the hamlet by Mique (1783). This consisted of eleven straw-roofed houses, among them the house of the queen, and a mill.

# LOUVRE EAST FAÇADE, PERRAULT, PARIS (1667-70)

Claude Perrault (1613-88) was a physician and amateur architect (he had no formal architectural training). He published a French edition of Vitruvius in 1674 and a work on the orders in 1683. His Vitruvius is interesting because he deviated from the accepted theory of harmonic proportions in (Ancient) architecture. This was based on the analogy between visual and musical harmony. Perrault insisted that if such a thing existed there would be no variety in buildings, and instead proposed that proportions were taken from the human body. Since there are different human bodies, there are also different sets of proportions.

Architectural proportions are part of the beauty of a building. Instead of the Ancient rules, Perrault established a system of positive and arbitrary beauty. Positive ones are the richness of materials, magnificence of the workmanship, and symmetry; arbitrary ones are based on taste. Positive beauty can be appreciated by common sense; arbitrary ones result from the special talents of the architect, his skills in the operation of imagination. Thus, the architect's skill was not in the realm of reason, but in that of taste.

Perrault also promoted a vision of Antiquity that centered on orthogonals, columns, and entablatures, sparsely broken by curves produced by the plan or decorative details. Perrault's theories heavily influenced this design. It marks a turn toward an architecture in which structural truth controlled the visual effect of a building.

The Louvre was the King's palace in Paris. It had grown in a piecemeal fashion. In the early 16th century, it was still basically a medieval castle. In 1661, there was a fire, which sped up construction of the new palace. The new Louvre was to express the absolutist governing system of Louis XIV. Part of the successful realization of this attempt was due to the site of the Louvre outside the original city. This allowed the demolition of "unimportant" houses and the use of this space for the new palace.

After the fire, it was decided to close off the eastern end of the existing building. Le Vau drew a project, which however was not liked by Colbert. A few other French architects presented plans, but it was decided to search for feasible projects in Italy (da Cortona, Rainaldi, and Bernini are known to have presented plans). In 1665, Bernini was invited to Paris, but his scheme was ultimately rejected (in 1667), for the feeling for plastic values was less intense in France than in Italy, most probably due to the strong Gothic tradition of dematerialized, diaphanous walls.

At this moment, a team of French architects (Le Vau, Le Brun, and Perrault) was hired. Their design consisted of a traditional five-part façade scheme with central and end pavilions and connecting wings. Between a tall base with windows and a flat roof is the stately colonnade of paired columns. It was among the earliest 17th-century instances of a colonnade in France. The individual elements are more strictly Classical than ever before. They include the octastyle pediment in the center, emphasizing this part in true Baroque fashion, and the reference to the triumphal arch in the basement below it.

This change was furthered by architectural pattern-books during the 17th c. In these books, fantastical designs appeared which helped free architect's imaginations. In France, this situation produced the rococo from ca. 1730 to 1750.

# ST. PAUL'S CATHEDRAL, LONDON, WREN (1675-1709)

The architect's profession was established as an independent one in Italy during the mid-15th century. The same happened in France a century later. In England, it occurred during the 17th century. This meant that the architect was considered to be the chief advisor of the building craftsmen and workers. Architects were learned especially in Neoplatonic philosophy of numerical harmonies. The universe was considered to be subject to the law of numbers; the architect being familiar with these numbers was highly esteemed. Inigo Jones was among the first architects so looked upon. The profession of the architect also received a boost from the growing practice of freemasonry.

Wren produced a design for a domed remodeling of the old structure in 1666, prior to the fire. This was a crude forecast of the eventual conception, including the cruciform plan, the colonnaded drum, and the dome with lantern. At first, it was decided only to add a new choir and crossing to the existing nave. After this partly fell down, a complete rebuilding was decided upon.

This is a church on a Greek cross plan. There were a number of stages to this design, all except the first one using cruciform plans. The first cross plan dates from 1673 and consists of a dome supported on eight piers. Eight vaulted or domed spaces surround the domed area, serving partly specific functions and combining to form a continuous ambulatory. The exterior was an alternation between four straight and four concave façades. Subsequently, an apse was added to the choir and a vestibule with portico to the western entrance. In 1675, due to lack of public support for this project, the final basilican scheme was presented. The ecclesiastical authorities wanted a design in "cathedral fashion," not in the modern "Renaissance" mode. Consequently, the final design combined a centralized space with an almost medieval plan.

A cupola sits over the crossing, covering both nave and aisles. The dome is made of three shells. The final solution for the dome exterior was based on Bramante's Tempietto, with a peristyle enclosing a cylinder. This system is combined with buttressing, in that every fourth intercolumniation is a solid wall. The section of the dome took into consideration its interior function. This eliminated a single shell dome. The solution consisted of an inner masonry cupola with an oculus, an intermediate chain-girdled brick cone to support the lantern, and an outer cladding of wood and lead to give the needed silhouette for exterior effect. The brick cone is exposed for the most part to compression forces, not tension forces.

A portico forms the entrance façade. Its double columns were inspired by the eastern façade of the Louvre (Wren saw preliminary drawings of Le Vau's scheme on a trip to Paris). The lower order is Corinthian, the upper Composite. The two towers add a Baroque element. To counter the discord between the high dome and the low church, Wren raised the exterior walls with screen walls, which also hide flying buttresses supporting the clerestory walls of the higher nave, and suggest a two-story building.

The whole design blends medieval, classical and baroque features.

# TOWN HALL, ELIAS HOLL, AUGSBURG (1615-20)

At the beginning of the 17th century, the regional variation of the Renaissance style in Germany is replaced by a Classicism based on Palladio, characterized by cubical blocks with clear proportions.

Holl combined the Classical block articulation with towers, two features of earlier town halls. Plan and elevation are articulated in a biaxial symmetry. The plan is based on the Greek cross, with a larger and smaller cross arm. The main axis goes from front to back. This central part is the highest of the building. The smaller cross arms house staircases. In the corners between the arms are service and auxiliary spaces. The larger arms contain on all floors the representative spaces. Its termination is done with a pediment flanked by volutes. The staircases are indicated in the cubical forms underneath the towers.

# MEANING

The main purpose of Baroque architecture was to symbolize the strict organization of the system, as well as its persuasive power. It thus appears as a synthesis of systematization and dynamism.

**FIGURE 18–1.** View on to the square in front of St. Peter's Cathedral, Rome.

**FIGURE 18–2.** Santa Maria della Salute, Venice, exterior.

FIGURE 18–3. Santa Maria della Salute, interior

FIGURE 18–4. Castle, Vaux-le-Vicomte, showing main building.

FIGURE 18–5. Castle, Versailles, court of Honor with main entrance.

FIGURE 18–6. Castle, Versailles, view from garden with fountain of Apollo in foreground.

FIGURE 18–7. St. Paul's Cathedral, London

**FIGURE 18–8.**  Louvre, Paris, East Façade

**FIGURE 18–9.**  Town Hall, Augsburg

# Chapter 19

# 17<sup>th</sup>-Century Global Architecture


## JAPAN

### KATSURA IMPERIAL VILLA, KOBORI ENSHU, KYOTO (1620-1658)

Zen Buddhism came to Japan during the 13th c. Among its precepts is the tea ceremony. Tea drinking was first practiced by monks to keep awake during meditation. Later, it became an active part of Zen rituals. Subsequently it came to be a gathering of friends in an isolated atmosphere, drinking tea and discussing aesthetics. It became an outlet for the products of the artist-craftsman. A specific discipline for behavior was established. Everything used in the ceremony was rustic, simple, rough, and unrefined.

The setting for the ceremony was unpretentious. The tea house was a separate building, approached through a small garden. It is a thatched building with plaster walls and openings of various sizes and placement. No two teahouses should be alike. The building was closely integrated with its setting.

This complex is situated at the Katsura River, which supplies the water for the various ponds. The estate covers about sixteen acres. Bamboo fences and hedges completely enclose the area. The ideals governing this design were rustic simplicity and picturesque nature.

The architect was a tea ceremony master. The landscape around the building has been expressly created. The ponds and miniature hills are intended to create a feeling of depth.

There are three main buildings, the old, middle, and new shoin, joined together in a sawtooth pattern, imitating "files of flying wild geese." This zigzag pattern was chosen so that the L-shaped rooms of the three buildings could be arranged en suite. The old shoin was used as guest quarters, the middle one served as residence of the owner. The buildings are raised. Walls are either plank-doors or sliding frame doors. The moon-viewing platform is oriented toward moonrise. The buildings are partly designed for moon and garden viewing.

The architectural forms express their function simply and without disguise. Proportions are subtly adjusted between adjoining buildings, and façades are compositions of solids and voids.

The palace has four tea pavilions, one for each season. The principal one, across a pond from the old shoin, offers an overall view of the garden. It has a thatched roof, as it is fashioned in the style of a rustic house for a common man. Inside, raised sitting areas are arranged around earthen-floored areas. Another teahouse has a shingle roof, imitating the residence of a nobleman. The third one imitates a farmhouse. One teahouse was close to the boundary of the estate, to provide views into the adjoining agricultural community, another at the river border to provide glimpses of fishermen and their work.

The houses are constructed of unfinished wooden posts, thatched and shingled roof, embodying unscathed nature. The overall effect is created by the use of natural materials and a compositional sense. None of the ornate Chinese trabeated forms are used.

# INDIA

## TAJ MAHAL, AGRA (1631-1648)

This building stands outside the northern boundary of a paradise garden. It is flanked by two red sandstone buildings, the guest house to the east and the mosque to the west. It has white marble facing over rubble masonry.

The plan is square with chamfered corners. It is based on a nine-square mandala, and refers therefore to a venerated Indian practice and symbol.

The main hall is placed in the center of the building, and gives access to the crypt beneath. The crypt is covered by a cloister vault. The main hall is octagonal. Square chambers on the sides and octagonal ones in the corners surround this space and turn the outer form into a square. The central space is covered with a cupola. On top of this is a drum with an onion dome. Four smaller domes are in the corners. The entire tomb is on a terrace, with four minarets in the corners. The corbelled dome swells in its upward curve. The exterior surface blends the building perfectly into any time of day. Decoration consists of arabesques and Koranic inscriptions. On the dado, however, the decoration depicts flowering plants, as if the tomb rises from a flowering field.

# NORTH AMERICAN COLONIES

## GOVERNOR'S PALACE, SANTA FE (1610-14)

This was built by first European settlers and combined European planning methods with local building technology. The mass of this building is low, the walls taper and the roof rafters project from the walls. A loggia is set between two square flanking building parts.

## S. FRANCIS OF ASSISI, RANCHO DE TAOS (18TH C.)

Spaniards saw that no money could be made in New Mexico. Hence, it became a field for missionary work. This church shows the same combination of European and local feature as found in secular buildings. The walls still demonstrate the molded surfaces stemming from its local construction material and method.

## PARSON CAPEN HOUSE, TOPSFIELD (1683)

New England had a cold climate, hence buildings were of a timber frame with boarding on exterior and interior and small windows. The chimney was the center. There was also the lean-to or saltbox to enlarge.

This is a two-story clapboarded house with a steeply pitched roof and a broad chimney. This chimney divided the interior into two rooms in each half. Stairs to the upper floor wind around the chimney and fireplaces. The upper floor contilevers over the lower one and have drop ornaments at the ends.

## OLD SHIP MEETING HOUSE, HINGHAM (1681)

Churches were independent and served as both church and meeting house. At Hingham, this is an almost square block with an entrance porch. Its pyramidal roof is topped by a belvedere with an octagonal belfry. Inside, the pulpit is opposite the door, and an impressive open timber frame supports the roof.

## BACON'S CASTLE (1655)

This was a house of a prosperous planter in the South. It consists of a two-story rectangular block with a steeply pitched roof. An entrance tower protrudes from the center of the main façade and reaches into the roof level. On the rear is a similar tower for the stairs. The walls are of brick construction with a stone stringcourse dividing the two floors. The sides have Flemish gables. Two chimney stacks on either end make for a varied roofline. Inside, asymmetrical rooms occupy the entire area between the exterior walls. Window and door decoration are almost Classical.

## St. Luke's (1632)

Churches took up the English tradition. St. Luke's has a Gothic nave with an attached tower. The nave has a high pitched roof and terminates in a Flemish gable on the eastern end. Round-arched windows are divided by brick tracery into doubled pointed-arched windows, which are placed between projecting wall buttresses. The eastern end has three rows of arched openings form a large lancet window. The square tower is divided by stringcourses and lined with quoins. The pediment over the entrance door adds a Classical flavor to this building part. Inside is a trussed wooden ceiling. Tie beams connect the bases for the trusses.

## John Brocket, Plan, New Haven (1638)

Settlements on the Northeastern seaboard were organized into townships, the earliest of which consisted of houses along curved and bending roads that followed the contour of the land: examples are Boston and New York. Shortly thereafter, in first half of 17ᵗʰ c. the grid system was instituted, which was to become the dominant scheme for American city planning.

The grid plan for New Haven was based on a perfect square divided into nine smaller ones (grid is aligned with the four directions of the compass). The center square reserved for meeting house: hence square plan for these meeting houses. This was common land and was called the "Green."

## Plan, Wm. Penn, Philadelphia (1682)

A grid plan for a large city. Intentions: establish a spacious city with provisions for future growth. The whole grid divided into four parts by N-S and E-W thoroughfares. A large open square reserved for public buildings at intersection. Similar public squares in center of each of the four parts. City blocks to be subdivided into wide, deep lots with house set in the middle, with gardens: reason was to prevent fires from spreading.

Copyright © 2008 by Sam D Cruz. Used under license from Shutterstock, Inc.

**Figure 19–1.** Imperial Villa, Katsura, view of one of the teahouses in this garden.

**FIGURE 19–2.** Taj Mahal, Agra.

**FIGURE 19–3.** Parson Capen House, Topsfield, MA.

# Chapter 20

# Compositional Innovation and Stylistic Changes in Late Baroque Architecture

At the beginning of the 18th century, the reigning style, Baroque, was replaced. Two elements were responsible for its defeat: (1) An emotionalist, naturalist Romanticism and (2) a Rationalism. The new ideals were simplicity and purity. In architecture, this meant for the most part a step from decoration toward expression.

## ENLIGHTENMENT

Preconceived ideas and principles no longer govern and dominate investigation, which instead was the result of critical inquiries. Phenomena are investigated in their own right, not in how much they conform to a preset principle. The protagonist of this new way of thinking was Newton, who replaced metaphysical explanations with systematic description of phenomena.

In the course of the 18th century, there was a need for a new form of art and architecture, namely one that educated, not just delected. Such ideas were promoted by the "philosophes," a group of progressive members of the middle class who believed it was necessary to strip away the corrupting influence of the past culture in order to arrive at the natural condition of humankind. Denis Diderot, one of their members, compiled the Encyclopedia, which offered a detailed, rationally described view of the productive community.

Moreover, the philosophes attempted to create a new social order through rational design, and concurrent with this a new pure, functionally and structurally expressive architecture.

The philosophes had faith in reason, which, if pursued, would lead to enlightenment. Supernatural religion and the notion of a Divine plan were rejected in favor of the power of enlightened human reason. They believed that knowledge came from a close study of the natural world. Certain knowledge was only what could be demonstrated by scientific observation and measurement.

The difference between Enlightenment and Romanticism is that the Enlightenment studied scientifically the visible parts of reality (see what can be seen, calculate what can be calculated.). Romanticism is interested in the invisible parts, the underlying forces.

In architecture, (Baroque) persuasion was replaced by (Rococo and Neoclassical) sensation.

# STYLISTIC CHANGES

The architectural development in 18th-century Italy was a change of system, that is, a change in the interrelationship of the parts. This can be noted in the arrangement of, and the relationships between, the various parts. In individual parts, there is not much change to the earlier Baroque. The Renaissance and Baroque systems (of parts) were defined by concatenation (combination of parts), integration (formation of an entire body), and gradation (differentiation to distinguish dominant and subordinate elements). 18th-century architecture exhibits a movement away from Baroque integration and unification, toward a more individualistic treatment of the various building parts, an individual characterization. A new order of the components became the main concern of architects, namely the principle of isolation between the elements. Cubism in terms of architectural forms began playing an increasing role. Textural differentiation, and contrasts in shapes and sizes and other incongruous features were accumulated. It was stated that pleasing the mind was more important and lasts longer than pleasing the eyes. Thus, the rise against tradition was born out of reason. The new style was one of masses struggling against one another, and is not based on ornamentation. Through surface articulation and decoration, these systems can be expressed. During the 18th century, this system was replaced through the invention of new forms of coexistence of parts. First, clashes between horizontals and verticals were emphasized. This led to conflicts between framework and filling. The frame gained dominance during the 18th century. This led to the emphasis on spatial interrelationships and the combination of various rooms. In the final stage, individual parts became completely separated. The old all-embracing unity was no longer possible in architecture, not even in the integration of a building into its context.

## SUPERGA, JUVARRA, TORINO (1719-31)

This is a monastery complex on a hill overlooking Turin, Italy. It was commissioned as an offering in thanksgiving for the victory of Vittorio Amedeo II over the French in 1706.

A church precedes an elongated monastery complex. The church presents the design solution that resulted from the reconciliation of the two features vying for dominance in a Catholic church, namely architectural dominance through the dome, and liturgical dominance through the ritual focus of the altar. On the exterior, the longitudinal axis is reinforced by the elongated portico. The entire church shows the reconciliation of the two dominant features. The horizontal extension communicates with the surrounding landscape, whereas the vertical one represents the religious axis.

In plan, the church consists of a circular core to which are attached choir, entrance portico, and transept wings. These latter are, however, just screen walls to hide the monastery. The dome sits on a high drum. While showing influences from Michelangelo, the building also exhibits Neoclassical features, especially in its resemblance to the Pantheon. It can be considered the beginning of 18th-century Neoclassicism. The towers are a Baroque feature. On the whole, there is an intimate fusion of historical elements from different periods.

## SPANISH STEPS, F. DE SANCTIS, ROME (1723-25)

This is an urban design emphasizing a theatrical treatment of its purpose. It has also been called a piece of scenographic town planning. The stairs had to provide a setting for festivities, form a promenade for the citizens, and provide good drainage.

Its purpose was to unite a street leading from the Piazza del Popolo with one of the streets planned by Sixtus V, which are at different levels. At right angle to their joint is the direction towards St. Peter's. In front of the church, an obelisk marks the confluence of the various directions crossing on this square.

The whole stair consists of an interplay of convex and concave curves, a return to a Borromini motif. The plan is based on a pattern of elliptical curves anchored by rectangular and trapezoidal forms. A convex-concave motif is doubled in depth. The protruding (convex) volume is flanked by stairs and has a straight flight of stairs in front. The upper unit introduces this motif, while the lower one presents a livelier and more articulate variation. In front of the lower one is an area with concave steps, the theater. The beginning of the stairs is flanked by two buildings, which were part of the original design.

The whole stair is an interplay of rising and falling movements, inviting slow passage through it. The design makes the user more aware of the rests than of the climbs. The forms and curves suggest the dynamic movement of its users. The design also brings out better the façade of Santa Trinita dei Monti. In its totality, this stair design synthesized the characteristic Roman monumentality with the grace and sinuosity of the new artistic medium. The irregularity and adaptability of the plan points to Rococo design.

The stairs were heavily damaged in 1728; de Sanctis was sued, but died in 1731, before the lawsuit was decided.

## FOUNTAIN OF TREVI, N. SALVI, ROME (1732-62)

This fountain has a long history dating back to Roman times. The name Trevi means tre vie, or three streets. The fountain was commissioned by Pope Clement XII. This is a synthesis of Baroque and Classical features. A triumphal arch flanked by colossal pilasters forms the backdrop. The whole is a Gesamtkunstwerk (= total work of art), combining architecture, sculpture, and nature. This fountain was on the site of one of the supply points of the Aqua Virgo aqueduct, constructed by Agrippa to bring water from a spring to the Baths of Agrippa behind the Pantheon.

On top of the backdrop is the coat of arms of Pope Clement XII. On the attic level are statues of the Four Seasons with their characteristic vegetation. The central arch is flanked by two reliefs, one showing Aggrippina approving the design of the aqueduct, the other showing the Virgin Trivia pointing out the source to soldiers. Beneath these are statues of Abundance and Salubrity. The central figure is Oceanus, ruler of all waters. Illusionist stone carving suggests natural forms. A scene of tritons and sea horses in a rocky landscape inundated by three cascades forms the base of the design.

Advanced hydraulic engineering was necessary for the cascades and pools. The water from this fountain also flows to the fountains on the Piazza Navona. This monument appeals to more than one sense.

Salvi died in 1751, the fountain was then completed by Giuseppe Pannini.

## BLENHEIM PALACE, VANBRUGH & HAWKSMOOR, OXFORDSHIRE (1705-22)

This palace was offered to the Duke of Marlborough for his victory over Louis XIV in 1704 in the War of the Spanish Succession. The Queen donated Woodstock Manor for this building. It was meant to be both a dwelling and a monument to the Queen's glory.

The general layout is traditional, with a large forecourt. However, the plan is rectangular, that is, the side façades are formulated as full elevations. Consequently, there are two interior courts within the building proper, the kitchen and stable courts. The main parts of the palace are the central pavilion of nine bays and the corner towers. This arrangement of volumes merges a fortress with watchtowers with the more flowing palace scheme. The whole is made of differentiated parts united by common properties. The exterior shows an integration of heterogeneous elements, both in interlocking volumes and in heavy colonnades. The central parts are connected through the giant order and the frieze (of the towers), which are both of the same height. The whole is an amalgam of oversized forms plucked from the history of architecture. There is a richness of texture in materials and surface articulation. The windows, for example, are punched into the wall and not primarily aligned with the façade elevations into a coherent system. The ornament used is mostly abstract. The scale is titanic. In terms of sculptural architecture, this is a simple piece with receding and protruding parts. A temple porch is set before a Renaissance façade, both united through the colossal order. The intention was to create something both heroic and romantic. In terms of lines, shapes, and masses, Blenheim is coherent.

The rear façade consists of an unpedimented portico in the form of a triumphal arch. This is topped by a statue of Louis XIV captured in the war in France.

## CHRIST CHURCH, HAWKSMOOR, SPITALFIELDS (1714-29)

The tower of this church is an example of sculptural architecture. It is a combination of contrasting forms. It is rather massive and flat, an impression that is undermined on the side façade where one sees wall buttresses, not masses. The niches on the front façade suggest a massive configuration.

The portico is a vertical plane, which, however, does not hide the things that are behind it. It is more a symbol, half a Venetian window, half a triumphal arch. It also imitates the belfry above.

With the three circular and ten arched openings, the whole western façade becomes a geometrical exercise. Patterns move up and down the façade. In totality, it is also a visual conceit.

The church is laid out along an east-west axis. Inside, there are columnar screens at the east and west end. Four larger piers introduce the corners of a smaller rectangle within the nave, articulating the north-south direction. This resulted in an interior that simultaneously is a basilica and a central plan.

**FIGURE 20–1.** Superga, Torino.

**FIGURE 20–2.** Blenheim Palace, main façade.

**FIGURE 20–3.** Blenheim palace, garden façade.

# Chapter 21

# Rococo: Sensuality in Architecture

## STYLISTIC SOURCES

In 1715, Louis XVI died, leaving a five-year old heir. In the resulting uncertain political situation, the "absolutist" taste was replaced by the Rococo. J. Rykwert proposes an interesting genealogy of this style. Among the origins for the typical decorative patterns of the Rococo style are the S and C shapes, with which empty spaces in the drawings of buildings in pattern-books are filled. Similar lines can also be found in the wall decorations of Ancient Roman villas. These sources led designers to experiment with free ornamental fantasies that continued into the design of grottoes. There, walls were covered with pebbles and shells, from where the new style got its name. Decorative aspects became dominant during this period. It was based on flowing lines and arabesques, contained within a panel. A source for this feature could have been the metal edgings of pieces of furniture, as well as the characteristic forms and elements of wood paneling.

Rococo dissolved the Classicism of the Baroque. This had already begun in Baroque with the debasement of the Classical support system. Rococo merely changed supports and turned them into frames, thus elevating ornament to a significant position in architectural evolution. The frames begin to unravel at the edges, the projections curl up and pierce through other frames, figures are interwoven into these linear fabrics, and finally the architectural forms on which these ornamental fantasies happen, lose their geometric clarity. Consequently, ornament gained a greater influence on the appearance of a building. Ornament is conceived as a generator of forces, and as being quite decisive in creating the architectural impression.

The exterior of buildings was rarely affected by the Rococo. Façades were still governed by the Classical orders. This contrast, between inside and outside, points to the fact that there was no clear ideal at the time, no common denominator. Such an eclectic approach indicates the mixing of the classes occurring at the time.

The hôtel replaced the palace as the dominant building type. Novelties were introduced in the plan. Rooms en suite were abandoned in favor of smaller rooms with greater articulation in their arrangement. Houses were planned for convenience, not for ceremonial display.

On the inside, the use of the classical orders as constituent elements of the building's skeleton was abandoned in favor of a skin-like wall perforated by large openings. The impact of architectural features was lessened in favor of lighter paneling. The grammar of Classical architecture was replaced by motifs abstracted from natural forms or the grotesques of ancient Roman ornament. This became a constituent element of Rococo architecture.

Up to 1760, Late Baroque and Rococo dominated architectural style. The Rococo was a transitional style, aiming to produce sensations while at the same time still residing in Baroque design intentions. On the other hand, Rococo buildings – and interiors – attempt to provide comfortable living based on empirical study. In the new hôtels, rooms were distributed more practically, no longer according to principles of symmetry or ostentation. Rooms were disengaged so that they can be reached individually. Spaces are differentiated according to their use, and are given different names, such as: ante-chamber, salon, bedroom, and so forth.

## HÔTEL DE SOUBISE, INTERIOR, G. BOFFRAND, PARIS (1735-40)

The exterior was designed by P.-A. Delamair in 1705-9. It is Classical in nature. The numerous windows, however, allude to the luminous interior.

In the oval Salon de la Princesse, the wall consists of large window or mirror panels alternating with narrow bands. Moldings are gilded. The walls were creamy white, the ceiling pale blue. Wall and ceilings are united by means of paintings. Indoor and outdoor characteristics become indistinguishable.

Some of the wall openings are filled with mirrors. Interestingly, while these are functionally part of the wall/openings system, the image they bear is part of the system of spatial perspective.

# AUSTRIA AND SOUTHERN GERMANY

In both Austria and Southern Germany, this movement came out of local craft traditions. It also revived medieval German architecture. The German bourgeoisie was still weak in the 18th century. While German Rococo is a straightforward imitation of the French version, it was used by those classes – aristocracy and church – against which this style had been directed in France. Among the main design intentions was the creation of a "Gesamtkunstwerk" (total work of art). Churches used the system of a double layering of spatial zones, articulated through architectural parts. Decorated ceilings served both as that, and as baldachins over the altar. One of the intentions of the interiors was to emphasize the sight lines to the altar. The eye was to slide easily along the walls to the dramatic focus.

## AMALIENBURG, F. CUVILLIÉS THE ELDER, MUNICH (1734-39)

This building is a long rectangle with a circular salon in the center. It was named for the electress, Amalia, and used as a pleasure pavilion in the Nymphenburg gardens. The salon protrudes on the front façade, contained by a concave curving out of the walls and connected by the convex curve of the entrance. The pediment above this has an open entablature supported by four Ionic pilasters, and is set on a convex plan. This portico is open in the center, and has garlands and swags between its pilasters. Above the door is a sculpture of Diana. The remaining façades are articulated very much in the traditional Rococo manner. The windows of the wings are topped by cartouches underneath segmental arches. Additional decorative pieces are placed between the windows. On top of the salon is a circular balcony from which pheasants could by shot.

The salon interior is articulated by arched doors, windows, and mirrors. A riot of Rococo decorations covers everything. The main color is blue; the decorative reliefs are colored in silver. Flanking the salon are a bedroom on one side and a hunting room on the other. The electress's bedroom is yellow with silver ornament. There is also a room decorated in Chinese motifs. Behind are spaces for the guns and dogs. Throughout, the decorations depict the pleasures of the hunt, and of country life.

## ST. JOHN NEPOMUK, ASAM BROTHERS, MUNICH (1733-46)

These two artists continued the Italian Baroque tradition of Bernini. This comes out in their frequent use of marbling and their architectural details.

This church was built next to their house, and served as their private chapel. On the opposite side is the house for the priest, also designed by the Asams. It was probably meant as a showcase for the brothers' skill, and a private votive offering.

The exterior shows some quotations from Bernini and Borromini, work that the Asams saw during their training in Rome. The front protrudes between two giant pilasters. Their capitals appear to melt down the shafts. The church rises from a stable foundation of symbolic rocks. Free-form pediments frame entrance door and upper windows. The entire façade derives from Classical features that have been transformed into a freely modeled plastic articulation of "melting" architecture. The rocks symbolize the "foundation" of this church, as well as St. John Nepomuk's Church on the Rocks.

The interior is tall and narrow, and has two levels with a gallery. Light enters through concealed openings. Various means are employed to create a supernatural environment meant to heighten religious experience. Ornament seems to drip down like stalactites. Both on the ground floor and the gallery are altars. The one on the gallery level is flanked by four twisted columns. The cupola bears a mural depicting St. John Nepomuk's presentation in Heaven, together with scenes from the life of the saint.

There is an oval vestibule in front of the nave.

## Vierzehnheiligen, J. B. Neumann (1743-72)

This church is dedicated to the assumption of the Virgin Mary. A shepherd had visions of the auxiliary fourteen saints there.

The first project for this church featured a dome supported on coupled columns, which continued the nave colonnade and resulting in the insertion of a skeletal system into an outer shell. However, the supervising architect built the foundations for the choir too far to the east. Thus, the sacred spot of the fourteen saints no longer would have corresponded to the crossing, and became the center of the nave.

The exterior appears as a Latin cross church with a twin tower façade. The central portion of the entrance façade is convex and decorated with engaged columns in the upper story. The side walls have two rows of windows.

Totally contrasting is the interior, where a series of oval baldachins are placed. In this way, the conventional plan was completely obliterated, and the importance of the crossing suppressed. Colossal columns and pilasters provide support. Both longitudinal focus and center are emphasized, thus uniting a number of basic concepts of Baroque church architecture into a synthesis.

## Wieskirche, Dominikus Zimmermann (1746-54)

This church provides the site of a popular pilgrimage.

The exterior shape resembles the surrounding hills. The façades are simple, and appear as membranes. Freely shaped windows pierce the walls. The columns at the entrance have symbolic function. The bell tower acts as a joint between the church and a convent behind. The building is not a center, but the end point of a journey. It is constructed of wood.

The interior is ovally disposed, with a central part within an ambulatory. Support is provided by pairs of slender columns. The lower part of the vault is hollowed out and perforated. A deep presbytery forms the chevet.

Art Nouveau is a later style, that can be introduced for comparative analysis of design intentions and perception.

**Figure 21–1.** St. John Nepomuk (Asam Church), Munich.

FIGURE 21–2. Wieskirche, with scaffolding.

# Chapter 22

# Historicism I: 18<sup>th</sup>-Century Neoclassicism

## JOHANN B. FISCHER VON ERLACH (1656-1723)

He was trained as a sculptor, and went to Italy in 1674. He returned to Vienna in 1685, and was appointed Royal Architect in 1704. In 1721, he published *Entwurff einer historischen Architektur in Abbildung unterschiedener berühmter Gebäude des Altertums und fremder Völker*. This book was probably begun in 1705. It dispensed with the traditional sections on the orders of architecture. Instead, it presented a universal history of architecture, and contained the following five chapters: 1) On Buildings of the Ancient Jews, Egyptians, Syrians, Persians, and Greeks, including the Seven Wonders of the World (Fischer added the Temple of Solomon in Jerusalem as the eighth), 2) On Lesser Known Roman Buildings, 3) On Arab, Turkish, Persian, Siamese, Chinese, and Japanese Architecture, 4) On His Own Designs, and 5) On Vases. Many of the designs are based on coins Fischer saw in Rome. The descriptions of his plates are mostly informed by Ancient travel writers, especially Pliny and Strabo. With this unprecedented layout, this book is part of the oriental craze in Europe begun in architecture during the 1670s. The book demonstrated the new expressive means found in 18<sup>th</sup>-century architecture, here derived from an historical synthesis. Fischer's book is a forerunner of the voracious, encyclopedic, and eclectic mentality of 18<sup>th</sup>-century Enlightenment.

## ST. CHARLES BORROMEO (KARLSKIRCHE), VIENNA (1715-37)

This design shows the implications of Fischer's method, as exemplified in the *Entwurff*. The idea for its form goes back to the Triumphal Arch of the Foreign Merchants, which Fischer designed in 1690.

The church was commissioned by Emperor Charles VI, who had vowed that, if Vienna were delivered from the plague in 1713, he would build a church dedicated to St. Charles Borromeo. All Habsburg dominions had to contribute to its costs. A competition was held, and at the end of 1715, Fischer's entry was accepted. The foundation stone was laid in February 1716; the building was completely finished in 1738. The first design was published in Fischer's *Entwurff*.

The complex formal and symbolic structure of the main façade attempts to satisfy the two functions of this church: as a votive church and as a monument to the greatness of the Habsburg dynasty. The spiral reliefs on the columns represent scenes from St. Charles Borromeo's life. In between the two columns, on top of the entrance pediment, are statues symbolizing the virtues of the saint: on the apex of the pediment is charity, on the two flanking towers, faith and hope. Additional statues that are allegories of the virtues of the saint are on the attic above the pediment. The dome symbolizes the apotheosis of the saint through its soaring outline. It is guarded outside by statues of angels; inside a fresco depicts the glory of the saint. The Emperor is symbolized through the two triumphal columns, which was his emblem, alluding to the Pillars of Hercules.

The sources for the building are varied: Temple of Jerusalem (indicated by the statues of Ecclesia and Synagogue flanking the entrance steps), Pantheon and other Roman temples, Hagia Sophia (minarets), St. Peter's, Rome, Dome des Invalides, Paris, St. Paul's, London.

These sources allude to the Emperor, who is extolled as the second Solomon and Augustus (= bringer of peace), and to the city of Vienna as the New Rome. The entrance pediment sculpture depicts Vienna's deliverance from the plague.

The individual parts of the front are unified through proportional relationships and dynamic tensions. The whole is a synthesis of the main 17th-century styles and Ancient details. The building forms a visual unity. There are no façades in the usual sense, but a frontal view and composite structural groups with different aspects.

The plan is organized around the central oval with a dome over a high drum. The transepts are barrel-vaulted, and there are oval side chapels in the diagonals.

Fischer brought contrasting features together and harmonized the heterogeneous parts into a unified whole. His final designs were usually based on a thorough examination of earlier solutions. His architecture was influenced by Leibniz's system of philosophy. His conception of architecture developed under the influence of the syntheticism of Late Roman Baroque, and the rise of archaeology. His conception was idealistic, often sacrificing comfort for iconographical purposes and ideal plans. Interestingly, Fischer saw himself as the end point of previous architectural development, not as a modern architect. His buildings were historical architecture. They were above all else functional, that is, determined by their purpose and iconographical requirements. The basis of his architectural conception was the intact spatial element of simple shape and ground plan. In his buildings, form and content are fused together.

# PALLADIANISM

In 1714, after Queen Anne's death, George I assumed the throne of England. The Whig party gained control. During the 18th century, England's political system was changing from feudalism to modern capitalism. This partly explains the stylistic progressiveness found in Palladianism. The Venetian sympathies of the king's Whig advisors became a dominant factor in the formation of taste both in Britain and in North America. These were all enlightened citizens, eager to work for a new beginning.

Furthermore, it saw itself separated from the European continent not only physically, but also politically. Hence, there was the intention to create a new, individual style for its buildings. In fact, the earliest anti-Baroque features are found in English 18th century architecture.

After 1720, England witnessed a revolution in architectural thought that changed future development. This nation had hardly any Classical tradition, with the exception of Inigo Jones during the 17th century. Stylistically, an Italianate Classicism, derived from Palladio and Inigo Jones, became fashionable.

An early indication of the yearning for clear forms and proportional relationships was the revival of Palladian architecture in England. It is interesting to note the difference of this sense of order from the "organic" unity of Rococo design. At this point, architects replaced publishers as writers of architectural treatises. As a consequence, the earlier unscholarly translations of Italian treatises became better. An English translation of Palladio's *Four Books* appeared in 1715. In the same year, Colin Campbell published *Vitruvius Britannicus*, a portfolio of Classical designs from England, which was a sign for the independent intentions of English architects. The Palladio was edited by Giacomo Leoni. It did not contain literal transcriptions of Palladio's original illustrations; rather, Leoni changed them to a Baroque flavor. Consequently, Boyle began a new edition, after having traveled to Italy and returning with Italian editions. He employed a number of architects on this project, ultimately producing an edition by Isaac Ware, in 1738. The interesting aspect of these events is that at this time, the main examples of Palladian architecture – Chiswick House, Assembly Hall, Haughton Hall and Holkham Hall – were either finished, or well under way. Campbell's book was intended as a protest against Baroque extravagance, and praised Palladio's architecture as a remedy.

These books became the cornerstones of the new movement. Incidentally, these books appeared five years after the completion of St. Paul's. With this, architectural history disregarded both the Baroque and (continental) Rococo achievement and returned to Palladio and English medieval architecture. Palladianism was a quest for absolutes, a feature that aligns it with the age of reason. Its stylistic premises were the purity and separateness of each individual unit. These efforts all happened in the intention to create a new national style influenced by the achievements of Ancient Rome. As a telling sign of the time, the new style was to emphasize simplicity, uniformity and universality. This was continued into Robert Morris's advocacy of elementary geometrical forms and subsequently into late 18th-century Neoclassicism.

## CHISWICK HOUSE, LONDON (1725-30)

Richard Boyle, third Earl of Burlington, was among the leaders of this new stylistic movement. He was a practicing architect, and independently wealthy. He used his country estate at Chiswick to create a showcase for the new style. This was the intention behind the design of a wing to the existing residence. The design was mostly his own. Entrance stairs with bridges are at the end of each arm. The form of the addition was inspired by Palladio's Villa Rotonda. The proportions are the same, but the English foot was used, resulting in a slightly smaller building. A much closer source is Scamozzi's Villa Rocca Pisani, Lonigo. By using the simple formulas of Palladio, Burlington aimed to fashion the English response to continental Baroque as an expression of absolutism.

However, Chiswick House is not simply a transcription of the Villa Rotonda. It is only superficially patterned on the earlier example. The plan, centered around an octagon, shows contrasting sequences of rooms on the two fronts. The façades do not use the same articulation, and are not centralized. In the garden façade, three Palladian windows are contained within arches. The octagonal drum holding up the cupola, pierced by thermal windows, adds an extrusive element to the overall composition. By treating each part as a distinct unit, the building shows the new order. Boyle was fastidious, and had a pedantic feeling for the separateness of each component. As a result, his designs show an over-articulation, both in plan and elevation. Moreover, the addition of stairs makes the design more picturesque, and links it to the environment.

Inside are mostly staterooms. Rooms are laid out en suite flanking a central octagon. Along the garden façade, a rectangular room with apsidal ends is flanked by two circular ones, pointing already to the more informal sequences of later periods. The interiors are derived from Jones, rather than Palladio. Kent was employed for the interiors and furnishings.

# COLONIAL GEORGIAN ARCHITECTURE IN THE AMERICAN COLONIES

## GOVERNOR'S PALACE, WILLIAMSBURG (1749-51)

This Palace is a typical example of a Georgian house. It is based on a number of abstract norms and principles. The whole is bilaterally symmetrical along a center axis, both in plan and façade. This axis is marked by a central hall, which runs the full depth of the house. Reception room and family dining room are to each side. In the back of the house are the state dining room and the main staircase. Bedrooms are on the second story. This axis even determined the layout of the garden. The overall shape or volume of the house is cubical and restrained. The façade elevations are horizontally divided through the use of hipped roofs, balustrades, cornices, string-courses, and the foundation. The building is assembled of distinct elements – building parts, as well as, façade ornaments – carefully proportioned with the whole. Ornamentation is based on antique devices. The parts of the building are clearly articulated in edges, windows, and the central pavilion. This type of design is derived from Renaissance and Baroque architecture.

The Governor's Palace was one of the most sumptuous residences in the colonies. Its plan: central hall, reception room and family dining room to each side. In the back of house: state dining room and staircase. Bedrooms were on the second story. This axis even determined the layout of the garden.

## REDWOOD LIBRARY, HARRISON, NEWPORT (1748-50)

Straightforward Palladianism begins in North America around the middle of the century. Before that, there is still some influence from English Baroque, which came especially from James Gibbs's treatise. The common sources for the American development are architectural treatises published in England: Palladio's *Four Books of Architecture, Vitruvius Britannica,* and Gibbs's *A Book of Architecture* (1728). Gibbs' book does not faithfully reproduce Palladio's originals. The engravings are more sculptural, and hence reflect rather the late 17th-century Baroque style. This influence was mostly visible in the South, as the wealthier landowners moved there. In most cases, architecture was practiced by gentleman amateurs, and was a pastime for the wealthy.

Peter Harrison, the first "professional" American architect, lived in the middle of the 18th century. Harrison had drafting and engineering skills through his profession (merchant and sea captain). He was the most learned and accomplished of the contemporary gentleman-architects. He had accumulated wealth, and could devote his time to pursue his hobby, architecture.

His first building was Redwood Library. The design was based on an illustration in Palladio's *Four Books.* The building is a rectangular block with a pitched roof. A Tuscan Doric (with base) temple front on a base is superimposed onto the lower building. Two wings flank this portico, in a manner similar to Palladian designs. The entire building is of wood, but imitates stone masonry. The planks are cut to suggest ashlars, and sand is mixed into the paint to give it the appearance of stone. It was the first American building with a temple front. The Classical forms were meant to suggest the simple, pure, regular, and ordered sense of 18th-century America.

## VIRGINIA STATE CAPITOL, JEFFERSON & CLÉRISSEAU, RICHMOND, VA (1785-89)

Thomas Jefferson and his architectural designs offer an example of anti-English feeling after the declaration of independence. He was a scientist and politician (a number of ministerial functions, President 1801-09). Because of his dealings with the English in his political capacities, his antagonism toward English was pronounced. His involvement with the new nation's political affairs also made him aware that it needed structures with which it could identify itself. In general, Jefferson was still one of the 18th c. gentleman-architects.

While working on Monticello, in 1776, Jefferson had proposed that the capital of Virginia be moved to Richmond. Williamsburg and its buildings reminded him too much of the colonial exploitation; in addition, Richmond was more centrally located. He proposed that a separate building should be constructed for each branch of the state government. To save cost, the legislature asked for just one building, which was to contain all government services. Jefferson was asked to find an able architect to work out a design. He did more, and with the help of French architect Charles-Louis Clérisseau submitted plans and a plaster model to the State of Virginia. This design had a central foyer, offices, and halls, all contained within an Ionic hexastyle temple.

The model for the building was the Maison Carrée. To adapt this plan for the purposes of a capitol, Jefferson simplified the original building. Differences include a different order, a smaller portico, pilasters instead of engaged columns, variations in size and number of interior spaces. On the rear façades, pilasters replace the original engaged columns. These created problems later, because the temple form did not lend itself easily for the new purpose. This was the first genuine attempt to move away from Georgian prototypes in a public building. The Capitol was among the first buildings that were literal reinterpretations of the classical temple, and that were full-scale useable structures. The Madeleine in Paris, for example, was built twenty years later. To imitate a Roman building also disassociated the Virginia State Capitol from the old colonial rule, and instead aligned it with an earlier example of a republican government. The Maison Carrée was built under Emperor Augustus. This symbolism points to another influence on Jefferson's architectural designs, namely French Revolutionary Classicism.

The building was completed in 1789. Its achievement brings a change to Jefferson's relationship with Palladio. Now that he had seen the originals himself, he became equal to Palladio, whereas before, Palladio was his only source. The choice of this source was also facilitated by the abstract, geometric quality of the Maison Carrée, especially its clear articulation of simple rectangular volumes. This return to Classical architecture was aided by the current excavations of Roman sites. Herculaneum started in 1738; ten years later, Pompeii was discovered. Publications of the findings helped spread the knowledge about Roman architecture.

The building was refurbished in 1904-5. It was at this time that the two side wings were added.

FIGURE 22–1. Karlskirche, Vienna, main façade.

FIGURE 22–2. Karlskirche, interior.

FIGURE 22–3. Virginia State Capitol, Richmond.

# Historicism II

## THEORY

By mid-18<sup>th</sup> century, the artifices of Baroque and Rococo were viewed in France as symptomatic of the artificiality and corruption of the reigns of kings Louis XV and XVI. The industrial and social revolutions confirmed the decline of the old world. With the loss of identity of the old integrated settlements came the need for a new form of art and architecture, namely one that educated, not just delected. The Baroque style was blamed for lacking in the study of nature, for preferring the imitation of other masters, and for emphasizing practice (of painting) instead of serious study. (This was a reaction against mannerism, or against the personal manner. Classicism eliminated subjectivity in favor of idealism.) The new ideal oriented itself according to Antiquity, which was interpreted as having promoted a purified, refined reality (nature).

An almost sacred importance was attributed to primitive nature, as it was characterized by purity, originality, and uncorruptedness. Translated into architecture, this meant that the purest architecture was what had appeared at the dawn of civilization. Studies focused again on Vitruvius' treatise, and especially on its emphasis on the column as the basis of architectural structure. As this was not used in Baroque architecture, it was proposed that ornament be stripped away and that architecture go back to its essentials. In opposition to Baroque and Rococo, writers of treatises stressed that architecture was the art of pure structure.

This necessitates the acceptance of an idea of the beautiful. This idea represents the original image of all creatures. The artist, imitating the highest creator, must approach these ideas. (This is neo-Platonic aesthetics.) These ideas have their origin in sense perception, but aim for a more refined reality. The idea is the perception of nature cleansed through the mind. Hence, Classicism criticizes both mannerists (for disregarding nature study) and naturalists (for adhering too closely to visible nature).

### Carlo Lodoli (1690-1761)

Lodoli was the spiritual leader of the Venetian "rigorists." He formulated a novel theory during the 18<sup>th</sup> century (first published in 1759, but already taught in courses for young noblemen Lodoli held during the 1740s). This theory attempts to apply a scientific outlook to architecture. Human control over nature was expressed in mechanics. Statics, as part of this discipline, was one aspect in which architecture could be taken out of transcendent, divine nature.

Sometimes labeled "functional," it is rather a rational theory, demanding in essence that architecture should consist only of parts that have a definite function and are strictly necessary (in general, nothing that is not a working part should appear in a building). Furthermore, architecture had to conform to the nature of materials and express their poetics. The nature of buildings is based on statics, materials, and function. Function is understood as how the structure of the building works and how each part relates to another in terms of statics. This theory resulted in the condemnation of Classical architecture, as it imitated wood structure in stone. Hence, since Ancient architecture thus was not correct, its ornamental vocabulary was false as well. The elimination of ornament was one of the effects of this theory. Lodoli was against the authority of earlier theoreticians, especially Vitruvius; he was contemptuous of popular taste, and disdained Baroque architecture as too plastic. His outlook was dominated by a belief in progress. While not having an immediate impact on the built environment, these new theories were discussed around 1750. Architects and intellectuals became aware of the historical necessity for change. Lodoli's theory paralleled the change in the social structure from the aristocracy to the bourgeoisie during the 18<sup>th</sup> century.

## MARC-ANTOINE LAUGIER (1713-69)

In France, beginning with Claude Perrault, architectural theoreticians advocated, above all, the use of a trabeated system of support structure. Into this, they also inserted Gothic principles, resulting in the use of trabeation to support barrel vaults. This architecture was related both to the Gothic cathedral and the Greek temple.

Laugier's *Essai sur l'architecture*, published in 1753, was an attempt to purge and invigorate architecture through a return to the sources, namely the Vitruvian hut. Nature is the only authority Laugier accepted. His attempt was to give architectural principles the same certainty as scientific/natural principles. Art is developed out of imitation of nature. Translated into architecture, this idea identified the essential elements of architecture as the freestanding column (support), the lintel (beam), and the pediment (roof). Hence, architectural beauty is found in the forms, not in the decoration or proportions.

Laugier formulated *a priori* principles of architecture. Laugier's ideas regarding the origins of architecture in the primitive hut are interesting. The features of his primitive hut suggest the details of Greek architecture. The uprights point to the columns, the horizontals to entablatures and the roof to the pediment. These are the essential elements of architecture. All other parts that are found in a building are like ornamentation, i.e., added due to human caprice. Laugier's primitive hut is the mediation of nature through instinct and reason. The quest for the primitive hut was also justified by thoughts on the innocent state of human beings, uncorrupted by susequent historical development. Laugier's theory presented architecture as free from caprice and individual taste. Laugier's hut was attained by speculation, not by data research. It is a distillation of nature through unadulterated reason, prompted only by necessity. Laugier's primitive hut is notionally primitive, not in the sense of longing for the primitive life.

He believed that the beautiful in the arts was based on reason. The Greek orders and their functionality were proof of this theory in architecture. The architect had to accept this axiom, especially the proportions, and design his various buildings within this limit. This also allowed the architect to express more than the elements of Laugier's primitive hut, giving him the means to make his architecture "speak."

The frontispiece shows a female figure leaning on debris from Classical architecture and directing a genie's attention to a primitive hut built by nature. The figures illustrate the biological relationship between mother and child, thus referring to the pedagogical duty of parents. The female can also be read as the guardian of tradition. The picture is ambiguous, leaving it to the viewer to decide whether architecture here is considered representation or building (= the act of).

## GIOVANNI PIRANESI (1720-78)

He was a pupil of Lodoli's. He chose to become an engraver as this allowed him to design on a larger scale than contemporary taste and means would allow him, a scale, furthermore, that was inspired by the monumental Roman ruins, for which he had a great passion. His collections of engravings appeared during the 1740s, beginning with architectural projects, depictions of ruins, and finally the prisons. Piranesi established himself as a recorder of old and new buildings in and around Rome. In these, Piranesi gave up the existing architectural order through the force of inspiration, not rationality. His content was the archaeological experience. His drawings of Ancient ruins arise out of a combination of archaeological curiosity and Romantic emotion. The crumbling ruins are not intended as models of geometric order, but as stirring spectacles of transience and decay.

During the 1750s, Piranesi began to publish engravings of Ancient Roman ruins. These are assemblages of Classical details in unordered arrangements. One of his aims was to prove that Roman architecture owed nothing to Greece, but instead derived from Etruscan building. His main argument was the engineering skill that distinguished Roman from Greek architecture. This skill, according to Piranesi, came from the Etruscans, as still existing civil engineering structures in Rome, such as the Cloaca Maxima, demonstrate. Besides, Roman architecture was more varied than Greek. The Romans had been true builders, not designers such as the Greek architects. Romans understood the poetics of stone; they did not simply translate wooden forms into stone.

In 1765, Piranesi's architectural treatise was published. This – the Parere – was presented in the form of a dialogue between a traditionalist and a rigorist, with the traditionalist gaining the upper hand.

Nevertheless, in his designs, Piranesi proved to be more prophetic, as most consist of heterogeneous, incongruous assemblies of Classical details. Nevertheless, he intended formal accuracy; as in other contemporary publications, outline and silhouette modeling are used.

Piranesi was most probably influenced by French architects who had won the Grand Prix and spent their earned time in Rome.

## ST. SULPICE, OPPENORD & SERVANDONI, PARIS (1646-1732)

In France during the 18th century, Ancient Roman architecture, presented through Piranesi's publications, engendered Neoclassicism.

The change toward more rational forms can be noticed in this building. Meissonier, who had gone furthest in his rejection of the orders, presented a plan in 1726, which was a combination of Baroque wall-architecture with Rococo decoration. It was rejected, and the subsequent competition won by Servandoni.

Servandoni was trained by a forerunner of Piranesi and, thus, brought out the Roman connection. His competition design featured a two-story portico framed by two three-story towers. The choice and position of the orders followed tradition. It was one of the earliest Neoclassical designs.

Work on this scheme began in 1732, but already in 1742, Servandoni altered his design. The pediment now covered the five central bays, and the columns of towers and central part were combined at their juncture. The columns were freestanding. In this, he followed Perrault.

This scheme was built up to the second story by 1745. Then, it was decided that this structure could not support the heavy pediment. The decision was made to replace it by a balustrade.

This is the design as it was finished by Chalgrin after Servandoni's death in 1766. When it was finished, this church appeared with the firmness of geometry, the regularity and the columnar rhythms of a Greek temple. The orders, the coupled columns, the straight entablature, and the appeal to a conventional, unspecific Antiquity were influenced by Perrault. The western façade has no climax within itself. The individual parts are independent. The towers are not tied into the façade articulation.

In plan, this is a basilica. Inside, Classical details blend with Gothic forms. Piers decorated with Ionic pilasters support a second row of piers, which in turn hold up domical, ribbed stone vaults.

## STE-GENEVIÈVE (PANTHÉON), SOUFFLOT, PARIS (1756-90)

This building can be seen as an illustration of Laugier's theories. It was intended to mark a new beginning in architecture, based on the freestanding columns supporting an entablature. This begins with the entrance portico and continues inside the building.

When this building was finally begun, there had already been a number of designs for it, all following a Greek cross plan with a dome over the crossing. To this, two bays and flanking towers were added in the east. Soufflot's design dates from 1764. The crypt was constructed in 1758-63, the church begun in 1764.

Inside, the nave was separated from the aisles by screens of Corinthian columns. These supported a continuous entablature, which in turn carried the vaults and domes. A total of five domes are found inside, four over each cross arm, one over the crossing. This one is set on top of a drum; the four smaller ones rest on arches over slender Corinthian columns.

In a second project of 1777, Soufflot added the circular colonnade around the drum. The aim was to combine under one roof the lightness and transparency of Gothic structure with the purity and correct taste of Classical architecture. The final product has an archaic character (openly), but a Gothic structure (hidden). The exterior walls were crowned by a cornice and balustrade, which concealed the roof.

The important issues around this building were, first, the contemporary reevaluation of Gothic architecture as a national French style and, second, the detached column as the most superior building element. The intentions behind Soufflot's design were to link the French 18th-century church to the earliest periods of Christianity. The four piers supporting the crossing dome carried statues of the eight church fathers (four each from the west and east).

Detailed studies and tests of materials were conducted to create the lightness of structure intended. Influenced by this activity, Soufflot proposed the development of abstract (not empirical) theories based on experiment and mathematical calculation. In the building, iron rods are arranged according to rationally calculated stresses. This points to the dual origins of Soufflot's design – on one hand, the traditional language of Classicism; on the other, a typical experimentalism brought by the Enlightenment. The lighting requirements of Ste-Geneviève were solved by scientific planning, whose results were applied to Classicist structural elements.

In 1791, Quatremere-de-Quincy demanded that the windows in the exterior walls be blocked so as to give the building a more serious character. This was also the time the church was renamed and dedicated as a national monument to honor the great men of France. All Christian ornament was replaced by symbols of freedom, equality, and fraternity, which were the ideals of the new post-revolutionary France.

### PETIT TRIANON, GABRIEL, VERSAILLES (1761-68)

This building was the architectural focus of the farmyard where poultry and botany were kept within the parks at Versailles. This was given by Louis XVI to his queen Marie Antoinette. Originally, a menagerie of domestic animals was installed. This was a signal for the victory of the Neoclassical style. It gives an indication of the refined taste of this period. While being as chaste and pure on the outside as the earlier hôtels, it nevertheless is more delicate when compared to the large scale and massiveness of traditional French palaces. The decoration does not emphasize any part. It is intended to express the original purpose of the building and is derived from the vegetable kingdom. The whole area was later conceived as an English garden, with the intent to increase the pastoral quality of the gardens. The pavilion and the gardens immediately surrounding it are still in a Classical mode. In there, a circular temple of love was added by Mique in 1777-78. In 1774, an Anglo-Chinese garden was added, laid out along a meandering river.

The building is new in form, with the strictly cubical volume isolated from its environment. A change in site allows two sides to have three stories, and two to have two stories. The façade articulation is created through textural varieties in the masonry, which is used for the rusticated base, the fluted pilasters, and the entablature, as well as for the undecorated walls.

The interior is informally laid out. The top floor contains eighteen bedrooms, some not bigger than cabinets, while public and dining spaces are on the main floor. In its decoration, it still contains part of the Rococo spirit.

### KEDLESTON HALL, DERBYSHIRE (1760-70)

Robert Adam (1728-92) was the first to successfully create a new language based on Antique architecture. In 1757, he prepared measured drawings of Diocletian's Palace at Spalato (published in 1764). He also combined Picturesque elements with his Classical vocabulary.

Many examples of 18th-century Neoclassicism consist simply of redecorations all'antiqua. The use of the Classical style expressed an up-to-date fashion reflecting the archaeological revelations of the century. Classical allusions are grafted onto outmoded forms. Individual columns can be traced back to contemporary published illustrations of Ancient examples. Some are even genuine examples, excavated in Rome. Thus, conventional historical boundaries are transcended.

A number of different architects were involved in this design. The plan derives from that used at Holkam Hall. The main building is square. The corner pavilions have a central three-part pedimented porch flanked by side wings.

The garden facade is derived from the Ancient triumphal arch motif.

The entrance hall is treated as a great columned basilica.

### SYON HOUSE, ADAM, MIDDLESEX (1762-63)

This was an interior remodeling of an existing 16th-century house. Adam left the exterior shell, but inserted a vast rotunda in it as a central court.

Robert Adam destroyed the movement of Baroque architecture by making certain details too heavy. His exteriors tend to be "confectioner's" trimmings, inspired by a desire to please. But, by inserting cylinders into cubes, he shows some novel "cubistic" exercises.

His approach was empirical, not one that fixes a definite entablature for each order. At Syon, individual columns can be traced back to contemporary published illustrations of Ancient examples. Some columns are even genuine examples, excavated in Rome. Thus, conventional historical boundaries are transcended.

The interior spaces are either domed or vaulted in the manner of an Ancient Roman bath building.

# GREEK REVIVAL

This development originated in the knowledge about Greek architecture begun in mid-18th century (Leroy, Stuart & Revett, Dumont). Between 1748 and 1750, there was particular interest in the temples at Paestum. This knowledge had already been present in the 17th century, but the philosophy of the picturesque renewed interest in these monuments.

The fact that these Greek examples seemed less refined than the Roman ones brought with it a reversal of views regarding history. Whereas before history had been interpreted as a slow but steady evolution, now it was thought that history can evolve in stages or cycles. This also had some impact on the evolution of architectural theory, as it led to the decline of Vitruvius's authority.

The triumph of Greek Revival came in the 19th century; after 1820, the style of the Periclean age was the model to be emulated. In the United States, the Greek passion also was influenced by the Greek war of independence and links between this struggle and the earlier American war of independence.

## BRANDENBURG GATE, LANGHANS, BERLIN (1789-94)

This gate served as the western entrance into the city of Berlin. It was the first example of Greek Revival in Germany. The design was based on the Propylaea, a source suggested by King Fredrick Wilhelm II. It is not totally accurate in individual details. It was most probably based on French treatises on Ancient architecture. The order used is not Greek, but Roman Doric (the corner triglyphs are over the centers of the columns). The metopes are decorated with scenes from the battle between the Lapiths and the Centaurs. The entire complex is laid out symmetrically. Above the columns is an attic story in the form of a monument. A series of steps suggests a Hellenistic mausoleum, as well as a pediment. This is crowned by a quadriga. In its gigantic size and in the superstructure, it is influenced by Boullée.

The gate has a long history as a symbol, for the various aspirations that governed Berlin since its completion.

FIGURE 23–1. Ste-Geneviève, Paris, exterior.

**FIGURE 23–2.** Ste-Geneviève, Paris, interior.

**FIGURE 23–3.** Brandenburg Gate, Berlin.

# Chapter 24

# Visual Arts and Architecture

With the Late Baroque and Neoclassical search for origins came also a new sensitivity to nature. A particular natural setting was seen as evoking associations. Applied to architecture, this meant an interest in earlier periods, to exploit the emotions and feelings associated with earlier ages. In broad terms, architecture was interpreted as having evocative and narrative (or literary) powers. Romanticism reacted against a strictly rational view. The new philosophy of the sublime was formulated. It stated that the most powerful emotions and associations did not arise from traditional elements of beauty; but rather that a heightening of the senses was caused by darkness, danger, and great natural forces. This danger was seen as awe-inspiring. Thus, the sublime could be called the romanticized awe of natural power. It was felt that architecture derived its value through literary associations. Eclecticism became one of the bases of architectural design. The associational connection between the form of a building or its details, and those of an earlier building, became important. Eventually, various historic styles from a range of periods could be used in the same building. Especially, Classical buildings concretized a general longing for a golden age when wo/man lived in close contact with nature and was guided by his/her natural faculties. On a more pragmatic level, eclecticism can be explained as the solution to quickly find new forms for the multiplicity of new building tasks.

The Romantic movements in 18th-century architecture were subjective periods, allowing for personal taste and expression. In this, they partly reacted against the earlier normative styles. Romanticism was a revolt of feeling against the coldness of reason. This was especially directed against the narrow decorative vocabulary of Palladianism, which was seen as a Classicist tyranny. Taste was no longer the only faculty needed to appreciate a work of architecture; passion became as important. "One needs taste to be sensible to Ancient architecture, but only passion to feel Gothic." (Walpole)

New design principles that were established through the picturesque were novelty and surprise, and the avoidance of symmetry.

Architecture designed according to Romantic principles is usually not characterized as beautiful (in the Neoclassical sense), but rather as crude. Aesthetic standards were now based on subjective reactions, not on harmony or proportion. An aesthetic reaction was described as containing an emotional part. Romanticism was revealed as emotionalism, since emotions are part of one's own personality that cannot be subordinated by others.

## PICTURESQUE

This stylistic movement was influenced by an interest in the "pleasures of the imagination." The sense of sight became important. The most lasting impact of this movement was the emphasis it put on architecture as part of an environment. There was an intimate connection between the villa type and the informal landscape. After 1750, the country villa became a dominant building type.

In broad terms, architecture was interpreted as having evocative, narrative or literary, powers. This encouraged the view of architecture as having flexibility and also brought a ruin mania. Picturesque buildings have the advantage of being capable of being added to without destroying the existing ensemble. Picturesque theory dissolved the compositional techniques of Palladianism and Baroque architecture. The three main points of the picturesque are: (1) buildings can bring the past back to life more vividly than written records, (2) buildings can be composed as an integral part of a landscape and (3) buildings and trees should be mingled like those in 17th-century landscape paintings.

## ENGLISH GARDEN

The first result of the picturesque was the English garden. Its pavilions were of three types: 1) reconstructions of Antique temples (Antiquity in its glory), 2) ruins of Antique temples (Antiquity in its decline) and 3) rustic dwellings found in the Italian countryside (buildings associated with a pastoral life). The closer connection of the main villa to its environment also influenced their design. No longer were these cubic boxes to be adorned, but projections and shadow effects now made up the façade articulation. An interesting paradox is expressed in the English garden. It may represent the concept of looking for one's future in the past. Like the museum, this garden type offered a collection of architectural history, but was meant to indicate a future direction for architecture.

### Blenheim Palace Gardens

Capability Brown began working there in 1764 and changed the existing formal gardens. He dammed the river and excavated two lakes. A cascade was added to the western border of one of the lakes.

## CHISWICK HOUSE, GARDENS (1717-24)

The new English garden ideal was at play in this design. This transformation from the French garden was brought about by a mythological fantasy derived from contemporary art, which allowed the discarding of the straightjacket of ancient rules. Similarly, a taste for the exotic, especially for Chinese gardens, had an influence. Gardens were considered as framed pictures (framed by windows). The new mood was mainly influenced by literary discoveries, that is, written descriptions of Chinese and Ancient Roman gardens. Gardens recreated tragic visions of the ultimate physical expiration of a dead civilization. Changing sets of an opera are parallels to the evocative possibilities of such a garden that offers an illusionary landscape of all times and places.

At Chiswick, there were still some residues of the French garden. The traditional geometrical principles are blurred. The main lines of the garden are related to the interior of the house. However, wilderness is allowed to enter the whole pattern. The garden wall is discarded and replaced by sunken fences. The new garden arrangement also had repercussions on the buildings, as they were no longer the only commanding aspect of a country seat. Now, they were simply among the various objects of the garden.

A paradox is introduced by the distinction of a strictly formalized Classical building placed in a Romantic garden. However, both directions arose out of the intention to liberate oneself.

This new development marks the beginning of the picturesque. One source of the English garden can be found in the grottoes, groves, nymphaea, and irregular areas of Italian Renaissance gardens. Chiswick garden was partly influenced by Chinese garden design. Informal gardens had been used in China and Ancient, that is, Republican, Rome. The English garden is therefore not an original creation. Another influence was the paintings by Poussin and Lorrain, which were taken as contemporary interpretations of Ancient bucolic literature.

The little temples in Chiswick garden were built by Boyle between 1717 and 1724. They were all derived from Classical or Palladian sources. The Bagnio was the first pavilion; others included a domed Ionic temple and the portico of Inigo Jones's Covent Garden church. Kent added the landscape features, among others the cascade. A classical exedra hedge with statues of Roman worthies is in direct line with the garden façade. Partly, these were conceits meant to stimulate a variety of literary associations. The pavilions (and the main building) were meant as beautiful or curious incidents in a scene of controlled wildness. Controlled vistas produced small views of varying styles and moods. English gardens were not uniform, but combined natural aspects in the landscape with artificial ones in the human intervention to nature and the pavilions. Gardens were intended to induce a mood. Wild nature alone was not enough stimulus. The current fashion was influenced by painting; and nature was to be presented as if it was a painting.

Especially in France, the new English garden was applied as a combination of Neoclassicism (in the pavilions) and picturesque (in the garden layout). Here, the Classical miniatures show the contrast between geometrical clarity and organic nature. In this way, Antiquity was seen as a source of new forms and new societies. Classical forms were invoked to counter the decadence of the old monarchic system and its style, the Baroque.

The first phase of this movement began in the 1710s, reaching a climax in William Kent's designs of the 1730s. The second phase coincides with the work of Capability Brown. He reduced the new system to one of his own, the main elements of which were clumps, belts, and lakes distributed in an otherwise close-shaven terrain.

## STOURHEAD, HOARE & FLITCROFT (1744-65)

Here, poetry, painting, gardening, architecture, travel, the study of antiquity, and topography were all combined in the design. They all merge to form an idyllic, narrative, cultural picture dominated by a sense of place. The main design intention was to provide a chain of responses, which were linked into a narrative. The various pavilions stood, as in a painting, directly in the landscape. They were crystalline incidents in a continuous, quasi-natural landscape.

Henry Hoare, a rich banker, first built a Palladian villa designed by C. Campbell (1718). In 1743, his son Henry began work on a Picturesque circuit tour around the valley. The river was dammed to create an artificial lake. The gardens are laid out around a lake and offer surprising views on temples, water cascades, and bridges. The inspiration may have been Lorrain's painting "Coast of Delos with Aeneas" (1672). Henry Flitcroft designed a few of the pavilions. The path around the lake is an allegory of Aeneas's journey through the underworld. Pavilions include a Temple of Flora, a grotto, a Pantheon, a Temple of the Sun, and even an existing medieval village. The story told begins with birth at the Temple of Flora, opposite the Pantheon, passes the grottoes of the underworld, reaches the Pantheon of earthly glories, and continues through the rock arch, suggestive of mortality, to ascend heavenwards to the Temple of Apollo. The Gothic cottage was added later. The lake reflects the sky and is the natural center of this tableau. From the Pantheon, one sees the old village church or the temple of Flora.

# CIRCUS (WOOD THE ELDER), ROYAL CRESCENT (WOOD THE YOUNGER), AND LANDSDOWNE CRESCENT (PALMER), BATH (1764-93)

Bath had a local wool industry and its waters at the beginning of the 18th century. During the summers, when the court was away from London, London society came to Bath as a summer amusement center. This development brought the need to expand upper-class housing in the city.

A square, a circus, and a crescent were planned for the perimeter of the town. John Wood Sr. began construction with Queen's Square in 1729. His goal was to expand Bath, giving it the character of its ancient Roman predecessor. He wanted to re-endow Bath with a Forum, a Circus, and a Gymnasium. Queen's square was on a sloping site, thus making each side different.

The site for the Circus was leveled. The Circus combined row houses into a monumental unity. It is a simplified, smaller, and inverted Colosseum. Thirty houses are combined in three circle segments. The façades are articulated by double columns of three superimposed orders, Roman Doric, Ionic, and Corinthian.

The younger Wood built the Royal Crescent (1767-75). The elliptical curve follows the curvature of the Roman Colosseum more closely. Through the use of colossal Ionic columns, the scale is greater than in the Circus, and the monumentality more effective. The style here is Neoclassical, not Palladian as in the two earlier schemes.

In the Circus and Crescent, Apollo and Minerva are evoked, hence celebrated.

# GOTHIC REVIVAL

A scholarly interest in archaeology followed by a delight in decay are the sources of this revival. The Gothic style was still widely practiced in England during the 16th century. In mid-17th century, it was officially named Gothic and, thus, became the object of a revival. While it never completely died out in the meantime, by this time it was no longer the prevalent fashion. It survived in the use of Gothic ornamentation to buildings of primarily other styles, in its continuation by local craftsmen, and in an antiquarian interest in this style.

Interest in the Gothic style arose from delight of the large or the ingenious, religious fervor, and a literary impulse. Poets began to exploit the Gothic mood in the 18th century. This mood is characterized by melancholy and the combinations of ruins, ivy, and owls. It was a love of dramatized decay (of Gothic ruins). Toward the middle of the 18th century, this literary interest in Gothic was combined with an archaeological interest. This combination had great impact on the Gothic Revival. Horace Walpole was archaeologically less scientific than the others, but attempted to analyze the aesthetic value of Gothic as compared to Classical architecture. He focused on the structural improvements of the pointed arch, and the variety of impressions evoked by Gothic buildings.

## STRAWBERRY HILL, R. ADAM, ET. AL., TWICKENHAM (1749-77)

Horace Walpole bought this building in 1747. He was the writer who wrote the first Gothick novel of the 18th century, *The Castle of Otranto,* and had a particular curiosity about the medieval times. Serious enlargement began in 1750, with the first stage completed in

1753. The initial idea was to enlarge the house in a spirit of caprice, of making the fabric of the house reflect the studies Walpole was conducting at the time: topography, county history, and the antecedents of his own family. The enlarged Strawberry Hill then became a Gothic castle that celebrated his family history. The design is a product of the reigning fashion for Gothic as stimulating imagination or as decorative form. In this respect, the stylistic choice was a matter of taste. Inspiration came rather from a superficial Gothic-Rococo mode used in prior sham ruins for gardens.

Developing the garden into a scenic landscape was the first step in enlarging this building. Construction of this building continued for almost 40 years. This aspect was emphasized in the villa, so that its growth can easily be noticed. The first designer used was Richard Bentley. In 1761, he was replaced by John Chute (he designed the library). At this time, a change from the Rococo direction to a more strictly archaeological one occurred. Later on, even Robert Adam provided design support. His work began with the tower in the south-west corner (1759). What was originally a small villa was enlarged into a sprawling Gothic castle. It is a mixture of every conceivable expression from the Middle Ages. Features range from battlements, turrets, towers, galleries, and corridors to Tudor moldings. It includes a library in a new "Gothick" style. This attests to the high archaeological knowledge about Gothic architecture. Strawberry Hill was a kind of paper architecture, since many of its details were copied from engravings of medieval buildings. Inside, a gallery imitates the Chapel of Henry VII at Westminster Cathedral (16th century). The rooms inside were organized by themes. These were placed along a circuit that provided the visitor with a series of vignettes illustrating the links between Walpole's ancestors and English history.

The whole is an assembly of unruly, unscaled Gothic quotations, even including bits and pieces from actual ruins. The building is full of sham construction, including papier mâché and stamped wallpaper imitating stucco. The long building campaign and the many designers resulted in this medieval hodgepodge. The building is laid out completely asymmetrically. In the gradual extension, the merits of an irregularly designed building were exploited. The asymmetry began with the projecting round tower in the west. In this, it was an example of the new freedom from ancient rules, which was so influential on contemporary garden design. The first addition to the existing symmetrical building continued its level roofline with crenellations. Chimneys are clustered together, and windows use the pointed arch.

### FONTHILL ABBEY, WYATT, WILSHIRE (1796-1807)

This building was commissioned by William Beckford, an author. It was originally conceived as a piece of scenery. Wyatt believed that Gothic should have a sudden, overwhelming emotional effect, and tried to accomplish this by unimpeded vistas. The appeal of the building is primarily to the imagination. This then developed into long halls (120 feet in height) extending on four sides of a central 276 feet high tower. Fonthill Abbey was intended to be a ruin. Wyatt was asked to design a ruined convent, of which only the chapel parlor, the dormitory, and part of the cloister had survived. This was deemed too small, and a great wing with octagonal tower were added. In 1807, Beckford made this building his residence and the eventual building was constructed.

The plan is too symmetrical to be Gothic. In some details and in the construction, the building was not soundly Gothic. Construction proceeded speedily and was therefore not of the best quality. The tower foundations were faulty and in 1825, the tower collapsed. The building then was left to decay.

The building is Gothic both inside and outside. Wyatt, the designer, was a trained architect with complete knowledge of the stylistic and structural features of Gothic architecture. Wyatt was essentially a Romantic, but he also designed Neoclassical buildings. He worked on many restorations of Gothic cathedrals. As many restorations he supervised fell to pieces, he acquired the reputation of "Destroyer of the Gothic." The sculptural quality of an original Gothic exterior is accurately captured in the wall buttresses. Vaults inside were of wood of plaster. Here, the lightness and variety of Strawberry Hill are changed into horror and mystery.

# INTERNATIONAL STYLE

Influence form the usual arts was also notable in the architecture of the 1920s. The technique of using abstract pictorial and sculptural devices to form new architectural forms was noticeable. There is a general concept that to be a creative architect one needs to be partly a visual artist; without this capacity, one would merely be a builder or worker. At the beginning of the International Style, this relationship was particularly explosive because of the previous development in the visual arts. Since abstract art was no longer "useful" (= representing something), its forms were seen as significant. This concept of "significant form" was applied to architecture, partly resulting in the rejection of Rationalist or Vitruvian definitions of architecture. A different reading of "significant" may be to understand it as open, namely open to the viewer's interpretation in the sense that the creator did not impose a particular reading on his forms. Buildings in themselves rarely have a representational function. Due to the influence from the visual arts, architecture was no longer ornamented structure, but structure conceived aesthetically like sculpture.

In view of this relationship, there are a few aspects of abstract art which seem important. These include the view of art as a form of research. Art also became self-referential, or an end in itself. Concepts of modernity and avant-garde were associated with it. Other ideas were that of surprise and purity. On a detailed level, it was mostly Cubism and Expressionism, which had any direct influence on architecture.

# PIET MONDRIAN (1872-1944)

# BASIC PHILOSOPHY

"Always further." His design theory – his striving for a suprapersonal culture – was influenced by the precision and division of labor brought by technology and especially the resulting significance of abstraction. Architecture and music, for example, are created through abstract thinking and designed in abstract languages. Consequently, Mondrian believed that abstract life was characteristic of his age. He rejected the phenomenal forms of nature, which constituted the decisive step toward abstraction. He expressed – at least in his paintings – an aversion to the sensuous attraction of the world. He wanted to demonstrate in a geometrical manner the ethics of the new age. For him, art was above nature. The artist rises above reality toward reason. Art had to reveal the universal so that it could be plastically contemplated.

Mondrian attempted to depict universal harmony, the laws that govern the universe. Since this is only partially visible in nature, he distills them in their purity through his intuition. From the expression of things, he wanted to go to the expression of relation.

After his training, he began by painting landscapes. He joined the Theosophical Society in 1909. This society promoted neoplatonic and pantheistic ideas. In 1910, he joined the Modern Art Circle, which was conceived as an avant-garde association. In fall 1911, he saw Cubist paintings for the first time. This changed his life and work.

His paintings became frameworks of pictorial signs, or a notation of a formula. He adhered to a strict universalism: reduce all diversity to a small number of signs. The depicted object does not play a big role in the painting. Instead, he created an independent world on the canvas, the central point of which is its composition. The painting is independent of perception and the temperament of the artist. Form was stripped from the object.

He joined the De Stijl group from 1917 to 1925, at which time he felt that Doesburg had moved away from this group's founding principles. Characteristics of this work were its foundation on total abstraction and the confinement on the elements of painting: straight line, right angle, three primary colors, and three primary non-colors.

Starting point of these mature works was the principle that absolute harmony can only be constructed by abstract means that were objective and generally valid, not derived from a fortuitous existing object. Work proceeded along a continuation of a constant refinement. Ultimately, Mondrian found a language to represent the grandeur of nature in painting, namely one of simplifying color and form.

### The Red Tree (1908)

There is a simplified color range and a trend to nonnaturalistic colors. The painting rejects tonalism. Formally, the tree is flattened out into the picture surface. The linear structure of the brush strokes enforces this flat impression. The colors indicate protruding (red) and receding (blue), yet the entire painting symbolizes calm equilibrium.

### The Grey Tree (1912)

Color has been reduced, and form and rhythm dominate. The aim in this painting seemed to be to bring the three-dimensional form of the bare tree onto the flat surface of the picture, transforming a real object into the rhythmic structure of a sign on a surface. The lines no longer have a "thing" value.

### Flowering Apple Tree (1912)

Here, the descriptive function of the pictorial language has been discarded. The painting has become a pure sign. Painterly technique has been reduced dramatically.

### Composition (1916)

A new synthesis is produced between the rhythmic pattern of lines, and refined color.

COMPOSITION WITH RED, BLUE, AND YELLOW (1930)

Here, Mondrian had reached his mature level of purity and sobriety.

# VILLA SAVOYE, LE CORBUSIER, POISSY (1929-31)
# PURISM

Such thoughts about abstraction are also at the root of Le Corbusier's characteristic designs of the 1920s. Part of Corbusier's formation happened through his encounter with Ozenfant after his move to Paris. For the duration of World War I, Corbusier mostly painted. Together, the two developed purism, a style favoring mathematical order and precision. In 1918, they published *Après le Cubisme*, in which they proceeded to revise cubism by liberating it from decorative excesses. They saw cubism as too ornamental and not really adding new dimensions to perception. In their opinion, one should not dismember objects to rearrange them on a flat surface. Instead, the artist should respect the plastic continuum of three-dimensional objects. Paintings must stimulate the intellect. Objects represented should be "objects types," because they really express the virtues of the new industrial world. Purism's general outlook was based on reason and idealism. Corbusier's interest in machines and their beauty developed.

In his paintings, sculptural effects were created through sharp shadows. Objects were incorporated to the overall composition through a "marriage of contours" and a limited choice of colors.

### VERS UNE ARCHITECTURE (1923)

These influences were then combined in his mature International Style work. In addition, he required forms with a universal character similar to the eternal impressions he had received from traditional architecture. Consequently, pure, precise, geometrical forms were seen as appropriate for the Machine Age. This theory is expressed in "Towards an Architecture," a collection of pieces published in *Esprit Nouveau* between 1920 and 1921. Corbusier's main point is that the true architecture of the age is created by engineers. Architecture is defined as the "masterly, correct, and magnificent play of volumes brought together in light." Egyptian, Greek, and Roman architecture were then seen in terms of the same geometric figures. Corbusier also introduced his theory of regulating lines, meant to ensure proportion and order in the architectural composition. The book succinctly equated machine forms and those of Classical architecture. Platonic geometry was also seen inherent in mechanical design.

Le Corbusier extolled the mechanical perfection of industrial machinery as the supreme expression of the beauty of form, if form is determined as absolute response to function. In a similar manner as industrial design, he attempted to define the purpose of the modern house and then simply designed a shape or container for these functions.

Villa Savoye is the most "pure" of his 1920s houses. It was to be a weekend retreat. There are powerful references to Classicism through its similarity to Palladio's Villa Rotonda: the main floor is raised to piano nobile level, all four façades are identical, and the geometry of plan, form, and structure are similar.

### FIVE POINTS OF A NEW ARCHITECTURE (1927)

These were based on a structural argument. The pilotis were the essential part. They raised the building, reserving the ground for vegetation and moving objects. The roof garden serves moral and physical regeneration through hygiene and exposure to sun. Pilotis structurally allowed the free plan and free façade, allowing interior and façade layouts according to function and necessity. Corbusier's favorite façade elements were the windows in bands, because they admitted most light.

The Villa Savoye is a perfect illustration of his five points: (1)The building is raised on pilotis, (2) uses the free plan,(3) free façade, (4) windows in horizontal bands, and (5) a roof garden. The structural system goes back to the Domino system. There, Corbusier had produced a way of building – a bone structure – which is completely independent of the functional demands of the house plan. Thus, he recognized the natural connection between skeleton construction and open space. The design combined structural rigor and spatial freedom. The above five points list basically the advantages of this structural system. The roof garden returns the ground lost under the building, the free plan allows for an efficient use of space, continuous windows make spaces open and create contact with nature outside, and the free façade transforms the massive wall into a screen, which can be opened or closed at will.

The ground floor level houses maid's and chauffeur's spaces, a dogleg stair for the servants, a ramp for visitors, and a three-car garage. The vertical circulation features assume sculptural significance. The curvature of the exterior is determined by the curving radius of an automobile.

The main floor houses living room, dining room, and bedrooms, as well as the kitchen, and has also an open area. On top is another balcony/solarium, partly enclosed by curving walls. The ramp connecting all floor levels thus introduced vertical extension of the open space.

The interior arrangement is free, but is contained within an almost perfect square. Corbusier thus satisfied two intentions, the desire for spatial freedom and for elementary form. This building is not a radical new invention, but rather the perfection of earlier attempts. The ramp, serving as the spine of the house, is in fact an architectural promenade: the higher one gets, the more open the space becomes. Circulation within the house is dramatized by way of stairs and ramps that are treated as independent sculptural objects. The language of this building derived from modern structural technique, and its imagery referred to modern engineering. Details come from ship design, and the smooth surfaces indicate machine surfaces. It attempted to idealize a modern way of life, positing a Utopian social order. It was also a quest for the roots of architecture. The distinction between outside and inside was made minimal, thus creating partly an ambiguous design. Nevertheless, this distinction could be there to allow the discovery beneath the logic of everyday life of the alogic of dreams.

# TRANSPARENCY IN MODERN ARCHITECTURE

Exists as material transparency (in glass, e.g.) or organizational/compositional. This concept was discovered in cubism. Already in Cezanne, one notices a non-traditional perspective, characterized by the suppression of pictorial depth. The represented objects are fragmented, and the painting surface is divided into a grid system, in which horizontal and vertical lines point to the depiction of frontal parts, diagonal ones to a spatial receding.

At first sight, transparency in architecture seems to be relegated to the material kind. Glass walls allow the simultaneous viewing of different layers.

Phenomenal transparency can be found in Le Corbusier's Villa Stein. In its garden facade, a number of different layers is alluded to and clearly visible. The recessed ground floor plane is repeated on the roof in the slightly set back side walls. In the side facades, this recessed plane is made visible through the doors that end the rows of windows. These features allude to the existence of a spatial slice behind the facade, again bounded behind by an interior wall. A third layer is articulated by the back wall of the terrace and the roof structures. The stair balustrade introduces another parallel level, as does the balcony of the second floor. This "layering" can be found in sections and floor plans as well. Reality and allusion play a dialectical relationship.

FIGURE 24–1. Blenheim Palace Gardens, showing entry bridge and artificial lake.

FIGURE 24–2. Villa Savoye, Poissy, exterior.

# Chapter 25

# Architecture and Industry

The architectural situation in the 19th century is characterized by the creation of numerous new building tasks – especially those that involve large, open interior spaces – and the arbitrary use of architectural forms borrowed from the styles of the past. Industrialization and economic growth brought building tasks which provided the greatest use for the greatest number, the greatest public service to the community. Industrialists and governmental bodies became the new patrons of architecture. The environment during the 19th century could be characterized as consisting of the factory, the railroad, and the slum. Open space became the main spatial conception of the 19th century. This space expressed a new ideal of human freedom. The slogan "liberté, égalité, fraternité" defines this new ideal. The main purpose of eclecticism was to draw analogies between the new building types and similar ancient examples. The emphasis was now on revivalism, that is,, on archaeological accuracy. In addition, new building materials were introduced by industry. In general, church and palace lost their importance as leading tasks and were replaced by monument, museum, dwelling, theater, exhibition hall, factory, and office building. After the middle of the 19th century, the large hall, the office building, and the dwelling became the leading tasks.

The main problem posed by this union was that industry was pragmatic and modern, whereas architecture found itself rather in a conventional frame of mind, one that was oriented toward the past. The industrial revolution brought changes in society, whereas architecture continued to fashion Neoclassicism. Architecture can be criticized for not reacting fast enough to these changes. Part of this situation lies in the nature of Neoclassicism: its rules were based on Antiquity and were given similar value as nature, namely universal and eternal. Industry also brings a separation of those in charge of building into architects and engineers. A separation of theory from practice occurs through the publication of textbooks containing the new laws, rules, and principles. Given these circumstances, 19th-century architecture is mostly the effort to devise a style adequate to the Industrial Revolution. The impact of industry on architecture is notable in a separation of this discipline into construction and design. The detailed changes are seen in technology, where new materials are introduced. New insights into geometry led to better drawings and calculations. The influence of new scientific methodology came out in the more accurate calculation of elastic tension forces, and the institution of a unified system of measurement.

## SEVERN BRIDGE, COALBROOKDALE, T. PRITCHARD & A. DARBY III (1777-79)

The immediate change in architecture is found in the improvement in bridge design at the beginning of the 19th century. The new scientific insights allow a greater exploitation of the materials and favor the use of new ones. First, the structural change is one from trabeation to space frame. In masonry bridges, the volumes become smaller due to better calculations and to improvements in descriptive geometry. Iron is first used as reinforcements in traditional masonry constructions.

The new cyclical view of history lifted the air of a Golden Age from Antiquity; now it was simply a historical period like any other, without particular normative value. The previous conception of Classical forms as congruent with rational structure was dissolved through more detailed analysis, and the principle that exterior forms should reflect straightforward what they conceal. In view of this situation, the only arguments in favor of Classical forms were the preservation of traditional ideals of beauty, the educational importance of these forms, and the preservation of established taste and fashion.

Bridge construction was almost predisposed for industry, as there are iron ore, coal, and a water transportation system readily available. This bridge replaced existing passenger ferry service, and facilitated traffic for a major local economic thoroughfare. Iron was used because the arch had to be tall enough to let high-masted barges pass underneath. In addition, it solved the abutment problem created by unstable banks and could withstand periodic flooding.

The bridge spans 100 feet. It is assembled of two halves of an arch cast in a workshop before assembly on the site. Construction took three months. The arch is a perfect half circle. The design synthesizes successfully existing forms and techniques, including the masonry arch and dovetail joints to connect secondary iron members.

Later on, this type of construction is made less heavy by actually forming the individual parts in the shape of hollow cages.

# ROYAL PAVILION, BRIGHTON, J. NASH (1811-23)

This building had been a farmhouse, which was transformed into a Palladian villa in the late 18th century, with two lateral wings flanking a domed rotunda. Nash added domes, extended the wings, and transformed the interior. The end wings are covered just with the tips of onion domes. His roof outline is made of domes and minarets. The exterior derives from Indian architecture. It is mostly of brick with a stucco cover. The buildings are surrounded by verandas with webbed spandrels. It is mostly of brick with a stucco cover. The desired effect is that of a luxurious tent.

As the inside is decorated in chinoiserie, a stylistic conflict results. Inside, cast iron was used in the structural skeleton. The ceiling in the kitchen is supported by iron columns in the form of palm trees. The principal staircase has bamboo moldings. There are two state rooms in the wings. The banqueting room has a gasolier hanging from the claws of a silver dragon. The music room in the other wing has undulating serpents swirling around in a landscape.

The same material was used increasingly in railings, grilles, and ornaments.

# BRIDGE, MENAI STRAITS, TELFORD (1818-26)

The subsequent development in bridge design was the suspension bridge. These allow greater spans and elasticity to cope with the forces. This one is 100 ft tall and has a 580 ft span between the two towers. 16 chains that were anchored in tunnels dug into the rock on either shore were used. Rods hang from these chains and hold up iron bars which support the wooden plank road. Arches and piers were constructed of limestone masonry.

# BROOKLYN BRIDGE, JOHN & WASHINGTON ROEBLING, NEW YORK (1867-83)

The Brooklyn Bridge was the culmination of the 19th-century development in the construction of suspension bridges. Here, wire cables replaced the earlier chain links. This resulted in a further lengthening of the bridgeable span. The first wire cable suspension bridges were constructed in the 1840s. One of the pioneers of this type of bridge construction in the U.S. was John Roebling (1806-69). Born in Germany, he was a graduate of the Berlin Polytechnic School and came to the U.S. in 1831.

His design for Brooklyn Bridge is a mixture of functional solutions and traditional, aesthetic features. The roadbed arcs gracefully over the East River while the spidery web of the suspension cables is draped from the tall towers. These take up architectural details from the Gothic style in their openings in the form of lancet windows. In addition, the capital-like tops imitate the cavetto moldings of Egyptian pylons. The reference to Ancient Roman triumphal arches is clear. All these features give the bridge a romantic silhouette. The piers are articulated horizontally through a narrowing of their circumference.

This bridge has become one of the icons for New York.

# CRYSTAL PALACE, PAXTON, LONDON (1850-51)

Industry also brought new building tasks. One of these was a large hall that could be used for industrial exhibitions. The first such building was erected for the 1851 World Exhibition in London by Joseph Paxton. With this building, especially its miraculous performance, industry actually saved its own show. These utilitarian structures of iron and glass reinterpreted the Baroque concept of an open and dynamic space. The Crystal Palace begins the age of large metal and glass exhibition halls. Its colossal size blurred the division between inside and outside; having sparrows and elm trees inside, one did not know whether one was outside or inside.

The Building Committee of the Royal Exhibition Commission produced its own design for the exhibition building in June 1850. It was intended for brick construction and a sheet iron dome. It would have required extensive foundations, been very dark inside, too expensive for a temporary structure, and probably impossible to construct in time.

Hence, traditional building methods were not capable of handling this building. Paxton approached the task by considering it a specific solution to a particular problem. He was a horticulturist and builder of greenhouses. He had already used a metal frame with glass infill in the great conservatory at Chatsworth (1837-40), which measured 277 ft. × 123 ft. × 67 ft high. In 1849, he followed this with his lily house. Though smaller, it had an ingenious roof design. Panes of glass were set at an angle to create a pitch, resulting in ridges and furrows outside. This roof was supported by wooden ribs on iron columns. The curved ribs also contained the gutters.

This is exactly what he proposed in June 1850 for the exhibition, namely a large greenhouse. To alter the reluctant Building Committee's mind, he leaked his design to the press, with a list of its advantages over the Committee's project. This resulted in overwhelming public support. On 15 July 1850, the Royal Commission rejected the Committee's design in favor of Paxton's.

The Crystal Palace was to be built with a ridge-and-furrow glass roof. The maximum size of glass sheet available – at that time 49″ × 30″—determined the base measurement. Two such plates, set at a pitch that prevented condensation from dripping, bridged an 8 ft. gap, which became the module. This was translated into a 24 ft. structural grid. The building was thus designed from the roof down. Fox & Henderson, the iron manufacturers chosen to fabricate the parts, offered to construct it at half price if they were allowed to keep the parts after the dismantling of the building. It was to be constructed of standardized iron posts and beams and glass panes. All parts were made with coordinated dimensions. The building was erected in nine months, three of which were spent prefabricating the parts.

After design changes, such as the vaulted transept to preserve an existing tree, construction began on July 30. The first column was raised on Sept. 26; the structure was complete in January. In November, the building was christened Crystal Palace by a journalist.

A cloth awning was stretched over the roof to protect the interior from too much sun. On warm days, the cloth was moistened to provide additional cooling.

The interior was decorated by Owen Jones. He used color to give body and depth to the framework. Inside, the iron skeleton was painted blue. This reduced the contrast and blended the frame with the sky, in a manner transforming materiality into atmosphere. The underside of the girders was painted red, and yellow was used for columns and some details.

The building basically consisted of a recurrent iron skeleton of extreme lightness and delicacy. An arched transept was introduced to preserve a tree.

Its real significance lies in its construction methodology. Ruskin was against the building because it did not reflect handwork and did not have mass. Function and form are independent from one another in this building. Architectural considerations did not depend on utilitarian requirements. This independence results in indifference where space has one logic and events another. The neutral shed of this building could accommodate anything from elephants draped in rare colonial silks to international boxing matches.

# MEUNIER CHOCOLATE FACTORY, SAULNIER, NOISIEL-SUR-MARNE (1869-72)

This building, an addition to an existing factory, had to be stretched over a river so that three turbines could be moved by the water flow. Saulnier chose to use an iron frame to support the building. The building is three stories high. Each floor is divided into three naves. The exterior walls consist of an iron frame with brick infill. The frame consists of vertical posts, horizontal beams, and diagonal braces. The brick walls were completely planar. To express that they are infill, Saulnier did not use the different colors to paint the semblance of a traditional articulation on his façades, but used a carpet motive that enhances the diagonal lines of the structure. The diagonal bracing, although of iron, imitates earlier wood construction.

# EIFFEL TOWER, GUSTAVE EIFFEL, PARIS (1887-89)

This tower was erected as the gateway to the 1889 International Exhibition, which also commemorated the 100th anniversary of the storming of the Bastille. Eiffel's design won a competition that had attracted 100 entries. It was the culmination of his previous work in arch railroad bridges, which were characterized by large spans supported by light, graceful pylons. This structure is a work of engineering, but has captured human imagination. It has become an integral part of Paris, like a phenomenon of nature. The tower is a universal symbol for Paris and belongs to the universal language of travel. Apart from this meaning it is an inexhaustive cypher, symbol of modernity, communication, science, the 19th century, rocket, stem, derrick, phallus, lightning rod, and insect. It expresses that line whose mythic function is to join earth and heaven. It is an object that becomes a lookout when visited. From Paris we look at it, and from it we look at Paris. The tower is a complete object that achieves the circulation between seeing and being seen. It is an open signifier into which constantly new meanings are filled. To accomplish this, the tower must escape reason. It is uselessness, as any conceivable uses are overwhelmed by its mythic power. It is both expression of the utopia (of height) and an instrument of a convenience. Like the Tower of Babel, it has shed its usefulness and risen from the great ascensional dream, making it live in men's imagination.

The tower provides an adventure of sight and of intelligence. Climbing it is ascending to a view. Like a belvedere in a garden, the tower makes the city into a kind of nature. The city joins with the great sublime themes of nature: ocean, storm, mountains, snow, rivers. The bird's-eye view from the tower gives us the world to read, not just to perceive. We are able to transcend sensation toward seeing things in their structure. To understand the city from this vantage point, we must decipher it by separating and grouping known points, identifying landmarks. Memory, knowledge, and perception interact with each other to form a simulacrum of Paris. Viewing this panorama gives us both the euphoric vision of the entire view, as well as the intellectual work of recognizing it. We also begin to imagine the history of Paris, as duration becomes panoramic. Landmarks become both points of history and space. We can also survey the functional zones of Paris.

As a public monument, the Eiffel Tower does not have a traditional inside. Instead, the tower gives the visitor the consumption of technological performances, making him a hobby engineer. The bases, their connection to the pylons, the elevators, the small parts of the tower frame serve to demystify the appearance of the tower from afar. The tower also constitutes a little world. All kinds of commercial establishments help increase the level of familiarity in using this strange object. In this respect, the tower provides the essential function of all human sites: one can feel oneself cut off from the world and still be the owner of a world.

FIGURE 25–1. Bridge over the River Severn, Coalbrookdale.

FIGURE 25–2. Brooklyn Bridge, New York.

FIGURE 25–3. Eiffel Tower, Paris.

# Chapter 26

# Architecture and Revolution

The interdependence between environment and social behavior became important for architecture in the Enlightenment. This premise suggests that, since man draws his knowledge from sensations and experiences, an environment can be designed that perfects him. This idea was partly behind the projects of the Revolutionary Classicists. These architects intended to shape the proper milieu for social happiness. Their projects were part of the reform of the physical, as well as, social environment. In Ledoux' case, the projects were also intended to communicate social place through architectural form.

For this formulation of a social architecture, freemasonry was influential. The form of their meeting places, their lodges, was important to them and to future architectural development. In the beginning stages, during the mid-century, lodges were not architecturally determined, but composed by their members and items of ritualistic equipment. Spatially, lodges were arranged along the "route of initiation," consisting of a waiting area, a purification area, and the initiation area which also served as meeting place. Added to this was a recreation area for the communal dinners and festivities.

While architecturally not distinguished, the lodges were important as concretions of ritual in space. In the later stages of the 18ᵗʰ century, initiations were more closely modeled on Ancient rituals, among them the Eleusinian mysteries and the journey of Sethos into the underworld. This led to the belief that the Egyptian ruins were prototypes of initiatory architecture. Egyptian temples were seen as consisting of a series of doors and vestibules, arranged along a route leading to the sanctuary. A second form of initiatory architecture was perceived in the landscapes laid out along the English Garden type. The next step in this development was the construction of initiation lodges in these gardens. (Examples include parts of the Desert de Retz and projects by Ledoux). Freemasonry evolved from the medieval guilds of stonemasons. After the decline of cathedral building, lay members were accepted. During the 17ᵗʰ and 18ᵗʰ centuries, rites of ancient religions were adopted by the Freemasons.

After 1763, some changes can be noticed in French architecture. These relate to the massing and the treatment of wall surfaces, and to planning (from enfilades to interlocking arrangements). Similarly, projects became large in scale, and delighted in formal geometry. There was indeed a visionary splendor in late 18th-century France. Toward the end of the 18th century, some French architects translated the aim for pure, elementary architecture into buildings of pure forms expressing function. They proposed boldly scaled and austere buildings whose forms evoked a sense of function. This architecture was intended to communicate its purpose directly to the viewer, to be "architecture parlante," or speaking architecture. During the 18ᵗʰ century, there was, thus, a change from a stylistic movement characterized as an art of virtuoso technique (Rococo) to one of social comment. This development of expression culminated in the architecture parlante. Architects did not only rely on the study and theories of Ancient architecture, but also on the study of nature.

## ETIENNE-LOUIS BOULLÉE (1728-99)

He began as a "conventional" architect. From early on, he worked as a teacher. After 1782, however, he resigned from all official posts and commissions, and devoted himself to fantasy projects. These later ensured his continued fame.

At first, they look simply like stylistic exercises, although on a monumental scale. Initial projects of the early 1780s were presented as reworkings for existing projects, for example, Soufflot's Ste-Geneviève (Panthéon). They are generally beyond the means of 18th-century technology. Partly, this reduced architecture to pictorial representation.

In Boullée's projects, a direct relationship between forms and the sensations they evoked was intended. Thus, a fortress should not just excel in fortification technology, but also terrorize through its form. Partly, the intention was to create architectural character. His projects are guided by a desire for order and regularity. His ideal figure was the sphere, not only for its regularity, but also for its capacity to assume a variety of reactions to light.

Boullée's theory shows the impact of his interests into the sublime. He wanted to formulate a theory of architecture as art, not as science. This was defined as the art to create effects through the distribution of the masses. Thus, by working like an image, architecture is connected to the other arts. Architects compose with light and shadow, which bring out the volumes of their buildings.

# NEWTON CENOTAPH (1783)

Here, Boullée's passion for the sphere is combined with the new cosmology. The whole consists of a hollow sphere resting on a terraced and landscaped cylindrical base. The vault of the interior was pierced by openings arranged to create an illusion of the star-filled sky.

# CLAUDE-NICOLAS LEDOUX (1736-1806)

Ledoux began his career in 1762 with traditional hôtels. His era is that between Baroque and "autonomous" architecture. Certain features of his designs still point to the old taste: the use of Classical details and the plans. However, in the lack of unity in his designs, the "new" autonomy can be detected.

Ledoux' designs are part of the frenzy for the extraordinary during the second half of the 18th century. The intention was to create an effect mostly through megalomaniac size. Buildings should also speak of their function. A prison should terrify, a church elevate. Pure geometrical forms were meant to express the purity of the new societal formation.

### Salt Works, Arc-et-Senans (1775-79)

This is the beginning of his mature work. In 1771, Ledoux was appointed General Inspector of the Salines of Franche-Compte. This appointment was pushed by Madame Dubarry, who was a favorite of Louis XV and had employed Ledoux for her own houses. This appointment brought him the commission for the salt works.

This project is based on heavy, simplified masses and unadorned wall surfaces. The buildings were arranged to enclose an oval. This layout indicates cosmic implications (path of the sun) and is related to the plans of ideal cities from earlier periods, as well as to the Vitruvian theater. The individual buildings are united in a heterogeneous, inorganic assembly, indicating an harmonic whole put together from autonomous parts. Moreover, this expressed the new form of monarchy, that is, not absolute but formed of various independent forces. Thus, it mirrored the new ruling class, the bourgeoisie. The individual buildings are no longer connected to one another, but isolated. The system of arrangement is the pavilion system. The architecture is Classical, but a new spirit is here hidden behind traditional garb. The choice of a Classical vocabulary was probably a concession to the ruling taste.

The program was dictated. The entire complex had to include boiling houses, drying halls, water containers, warehouses, apartments for employees and laborers, canals, sleuce gates, and other hydraulic facilities.

At the center was the director's house. This building was square and symmetrical and inserted between the two buildings for salt extraction. In addition, it housed the communal chapel and a corridor connecting the two salt-extracting buildings. The entrance lobby and the staircase were used as the chapel on Sundays. The sloping rooflines complete to a pyramid when continued up and down, making the building also refer to the shape of a truncated pyramid.

All houses were formed of stark geometrical shapes, and had overscaled details. All consist of a massive central part to which were attached two flanking wings. The central part is the production space; the wings house apartments and storage space.

The entrance building looks like all others toward the courtyard. One of its wings houses the guardroom, the other, the prison. Outside, the columnar porch makes this into a monument to industry. The grotto behind turns this entrance into an expression of harmony between human beings and nature.

The only ornaments were openings from which protrude carvings of a thick fluid, the representation of the brine. The roofs have mansard windows. Thus, Ledoux tried to use archetypal characters to give meaning to new building tasks.

Ledoux' architecture derives from a unity of beauty resulting from the relationship between mass and ornament, and the uninterrupted line.

## IDEAL CITY OF CHAUX (1790)

The salt factory was later developed into an ideal industrial city named Chaux. This transformation was influenced by his theoretical treatise and begun probably in 1790. Ledoux now put his talents as an architect in the service of the new post-revolutionary state. This city thus also became a city of liberty. It organized all instruments needed for the formation of a new social order.

The salt works, as built at Art-et-Senans, but doubled, were in the center, framed by the residential apartments for the workers, with individual gardens. Beyond this zone were to be communal facilities, markets, and agricultural land. The buildings were arranged to enclose an oval. This layout indicates cosmic implications (path of the sun) and is related to the plans of ideal cities from earlier periods. While the overall layout of the city is formal (hinting at an authoritarian regime), it does reflect the new sensitivity to nature that arose in the Age of Reason, through the protection of open space around it. However, the city was meant as a traffic junction. East-west and north-south axes intersect in the center. Nature is in this way subordinated.

It is interesting to note, however, that houses for the workers are given equal treatment as public monuments and buildings. The various buildings form an array of the issues dear to the society that would arise from the revolution. The various institutions are all given architectural form. Public buildings were given a character, which was furthering decent behavior.

The entire plan is no longer derived purely from esthetic considerations. Instead, Ledoux incorporated the needs of the new post-revolutionary society, which was still building its infrastructure. Architecture became a public right. Nevertheless, considering that many theorists in the past saw the city as a male body, Chaux can be looked at in this perspective as well. Because Ledoux disrupts the dominant center in his city with satellite developments, it could then be interpreted as a body without head. Thus, the city represents a hybrid between (pre-Revolutionary) monarchical centralization and (post-Revolutionary) democratic dispersion.

## OIKÉMA

Among the structures is this phallus-plan "Temple Dedicated to Love," intended as a theater where male youths could abandon themselves to the pleasures of all kinds of sexual practices, so as to be transformed into monogamous adults. Oikéma means originally house, temple, prison, or place of debauchery, but also refers to economy, thus indicating this building as referring to both women as commodity and the house as their prison. As such, the design could be taken as celebrating men, in a reaction to the power of courtesans before the Revolution. In its stead, the revolution elevated virility, clearly expressed in Ledoux's plan, which becomes therefore a symbol of liberty. In addition, the building documents the revolution's preoccupation with the polarities of vice and virtue. Due to the difference between the plan and the exterior shape, the Oikéma represents a veiled phallus, so as to increase the potential of its content. This project was published in 1804.

## BARRIÈRES, PARIS (1785-89)

Ledoux had in the meantime become architect of the tax authority. This brought the commission for the customhouses. These come out of his work at the saline of Arc-et-Senans. Ledoux changed the scale and measures of traditional forms, and assembled these simplified geometric forms in bold, complex arrangements. Ornament is applied only sparingly, and exhibits a new relation to surface or mass.

These buildings go beyond their immediate purpose. Ledoux planned this ring of customs houses for the city of Paris to help shed the village character of this city. The style is severe, and the individual buildings are monumental, colossal.

At the beginning of the French Revolution, Ledoux was fired due to his association with the hated tax system. In 1793, he was jailed for a term that lasted until January 1795. During these months in jail, he conceived his theoretical treatise. Already in 1782, he had intended to publish his work. Now, this enterprise changed to a work of theory. The main intention was to demonstrate what Ledoux's practice could teach future architecture, its roles and tasks. The first volume of this work was published in 1804. It contained the theoretical part and prints of works, mostly of the salt works at Arc-et-Senans, the Theater at Besançon, and the city of Chaux. The book was titled *Architecture, Considered in its Relationship to Art, Customs and Legislation*. It helped support belief in Ledoux as an untimely, that is, progressive architect who was only stopped by his more powerful clients to complete his new "social" architecture. His prison experience had taught him the new power of the people.

Characteristic achievements of Ledoux' architecture were a reorganization of the building volume, and a clear-cut system of arranging large building complexes. The individual parts become independent. They thus express democracy or a community of independent beings. Buildings are completely undecorated, in reaction to the Baroque practice of imitating organic aspects in stone. The individual forms are derived from elementary geometry, and forms are treated as autonomous. Even plans become autonomous. In his theory, Ledoux synthesized the realities of his day into something new. In his opinion, the creation of space was to be the cause of all scientific disciplines, and especially of the people.

# MODERNISM

Ledoux' architecture shows striking similarities to Modern architecture. The question arises whether this is a pure coincidence or whether the two have more in common. The principle of autonomy was widely used at the beginning of the 19th century, but then became increasingly weaker until it was reestablished in the early 20th century. Durand's system was definitely inspired by Ledoux. Durand attacks tradition, mocks the orders, and replaces these with functionalist ideas related to utility and structure. Hence the importance in which the plan is held. Plans should derive from rectangular systems of coordinates, resulting in elementary schemes. The two basic plans are the pavilion system and the assembly of blocks. The latter is rather important for Modern architecture.

Throughout the Neoclassical development of the 19th century, the autonomy of individual parts and the block assembly of buildings can be detected. Ledoux' principles then were used again, beginning with Berlage in Holland and Loos in Austria. From there, it continued above all into the work of Le Corbusier.

## ADOLF LOOS (1870-1933)

He was against the Vienna Secession. His design theory emphasized propriety over originality. His appeal was to reason. He did not consider the Modernist beginnings of the Vienna Secession enough and aimed to continue these toward an extreme geometric purism. His move was toward rectilinear and volumetric simplification. He clearly saw the willful, personal, and decorative excesses of Art Nouveau and did not feel that it would ever achieve a lasting existence. His vision was also partly influenced by the simplicity and practicality of everyday objects, which he praised in many of his writings.

He demonstrated a dialectical way of design, advocating in some respects adherence to architectural traditions, in others a complete acceptance of the conditions of modern life.

## "ORNAMENT AND CRIME" (1908)

Loos proposed to completely eliminate ornament. In this essay, ornament is associated with graffiti and tattoos, that is, as infantile, primitive, erotic, or criminal. Loos associated the evolution of culture with the elimination of ornament.

## STEINER HOUSE, VIENNA (1910)

The geometrical articulation is quite bold and the massing assertive and compact. The architectural effect relied on the adroit placement of plate-glass windows into stripped and undecorated surfaces. Every non-structural element is eliminated. In fact, the plaster walls of this house leave no room for representation and resemblance, making them nothing more than cladding. The window arrangement appears functionalist. In the corner view, the window patterns form a whole, as they are interconnected through a collage method in a form of interweaving. The round roof over the entrance reminds one of a railroad coach.

Here, Loos reinterpreted the typological tradition of the dwelling, but also remained within the tactile and esthetic aspects of the traditional dwelling interior. According to Loos, a "building should be dumb on the outside and reveal its wealth only on the inside." While the interior is dressed to the practical and psychological needs of domesticity, the exterior simply affirms the solidity of the building. Loos proposed that even in the age of industry, architecture needed to express labor, not just capitalist use value, as the Werkbund had demanded. Industrial rationalization did bring the rejection of ornamentation from architecture. It also brought a division into the design profession. While the architect deals with walls, the cabinetmaker deals with interior furnishings. It is impossible in the modern age to forge a synthesis from these design languages. Loos's exteriors are therefore expressing function, calculation, and use value, while his interiors are determined by lived experience, by memory. This makes the interior more significant than the exterior. His style is therefore characterized by the autonomy, with which each part is treated.

# INTERNATIONAL STYLE

Around 1920, the various pre-WWI strands of modernist intentions tended to converge, and became the International Style. Revivalism clearly was relegated to a secondary position. Most important in this development was the influence of Cubism and abstract art. The obvious paths of impact are from Cubism to Russian geometrical abstract painting to Constructivism, and from Cubism to Purism to Le Corbusier and the De Stijl movement in Holland. Other areas of contact include the purification of expressive means through abstraction, the emphasis on underlying tectonics, the belief in a spiritual meaning, the idea of an avant garde jettisoning the past, and the notion of empathy (= the capability of expression without anecdote). In its heyday, International Style design emphasized simple cubic volumes, stripped planar shapes, open plans, and machine-age details. Typical features of Modern buildings were strip windows, flat roofs, grids of supports, cantilevered horizontal planes, metal railings, and curved partitions. More general aspects include the tendency to use simple rectangular volumes articulated by crisply cut openings, and the emphasis on hovering planes and interpenetrating spaces. An interesting aspect of the International Style is its functionalism. Hardly any one of the famed examples is a straightforward functional solution to the given program. Rather, they use a priori images, resulting in a style of symbolic forms, which referred to the notion of functionality.

# RUSSIAN CONSTRUCTIVISM

In Russia, the new architectural style went together with a new social order. Problems were posed in finding an architectural language appropriate to the new situation. Interestingly, it was the avant-garde that was put in charge of this effort. Artists were committed to working class revolution. They saw the value of art lying in its relationship to the community. Artists must abandon the conventional sense of the work of art and participate in the development of new forms of community. Artists shared in the task of rebuilding the political and social structure.

Modern architecture in Russia was somewhat more pronounced than in the other countries. It occurred immediately following the revolution and was partly meant to express the new social and political order. Thus, social and utopian ideals were more consciously addressed in Constructivist architecture, and the break with history more stated. The economic shortages also required that costly aspects of decoration be abandoned toward practical, efficient buildings.

# SUPREMATISM

In detail, the new language derived from similar attempts in Western Europe. Both abstract art and Futurist attempts were emulated. Suprematism worked with the basic elements of design. It expressed non-objectivity, that is, forms that were removed from natural forms. The supremacy of feeling was seen as the essential thing in art.

Immediately following the revolution and the end of World War I, the arts assumed the duties of propaganda, communication, and education. The resulting emphasis on posters and typography may have led to the simplification of expressive means, and hence to abstraction. Lissitzky's *Beat the Whites with the Red Wedge* [1919] illustrates this phase. There was a period of frenzied visual experimentation, producing a rash of paper projects. All were attempts at finding new forms. An abstract vocabulary was developed, focusing on basic design and the creation of an universal language (Malevich and Lissitzky's Prouns). Proun works combined pictorial art and architecture.

Machine worship was practiced, influenced by Futurism. The machine was the symbol of the new society and the means to realize the new society. An iconography was worked out that blended the floating planes of abstract art with direct quotations from the factory floor and the production line. Constructivism looked for the social value of structures. Art was to come from technology and engineering, and move toward organization and construction. Constructivism replaced the imprecision of freehand drawing with the clarity of diagrams or engineering drawings. Art works were no longer composed, but constructed.

## MONUMENT TO THE 3ʳᴰ INTERNATIONAL, TATLIN (1919-20)

Demonstrates this new direction. Two interlacing spirals of open structural latticework support four geometric bodies – cube, pyramid, cylinder, and sphere – all containing various halls for the congress. They were to turn at different speeds, to emphasize the cosmic importance of the new social and political order. The whole was intended to be 300 meters high and painted red.

The spirals were meant to express a line of liberation. The double spiral may be an interpretation of the (Marxist) dialectical process, between synthesis and antithesis.

# DECONSTRUCTION

Deconstructionist buildings look like blown up versions of Russian Constructivist reliefs, or three-dimensional versions of sketches and paintings. They understand irregular geometry as a structural condition. No longer are pure forms placed in conflict with one another, but conflicts are created within the forms. They are infiltrated with skewed and distorted geometry. These distortions seem to have been generated by organisms within the forms, not by external intervention. It is an architecture of disruption, dislocation, deflection, deviation, and distortion, not one of demolition or dismantling. The traditional solution of stacked, parallel horizontal floors is twisted. The frame is warped, the structure is shaken. These designs stretch the boundaries of architecture by casting doubts on the basics: walls, floors, ceilings, and even gravity. The projects are purposely accidental and are about the erosion of architectural certainty. In this respect, the projects mirror an unruly world in which moral, political, and economic systems interfere with each other.

## HOUSE II (FALK HOUSE), EISENMAN, HARDWICK, VT (1969-71)

Peter Eisenman works within an attitude toward architecture that has been existing for the 500 year-old tradition of Humanism. This defines architecture by function (or program) and form (or type). Humanist architecture constantly vacillates between a concern for internal accommodation and a concern for articulation of ideal themes in form. Eisenman sees architecture as problematic, because it has only a weak sign language. Anything outside the discipline of architecture cannot be expressed, and there is a close connection between signifier and signified. To generate a greater transparency, meaning and carrier of meaning must be separated. The close connection between structure, form, meaning, content, and so on, must be broken to create multiple meanings. This separation can be called displacement, condensation, and shifting. This is necessary, because architecture is no longer capable of representing reality. Information and communication technology have distorted this reality dramatically. The media are determining reality. Consequently, architecture has to rethink its reality to persist in this media-created world. Architecture can no longer continue the traditional concepts of reasonable, comprehensive, and functional solution. A building still must function, but it must no longer look like it does.

Eisenman's interest is to develop multiple autonomous structural and visual systems. The rationality of geometry is turned into the irrationality of highly complicated structures. Formal issues become more important than content. Noteworthy is the avoidance of historicist forms. The paradox of architecture is produced through its difficult task of dislocating that which it locates.

House II carries the syntax of Terragni forward. In two articles on Terragni's work, Eisenman had articulated the difference between Terragni and Modernism, which he saw as a change from semantics (in Corbusier's Domino House) to syntax (in Terragni). While Corbusier symbolizes modernism's intentions with his geometric forms, Terragni assembles these same forms into a syntagmatic assembly.

The Falk house is based on parallel cubical grid systems, which are played off against each other. One was allocated the structural grid, the other the planes. Every part of the form can belong to two different systems. As a result, the house is a complex arrangement of closed and open cubical spaces in a similarly broken (or incomplete) grid of posts and beams. Structure is exaggerated through redundancy, that is, having simultaneously columns and walls. The house is full of empty signs, such as columns that become walls. The building is no longer created by following conventional architectural methods, but by inventing a process – a new set of rules governing the turning, breaking, and intersecting of the various features – that creates the design.

It is an exploration of basic formal syntax and the logical structure of space. Thus, the building expresses a kind of grammatical system, not values related to life and home. Partly, the building is also a polemical statement about architecture. Eisenman believes that the role of art is to dislocate, alienate man from his environment, so that he is forced to really see what this environment is. He tricks the occupants into seeing architecture in a new way by introducing certain unsettling features, such as stairs without railings, and hanging columns.

There is no acknowledgement of any contextual fact in the Falk House, neither of the regional style, a clapboard colonial style, nor of the natural setting, nor of the family. In fact, this building could be laid on its side and it would not look much different. The individual parts of Eisenman's houses can only be completely understood when seen as part of a sequence. Similar to the linear reading of a text, the houses then allow the viewer to reconstruct the individual steps in the composition from beginning to end, and vice versa.

FIGURE 26–1. Salt Works, Arc-et-Senans, showing director's house and production building.

FIGURE 26–2. Salt Works, showing workers housing.

FIGURE 26–3. L'Enfert Toll Gate, Paris

FIGURE 26–4. Vincennes Toll Gate, Paris.

FIGURE 26–5. Steiner House, Vienna, street façade.

# Chapter 27

# 19th-Century Neoclassicism

Immediately after the turn of the 18th century, there existed two modes in French architecture, a Classical movement and the Empire style. The Classical direction came directly out of the 18th century development. Its characteristics were: a preference for simple, geometric forms and smooth, plain surfaces; a devotion to the "functional"; the isolation of buildings; the emphasis on direct structural expression, not on expressive exploitation of exterior surfaces and the impersonality and internationality of expression. Earlier traditions were continued in France; there was no notable desire to overthrow them.

Neo-Classical forms can be associated either with revolutionary aspirations to primitive democratic purity, or to imperial ambitions for unshakeable authority.

## ARC DE TRIOMPHE, J.-F.-T. CHALGRIN, PARIS (1806-1836)

This was a commission meant as a memorial to Napoleon. He commissioned it to celebrate the victory over the Austrians at Austerlitz in 1805. The whole form and articulation promote Imperial Neoclassicism. Contemporary arches in other European countries were based rather on Greek examples, such as the Propylaea. Chalgrin had been associated with the first architect commissioned with this project, J.-A. Raymond. When becoming sole designer, he imposed his own astylar project. The arch is influenced by Roman prototypes, and broke with the traditions of the Louis XIV style, as seen in Blondel's Porte St.-Denis (1680). Chalgrin's design is not as decorative as these earlier arches. The proportions are square..

Construction stopped after Napoleon's defeat at Waterloo in 1815, and resumed only in 1823. The additional attic with shields inscribed with the major battles of the French republic and empire was the work of G.A. Blouet, who was in charge from 1832 to the completion of this structure. Otherwise, the finished structure is faithful to Chalgrin's initial design. In the meantime, the arch had been rededicated a few times.

The sculptural additions were done by F. Rude in 1833-36 (under Louis Philippe). Four high-reliefs depict "The triumph of 1810, Peace, and Resistance," and the main piece, which is titled "La Marseillaise." It consists of colossal figures representing volunteers of 1792. They are shown dressed in Classical armor, and are led by the Roman goddess of war. The design is characterized by Baroque features: the figures are densely packed, the contours jagged and the whole expresses violent movement. The liveliness of the sculpture nevertheless adds Romantic elan to this monument. Above the main reliefs are six bas-reliefs. The frieze in the entablature depicts the departure and return of the Grande Armée. On the vaults are inscribed the names of 660 generals. The arch demonstrates the mixture of visionary Classicist forms and crispness with Romantic imagery.

The gigantic mass of this structure creates a majestic effect. Mass and details show a degree of nobility. The hardness of stone comes out clearly, emphasizing the solidity of the construction. The applied decoration impresses through its beauty. Physical grandeur is among the main causes of value and effect in architecture. This design is appreciated through admiration. A feeling or idea of greatness is the dominant expression intended.

During Haussmann's 19th-century transformation of Paris, eight streets were added around the square, making the arch thus the center of twelve radiating streets.

# LA MADELEINE, A.-P. VIGNON (1807-45)

Vignon (1763-1828) was a pupil of Ledoux. He had to place his church on the existing foundations of Contant d'Ivry's earlier project. While begun as a church in 1763, in 1806 Napoleon decided to finish it as a temple to himself and a monument to the glory of the French armies, hence the classical form (After the first defeats of Napoleon's army ca. 1813, the original church purpose was reinstated). A competition was held for new designs. Vignon's entry finished 3rd and was chosen because it was less church-like than the first two places. The design is a paraphrase of a Roman temple using the Corinthian order. In this way, it links Napoleon I to Julius Caesar. It is an octastyle peripteral temple. A deep porch is set in front. While continuing the cubic clarity of 18th-century Neoclassicism, the individual forms are now more delicate and more ornate. The pediment is decorated with the Last Judgment. The rear pediment remains unfinished.

The interior was designed by J.-J.-M. Huvé (1783-1852) from 1825 to 1845. The first room entered is a vestibule. A series of three square bays are covered by domes on pendentives, supported by giant Corinthian columns. This provided a structural solution, which was technically Byzantine, but impressed rather like an imperial Roman interior. Light only enters through the cupolas. Each primary bay is further divided by fluted Ionic columns on its side into seven secondary bays. In the middle of each bay is a side chapel. The altarpiece depicts the rapture of St. Madeleine, and there are mosaics and murals depicting events in the Christianization of France. The seating capacity is 2000-3000.

The building is superbly sited. It is partly an urban design, since it terminates one end of the cross axis of the Place de la Concorde. The area had been annexed to Paris in 1922, and needed this building to balance the Palais Bourbon, now the National Assembly, at the other end of the Concorde axis.

Interestingly, both the Arc de Triomphe and the Madeleine, which were begun under Napoleon I, were not completed until the reign of Louis Philippe, who wanted to associate himself with the glory of Napoleon and undertook these completions.

# STATE THEATER, SCHINKEL, BERLIN (1819-21)

As in other western European countries, Durand's publications retained their authority in Germany as well. At the end of the 18th century, French influence was already widespread. After the Napoleonic wars, however, Germany, fearing that Napoleon would bring the achievements of the revolution with him, turned reactionary.

Schinkel's genuine architectural career began in 1816. Before that time, he worked as a stage set designer and painter. In 1815, he was named State Architect.

Schinkel was among the most prolific and eclectic architects of all time. Most of Schinkel's Classical designs were in the Grecian manner. His work encompasses two phases of Romanticism, namely the Greek Revival and a more eclectic mode of design.

Schinkel also developed a functional interpretation of Classical architecture. In 1826, he took a tour of England, which may have exposed him to novel (= industrial) types and technologies. After his return, he proposed a system for fireproofing buildings, consisting of a brick skin wrapped around an iron skeleton.

This is a building of complex masses. The articulation is characterized by a clear geometric order. The intention was to use Greek forms and methods of construction as much as was possible in this complex work. The main façade has an Ionic portico. In most other instances, the dominating feature is a (functionalist) pilaster strip.

The theater proper occupies the high central block, while the lower wings contain rehearsal and concert halls and other utilitarian rooms. Inside, simple but heavily scaled structural framework combined with delicate iron supports for the box ranges.

# ALTES MUSEUM, SCHINKEL, BERLIN (1824-28)

During the 19th century, the museum was conceived as an aesthetic church where all the works of mankind were brought together as a kind of art pantheism. Museums emphasized their educational purpose. Classical art was seen as having an uplifting and moralizing effect on the viewers. Making Classical art available to the public would improve the moral consciousness of the nation. Museums were generally built in the Classical style, as this style embodied the association of knowledge and learning.

The Altes Museum accomplished this expressive requirement two-fold. The rotunda contained statues of philosophers and poets, indicating that wisdom, intellect, and imagination are the most revered attributes of mankind. Murals inside the entrance colonnade depicted mythological subjects. On the right side of these walls were frescoes depicting the cosmological development, the lives of the gods. On the left were the subjects of human life, the creation of culture, and the seasons. On the walls of the second floor landing were the subjects of civilized man fighting against natural forces and barbarians. Sculptural groups depicting an Amazon and a Lion-killer flank the central entrance stairs.

The Altes Museum was designed in 1822, built between 1824 and 1828. It is a large rectangular block on an island in the river Spree, and is basically a collection of simple geometric volumes. Its front closes off the end of the royal pleasure garden, and faces the Baroque palace. The building approach is on axis. The stairs are visible as a truncated pyramid through the façade colonnade, thus indicating the centralized plan. The building is given a façade in the form of a Greek stoa, since it closes off a public square. Instead of acroteria, Prussian eagles stand on top of the entablature. The side and rear façades are articulated by corner pilasters, set apart by deep recesses.

The exterior is designed as a crisply and accurately detailed Greek envelope. The Ionic colonnade at the front is placed in between antae. This, together with a narrowing of the corner bays, allows this colonnade to be perceived as a whole. In addition, it is also seen as a figure-ground relationship. If one perceives the colonnade as a whole, then the spaces in between become the figure, thus turning this façade into a multi-wave visual oscillation.

Behind the portico was a small vestibule containing a recessed stairwell. This forms a visual and experiential transition from outside to inside. It slows the visitor's pace down, enabling him/her to enter into the appropriate mood for contemplating works of art. The pediment/stairs indicate movement forward, upward, and sideways. When exiting, the opening allows one a view of the city through columns of a dimension similar to that experienced in the paintings inside. The rising stairs form a pediment with either an open door, or a decorative plaque (when the entrance door straight ahead is closed). Since the lower flights of the stairs are behind the visible upper ones, a degree of mystery is associated with this entrance sequence. Entering this building provided the spectator with a brief history of Ancient architecture. One approached a Greek stoa, through which one could make out an Egyptian pyramid, and ended up in a Roman rotunda. On the second floor, one received the chance to look at a column halfway up. Thus, the building offered an actual experience of architectural time. The building was divided into two zones: a rotunda to house sculptures, and surrounding galleries for the paintings. These galleries were disposed around interior light courts. Large windows open outside to these yards and the paintings were hung on spur walls arranged perpendicularly to the walls. The whole interior arrangement was laid out with a view to function. The rotunda also formed a static termination of the entrance sequence on the ground floor. The rotunda in particular aims to present Ancient statues in their historical setting.

The stairs viewed from afar are understood as part of the mass of this building, while close up they become an object occupying the middle of the vestibule. The inscription on the building reads: "Friedrich Wilhelm III founded this museum for the study of antique objects of all kinds and the fine arts."

# WALHALLA, VON KLENZE, REGENSBURG (1831-42)

Based on the Parthenon. Original designs were drawn in the 1820s. The building is situated on a hill, on a tremendous substructure of terraces and stairs. In this, it is a realized version of the dream of a Greek temple set in a high place. The whole design incorporates elements from Revolutionary Classicism and the Picturesque. In its whole setting it can be considered the grandiose descendant of the follies in an English garden.

The design is of an attitude that rejects contemporary experience. Urban realities are not at all permitted to enter this building.

Inside is an openwork timber roof. The Walhalla is a mythological place where the souls of the slain heroes feast (in Norse mythology). It was as much a monument to Germany. Inside were portrait busts of politicians and intellectuals. Among the decorations were metopes depicting victories by the various historical German armies. The aim was to make the visitor a better German.

# BRITISH MUSEUM, SMIRKE, LONDON (1824-47)

Grecian simplicity was the result of a taste formed by scholarship. It was only during the 1830s and 1840s that styles and details were controlled by qualities deriving from sentiment and association. Greek Revival was as much a picturesque as a classical movement. Architects began to realize that a sensual and intellectual judgment was required for good architecture. The general rule was that public buildings were expected to follow the Greek mode, churches the Gothic.

Neo-Classical architecture expressed the changing social situation. At the end of the Napoleonic domination, England had changed from an aristocratic society with bourgeois leanings to a bourgeois society with aristocratic yearnings. The time for an architectural elite was therefore past. It was rather time for the general practitioner in historical styles. The Greek Revival was mostly used for the new urban building types arising out of the expanding town-life of post-Waterloo time. Nevertheless, most architects were preoccupied with style and its significance, rather than with the new situation brought by the industrial revolution.

The collections, which would be housed in this building, began in the middle of the 18th century. A new building for the growing contents was begun in 1823. The Classical style was chosen as conventional for this building type.

The plan is based on four wings enclosing a central courtyard. The south façade consists of a temple portico with flanking wings. A total of forty-eight columns continue the front into the wings.

A glass and iron dome covers the circular reading room, which was placed there.

Cast iron construction is used inside, but totally hidden behind its classical veneer. This construction was used in the main interior feature, the domed reading room. Here, during the mid-1850s, Robert's brother Sydney built a cast iron skeleton in the courtyard of the museum. The iron supports are encased in stacks.

# TRAVELERS' CLUB, BARRY, LONDON (1829-31)

During the second quarter of the 19th century, appreciation of the Greek mode decreased. Ensuing was the so-called Battle of the Styles. Immediately, the Italian Renaissance was elevated to most important model to follow.

Barry chose a Cinquecento Palazzo style for this commission. Partly a return of the Italian taste of Palladianism, although not favoring Palladio, this building was a meeting place for those having taken the European grand tour. The model chosen was Raphael's Palazzo Pandolfini in Florence. The design emphasizes the aedicular treatment of the windows and the top cornice above the orders of Classical architecture.

# REFORM CLUB, BARRY, LONDON (1837-41)

This building was commissioned by parliamentary Radicals who needed a meeting place for Reformers in London. It was to surpass the existing clubs in the vicinity. Originally, Classical and Italianate designs were in competition for this commission. The model for this building was the Palazzo Farnese in Rome. Changes are in the unaccented entrance, the balustrade on street level, the simpler top story and the corner emphasis. This choice pleased the users, since successful businessmen could see themselves as the successors of the Medici. The building shows its stone masonry openly, and is articulated through high relief. It aims at sublimity.

The planning is partly novel, since the original open courtyard is here roofed in to provide members with a comfortable salon to suit the local climate. The metal-and-glass roofing is interesting.

# MONTICELLO I, JEFFERSON, CHARLOTTESVILLE (1769-82)

Jefferson's country house, Monticello outside Charlottesville, was built nine years after he had begun to study architecture. He developed his ideas in a systematic manner through a series of preliminary drawings. The building was an experimental laboratory in which he could test his ideas. The entire house was thought out and planned to meet the practical and social needs of himself and his family.

This design incorporates stylistic details from both Colonial Georgian and Classical architecture, and combines them with a functional arrangement of the interior spaces. The Colonial Georgian features include the flat surfaces with little ornamentation, the emphasis on horizontal decoration, the symmetrical arrangement of the façade, and the hipped roof. The horizontal emphasis is further pronounced in the low building height and the widely spread additions. One may also adduce the emphasis on the central axis through the addition of two porticoes, to Georgian influence. Differences to the colonial Georgian style include the plan, which is cross-shaped, the octagonal end pavilions, the use of new geometrical shapes, and the siting of the house on top of a hill. The Classical features include the columned portico, the pediment, and the metope-triglyph frieze. The house is functional: there is a cross-shaped assembly of rooms so that each room has three sides to the exterior, and so that turbulence of the summer breezes is created in the corners, which helps to cool the house in the summer. The porticoes in front and back are from Palladio, but the wings are different; as they do not enclose a court. The auxiliary buildings are pushed into the earth, and extend behind the main building.

The leveling of the building site took place in 1768, and plans were fairly developed in 1770. The first building designed was the Honeymoon Cottage at one end, in 1771. This was constructed in brick, and consists of one room. It takes up the form of existing Virginia log cabins. At this time, the plan for the entire house was finished. The plan proper was derived from a plate in Morris's *Select Architecture*. Monticello I was finished in 1782. Afterwards, Jefferson was preoccupied with affairs of government.

# MONTICELLO II (1793-1809)

After his return from France, Jefferson began to enlarge Monticello. This rebuilding reflects his education in Paris. The design gives the impression of a single story with a rather horizontal arrangement of the building volumes and the emphasis of the balustrades and entablature. The central dome interlocks the various horizontal volumes. The final result produced a monumental, more coherent and broader version than the earlier building.

In plan, he basically doubled the side wings and added a low dome, influenced by the Hôtel de Salm. There is a distinction between the core rooms (those used for public functions) and the more private rooms, which is articulated on the exterior. Jefferson shifted from an architecture of surface to one of mass. It is still an abstract design, mostly depending on geometrical shapes. There are very strong, heavy, and sculptural details, which take up Harrison's building style and substitute a Classical vocabulary for the earlier Georgian one.

Inside, the public spaces are two stories high, the others lower. Related rooms are connected, unrelated ones closed off. There is a clear functional layout of both plan and size of the rooms that is based on their use. This arrangement is hidden behind the symmetrical façade. Windows also indicate the interior uses, that is, whether a room behind is two stories high or just one.

One of the sources of Monticello was the Ancient Roman villa, especially its more practical and visual qualities. This is seen in the widespread, but coordinated, plan. Auxiliary buildings are pushed into the earth, and extend in U-form behind the main building, terminating in a small brick pavilion on each side. Also Roman are the underground passageways connecting the service wings to the main house. Also, the location on top of a hill is Roman-inspired.

There is gadgetry inside – wine elevator, door with mechanical opening mechanism – but also functionalism: each feature designed for its later use: alcove bed, gallery only where one needs it, not for aesthetic reasons.

Jefferson worked and reworked his own house, Monticello, from the age of twenty-four almost until his death at eighty-three in 1826. Wills points out that Monticello, in some ways, was a test run for the university. It too is a hilltop complex with a dome at the center, arms reaching into the natural world and an open view to the horizon.

# UNIVERSITY OF VIRGINIA, JEFFERSON, CHARLOTTESVILLE (1804-17)

The third major work of Jefferson's was his design for the University of Virginia in Charlottesville. Jefferson had been thinking about a university beginning around 1800. He considered education a fundamental prerequisite for responsible citizenship. In 1817, his dream came true when the Virginia legislature passed a bill establishing a Central College. While the new university was not the first in America, it was to be of a new plan, based on Jefferson's new education system. Earlier colleges had been large scale, multi-purpose versions of domestic houses: Harvard, College of William and Mary. These buildings were added to when need arose. Jefferson wanted something different: he rejected both English and American prototypes because they were either too British, or they were not ordered enough for his own purposes. Jefferson wanted an "academic village." The university is the culmination of Jefferson's architectural intentions: buildings were used as a medium to bring about social reform and to educate and enlighten the people. Architecture is a form of visual education meant to promote the democratic ideal.

The original plan called for a U-shaped arrangement of buildings. Two rows of dormitories face each other across an expansive lawn, with arcaded, colonnaded walkways in between pavilions, with dormitories. At regular intervals, ten pavilions, with professor's houses and lecture rooms, were inserted into this arcade. At the center of the closed side, a rotunda with a projecting portico was placed, containing library, lecture room and other facilities. Gardens enclosed by serpentine walls were behind student dormitories, closed by another row of dormitories. Inserted in the second row of dormitories were six additional pavilions, containing dining halls.

This layout may have been influenced by Union College, by Rameau in Schenectady (1812), as well as the Chateau at Marly (1679-86). Another source is probably Jefferson's intention to design a genuine American plan, thus, the whole arrangement takes up the traditional feature of the common green. The plan also derives from the Greek agora and the Roman forum, especially the one at Pompeii. On the whole, it is a practical plan that can be infinitely extended.

No two pavilions are alike. This expressed the diverse schools and professors at the university. Each pavilion is based on a well-known example from the architectural past. The whole was intended to be an architectural encyclopedia for the benefit of architectural students. Models imitated were Roman, and the Palladian orders. The pavilions start as cubical Classical temples near the central Rotunda. The farther away from the Rotunda they are, the more modern they become, until they are examples of Neoclassicism, rather than Classicism.

The rotunda is based on Pantheon, but changed to accommodate it to the other structures and a new use. Its size is a half-Pantheon, the colonnade is reduced by two columns, the portico entablature carried around cylinder, and the windows are a new addition. The library is treated as the important part of the campus. The drawing suggests an interest in pure geometry: sphere inscribed in domed cylinder. It shows that Jefferson introduced the use of graph paper for architectural design: to study proportion in preliminary designs. While this is the system also used in the Pantheon, there is a second influence on Jefferson's design: Boullée's Newton Cenotaph with its pure geometry.

The decision not to build a large structure was also based on economic purposes; building a complex of smaller pavilions was cheaper. The serpentine garden walls are one more indication of such thinking: through the curves, they are structurally very stable and can be built lighter than if they were straight.

Aesthetically, interlocking the connecting arcade with the porticoes of the individual pavilions makes the arcade an interface between the green and the buildings. When passing underneath a pavilion, the viewer has two simultaneous spatial experiences, namely the arcade tube and the view into the green through tall columns.

Wills suggests one image that comes straight out of the 18th-century Enlightenment. He argues that the university resembles an orrery. An orrery is a physical model of the solar system showing the motions and relationships of the planets, satellites, and sun. Just so, the university is a physical model of the proper order of an academic society – with the library at the focal point, be it noted, and no chapel anywhere. Reason, not religion, would govern here. Another metaphor is that of a clearing in the forest. The long rows of columns that frame the Lawn on three sides can be viewed as representations of the trees of the American virgin forest, out of which this clearing of civilization, like so many others in early America, has been carved.

# GIRARD COLLEGE, WALTER, PHILADELPHIA (1833-47)

Walter was selected from among other competitors as architect for this building. The school was financed through the bequest of a wealthy Philadelphia banker, who clearly specified the dimensions of the proposed college building. Walter made a trip to Europe to study solutions of similar problems there.

Founder's Hall: Corinthian order, peripteral, with four rooms on the three floors. Rooms are groin-vaulted in masonry. Third floor rooms lit by skylights. Material used was marble.

Flanking this building are four dormitories, two on each side, each in the form of an astylar, pedimented block.

FIGURE 27–1. Arc de Triomphe, Paris.

FIGURE 27–2. La Madeleine, Paris, Main entrance.

FIGURE 27–3. State Theatre, Berlin, main façade.

FIGURE 27–4. Altes Museum, Berlin, exterior.

FIGURE 27–5. Altes Museum, interior rotunda.

**FIGURE 27–6.** Walhalla, Regensburg, distant view.

**FIGURE 27–7.** British Museum, London, central portion of main façade.

FIGURE 27–8.   Monticello, Charlottesville, VA, garden façade.

FIGURE 27–9.   University of Virginia, Charlottesville, VA, library.

FIGURE 27–10.   University of Virginia, main lawn with flanking pavilions and loggia.

# Chapter 28

# Gothic Revival

The major alternative to Neo-Classicism was Gothic Revival. Especially in northern Europe, Gothic architecture was viewed as being inherently national in expression. In fact, it had been cultivated as a "second" language already during the 18th century. The Gothic style was mostly used for religious and educational structures. There, the main justification for its use was that of environmental propriety. The Gothic Revival was associated with the theory of the picturesque. The principles of this theory were: irregularity, variety, intricacy, movement, and roughness. Other types of buildings in which the Gothic style was used were castle and villa architecture. There, the appeal of the style lay in its lack of plain and boring simplicity.

A particular characteristic of the Gothic Revival is that it had literary origins. Apart from Romantic Gothick novels, a number of influential anthologies were published during the 18th and 19th centuries. The 19th-century revival was influenced above all by a series of books on medieval architecture published between 1790 and 1830 by John Carter and John Britton. These not only provided accurate illustrations, but also a technical and stylistic vocabulary. In the quest for forms capable of adaptation to the new industrial building tasks, Gothic was judged extremely adequate, as it contained the principle of process within it. Gothic was not a normative style, but was seen as arising out of spontaneous creation by artisans, or the embodiment of rational principles. Hence, it could well express the values of an organic society, especially a society in evolution.

## AUGUSTUS WELBY PUGIN (1812-52)

Among the writers of treatises with the most influence in the 19th century was Pugin. His father was a draftsman, who worked for Nash in London after 1792, then did the illustrations for books on Gothic architecture. His son helped on these (finished and published them after his father's death); he was an accomplished designer and had commissions before the age of twenty. He was an architect, interior designer, and architectural critic. He converted to Catholicism in 1835. This led him to accept Gothic as the only true style. Importantly, Pugin did not promote to simply copy the Gothic style, but he advocated the revival of medieval building methods. Architecture must derive its character from the direct expression of structure.

In 1836, he published his book *Contrasts*. This book focused attention on the Gothic not as an object of antiquarian study, but rather as an architectural style conceived and executed in the service of the Christian church. Pugin developed moralistic ideas in the language of architecture. He illustrated his ideas with a series of paired contrasts between specific Christian and pagan examples. This marked a change in direction for the Gothic Revival. Pugin's Gothic was no longer picturesque, but moralistic. It was chosen because it was right to do so, not because it was agreeable to the eye.

In 1841, he published *The True Principles of Pointed or Christian Architecture*. In it, he proclaimed the Gothic as a dynamic style based on a direct relationship between structure and form. He established two principles: (1) No building should have features that are not immediately needed for convenience, construction, or propriety, and (2) ornament should consist only of the enrichment of the essential construction of a building. With such dogmas, Pugin obviously deviated partly from the picturesque, and associated himself rather with 18th-century French rationalist theory.

### HOUSES OF PARLIAMENT, BARRY & PUGIN, LONDON (1836-60)

In October 1834, a fire destroyed the medieval Palace of Westminster, which had housed the English parliament. An existing space in this palace, St. Stephen's Chapel, was used for parliamentary sessions, and over the years, parliament had adjusted its mode of operation to this space, which was not specifically designed for this purpose. The seating consisted of rising tiers of benches, as this arrangement offered most seats in the available space and allowed members to address the House from their seats. This seating was kept for the new parliament rooms. After the fire, which only spared Westminster Hall and St. Stephen's Chapel, it was quickly decided to rebuild parliament on the same spot. It was also decided to rebuild it in medieval style, so as to better incorporate the parts of the old structure that had not been totally destroyed, especially Westminster Hall. The surviving parts were incorporated into the new building as dramatic spatial entrance sequences for the queen and the members of parliament. The context, which was still medieval, appeared to support this decision as well. Most importantly, it was felt that Gothic was essentially an English style. This decision dates from June 1835. The competition reflected the sentimental romanticism of an increasingly nationalist age, and called for Gothic style to reinforce the medieval roots of English government.

This was a commission in which both painting and architecture were involved. The team of Charles Barry and A.W.N. Pugin was commissioned with this work. Barry had submitted a Classical design dressed Gothic, and had won the competition (announcement of the decision in February 1836) with drawings executed by Pugin.

Construction proceeded at a slow pace. The initial construction took place from 1837 to 1843, and was supervised by Barry. From 1844 to 1852, Pugin designed woodcarvings, furnishings, and other decorations. In 1858, Barry completed the clock tower. The House of Lords was opened in 1847, that of the Commons in 1852. The whole was finished by Barry's son from 1860-70. Victoria Tower was renovated in 1958-61.

Barry was responsible for the mass, silhouette, and plan of the new building. It was purpose-built. Certain irregularities in the exterior form (shape and placing of the two end towers) show that picturesque theory also played a role. The square tower indicates the entrance for the king/queen. The two wings indicate the bicameral legislature. Interspersed were a few light courts. On the riverfront are offices and a library, protected from the noise of the street. Pugin was responsible for the detail and interior decoration, which generally followed the English Perpendicular Gothic style. This style allowed the repetition of many small details, and provided for large banks of windows. The repetition and regularity of the exterior façade articulation are a remnant of the earlier Neoclassical tradition.

Iron was used for the roof trusses and roof shingles for fire protection.

An important contribution of this commission to future development was the revival of the crafts it engendered. Everything was carried out in the medieval styles, down to individual furnishings.

# HIGH VICTORIAN GOTHIC

Between 1850 and 1870, the Gothic Revival passed through a changing period, becoming by turns muscular and geometrical, naturalistic and polychromatic. Especially in England, it achieved lofty heights. This was partly due to the fact that there was no national architectural education, but that architects were rather trained as disciples.

### ALL SAINTS', BUTTERFIELD, MARGARET STREET, LONDON (1849-59)

Here, Pugin's call for truthfulness was translated into structural polychromy. This was a combination of 13th-century English prototypes with the polychromatic examples of medieval Italian churches. This church seems almost to want to shock. It was meant as a model church. It is flanked by a clergy house and a school, so that only the tower identifies it as a church. It is built of banded red and black brick. The polychromy is even more pronounced inside. Due to site restrictions, the interior is rather tall.

### KEEBLE COLLEGE, BUTTERFIELD, OXFORD (1866-83)

This is a complete entity. It forms a college for clerical students, around two quadrangles. Exterior walls are striated with bricks of various colors.

Butterfield added the chapel. This dominates the whole group through its size and verticality. The building is of smaller scale, and more decorative, than his earlier work. Its precedent is the upper church of St. Francis at Assisi. Windows are placed high up on the walls, increasing the impression of great height inside. The exterior walls are divided into four stages with increasing band width and a continuous lightening of the masonry.

## UNIVERSITY MUSEUM, DEANE & WOODWARD, OXFORD (1855-60)

The Gothic Revival was not only used for church or castle architecture, but also for other building types. Apparently, Ruskin influenced the choice of this Gothic design for the museum.

The exterior is disposed symmetrically with a focus on the central tower. The decoration is Gothic, emphasizing polychromy and abrupt angularity of detail and mass. This formula proved to be influential for other Gothic Revival structures.

The interior features a courtyard covered by an iron and glass roof.

## ST. PANCRAS STATION (1863-67) AND MIDLAND HOTEL (1866-74), SCOTT, LONDON

This is the Midland Hotel. It is partly overelaborated. The train shed was already under construction when a competition for this hotel was held in 1866. The two parts of this station are in drastic contrast. The train shed was among the first without intermediate supports. This part of the station is carried as a platform on columns above a street below. The hotel is among the largest Victorian Gothic structures. The style was obviously meant to refer to the Gothic cathedral and the air of institutionality it evoked.

## EUGÈNE-EMANUEL VIOLLET-LE-DUC

Together with J.-B.-A. Lassus the great French representative of the Gothic Revival. His contributions to this movement were literary and intellectual. In addition, he was the greatest restorer of the medieval churches damaged during the revolution. He was also important as an educator, as he trained most of the younger Gothic revivalists. In his own Gothic designs, he tried to prove how Gothic might serve as a basis for an adequate 19th-century style. Since much of his oeuvre consisted of restorations, one cannot speak of authentic 19th-century work.

In his later years, he tried to promote a new style that was Gothic in its principles but not in its appearance. He adhered to a widely held belief, that the generative forces of the 19th century were science, industry and commerce.

## RESTORATION OF NOTRE-DAME, PARIS (1844-66)

As part of this commission, a new Chapter House and other utilitarian structures were built. The chapter house was by Lassus, the Personnel House by Le-Duc. The chapter house is resplendent with murals and rich new furnishings.

## DE COURMONT HOUSE, PARIS (1846-9)

Here, Gothic details were applied to a typical Parisian street-front house. Stepped stringcourses, brackets, and moldings were intended to be functional, that is, as water channels.

However, although the houses fit politely into a stylistically different context, he (Viollet-le-Duc) decided that this was not an appropriate style for an urban environment, and subsequently used it only for churches and country houses.

# UNITED STATES HISTORICAL BACKGROUND

There where many aspects of the developing nation for which the Greek Revival was neither expressive nor appropriate. New and dynamic forces were adding diversity and a new, larger dimension to the American society. The American world was no longer simple and small. Enlargement of territory replaced the colonial isolation and gave way to the aspirations of a free and independent nation. This new spirit demanded more flexible and dynamic architecture than the simple, stable Greek style. There was motivation from a growing national awareness. The personal freedoms granted by the Constitution brought a diversification of ideas and beliefs, and a heterogeneous, fluid society.

This change of society and ideology was triggered by the influx of two forces from abroad: technology and Romanticism. The industrial progress, with its egalitarian elements, brought a longing for individualism. The Greek Revival as well was a rather regular, ordered style. These two developments were rather intellectual, and incited a fashion for romantic art and architecture. A romantic statement is a product of the sensibilities, rather than the intellect, of imagination rather than reason. Its appeal is to the emotions rather than to the mind.

## MEMORIAL HALL, WARE & VAN BRUNT, CAMBRIDGE (1870-78)

One of the most resplendent buildings in this style. It was built as a memorial to Harvard graduates who had died in the Civil War.

It looks like a church from the outside, but gives a clear reflection of the interior arrangement. There, we find a large rectangular hall for dining and assemblies, a central memorial hall under the tower, and semicircular auditorium. All materials are openly expressed both inside and out. Wood is used for the roof trusses. The façades are of red and black brick and stone bands. The slate roof is red, green, gray, and black.

**FIGURE 28–1.** Houses of Parliament, London, aerial view.

**FIGURE 28–2.** Memorial Hall, Cambridge, MA, exterior.

# Chapter 29

# Second Empire and Structural Rationalism

Napoleon III's architectural endeavors, executed by Haussmann, demanded a new breadth of scale and grandness of public performance. These demands brought forth the Second Empire style. The ambition was to revive the splendors of Napoleon I, and earlier kings. To line the new boulevards, rows of typically Parisian apartment houses were built during the 1850s. The style was internationally followed after the world had witnessed the New Louvre during the 1855 World Exhibition in Paris.

The most conspicuous feature of this style was the mansard roof. It always had a Parisian and palatial flavor to it, and symbolized cosmopolitan modernity. The main intention of this style was not that of a straightforward revival, as many contemporary aspects were inserted into its forms. The intention was to be creative, not archaeological. The style lasted into the 1880s.

Stylistically, Second Empire can be considered as a development out of the earlier Renaissance Revival. Changes are noticed in the richer and more plastic articulation, especially through the mansard roof and the pavilion system. The mansard roof appealed to architects because it provided for a more picturesque silhouette. The same argument also works for the pavilion system.

## THE TRANSFORMATION OF PARIS

This was not only the work of an ambitious ruler, but was also enabled by the particular situation of this city. By 1848, Paris had become the world's greatest manufacturing city. In particular, it had a new banking system consisting of institutions with networks of local branches, attracting the small investor.

The transformation was the work of Baron Georges-Eugène Haussmann (1809-1891). In 1853, he was appointed prefect of the Seine district, and was immediately commissioned to execute the emperor's proposal for the remaking of Paris. New streets and boulevards were laid out, public squares established at intersections, gas street lighting introduced, as well as a modern sewage system, and Paris itself was enlarged. The task was largely completed in 1869. It turned Paris into the first large city of the industrial age. The work was made possible by a law passed in 1852, which allowed the government to expropriate land for roads. During this task, the population of Paris increased from 1.2 to 2 million inhabitants. The transformation was financed by loans taken by the city of Paris. It was felt that these would be repaid by the higher tax revenues produced by the urban improvement.

This plan was the first example of an urban program that encompassed the whole city. Most probably, the preservation of order and the intention to win approval through imposing urban design efforts had some influence on the original decision. The old urban body is covered by a new grid of straight and broad avenues. New regulations guided the architecture lining these streets (height and roof pitch were prescribed).

## LOUVRE EXTENSION, VISCONTI & LEFUEL, PARIS (1852-7)

This project launched the Second Empire. It was to connect the existing Louvre, which was already an art museum, to the Tuileries. The Tuileries were the royal residence in Paris. The major design problem was to link the two façades of different width. This was achieved by oblong connections stepping back at intervals. The pavilion system that had already been used in the existing buildings was continued. Visconti died in 1853 and was followed by Lefuel.

The new addition is a mixture of both originality and eclecticism. The rich plasticity and the higher roofs are new elements.

## OPERA HOUSE, GARNIER, PARIS (1861-75)

Charles Garnier (1825-1898) was the premier architect of the Second Empire style. He won the second stage of the opera competition in 1861. There was a long development before plans for this building proceeded. The existing opera house had been destroyed in 1781.

The practice of stuffing new uses into old forms could not always succeed in the 19th century. A new design mode was developed, consisting mainly of using historic details in buildings otherwise planned strictly in accord with functional requirements. The Opera House in Paris is such a new building type decorated in historic forms. The Place de l'Opera was laid out by Rouhault de Fleury and H. Blondel in 1858-64. The location was intended to express the importance of this building as a social center. Haussmann's plan redesigned the city of Paris as a network of focal points and radiating arteries. Perspectives toward monuments became the city's aesthetic code. The Opera House was situated on one of the new boulevards, the center of the new bourgeois moneyed class.

The plan, an oblong rectangle, contains the four main parts of the opera: lobby and stairwell, auditorium, stage, and administration. Functional considerations required a solution for the approach and circulation pattern for visitors. This partly expressed a class society. Each kind of opera-goer had a particular entrance. The staircase leading into the upper story occupied almost ⅓ of the whole building, and in a way "makes the opera." The auditorium had both a parterre and galleries, so that opera-goers could be seen. The walls in the lobby were finished as mirrors. Everything seems to "drip." Garnier satisfied here the taste for bombastic luxury. The design celebrated grand opera, combining music, dance, painting, and architecture. It embraced tradition and novelty, theatrical expertise, and great expenditure. It catered to expectations of luxury and comfort.

Early on in the planning of the Opera House, it was required that it be big and magnificent, so that it could serve as a symbol for the cultural status of France. The building was meant to inaugurate a new contemporary style. Its characteristics were the use of a giant order on the flanking buildings, and of circular pavilions.

The interior structure of the auditorium is completely of iron, however, enclosed in masonry and stone veneer.

Garnier's taste was partly shaped by 15th and 16th century Italian architecture. During his stay in Italy, he was stationed in Florence, not in Rome, because Rome at that time was not safe. At the same time, he considered Classical architecture as full of emotion and human life, not as the ethical and perfect achievement that Winckelmann had read into it. Garnier was also partial to polychromy. These interests partly explain his solution for the opera, namely to accommodate a human spectacle. He saw no future in an architecture based on rationalism, science, engineering, or new materials. His design has a Neo-Baroque flavor, achieved with High-Renaissance details.

The various interior functions are expressed in the irregular outline of the building. These varied functions resulted in a rich contrast in massing in the exterior. The cupola covers the auditorium and the pitched roof the stage house. Lobby and stairwell are expressed in the side elevation. The main façade follows the "French" system as evolved in the Louvre.

However, expressive intentions were equally important for this design. Garnier saw the opera as the embodiment of man's most primitive instincts, namely to gather together in ceremony to share thoughts and dreams, to hear and to see and be seen (this began as gatherings around campfires). Theater thus involved not only the spectacle on the stage, but encounters before and after as well. The Opera House reflects society on show, a society that valued appearance above all. Paris was a theater and society was a spectacle.

Between 1962 and 1964, Marc Chagall painted new ceiling panels.

# VICTOR HUGO'S ARCHITECTURAL THEORY

The big idea was that buildings had lost the power to express human thought, a power that they relinquished to the printed word. A simple revival of one style or another was not the adequate response to this situation.

Hugo's concept treated architecture as beginning as a form of writing, not as shelter or primitive hut. The medium stone was chosen to perpetuate thoughts and ideals, which had been transmitted earlier through an oral tradition. The early forms of architecture were not imitations of nature, but letters. A pyramid was not a mountain, but a word. Carnac was a collection of sentences. Buildings were seen as books.

With the invention of the printing press in the 15th century, architecture was dethroned from this position. It consequently declined into revivalism and ceased to serve as the essential expression of society. All these Classical forms in post-15th-century architecture are simply grafts of foreign tissue that conceal the decay.

# HENRI LABROUSTE

Hugo's ideas had an impact on one of the major 19th-century buildings in Paris. Henri Labrouste (1801-75) had won the grand-prix in 1824 (project for a law court) and spent the next five years in Rome. Labrouste studied polychromy in the Ancient Roman buildings, and its possible application. Among other works, he did a restoration study of the temples at Paestum, and promoted new interpretations of these, based on social inquiry. The buildings were interpreted as reflecting their builders' social aspirations. He argued that one of the buildings was in fact a civic structure, not a temple. He based his reconstruction on a regressive theory of history. Regression was found in architecture as the degeneration from a primitive state of purity to one of conventional representation. Sculptural form was replaced by the written word. At Paestum, the religious programme had been replaced by a secular one. The Temple of Hera I was actually a public bulletin board. The walls functioned as the pages of an album for inscriptions of the citizens. The building needed the painted word to generate meaning. And, in the traces of paint found on the actual ruins, Labrouste had the proof for this theory. This was in fact a dismissal of the established ideals of Greek architecture held by the École des Beaux-Arts. He was also interested in the essence of materials and the spirit of construction, searching for the inner organism of structure.

During his stay in Rome, he wrote a critique of the educational methods of the Ecole des Beaux-Arts. After his return from Rome (1830), he opened an independent architectural school. As a result of his rebellion, he did not receive any official building commissions. The new times also had an effect on architectural education. No longer was training in an architect's office adequate, but students were educated in special schools. The instruction at the École des Beaux-Arts included structure and construction, and focused on plan organization with a view to the simplest circulation into and through the building, and on expression of the character of the function housed.

## Bibliothèque Ste-Geneviève, Paris (1842-50)

In 1838, Labrouste's dry period ended and he was appointed architect to the library of Ste-Geneviève. His initial plan (1839) was accepted in 1840; work on the foundations began in 1843, on the building in 1844.

The design was meant as a response to the issues raised by Hugo. As a Romantic architect, Labrouste agreed that architecture had declined. He blamed this decline on the lack of social and religious unity. Architecture had not only lost its medium, but also its content. Buildings therefore had to stop expressing architectural contents, and change to literary ones. Buildings had to become books, that is, a form of imprinted matter.

Labrouste's library was situated at the end of a public square, and thus had to contribute to its definition. The building was a narrow block that stretched like a blind aqueduct. It was entered on the street level. The ground floor contained stacks and offices. The vestibule separates the book stacks on the left from the manuscript collection on the right. A book-lined reading room occupies the upper level. There is seating for 400 people. Access to the reading room was through a stair hall in the back.

The vestibule is deep and cavernous. It is treated as a narthex and has a half-indoor, half-outdoor quality. The supporting piers look like trees with green iron boughs. Originally the ceiling was painted blue, and trees were painted on the walls. There are busts of eminent French scientists, artists, and intellectuals in a presentation of three-dimensional images of the names printed outside. A copy of Raphael's *School of Athens* is in the staircase.

The interior of the library is organized as a three-dimensional grid. The iron arches look like lines on paper. The reading room is the part of this building, which introduced a number of novelties to architecture. Its most obvious qualities are its lightness and openness. It is basically a double nave space. Since there was a need for daylight, the exterior walls are opened up by a partially glazed arcade. The reading room was covered by a double barrel-vault, supported entirely on a metal frame. A central row of slender, freestanding iron columns supports longitudinal and transverse truss arches. These hold up the barrel vaults, which were made of wire mesh covered with a layer of plaster, so as to let in plenty of diffused light. The arches are decorated in traditional architectural manner, although the individual motifs also express their structural function. The remarkable aspect of this interior is that the gravitational and lateral thrusts of the structure are contained within itself, thus not needing any extraneous buttressing. This structure is then covered by a sturdier metal truss and glass roof. On the outside, the transverse arches are supported by wall consoles. Three truss beams run the length of this ceiling, one supported on the central longitudinal arches, the other two at the apexes of the transverse arches. The architectural details follow the reigning Neo-Classical fashion. However, they are not applied, but are integral parts of the structure, thus producing an early example of "iron architecture." The general feeling of the reading room imitates both Greek and Gothic interiors.

Shelves were placed between the central columns and along the exterior walls, there below a gallery running around the room, giving access to a second level of stacks.

The interior circulation proceeds along an exposition of the evolutionary process of human knowledge. In the vestibule, the busts speak in front of nature and thus introduce us to oral transmission of knowledge. Raphael's painting introduces us to this form of communication. Finally, the reading room brings us to real light and real space needed to transmit information through reading.

The exterior does not conceal its blandness behind decoration. It expresses the two interior functions. The decoration is contained within the framework of the structural expression. It seems to be printed in its repetition. The exterior is compartmented in a grid of vertical and horizontal lines. The upper floor shows the opening through huge arches partly filled by windows. Each bay has vertical columns. The lower parts of the arches are closed by panels bearing the names of 810 famous authors and scientists. These panels list the contents of the building. A small window for an office is at the bottom. The panels also hide the shelves placed against the walls inside. A horizontal frieze defines the top of the upper level of shelves inside. The first floor window openings are smaller. A garland frieze between the two floors adds a dynamic element to the otherwise static rhythm of this façade. This is basically a building with an expressive surface that celebrates the building's function. The book in which the building is clothed is a catalog.

The most obvious source for the façade is Alberti's Tempio Malatestiana. As coffins were to be inserted between the arches on that building, so books are shelved between the arches of the Bibliothèque Ste-Geneviève. The interior is similar to the refectory of the Gothic Abbaye de Saint-Martin-des-Champs in Paris. The inscribed panels in the arches make the exterior look like the Temple of Hathor at Denderah. The vestibule is like an Egyptian hypostyle hall. No one stylistic identification works alone and convincingly.

This building exhibits a graceful introduction of industrial innovations to architecture. This emphasis was influential on the interior arrangement of Labrouste's library.

Labrouste's achievement in this building was fourfold. First, he provided a clear functional arrangement. Second, he included circulation straightforward into his design. Third, his structure exploited new building materials. And finally, he achieved a clear expression of the building's purpose without requiring historical ornament.

# UNITED STATES

The Second Empire style was popular in every Western country. This style is marked by a quality of cosmopolitan urbanity. It was just what America needed at a time of unprecedented urban growth. Its appeal, especially to businessmen and politicians, was based on the connotations of prestige, affluence, and authority. The Civil War (1861-65) marks a definite period in American architecture. In 1860, there were thirty-five urban centers with populations exceeding 25,000. Thirty years later, there were four times that many centers, and two dozen cities had more than 100,000 inhabitants. With the rise in size came also a transformation. The industrial, agricultural, and transportation revolutions changed forever Jefferson's ideal arrangement of land and public buildings. New building types came into being: commercial block, office building, town or city hall, opera house. The prevailing feeling in the large cities was one of wealth and commerce, the dominant social impression one of boundless material luxury; the atmosphere was thick with the emanation of those who hurry to be rich.

With the defeat of the confederates and the ruin of their agricultural production (mainly cotton), the U.S. emerged as a leading industrial country: the basis of a modern society was laid. A period not only of economic growth, but also of exploitation began. This was the time of the robber barons, when most of the great American fortunes were started. While the Civil War represents disunion on the political level, other events welded the nation together geographically, culturally, and economically. Telegraph lines spanned the continent in 1861. The first transcontinental railroad was completed in 1869. In the last four decades of the 19th century, roughly 400 million acres came under cultivation. With the industrial growth, land was no longer uniquely used for hunting and farming, but also as a source of minerals, lumber, and power.

Architecture reflected this development as well. Buildings were elevated to a level commensurate with European practices. Exteriors became more intricate and complicated, and architects began to explore new possibilities in various modes of buildings: especially public and economic structures became functional, that is, arrangement of interiors was more attuned to the particular requirements of the building task. The foremost interest lay in the expression of a building's purpose and importance in its exterior form. Whereas before, a particular style could be applied to all types of buildings, now there was a growing divergence between public and private architecture.

Moreover, the second Empire style suggested the world of cosmopolitan Paris. France was at that time a cultural center of the world, and its lifestyle was imitated everywhere: fashion, furniture, and language. French buildings furnished the Second Empire style with its two identifying features, the mansard roof and the pavilion motif. This motif is a forward break in the elevation, usually at the center and at the ends of the building. The general arrangement is of pavilions connected by wings, mostly in a symmetrical disposition. The mansard roof has a curb around the top of the visible slopes of the roof (the mansard roof has two slopes; the upper one is hidden). The strict adherence to Greek and Roman forms and their Renaissance/Baroque variations were abandoned. An appealing factor of this style was its modernity: it was a modern style that derived its prestige from contemporary Paris, not from any period of the past. Dormer windows are used universally (dormer window = window that projects vertically from a sloping roof and has a roof of its own). The decoration relies on superimposed classical orders and a number of Renaissance and Baroque features (window pediments) and on a florid, sculptural ornamentation that is overlaid on this "structural" decoration.

This style marks the temporary decline of Washington as the architectural trendsetter in the country.

## CITY HALL, JOHN MACARTHUR, PHILADELPHIA (1874-)

As the Louvre, which brought this style into the world, was used as government house, palace, and museum, this style became the official style of civic and municipal buildings.

One of the largest examples of a Second Empire Style building is the City Hall of Philadelphia. Its plan is simple and efficient. The building encloses a courtyard in the center. The courtyard is linked to the streets by high archways. Four wings, each in the familiar pavilion-arrangement, are laid out around this yard. The large mass of this building necessitated a greater bulk of the decoration. Pavilions have "smaller pavilions" added: the central pavilion has three mansard roofs in one. Motifs are doubled, for example, in the pairing of columns.

It was once the biggest building in the U.S., and until 1909 it was the highest occupied building. It is one of the world's tallest buildings of bearing-wall construction without a steel skeleton.

Sculptural decoration expressed American ideas: William Penn on top of a tower, around the rounded top figures of a Swedish settler, a Swedish woman, and Indian and Indian woman, and many more of such didactic examples, all carved by Alexander Calder's grandfather.

FIGURE 29–1. Opera House, Paris, main façade.

**FIGURE 29–2.** Library of Sainte-Geneviève, Paris, main façade

**FIGURE 29–3.** City Hall, Philadelphia.

# Chapter 30

# Theory, Philosophy, and Architecture

## ECOLE DES BEAUX-ARTS

After Napoleon I's demise, leadership in architecture passed into other hands. The government's architectural schools became the dominant promoters of the ruling theory.

### ANTOINE QUATREMÈRE DE QUINCY (1755-1849)

He first studied law. When he was in Italy from 1776-80, he began studying architecture. He eventually became a scholar and upholder of the Classical (esp. Roman) ideals. In 1791, he transformed Soufflot's Ste-Geneviève into the Panthéon. He was secretary of the Academy of Beaux-Arts from 1816-39, and, through this office, in charge of official building. The buildings he favored were rather boringly monotonous.

He wrote an *Encyclopedia* (1788) and a *Dictionary* (1825) of architecture. His ideas are important when it comes to the terms "character" and "type."

Character was introduced to architectural theory to distinguish the various building types. Quatremère established three kinds of character: general – expression of natural particularity brought by climate, mores, and civilization; essential – expression of moral and physical greatness; and relative – the specific expression of each kind of building.

The term "type" in architecture is similar to its use in printing, that is, it signifies a general model, an impression. In this respect, it has three features: it means looking for the original form, restoring forms back to the Greek temple, and finding the characteristic form for each task, easily understandable.

Quatremère defined type as "the root of," the pre-existent germ, origin, and primitive cause.

### JEAN-NICOLAS-LOUIS DURAND (1760-1834)

Foremost among theorists was Durand. He was trained under Boullée and taught from 1795 to 1830. He is considered the founder of the theory of structural rationalism. He also systematized the theory of design and established graphic formulas to simplify architectural representation. This is partly the result of his educating civil engineers, not architects.

Durand had two major publications. The first was an illustrated architectural history book of 1800. The second were the lectures he held at the polytechnic school in Paris, published between 1802 and 1805. The edition comprised two volumes. The first volume contains the elements of architecture: the goals and structural means of architecture and the principles that can be derived from them, followed by materials, detailed forms, and proportions. The second contains elements of composition – how to combine the architectural elements – and the various building types arranged in a hierarchical order. Durand divided architecture into its fundamental constructive elements, essential geometric forms, and then had a system by which these elements were combined to make up the whole building. According to Durand, the general principles of architecture are (1) the elements of the structures, (2) the combination of these elements, composition, and (3) the assembly of these combinations in particular structures. He combined trabeated, arcuate, and vaulting systems from all periods of history. Façade articulations derived from the Renaissance seem to predominate. Common to most proposals is the repetition of elements, both horizontally and vertically, the emphasis on a varied skyline, and the use of features adding voids into the articulation.

The main goal of architecture should be correct disposition. This was to be done following two principles, namely efficiency (or functionalism) and economy. Functionalism meant that the structure had to be strong, sound, and comfortable. Economy resulted if one considered simplicity, regularity, and symmetry. Architecture was to be built on a set number of principles. This was partly the result of trying to keep the design process as strict and clear-cut as possible, that is, free from intuitive aberrations impinging on the correct completion of a task. By thus elevating rationality to a position of importance for the design, Durand rejected earlier traditions, such as Vitruvius and nature. Vitruvius is accepted only as a historical source, not as an authority. Durand also discarded the primacy of aesthetic principles, decoration and distribution, in favor of construction. He proposed the use of colonnades over temple porticoes. The goal of architecture was to be useful for society. The choice of Renaissance over Classical sources also suggests his more functional orientation.

According to Durand, architectural beauty resulted from the nature of the task, from the construction, and from the adequately used materials. His aesthetic was normative. Following the general principles would result in beauty; one did not have to revert to decoration for this purpose.

Durand's historical significance lies in his proposing practical methods for the rationalization of building. This is done by providing formal rules to follow. In the examples he proposed, Durand favored vertical and horizontal repetition; the basic rule consisted of the combination of single, precisely defined elements. Similarly, ground plans were derived from accumulation, not from a composite idea. Each design starts with small elements, which are assembled into the whole. He proposed modular planning, based on a square grid system. These systems for ground plans were the graphic formulas of Durand. Modular planning allowed for variability in that the simple basic modules can be arranged in different systems.

# Chapter 31

# Domestic Revival

William Morris had revived the craft tradition and the appreciation for the modest, comfortable middle-class house, focusing on honesty and simplicity rather than on ostentation and eclecticism. Morris believed that if a culture could not make beautiful objects, either through inherited genius or through a craft tradition, it was finished. The importance of these ideas can be seen in the Prussian decision to send Hermann Muthesius on a fact-finding tour of this country. The detached house is almost a typically Anglo-Saxon invention, first found in medieval England and from there exported to the American colonies. Consequently, the Domestic Revival was a renewing agent in the late 19th century. The previous pomposity was replaced by honesty and human scale. Rationality and rectangularity are characteristic elements.

## RED HOUSE, WEBB, BEXLEYHEATH (1859-60)

This is informal architecture that develops toward abstraction and the interpenetration of space. In choice of materials and details this design is not very revolutionary, as the materials are local. It is inventive, but impersonal. Novel features are found in the plan. The overall layout is L-shaped allowing a crossed corridor inside and enclosing a courtyard outside. This layout creates its own context for the house. This is an informal, asymmetric interpretation of space. Composition is more important than functional expression. Spaces are linked. It attempts to be an example of ordinary house Romanticism. There is no pomp, just a celebration of domesticity. Partly, this design results from a reaction to industrialization and the engineering dominance of architecture, such as exemplified by the Crystal Palace.

This is simple domestic free-style architecture, that could have surrounded the Gothic cathedrals. The house recreates a romantic vision of the medieval world.

The northern side contains the entrance. This façade is clearly articulated. The other elevations are freely modulated, and express the nature of the main rooms, which are clearly identifiable through their particular window treatments.

The interior is continuously decorated and complete. The window treatment expresses use.

Living and sleeping spaces are separated, placed on top of one another. The main stair is in the tower, indicated by vertically emphasized windows. Interior corridors have rectangular windows. The living spaces are placed on a firm base, and the sleeping spaces are protected by a large, prominent roof. These various spaces interpenetrate each other and create the house in this manner. This would become the dominant domestic theme continuing into the beginnings of Modernism in Adolf Loos and Frank Lloyd Wright.

## LEYESWOOD, R.N. SHAW, SUSSEX (1868-69)

This was the "Old English" spirit in an impressionistic, rather than truthful way. Some of the decorative details are nevertheless archaeologically Late Medieval. There is ample fenestration in window bands and tall window-walls. There is a mixture of medieval forms and Classical decoration. Materials: brick on ground floor, half-timbering or tile hangings on upper stories, windows in ribbons.

Agglutinative plan which benefits the natural lighting of interiors.

# VOYSEY HOUSE "THE ORCHARD," VOYSEY, CHORLEYWOOD (1899-1900)

The layout with two cross gables is more symmetrical, and regularity is also introduced through the carefully balanced window bands.

# STOUGHTON HOUSE, RICHARDSON, CAMBRIDGE (1882-3)

This style refers to earlier American styles, namely those of the Colonial period. In 1876, the Centennial exhibition was held in Philadelphia, and the country embarked on a colonial revival. The Centennial was meant to celebrate the country's birth to freedom, with a grand exhibition that contained the "best we can do." It was seen as a dramatic way to impress the international community. The exhibition was held from May to November 1876, and total attendance was 9.9 Million. While the most up-to-date technology was shown, the buildings were rather traditional. But the exhibition generated a patriotic feeling among Americans, which developed into a renewed interest in Colonial architecture.

The plan is rather irregular; several spaces stick out. Inside is the main hall with the staircase, which is housed in the round stair tower.

The porch is recessed into the main mass of the building. By using shingles for the exterior, Richardson manages to present the whole building as a coherent, continuous shape: the shingles wrap around every turn of the façade. Thus, the Stoughton House was sheathed in a continuous skin, exactly as seventeenth-century colonial houses had been clothed. The cladding is no longer clapboard, but shingles, so that the whole surface becomes even more continuous than those of the earlier houses.

# Chapter 32

# Chicago School
# and the Skyscraper

## HISTORY AND ORIGIN IN NEW YORK

The skyscraper first appeared in the U.S. Three technological inventions are basic to the skyscraper: the elevator, fireproofing, and the self-supporting metal frame. The skyscraper can be defined as an elevator building supported by a fireproof metal frame. If height is considered, the birth of the skyscraper occurred in New York at the end of the 1860s. Before the invention of the elevators, tall buildings were mostly four or five stories high, as it was not expected that anyone would rent space higher up.

The elevator was invented around 1850, and was first demonstrated in the 1853 New York World's Fair. It was used spottily for the next 1½ decades, mostly as freight platforms. In 1868-70, with the completion of the Equitable Life Assurance Building, it made its break-through, specifically to increase the rentable space. Its success revolutionized New York office building. In 1865, the average commercial building was five stories high. By 1872, architects were planning buildings four times that height.

The development of the skyscrapers in New York happened in the office-building category. Construction played an insignificant role in the introduction of the skyscraper. Economics was a paramount factor. Space was considered a commodity in these buildings, that could be sold at a profit. The promise of high profits made builders invest in new technologies. A commercial reason for the "invention" of the skyscraper in New York was that the demand for high buildings was simply greatest in this city. Businesses started to become interested in the tall building: the desire for greater height was fed by the mystique of the corporate image, and the tall building began to become a status symbol. It signified position, power, and prosperity, and had publicity values. Height also had the capacity to excite the senses.

## TRIBUNE BUILDING, R. M. HUNT, NEW YORK (1873-75)

This building is nine stories, 260 ft high. It is still constructed in a traditional masonry manner with heavy walls on the outside and a framework of iron columns and beams inside. Hunt designed the Tribune Building basically as a blown up Second Empire house. He piled up successive two and three-story units: a number of Renaissance palaces on top of one another. While the expression of the height of the building is thus not very convincing, Hunt did attempt to express the weight of his walls through the broad segmental arches on the ground floor level and higher up, and the lightness of the wall parts in between the piers.

## CHICAGO SCHOOL

During the 1880s there appeared in Chicago a radically new technique for supporting tall buildings. This was the use of a metal skeletal frame both inside and outside the building. The masonry for the exterior walls was simply attached to this frame and did not any longer support anything. This technological invention reduced the weight of a building, and also eliminated the need for thick walls on ground floor level. In fact, the curtain wall was invented.

Two forces began to reshape commercial building after 1885. Technological inventions changed the arrangement and structure of buildings (steel), while architecturally, the expression of the structural and functional realities of the building was improved. What resulted was a mixture of blatant eclecticism with straightforward structures and functional planning. An additional structural improvement was the use of terra-cotta tiles for the floors. This was a lightweight and fireproof material.

The steel frame, on which many buildings of the 1950s were to rely, was perfected during the 1880s and 1890s in Chicago. Chicago School skyscrapers are conceived as single volumes, with rational façades exhibiting the underlying structure. The Chicago frame is different from Art Nouveau structures. The former is an economic, business-like solution to a given problem; the latter devised the frame as an aesthetic manifesto. The Chicago frame was part of economy, not of culture.

## HOME INSURANCE BUILDING, JENNEY, CHICAGO (1883-86)

This is still more or less a masonry building with iron reinforcements. It did not have an independent metal frame. However, Jenney developed a complete iron and steel frame for the upper floors, from which he hung the external brick and terracotta sheathing. The first two stories were of load-bearing granite masonry. From the third to the sixth floor, cast-iron columns and wrought iron girders were used, and on top of this, steel. These columns were inserted into masonry piers to relieve them, but not to support them. This radical support system is not fully expressed on the outside. Rather, exterior and interior masonry walls provided lateral support.

## MARSHALL FIELD WHOLESALE STORE, RICHARDSON, CHICAGO (1885-7)

Richardson's early work had partly contributed to the "commercial Romanesque." With the Marshall Field Store, he brought one of his masterpieces of this new urban style to Chicago. Because of its size, force, and austerity of conception, the building was quite impressive. It epitomizes Richardson's aim to design "quiet" buildings. The order of the façade elevations becomes the order of the whole building. The structure is a rugged masonry box. The materials used are red granite for the base and red sandstone for the upper parts. The building is of a U-shape, and fills a whole city block. Inside the block is an open courtyard. Its only exterior articulation is provided by the pattern of the arched window openings. Metal is used only inside, for supports and floor beams. The first floor is treated as base, with segmental arched windows. Above this, huge arches encompass three stories. On the next level, two narrower arches fill each bay, and the top consists of rectangular windows grouped in fours. The total height of the building is seven stories. The façade design is geometrical, and consists of an arrangement of horizontals and verticals, without one of the directions dominating. This creates both a geometrical rhythm and one of alternating aspects. The corners of the building give the impression of massive piers.

The building was demolished in 1930 to make way for a parking garage.

## SULLIVAN AND ADLER

Dankmar Adler (1844-1900) was born in Lengsfeld, Germany. His family had emigrated to Detroit, where he worked in the office of a local engineer. He served with the engineers in the Union Army during the Civil War. He was largely self-taught.

Louis Sullivan (1856-1924) was born in Boston. In 1872, he enrolled in the architectural program at MIT, but left after one year. He then went to work for Frank Furness in Philadelphia. In 1873, he was let go there and continued to Chicago, where he worked in Jenney's office from 1873 to 1874. In summer 1874, he traveled to Paris and studied at the EBA, but left in 1875.

His theory was one of structural rationalism, based largely on ideas expressed earlier by H. Greenough and R. W. Emerson. These were ideas that linked architectural beauty to function, and proposed organic forms for buildings (organic in the sense of juxtaposition of parts and subordination of details to the whole). Nevertheless, Sullivan was not a true rationalist. For him, function and structure alone were not capable of generating a new style, but needed to be complemented by artistic intervention. The classical division and the ornamentation are, in Sullivan's case, these individual interventions.

## AUDITORIUM, CHICAGO (1887-89)

This is a progeny of Richardson's Marshall Field Store, and not yet a typical Sullivan design. The Auditorium was built for a group of businessmen to house an opera, a hotel, and an office building (these latter parts to ensure a profit). The firm most probably was commissioned for this design because of Adler's proven ability in acoustical engineering. The design problem was that the diverse functions eliminated symmetry and required different façades on each side. The hotel was along Michigan Avenue, the offices along Wabash Avenue (left side of building). Entrance to the auditorium is underneath the tower. The building is ten stories high, in the forms used by Richardson in the Marshall Field design. As an economy measure, the clients had demanded that the exterior be as simple as that of the Marshall Field Store. The basement walls are rusticated, with tiers of windows. The presence of the wall, as it occurs in Richardson's design, is diminished through thinning of the piers and the use of smooth stones. The ornament is more crisp and linear. The vertical direction is emphasized. The whole building is in the form of a block, a cornerstone of Sullivan's design theory.

The interior is completely by Sullivan. The ornament comes close to European Art Nouveau design. In the metal grillage of the stair railings, the tile flooring, the stained-glass windows of the rooftop banquet room, and in the theater, the ornament begins to move. Here, Sullivan thought about line, rhythm, and plastic manipulation of surfaces.

The structure consists of traditional masonry walls outside, with an iron and steel frame inside.

## Guaranty Building, Buffalo (1895)

Here, Sullivan dealt esthetically with the structural system invented by the Chicago School in solving the problem of how to articulate the facades of ever taller buildings.

The Guaranty Building is carried entirely on a fireproof steel frame sitting on reinforced concrete foundations. Interior walls are movable partitions. On the outside, Sullivan's typical tripartite elevation is used: shops on ground- and second- floor level, uninterrupted, egalitarian office stack, top cornice. The building is arranged around an open light shaft. Every second pier in the office stack is free standing and does not represent the location of a skeleton upright. Spandrels separating the windows are recessed behind the vertical piers and carry the exterior walls on shelves.

The ornamentation intensifies the distinction among the major parts of the elevation by separating piers, spandrels, and cornice. The different treatment of piers and spandrels expresses their relative importance in the elevation. The top cornice provides a climactic termination of the building. The ornament here is embellishment designed to intensify awareness of construction and use, while simultaneously enhancing the expressive potential of the building.

The exterior is completely of terra cotta. The thinness of the exterior piers, and their linearity, make the exterior look like a skin. This exterior uses the same type of fluidity and extensiveness of the embellished surface as the interior of the auditorium. On the base, the ornament relies on the diamond shape. There is quite an abrupt division between base and office floors. There, the piers are decorated with rhythmic knobs, the spandrels with some kind of imitation of natural growth. At the corners of the top, abstract plant life seems to tie the rooftop to the corner piers. The top slab is related to the building volume by a cavetto curve.

The tall office building was conceived by Sullivan as a repetitive, orthogonal structure, which could be extended horizontally as well as vertically. The interior volumes were continuous.

## Carson Pirie Scott & Co. Store, Chicago (1899-1904)

This design was built in three stages. First, the low wing to the left of the corner tower, three bays wide was built; then, in 1903-4, the portion on top of this wing and the rest of the corner and other wing; then, in 1906, five more bays were added to the longer wing.

Here, Sullivan was faced with a different building type. A department store needed large, uninterrupted floors. Hence, this building was to be long, not tall. Neither horizontal nor vertical is emphasized; instead, the marble blocks of the horizontal and vertical masonry skin of the building are on the same level. Here, the horizontal line dominates only in the stringcourses lining the windows. The walls consist of a rectangular grid into which broad Chicago windows are set. The tripartite division still shines through in the lavishly decorated ground floor, the floor stack above and the flat rooftop. Material used is glazed white tile. In this composition, Sullivan used his most exuberant floral ornament, together with his most forthright expression of the structural nature of skeletal framing.

The corner tower provides a vertical pull against the horizontal wings. The ornament there mainly attracts prospective shoppers.

FIGURE 32–1. Auditorium Building, Chicago.

FIGURE 32–2. Carson Pirie Scott & Co. Store, Chicago.

# Chapter 33

# Art Nouveau

This style constituted a major break with the existing architectural situation. It deviated from the reigning Beaux-Arts classicism. Its achievements were a transformation of the anatomy and spatial character of architecture. Forms were controlled by functional discipline and a tendency to express structure and material.

There are a number of theories as to its origins. Some state that this movement originated in Belgium ca. 1892-4. Reasons for this view can be found in the avant-garde culture in this country at this time, the stylistic (and formal) impact of symbolist painting, and of the English Arts and Crafts movement. This latter movement also had a pedagogical influence. Others see its origins in graphics and the decorative arts.

Interestingly, there is also the attempt to derive the new style from the historical traditions of each country. Gaudi in Spain, Guimard in France, Mackintosh in Scotland, and Wright in the U.S. all exhibit this nationalistic trend.

## TASSEL HOUSE, VICTOR HORTA, BRUSSELS (1892-3)

The consolidating phase of Art Nouveau is usually associated with Brussels, especially the architectural work of Horta from ca. 1893-1905. This building is considered the event of this style's birth. It is a design without precedent, and exhibits the characteristic features of the style. It presented a synthesis of architecture and the decorative arts, and boldly declared new formal principles. Horta was partly influenced by Viollet-le-Duc's theories. This design rejected tradition and aimed instead at a new architecture. The new style was a synthesis of formal inspirations from the English Arts-and-Crafts, structural emphasis of French Rationalism, and shapes and structures abstracted from nature.

The building is one in a row of town houses. The exterior is not radically different from its neighbors, but impresses with the bowing central volume. The stonework is restrained, and an iron beam is discreetly exposed. The attempt was to subject modern materials to a traditional sense of craftsmanship.

Inside is a revolutionary staircase terminating in a winter garden on top. A metal skeleton supports wooden steps. The framework is frankly expressed and shaped in elegant flowing curves. Its forms are reflected in the floor and wall decorations. The formal vegetal motifs are gradually transformed into banisters, wallpaper, and floor mosaics. The emphasis is on the direct use of a modern material. The expressions of growth and tension recall contemporary interests in empathy and point to organic analogies of building.

## GLASGOW SCHOOL OF ART, MACKINTOSH, GLASGOW (1897-1909)

A spirit of conservatism and reverence for national traditions has always guided English culture. Mackintosh's designs were therefore partly influenced by Gothic architecture. However, he transmuted the typical Art Nouveau convolutions into geometric abstractions. He developed the floral Art Nouveau forms toward a more sober expression consisting of broad dispositions of simple masses and sequences of dynamic spaces.

The Scottish Art Nouveau development is a mixture of the rational/rectangular forms from the English Domestic Revival, and the sinuous shapes of continental Art Nouveau.

The eastern half of the main façade up to the entrance was built first; the western one was completed after additional funds had been secured. Mackintosh won the competition for this commission in 1896. The original building dates from 1897; it was enlarged in 1906-09. The long campaign allowed Mackintosh to modify his forms and details in tune with his evolving ideas.

The site is on an impossibly steep slope. The program included studios, a lecture theater, a library, a room and private studio for the director, and exhibition spaces. Mackintosh seemed to let programme determine the main scheme of this design. Especially the window dimensions are entirely determined by use, thus making this design a proto-Modernist example of architecture. Ultimately, the design is considering both what happens inside the building and what is demanded by the site and context of it.

The building has an E-shaped plan aligned in the east-west direction. Workshops in the basement are stepped down a deep slope on the southern side. Additional functional spaces are placed on the east and west façades. The south, or rear, part of the building housed the top-lit museum. This scheme results in a rich sequence of different spaces and different qualities of light. A central and two end staircases serve for access. The central staircase rises through the museum spaces, and seems to reach through the skylight frame. Thus, an entering visitor learns instantly about the purpose of this building. A library and meeting rooms take up the rear additions on either end.

The main façade was placed at the highest level. It is asymmetrical, maybe as a result of the long building campaign. Studios are at the front of the building toward the northern side, laid out in two tiers. As a result, it is mostly opened up, with huge studio windows. There is also an attic story. To the rear are hallways connecting these studios. The windows derive partly from Shaw's Queen Anne Revival, especially in their division. The whole wall suggests a functionalist, abstract building. The elevation of the main façade fuses symmetrical and asymmetrical articulation. The entrance bay is eclectic and monumental, combining a vernacular bay window with a Baroque aedicula and a manorial tower. The director's office is placed above the entrance. The entrance bay is a free-form sculptural design placed asymmetrically. The geometric severity of masonry and fenestrations is partly obliterated through metal screens of sinuous lines. The side façades are formed of large stone expanses, subtly articulated. They recall Mackintosh's interest in regional farmhouse prototypes and Scottish baronial halls.

The linear quality of Art Nouveau artwork was here used to define spaces. The building excels in geometrical control and a tendency toward abstraction. Imaginative play is introduced by the curvilinear metalwork, which forms a transparent screen in front of the masonry façade. It appears as if the internal space is allowed to burst through the skin. Mackintosh had a unique sense of combining sensuous and structural elements in the same piece. While the wooden structures inside are assembled from basic carpentry techniques, they impart a feeling of Japanese architecture. Inside, light and views are controlled by varying the height of individual spaces.

In 1906, a library wing was added to this school on the western side. It is two stories high and reaches to a third floor skylight. It is a completed hollow space, and a complete object. On the outside are tall vertical windows, inside rectangular wood brackets.

There is an overall expression of structure in the exposed brickwork, roof timbers, and columns and balcony beams in the library. There is an interplay of use and ornament.

There are allusions to Scottish architecture, especially to the tower-houses and baronial manor houses in the wings.

Ultimately the building draws distinction through its symbiotic combination of form and function.

# ANTONIO GAUDI (1852-1926)

His work begins with traditional eclecticism, but he was also influenced by Gothic architecture and structural rationalism. Generally, his work is bold and full of sensational effects, and shows a capacity to grasp the qualities of the materials used. He was rather original and idiosyncratic.

## Casa Battlò, Barcelona (1905-7)

His architectural works began as an abstraction of medieval forms. He then transformed these prototypes, motivated by his private imagery and his obsession with finding a regionalist style for Catalonia.

This house was a remodeling job. Its façade allows the playing of a sport of spotting analogies. There are maritime references, bones, jaws, and even a dragon on the roof. This imagery refers to Barcelona's patron saint St. George and the Catalan struggle for independence.

## Casa Milá, Barcelona (1905-10)

This building has stores on the slightly elevated ground floor, an owner's apartment on the second floor, and rentable apartments above.

Here, plan, interiors, and exteriors are all subordinated under a plastic conception of swirling curves. The façade is of cut stone, laid in traditional load-bearing manner. Deeply cut, overlapping ledges articulate the main façade. Wave and cliff images come to mind. The wrought-iron balconies mimic seaweed.

Due to the use of elevators, Gaudí eliminated a grand staircase for the upper floors. There are two oval light courts inside the building mass. The floor plans are independent from the structural system, and vary.

The structural system consists of point supports. Brick supports hold iron girders and beams. Curved peripheral iron beams isolate the façade from the building.

## Sagrada Familia, Barcelona (1884-1926)

This church was begun by Francisco del Villar. Gaudi took over in 1884. The crypt followed 13th and 14th-century models. The lowest visible levels were designed by Gaudi, still following a Gothic manner; however, slightly changed. From then on upwards, Gaudi's personal style emerges. From forms superficially resembling Art Nouveau, finally a language of evocations of vegetable stems and dream-like anatomies evolves. At the same time, Gaudi reconciled the fantastic with the practical, since all forms are rooted in structural principles, namely variations on the parabolic curve, thus eliminating the need for flying buttresses. Such seemingly practical laws of structure were seen by Gaudi, not only as derived from the physics of materials, but they also gave evidence to the Creator of all design. This exhibits partly a pantheistic view.

The plan consists of five naves with transepts of three naves.

Gaudi's work points to one reason that may have doomed Art Nouveau. This is the highly subjective approach to form.

# METRO STATIONS, HECTOR GUIMARD, PARIS (1899-1904)

These showed the public application of the style. Guimard received these commissions after a competition had produced mostly academic designs. Naturally inspired forms were used to shape banisters, lampposts, and furnishings. All were mass-produced by adapting three basic types. Type 1 consisted of a simple railing and open steps. The railing grows from the cement base and contains shields containing the letter M. Two stem-like forms form the arch through which the steps are reached. Type 2 (Porte Dauphine) has lava and glass panels supporting the roof over the steps. Type 3 was a pavilion with a waiting room.

Guimard successfully combined industrial prefabrication with creative individual design, thus bridging the opposition between Arts-and-Crafts and industry.

# PALAIS STOCLET, HOFFMANN, BRUSSELS (1905-11)

This commission was for a financier. It was to combine the functions of museum, luxury residence, and an exemplary setting for modern taste.

The box of this building is articulated through flat planes. Clerestory windows separate the lid of this box, making it appear lightweight. The volume of the building is broken down into squares, edged with dark bands. This system, which was worked out in his (Stoclet's) earlier furniture designs, is here achieved by marble slabs with bronze edgings. The exterior is picturesque, combining devices of formality and informality.

The plan linked rooms en suite, employing ingenious changes of direction and axes. Major spaces were expressed as protrusions from the façade.

Inside is an array of dazzling spaces. The whole is devoid of traditional ornamentation, but instead is incrustated with luxurious materials and murals.

**FIGURE 33–1.** Tassel House, Brusssels, exterior.

**FIGURE 33–2.** Casa Battiò, Barcelona

FIGURE 33–3. Casa Mila, Barcelona.

FIGURE 33–4. Casa Mila, interior showing parabolic arches.

FIGURE 33–5. Sagrada Familia, Barcelona, distant view.

FIGURE 33–6. Sagrada Familia, Barcelona, exterior showing parabolic transept entrance.

FIGURE 33–7. Sagrada Familia, interior showing columns supports for the transept vaults.

FIGURE 33–8. Bastille Metro Station, Paris, entrance.

FIGURE 33–9. Palais Stoclet, Brussels.

# Chapter 34

# Modernist Beginnings

## PRECONDITIONS FOR MODERN ARCHITECTURE

During the 19$^{th}$ century, the arrival of a new architecture was dependent on the invention of a novel structural system. New architecture, around 1850, always meant a contemporary style, or a style that would serve, and derive from, the present.

In the succeeding years, these demands were rejected in favor of eclecticism. Demands for a new architecture were, to a minor degree, instigated by the new materials and technologies and by a craving for originality. Notions about a modern style originated in the 18$^{th}$-century idea of progress. History was perceived as progressing through epochs, each of which manifested its spiritual core in cultural works. Similarly important was the 18$^{th}$-century development of empiricism, which resulted in the loss of the earlier authority of Renaissance and Antique norms.

Cultural and social reasons for the demand for a new style can be found in the attraction of invention, the ideas of progress, liberty, and reform. Technical innovators became the spokesmen for a new architecture. This may be the reason for the slow pace with which this new style came. Most practicing architects were too embedded in the existing traditions to attempt anything radically new.

Nevertheless, there were some architects who managed to transcend superficial issues of stylistic clothing. Schinkel, Labrouste, and Richardson were able to produce convincing syntheses of form and content by probing the principles of past styles and translate these into vocabularies of their own that were appropriate to the social state of their time.

Among the most promising development in the 19$^{th}$ century was that of a rationalist point of view toward the creation of a new style. This had begun with Durand and continued with Viollet-le-Duc. However, hardly anybody in this period was able to execute the leap from idea to form.

The architects of the 1890s and 1900s, in their proposals, drew on tradition and nature, but their methods involved a greater degree of abstraction than before.

During the early years of the 20$^{th}$ century, the European architectural mainstream was in close touch with reality, especially with the mechanomorphic world. In this period, geometric abstraction and Classicism were overlaid over one another. A lot of credit for this new direction must go to Art Nouveau, which had shown a way out of 19th-century eclecticism through abstraction and natural/structural functionalism. Nevertheless, the International Style, with few exceptions, was born out of a reaction against Art Nouveau.

Among the most important ideas that propelled the formulation of a modern style was that of rationality. Practicality, function, and structural rationality were promoted as those elements which, when strictly followed, would produce good design.

## STOCK EXCHANGE, BERLAGE, AMSTERDAM (1897-1903)

Hendrik P. Berlage (1856-1934) was trained in the structural rationalism of Viollet-le-Duc. His main theoretical contribution was to bring this architect's medievally inspired thoughts up-to date.

Berlage & Sanders won fourth prize in the competition of 1885. Berlage received the commission in 1897 and the building campaign began in 1898. The competition design was a palatial Dutch Renaissance building. When finally hired as artistic advisor, Berlage revised this scheme.

Stylistically, this building is a revival of Flemish Romanesque and Gothic, a choice based on Viollet-le-Duc. The entrance resembles a drawing for a door for the castle at Pierrefonds by Viollet. The style, however, served only as the basis of an original constructional analysis, and functional considerations played a great part. A number of decorative details are inventions by Berlage, and not copied.

Berlage was also interested in the handling of planes and volumes, as well as the role of mathematics in the coordination of elements. His concept of "unity in diversity" was not just meant to govern the building design, but also social structures.

Materials used were stone and bricks. Each material is given its own character and used according to its functional capability. Brick produced the modulated wall planes, hewn stone the transitional elements, and iron the wide spans.

# SECESSION BUILDING, OLBRICH, VIENNA (1898-99)

The attempt of the Vienna Secession was to find an alternative to florid Art Nouveau. The exterior consists of closed walls formed into a geometric massing with historical allusions and non-historicist decorations. The façade is Egyptianesque. This was partly influenced by Mackintosh. Viennese Art Nouveau at the beginning of the 20th century favored a straightening of forms, clearly seen in the Secession building.

The cultic, ritualistic decoration suggests roots in the turn-of-century interests in mysticism and primitivism. The decorative program is related to the Sacred Spring (Ver Sacrum), the Roman ritual of the consecration of youth in times of national danger. The laurel leaf dome creates associations to the myth of Apollo. The Medusa frieze above the door symbolizes the fertile force of the unconscious, and Minerva's owls guard the fortunes of the arts inside. Tree motifs on the building's corners reinforce the theme of the sacred spring.

In its forms, the building abstracts historic forms, primarily referring to pre-classicism, thus making the building an attack on the formal language of 19th-century Viennese historicism.

The interior is open and laid out around a sky lit courtyard.

The Secession building is across from Fischer von Erlach's Karlskirche, and the façade attempts to respond wittily to the earlier building.

Contemporary nicknames for the building included Golden Cabbage and Mahdi's Tomb.

# POST OFFICE SAVINGS BANK, WAGNER, VIENNA (1904-06)

The site demanded a trapezoidal plan.

The main façade is organized according to classical principles. The base is distinguished by the use of larger stones than those on the façade, and the roofline is set off by an attic and a balustraded cornice. The main entrance, as well as the corners, is framed by projecting wall parts.

These traditional features are balanced with modern details. The marble plates of the façade are bolted to the underlying iron frame. Metal is used throughout the façade, including aluminum for the female figures on top of the building (one symbolizing Business, the other Thrift).

The central interior space, the banking hall, is adapted from the basilica form. Slender piers, encased halfway up in aluminum, with lamp capitals, support the nave vault. Its floor is of glass tiles. There are many architectural details that have been designed strictly for function.

This building embodies the functionalist high-technology mechanomorphism of Wagner. The interior derives from the 19th-century ferrovitreous tradition of railway stations and exhibition halls. It was a non-historicist reshaping of engineering into monumental architecture. Piers taper downward, and curving and straight linear vocabularies are mixed. Rivets are used decoratively. This is a nuts-and-bolts rationality, no longer the dynamic tendrils and curves of Art Nouveau.

Wagner's philosophy here was a realistic one. To create a well-lit and spacious interior, one must on occasion use modern technology. This is like looking at a landscape painting done in the open, as opposed to looking at a historical painting full of mythological figures. Ornament was subordinated to function.

The rear portions of this building were added in 1910-12.

# ROBIE HOUSE, WRIGHT, CHICAGO (1908-09)

Wright's designs expressed discontent with the existing situation. He had a good deal of self-confidence, and basically invented his own architectural idiom. Contemporary houses for the upper class had become status symbols, stages for entertainment, and a measure of wealth. Wright proposed a new residential concept. This concept was based on his conviction that buildings should serve human needs and reflect human size, not be showplaces, status symbols, or museums.

This resulted in houses in which the scale was small. Walls reached from the ground, a water table, to the second-story windowsill. The roof projected widely, and the underside of the eave was painted in a light color to further reflect and diffuse light. While being two or three levels, the houses generally looked lower and began to associate with the ground. The outside reflected the interior, as the walls were screens that did not obstruct the interior flow of space. The façade hardly matters any more. The lower floors were generally treated as one room, cutting off the kitchen as a laboratory. Various portions of the big room were screened for domestic purposes like dining, reading, or social activities. The number of doors was reduced, except in the upper floors, where bedroom privacy still demanded traditional boxes. Interior trim was meant to induce a sense of lowness, intimacy, and warmth (by way of horizontal bands of plaster on the walls above the windows in the same color as the ceiling), as well as adding a feeling of movement, spaciousness, and flow (through continuous rows of contrasting trim). Wright wanted to combine a sense of rootedness and protection with a sense of freedom and mobility.

These houses also indicated a move away from historical styles, because Wright felt them to be unable to accommodate interiors demanding greater functional and visual variety. However, the Prairie Style was as emotionally reassuring as any other style. It had an elementary law and order of its own. The fireplaces, low intimate ceilings, rich primary colors, and natural materials, and its supreme common sense fulfilled a psychological need to feel at ease in knowable surroundings. The close association with the ground indicated the human impulse to live close to the soil. The horizontal line was the line of domesticity. The increase in window space (casement windows that opened outward) and their protection, through the overhangs, even from rain, symbolized a working partnership with nature. Wright thus destroyed the traditional box to achieve a dynamic interaction of interior and exterior space.

Around 1900, Wright's plans tended to become cross-shaped (he virtually introduced this kind of plan to American residential architecture).

The Robie House appears longer and lower than it actually is, mainly because of the widely cantilevered roof with sweeping, uninterrupted trim, and the extended fenestration on the second floor. Through the contrasting horizontals and verticals, this building remains in a state of perpetual tension. Nevertheless, the parts are proportionally fitted to each other, and the chimney serves as a major unifying feature.

The house is a safe, secure family place, strong and sheltering. The living quarters are raised off the ground, guarded by the long wall of the terrace. Thus, the building stipulates independence, without withdrawal, group solidarity without rejection of the community.

The main spaces on the main living level are arranged in a linear fashion, almost like in an ocean steamer, totally opened by windows.

# AEG TURBINE FACTORY, BEHRENS, BERLIN (1909)

Behrens was hired by the AEG Company, as probably the first industrial designer, in 1907.

The factory is structurally a series of steel arches. Each arch has three joints. One rests on the street side, on concrete pedestals, the other on the steel frame of the adjoining lower hall, and the third on top of the seven-pointed gable. The posts on the street side are square in section; the arches on top are of frame construction. The posts are pointed toward their resting points. A tie rod is inserted at the springing of the arches. On top of the building is a long shed window to air the interior.

This utilitarian shed was then converted into a noble architectural monument with a clear hint to a classical temple. With this, an industrial factory is given the same style as would have been used for a monumental public building. Nevertheless, the absence of overt historicism, and the incorporation of construction elements in the design, make this a prototypical modern building. Behrens expresses the engineering underneath this architecture. His architectural space is therefore reduced to the place of production. The classicizing façade alludes to the tensions of the soul, by giving them monumental significance. The façades set up the activities inside as special, as separate from the urban context. The entire building then becomes a sacred place of labor.

The "temple front" is not a supporting part of this building, but was simply added to the front. The massive-looking corner piers are actually of thin concrete walls with iron bands to articulate their function to fill in the corners. They are not load bearing. The tympanum is supported by the steel frame of the big window. The middle part of the resulting temple front consists of a glass curtain wall, flush with the pediment above, but clearly separated from the corner piers.

The whole is thus a mixture of old and new, but also of a careful orchestration of visual lightness and massiveness. Nevertheless, Behrens proved for the first time that a marriage between functional and esthetic/historicist design was possible. The windows on the side façade taper inwards, to prevent glaring light inside. The corner piers have the same taper. This detail articulates visually between the historicist, stylistic allusions and the novel construction of this building. To reinforce this point, the front window is flush with the (steel) entablature. Hence, the building consists of an interweaving of two buildings, one with vertical pieces forming the structural plane, and one with tapering pieces forming the supported wall. The steel supports rest on a joint at the bottom, further increasing the ambiguity of this design. On one hand, this refers to the Classical post-and-beam structure; on the other, it expresses the better potential of steel over traditional materials. Behrens promoted a new unity of technology and art. The classical allusions proclaim the architectural dignity of this industrial building. However, he abstracted the stylistic details, so that the building could be perceived according to the conditions of the modern, industrial world. According to Behrens, architecture needed to present solid, calm planes so that the viewer speeding by in the new transportation means could still get a complete image of the building.

# FAGUS FACTORY, GROPIUS, ALFELD (1911-3)

This is frequently given credit as the first modern building. Its modernity is revealed in the glass walls. The main intention was to be more modern than Behrens, making it then the antithesis to the Turbine Factory. Gropius's goal was to build a palace to labor. The workers must be given light, air, and cleanliness. The design must express the dignity of the communal idea that guides the entire enterprise.

Gropius was hired when the foundations were already built. He had just left Behrens's office and had sent out letters soliciting work to, among others, the owner of this factory. Gropius was to provide external improvements. He convinced the client to let him redesign the superstructure without reference to eclecticism.

The structure is a post-and-slab system. The exterior consists of slender brick supports, carrying a simple brick-faced parapet. The rest is made of glass curtain walls. These are innovative, as the parapet walls in conventional stone architecture was eliminated, by integrating its sheet metal panels into the window grid. A massive pavilion serves as main entrance, but the corners of the building are dissolved into glass. The glass panels are hung in front of the structural system, as in a reversion of Behrens's system at the Turbine Factory; Gropius here tapered the supports toward the inside.

The entrance façade, with a brick pavilion placed off center, is an exercise in abstract composition. It not only adds a layer in front of the cubical building mass, but also introduces a color and texture duality into this façade.

In fact, this building is purely esthetic, that is, the architect has composed his façade as a series of infinitely repetitive motifs, but has not given it the unbreakable contour, as well as the formal coherence and surface tension that we associate with conventional architecture.

# CENTURY HALL, MAX BERG, BRESLAU (1912-13)

This hall was built to hold large congregations of people, as well as to serve as a space for exhibitions. For reasons of fireproofing and economy, it was built entirely in reinforced concrete. In plan, it is a circle with four semicircular apses. It could hold 10,000 spectators. The dome provides a structure supporting the stepped rings of windows outside. These windows were placed vertically so that a distinct light atmosphere could be provided inside, instead of having merely walls broken by openings. The diameter of the skeletal dome inside is sixty-seven meters. It rests on a circular pulling ring, which is supported by four outward leaning arches, thus making this a dome resting on a circle. On top is a sixteen meter-wide pushing circle. There are thirty-two ribs.

This is among the rare buildings attempting a use of concrete more adequate to its potentials. Here, the material is understood to be poured and molded, and to perform best in arcuate structures. It contains a few echoes of the past, namely bridge structures in the base and a Pantheon-like superstructure. The only change to this source is the inversed lighting. Here, the oculus is dark while the lower parts of the dome are bright. The solid oculus improves the acoustics inside. The pendentives between the support piers and the circle supporting the ribs of the dome were filled in later.

# FUTURISM

This was the enthusiastic reaction of some radicals to the industrial revolution. Futurist architecture was to come totally out of industry. The old tradition was dead; the new one was that of the machine. This meant destroying the existing social situation between art and architecture, which were deemed academic and eclectic. Architectural inspiration must come from the new mechanical world. Similarly, architecture was to be part of the transitory and expendable equipment of the Industrial Age. It was to express new spiritual attitudes, but also find forms appropriate to new materials and means of construction.

## ANTONIO SANT'ELIA (1888-1916)

His designs were intended to show simultaneously destruction and construction. There is an emphasis on gigantism, verticalism, and structural dynamics. All conventions are destroyed, and the sketches are a kind of heroic swashbuckling.

## STUDIES FOR ARCHITECTURAL FORMS (1912-13)

These designs are developed out of geometrical solids into a combination of positive and negative shapes. This practice creates a contrast between open and closed forms. Flat planes are sometimes articulated as grids. Diagonal planes and cylinders are favored elements. New forms are invented by molding sculptural planes and eliminating flourish. The drawing style is literally cubist, emphasizing clearly defined planes, which are allowed to intersect. The spatial concept is total, radiating from the building volumes. Straight lines are used to suggest three-dimensional volumes, and the drawing style is economic.

Subsequently, Sant'Elia drew relationships between these forms and particular building types associated with industry: power stations and dams. Then, he evolved toward the terraced building and finally the Città Nuova. He thus used a Modernist subject matter.

These designs are symmetrical and axially arranged. Steel (with glass) and reinforced concrete are the materials. Reinforced concrete is simply used to create building volumes, not in any progressive structural articulation. The choice of perspective suggests that the effect of the drawing was considered, most probably in an attempt to appropriate visual techniques from Futurist painters. Sant'Elia was attempting to realize a three-dimensional notion of dynamism through creating dynamic sensations.

## CITTÀ NUOVA (1913-14)

The entire design is a perspectival compilation of Sant'Elia's earlier building types, not so much a clearly defined urban proposal. The two main components are terraced buildings and traffic systems. The sketches show interacting urban activities and the city is depicted as a fully three-dimensional structure. The buildings have a base of two stories, then step back. Elevator shafts are added, as well as masts, and so on, on top. The building volumes are seen as capable of expression. The traffic system relies on streets and other connectors that are articulated as movement streams.

Here, architecture and the industrial metropolis form a unity. This unity expresses a uniform lifestyle and the loss of personal intimacy. Individual buildings of this new city were meant for huge masses of people. Modern cosmopolitanism has no use for royal, religious, or spiritual monuments. New comforts, such as fast communications, hygiene, and so on, require new forms of architecture. As the essence of the machine is power and speed, the Futurist city was to be one of movement. The buildings shape an infinite spatiality and follow the large-scale movement patterns brought by mass transportation, production, and entertainment. They adhere to Futurist concepts, above all the idea that objects do not finish where others begin, and that they can be cut up or sectionalized by curves. The world of the Città Nuova is seen as in flux. Man and machine are united. Buildings could be imbued with kinetic energy. The new city was to arise like an immense and tumultuous shipyard.

Sant'Elia faced the formidable project of realizing the ideal conception of Futurist architecture in actual buildings. He attempted this by using metal frame construction with glass, to make his buildings transparent, floating, and moving. He used light in the form of actual lights and advertisements, and focused on mobile elements, such as elevators. The goal was to create seemingly mobile architecture, houses of air that appear to be suspended from the sky. This was called "atmospheric architecture." These designs diminish the importance of the façade.

Such dynamism is shown in the Apartment Tower project. Here, the whole structure arches backward over a maze of service features. Tiers of bridges, setbacks, and advertisements are part of the articulation. The building is part of a bridge spanning a transportation channel. The main emphasis is on circulation, not vista. The Central Station project brings out the sense of architecture in machine-like motion. This is not conventional architecture, but rather a new transportation hub, intersected by a network of movement. The machine world is accepted and realized, and symbolized in simple, powerful geometrical form. The architecture has strong links with function and leaves structural systems naked, without decoration. Individual forms follow principles of harmony and attempt to create beauty through lines and shapes. In this aspect the sketches portray a sensitivity and state of mind.

The architectural experiments of the first fourteen years of the 20th century in Europe were all characterized by the lack to find an aesthetic discipline that would make sense of transparencies, cantilevers, glass walls, and other technical inventions. This aesthetic did in the end not come out of architectural theory, but from the contemporary developments in painting, namely those toward pure abstract art promoted by the Cubists and Futurists.

**FIGURE 34–1.** Secession Building, Vienna, exterior.

**FIGURE 34–2.** Pos Officel Savings Bank, Vienna, exterior.

**FIGURE 34–3.** Post Office Savings Bank, interior banking hall.

**FIGURE 34–4.** Robie House, Chicago, exterior.

**FIGURE 34–5.** AEG Turbine Factory, Berlin.

# Chapter 35

# International Style

Around 1920, the various pre-WWI strands of modernist intentions tended to converge, and became the International Style. In its heyday, International Style design emphasized simple cubic volumes, stripped planar shapes, open plans, and machine-age details. Typical features of Modern buildings were strip windows, flat roofs, grids of supports, cantilevered horizontal planes, metal railings, and curved partitions. More general aspects include the tendency to use simple rectangular volumes articulated by crisply cut openings, and the emphasis on hovering planes and interpenetrating spaces. An interesting aspect of the International Style is its functionalism. Hardly any of the famed examples is a straightforward functional solution to the given program. Rather, they use a priori images, resulting in a style of symbolic forms, which referred to the notion of functionality.

Bourgeois society reached a state of autonomy for art. Sacred art had consisted of cult objects that were collectively produced and enjoyed. Courtly art had been made of representational objects that were individually created and communally enjoyed. Bourgeois art portrays the bourgeois self-understanding, is individually produced and enjoyed, and is separated from life, especially as l'art pour l'art.

Avant garde art tries to re-integrate art into life, by redefining the life-content not as an industrial means-end existence, but the opposite. Art presents the values that do not have a place in capitalist competition.

Art is sublated into life through a dialectical process of cancellation and preservation. On one hand, art projects the image of a better life; on the other hand, it is pure fiction without practical power, that is, it relieves society of the pressures these images would otherwise have.

These intentions are carried out in avant garde art by negating individual creation and reception. Generally, the avant garde tries to destroy the autonomy of art.

The main characteristic of an avant garde work is that of newness, that is, the complete break with tradition. The "new" refers not only to artistic techniques or stylistic principles, but also to the whole tradition of art. Thus, avant garde art is not a differently packed existing good.

The break with tradition comes out partly in the elevation of chance to the main creative element. Chance can be produced directly (action painting), or mediated (submission to the chance of construction).

Similar effects are created through fragmentation and re-assembly (in literature) and montage (in the visual arts). This principle was used as artistic principle in Cubist collages and by John Heartfield. By introducing fragments of reality into the artwork, the former unity of it is destroyed. Similarly, meaning is no longer provided, resulting in a feeling of shock in the viewer. Consequently, interpretation rather goes along formal approaches or the understanding of the construction process.

## SCHRÖDER SCHRÄDER HOUSE, RIETVELD, UTRECHT (1924)

This building was designed in collaboration with the client, Truus Schröder. It terminates a row of suburban houses. It is formed from intersecting planes, some of which appear to float. Everything seems to be in a state of tension. Wall surfaces are gray or white, articulating detail in primary colors and black. The design expresses austerity and simplicity as a more appropriate way of life for the Modern age. Inside, every aspect is integrated into the overall design intention and style. Upstairs are working/sleeping areas and a living room. The upper floor is flexible and partionable, and equipment and furniture are built-in. The lower floor houses studios and a kitchen/living area. Here, walls are fixed in place, but clerestory windows link the spaces. The whole building creates a wonderful contrast between the formal qualities of the exterior and the ingeniousness of the interior layout. The design was worked out in a model, using demountable cardboard panels.

# BAUHAUS BUILDING, GROPIUS, DESSAU (1925-26)

Modern buildings share a few characteristics. They derive from simple stereometric shapes, they appear as unitary volumes wrapped in a thin weightless skin, and they show a lack of material texture and articulating detail. In 1926, Gropius completed a new campus for the Bauhaus. It was built on an empty, unconstricted site. The layout of the building was determined by the goal to achieve maximum daylighting, ease of internal circulation, and clarity of the different functional façade articulations. Flexibility for future changes was also a factor. The plan consists of two L-shaped forms intersecting and overlapping one another. These were arranged in a pinwheel plan straddling an existing street. The building's asymmetry expresses the modern spirit. Classrooms were on one side, linked by a bridge of faculty offices to the workshop wing on the other side. Attached to the workshop wing were dining halls and student housing. The one-story connection housed the auditorium and the cafeteria, which could be combined through partition walls. The student residences were combined studios and living quarters. The plan is thus functional, while also opening the buildings into the exterior and creating a dynamic overall shape. Walking around the building reveals the three-dimensional character of the entire composition. The main volumes are broken down, and could be experienced from every angle without losing overall coherence. The various volumes are rectangular shapes of various sizes, linked by oblong pieces. All buildings are covered with flat roofs; that of the student wing was used as a roof terrace.

All surfaces were either of white stucco or glass. Fenestration brings out the functional differences. Façade articulation was achieved through windows, which were functionally (relating to size, use, and need of light for the rooms) sized. It appears that Gropius was given a large amount of plate glass, which had to be integrated into the design. This requirement seemed to go well with the design philosophy of the building. Glass either accentuates the skin quality of the exterior or, by being recessed, the hovering quality of the white walls. Each wing has a different articulation, expressing the different activities taking place inside. The workshop wing is completely glazed and transparent, allowing one to see the structural frame behind this wall. Gropius claimed that this building – because it was based on the school's programmatic requirements and spiritual life – had designed itself.

The design took clues from Corbusier's Dom-Ino structure and Mies van der Rohe's Concrete Office Building. Form and façade articulations derive from function, the structure from the materials, and surface from the materials. Thus, the exterior becomes space-defining, no longer articulating stories or emphasizing certain parts of the façade. The structure was of a reinforced concrete skeleton with floor slabs and brick walls. The interiors were furnished by the Bauhaus workshops. The building was damaged by the Nazis during World War II. It was renovated in 1976.

# GERMAN PAVILION, MIES VAN DER ROHE, BARCELONA (1929)

For Mies, space exists as a continuum. He promoted the theory that the artistic expression of architecture must derive directly from the crafts, which in his case was industrial technology. His architecture is based on the practice and skill of crafts, less on theory (although the designs were to present distilled ideals). He created a style of luxury born out of the simple factory shed. He demonstrated sensitivity toward materials. He integrated the universal precision of technology into the domain of culture.

The overall paradox in Mies's works stems from the fact that he dematerialized materiality. His buildings and projects are articulated as a balance between Classicism (in structure) and Modernism (in materials).

Mies was a rationalist who elevated his art to a form of visual poetry. His designs were lyrical demonstrations and realizations of the Modernist style. In this respect, he liquidated the traditional language of art in favor of that of technique. For him, there is no gap between the object and its representation, as he saw modern culture as representing its void through the loss of memory and intimacy.

His plans are either symmetrical and ordered, or based on dynamic rotation and centrifugal play of planes.

The German Pavilion had to represent the Weimar Republic by presenting an architectural space expressive of the industrial potential of the country. Mies received the commission through his client Hermann Lange, who mentioned his name to the director of the I.G. Farben concern, which was in charge of building the pavilion. The original building was only standing for eight months. It is primarily an aesthetic, not a functional, piece of architecture. The design embodies a synthesis of form and technique, of Modern and Classical values. It used the concepts of free plan and spatial continuum. Spatial effects were created uniquely by structural solutions. The entire aesthetic system derives its order from the structure. Walls, floors, and ceiling/roofs define space, but do not contain it. Walls are reduced to partitions. Expensive, reflecting materials were used to give this instrument of standardization a luxurious air. The pavilion is both opaque and transparent through the reflective surfaces. The ceilings were in white plaster. The roof plane is no longer a symbol of shelter. In its entirety, the design is a combination of structure, materials, technology, and the essential. There are no scale-providing details in this building. The whole complex is a compound where the perimeter is constantly fractured, that is, where forms inside seem to push through the enclosing wall.

As at the later Tugendhat House, here Mies presents a dialogue between column and wall. Walls symbolize their liberation from load-bearing duties, and only partition space. They are placed in a dynamic manner, offering a contrast to the regular symmetry of the eight columns. These two elements also introduce a contrast between tectonic and stereotomic elements, as well as between columnar and planar forms. The cruciform shape and the chromium-plated exterior skin of the columns also makes them part of the planar vocabulary of the building.

Similar impressions arise from the setting, the pavilion asymmetrically placed and contrasted with two pools. The Pavilion was a perfect expression of the time: the plan is similar to Mondrian paintings, the materials are employed factually, the wall surfaces are simple, and the space conception consists of floating planes, suggested illusions, and ambiguities. Schinkelian sources account for the reduction of forms to the simplest geometries.

It was recreated in 1986.

# TUGENDHAT HOUSE, MIES VAN DER ROHE, BRNO (1929-30)

The lot for this building is steeply sloped and faces south, overlooking a crastle and a city. Work on this commission proceeded together with the Barcelona Pavilion. The final design was presented in December 1928; construction began in June 1929, and the building was finished in December 1930. The Tugendhats lived in it until 1938, when they fled the Nazis to Venezuela. In 1963, the villa was granted status as a national cultural monument. It was renovated in 1969.

The interior layout intends to evoke a feeling of endless space. Floor and ceiling provided a spatial continuum interrupted only by the plate glass windows. The lower floor is designed as one large (living) room. It is subdivided by a freestanding onyx plane and a circular ebony wall. This wall encloses the dining alcove. These partitions organize a flow of space and circulation. The windows can be lowered into the ground, and a guardrail inside protects. A narrow conservatory flanks the narrow side of the living room and library. The upper floor had traditionally enclosed bedrooms. The entrance is behind a curved staircase wall. The entrance court is covered in travertine, and set between residential and service blocks. The house serves presently as a museum.

# WITTGENSTEIN HOUSE, WITTGENSTEIN & ENGELMANN, VIENNA (1926-28)

Paul Engelmann, a friend of the family, produced designs for a single-family house for Ludwig's sister, Margarethe Stonborough-Wittgenstein, in spring of 1926. In autumn of that year, Ludwig began to participate in the design, and subsequently produced its design independently. He received this commission from his sister as her attempt to offer therapy for his tormented mental state after World War I.

The building occupies the northern half of its plot, with the southern half becoming the garden. A high wall surrounds the lot, used to contain the landfill in the southern half of the lot to keep the whole grounds level. A curved pathway leads from the rear wall, to the main entrance to the house, on the opposite side. The house is built in reinforced concrete columns and beams, with walls either being reinforced concrete slabs or brick infill stuccoed over.

The entrance facade is vertically and horizontally divided into three parts. The main door is not placed axially, and projects from the wall of the house. There are a number of terraces adjoining the building on the ground floor and on upper stories.

On the ground floor are the living quarters and the bedroom for the woman of the house. The second floor contains the husband's bedroom, other bedrooms (also for the servants), and utilitarian spaces. The third floor contains the children's and guest bedrooms. The kitchen and laundry are in the basement. There is an elevator shaft that is enclosed entirely in glass. This allows the machinery to remain visible, and enhances the mechanical impression of the building.

Everything of, and in, the house was custom designed. Proportion was very important, as well as a look and mechanical precision that was machine-like. Door and window frames are of metal, and dividers are primarily vertical. The parts for all openings are the same, the measurements are different. The openings are proportioned to the walls in which they are set, and to their respective significance. The architecture consists only of a few parts: dark floors, light-coloured walls and ceilings, naked light bulbs. The light fixtures are placed axially and symmetrically. There are no carpets, chandeliers, or curtains. The design strikes one as being perfect, balanced, clear, rigorous, absolute, and non-subjective. The design is indeed the transposition of Wittgenstein's philosophical posture into architecture.

The door between the entrance hall and the salon demonstrates Wittgenstein's proportional design. In the hall, the connecting door is placed in the center of the wall, with its leafs having the same width as the framing wall pieces; in the salon, its dimensions determine all other wall dimensions. This connecting door then lines up perfectly with the exterior doors of the respective rooms. In the dining room, one wall is emphasized with four identical doors, one leading into the hall, the others to the outside terrace. A similar proportional rigor determines the columns in the house, which are full, half, and quarter ones.

In this house, Wittgenstein tried to eliminate stylistic concerns from architectural design. The house is composed spatially from within. Exterior and interior follow the same language. The house is non-expressive, and is indifferent to its materials. The building is simply present, without any social message.

# LOVELL BEACH HOUSE, R. SCHINDLER, NEWPORT BEACH (1922-26)

This building is generally considered one of the most important buildings of the modern movement in the U.S. In 1922, Schindler received the commission for the Lovell Beach House. He had met the Lovells through the sociocultural and educational activities of Mrs. Lovell. She was a kindergarten teacher at the Hollyhock Center, where she met Wright, and consequently also Schindler. Lovell was a fitness fanatic who believed in the power of nature and health, and advocated health food, exercise, abstinence from drugs, and nudism. He regarded himself as a modern person, and surrounded himself with members of the cultural avant-garde. He wrote one of the first fitness and health columns in the U.S.: "Care of the Body" for the LA Times.

At the time, Schindler was engaged in creating a new idea of "space architecture." He adopted the specific need of a family for a vacation house to create a "health house." The house is situated right next to the beach walk.

Exterior: The building combines structural efforts with a concern for space architecture. The form was influenced by local seaside pier architecture. The construction is functional, and the interrelations of the interior spaces reveal transparency. The building is raised on stilts to provide (1) privacy from the public beach, (2) a good view of the ocean and (3) the penetration of the beach underneath the house, as well as storage space underneath the house. The main features of the front facade are the cantilevered third floor and the five concrete frames. On the third floor, originally there were open sleeping porches. The entrance facade is partly transparent, with the concrete frames forming a portico and the ascending staircases a dissenting accent to this. The side elevation is dominated by horizontal lines and surfaces. The large windows are subdivided into smaller sections, to bring them closer to human scale. On the rear facade, the concrete frames are treated as pilasters.

Lovell wanted a progressive design that allowed as much sunshine as possible into the house, and Schindler was receptive to this demand. The concrete frames are kept outside the walls, so that the interior spaces are uninterrupted. The house consists of two rectangular volumes, a large open living space on the ground floor, and a number of small bedrooms lifted up under a common roof. The living hall is two stories high in the central part. Through the extensive use of glass, Schindler achieved a sort of outdoor living space with much light.

The structural system consists of the five frames, which function as both interior and exterior features. These frames support the interiors as "trays." Boards are laid over this frame to support the floors. The walls are two-inch thick cement plaster laid over metal lath and suspended from the frame. The exterior appearance is definitely "European Modernist."

# PSFS BUILDING, HOWE & LESCAZE, PHILADELPHIA (1931-32)

## COMMISSION

After leaving the firm of Mellor, Meigs & Howe, Howe practiced alone for a year. During this year, he got the commission for the PSFS Building. This commission had come to the earlier practice in 1926. Howe then designed a conservative, setback tower. The Society then conducted a test with a temporary structure, to make up its mind about what kind of structure to erect. At the completion of this test, Howe himself no longer liked his earlier design. In March 1929, he presented a more modern design, anticipating many features of the eventual building. In May, Lescaze joined Howe in a partnership. Howe was responsible for business relations, Lescaze for the drafting room and construction. William Lescaze (1896-1964) was born in Switzerland and studied architecture in Zürich. He came to the U.S. in 1920, worked for three years as a draftsman in Cleveland, and then moved to New York and opened his own office. Between December 1929 and July 1930, these two architects pretty much worked out the design and presented it in a model. Excavations began in February 1931.

## CLIENT

James Willcox, President of the Society, was instrumental in persuading the building committee to accept a rather modernistic building. He was autocratic, making many decisions about the building alone, with Howe. He accepted the building mainly because he felt it was practical.

## BUILDING

The building's massing can be accounted for mainly by practical features. The ground floor was given over to shops, the main bank room was on the second floor. This arrangement determined the base of the building: shop windows on the ground, cantilevered curved glass wall of banking room above. Topping this base are three more floors of bank spaces. Then follows the stack of rentable office floors. This tower is shaped to allow most light into the interior. On top is a huge billboard shielding the air conditioning exhausts. The office tower is basically a stack of equal floors. Vertical supports are pulled to the outside of the façades, thus eliminating the traditional horizontal layering associated with the International Style. This results in a balanced design, resting on both horizontals and verticals. There are separate entrances to the bank room and offices in two corners. Tower plan is in the form of T with separation of offices (in down stroke) and service/utilities (in cross bar of T). The structural columns for the office tower are supported on a deep truss (16.5 ft) that bridges the banking room in a sixty-three- foot span. This truss is supported on two rows of columns in the lower floors. The truss also houses the bank vaults and air conditioning equipment. Additional mechanical equipment is housed on the twentieth floor (window height reduced at this level). This is largely a masonry-sheathed building. Polished charcoal-colored granite on first two floors, sand-colored limestone on additional banking floors and tower piers, brick for the spandrels. Aluminum for window frames. Public spaces on the lower levels with marble inside.

# CASA DEL FASCIO, TERRAGNI, COMO (1932-36)

Modernism had come relatively late to Italy. In its use there, it did not emphasize functionalism and machine-aestheticism, but rather its similarity to stripped Classical forms. Terragni, during the 1930s, was the undisputed master at this combined Modernist/Classicist expression. He was able to forge a compromise between the traditionalist aspects of Fascist mythology, and modern, progressive ideas. Instead of continuing the Futurist break with the past, Terragni proposed that the new architecture should be the result of logic and rationality.

The Casa del Fascio was the local headquarters for the Fascist party in Como. It housed office and conference space, an assembly hall, a reading room, and a "sacrario." The building is a masterful essay in transparency. It presents a linear design as its main façade. This frame is a shell that defines the virtual volume of the building. Architectural effect is created by the juxtaposition of open and closed areas. While based on the Classical motif of support and load, it also symbolized Mussolini's intention to present Fascism as a glass house into which everybody can see. The open bays over the central courtyard allow the view of the surrounding hills from street level. The ground floor was opened with glass doors, which could be opened simultaneously. The plan (with interior courtyard) and material (marble) suggest a long-established iconography, rather than a machine symbolism. From the courtyard, party officials could be seen at work through windows. More purely architectural motifs were combined with the political expression. Terragni established dialectical relationships between trabeated and mural parts, strip and sash windows and natural and artificial light. The main façade, with its mural and open grid elevation, initiates a dialogue between Modern and traditional tectonic conceptions of architectural form. The same dialogue is articulated with windows on other sides of the building. The mural part may allude to the tower, which is a characteristic element of other Fascist headquarter buildings. In the end, the building was Terragni's personal interpretation of the political theme of this commission. He may have followed a strategy of indifference by treating form and function as independent from one another. Architectural considerations are independent from utilitarian requirements. The resulting building is an exercise in architectural language and a pleasant building, despite its original bad function.

FIGURE 35–1. Bauhaus Building, Dessau, Exterior showing workshop wing.

FIGURE 35–2. Bauhaus Building, Exterior showing dormitories and workshop wing.

FIGURE 35–3. German Pavilion, Barcelona, Exterior.

**FIGURE 35–4.** German Pavilion, Interior with statue by Georg Kolbe.

**FIGURE 35–5.** Wittgenstein House, Vienna, Exterior with main entrance.

FIGURE 35–6.  Lovell Beach House, Newport Beach, CA, Exterior.

FIGURE 35–7.  Casa del Fascio, Como, Exterior.

# Chapter 36

# Countermodernism

## EXPRESSIONISM

This movement should not primarily be seen as a revolt against the mainstream, namely the emerging International Style. It was rather the last flowering of stylistic developments before World War I. It is a style that rejects that architecture is conditioned only by utility, materials, construction, and economics. Expressionist designs were products of imagination and meant for the future. They were created in a visionary manner, by letting the hand draw automatically, and excluding the head. Expressionism was an attempt to invent a new and dynamic architecture that was symbolic. Its designs are characteristically sculptural. Architecture was the symbolization of inner human emotions realized in physical form.

Paul Scheerbart influenced the preference for glass and crystals among Expressionist architects. Apart from providing technical information in his book *Glasarchitektur*, Scheerbart also promoted glass building for its generation of a new morality. Glass stood for brighter awareness, clearer determination, and utter gentleness. "A person who sets eyes on the splendors of glass cannot do wicked deeds."

### GLASS PAVILION, BRUNO TAUT, COLOGNE (1914)

Throughout his life, Taut propagated his mythology of glass. The Glass Pavilion was built for the glass industry. It was intended to introduce a lighter building method, change spatial conceptions, and introduce the effects of glass to architecture.

A centralized building has an addition at the back with stepped roof. The pavilion consists of a geodesic dome on a concrete base. The structure is a three-dimensional reinforced concrete frame. Open stairs lead up to the terrace formed as a partly open fourteen-sided drum, which forms a ring around the central part of the pavilion. Prism glass in reinforced concrete frames was used for both the walls and the stair treads leading up to the glass hall. This is covered by a crystal-shaped dome assembled from reinforced concrete ribs and colored glass panels resting on prism glass. The dome is double-glazed, as reflective glass panes cover this interior glass system. At night the dome was lit from inside. Construction and form are identical. The floor of this hall is made of glass prism; round yellow and white ones articulate a diamond-shaped pattern. The glass used is colored, so that it lets light through, but closes off the exterior otherwise. Hence, the building creates a special interior world. Nevertheless, architecture has here freed itself from the solid exterior wall, and has therefore transcended matter.

Visitors took a predetermined path. From the base, two outside stairs ascend into the upper hall. Here, visitors saw the lower level, a cascade room. This was reached by two inside stairways, also constructed of prism glass between prism glass walls. On the lower floor was a rotunda with a pool in the center. The cupola is cone-shaped and made of red and gold glass. The vertical walls are of silver- and gold-colored glass and have a number of stained glass windows. Water cascaded down five glass steps, made of clear glass lit from behind. The circular fountain is lined with black glass tiles on the inside. The steps are made of residue from glass production. The floor of the lower room is of blue and black glass. The cascade terminates in a recess in which pictures from a kaleidoscope were projected. Purple cloth frames the projection plane. The procession through this pavilion was characterized by seductive anticipation and an increasingly intense experience of space. One exits the pavilion through two side doors, which lead out to the ground.

The whole is an aesthetically impressive reinforced concrete-and-glass structure, similar to the many prototypes of the 19th century. At night, sphere- and bell-shaped lamps were lit inside and illuminated the pavilion for those standing outside. The crystal here has become the final stage.

## EINSTEIN TOWER, ERICH MENDELSOHN, POTSDAM (1917-21)

This facility was intended to measure the spectrum of light in search of proof that light could be bent by gravitational forces. Einstein stated that as it travels, light loses mass, which results in a reddening of the light rays. In this observatory, the light measurements from celestial bodies was compared to two artificial light sources.

Mendelsohn wanted to communicate the dynamism inherent in Einstein's theory of relativity by attempting to capture a sense of movement in his forms. He realized that Einstein's theory would affect the relationship between mass and motion. In addition, the design serves as metaphor for the material properties of reinforced concrete.

The design presents an animated form, as if it were moving through space. The tower windows curve as if they were formed by wind. The round tower's details make it appear as if shedding mass. The tower presents an analogy between the industrial material reinforced concrete and the human body. The shaft resembles human vertebrae. This is a symbol of Promethean power.

## GROSSES SCHAUSPIELHAUS, HANS POELZIG, BERLIN (1919 BEGUN)

This building had originally been designed as a five-aisled market hall, and was later converted into a circus. The plan for the theater was taken over from this circus. The theater was to be used for stage plays as well as arena plays. The arena is covered by a stalactite dome meant to symbolize the sky of the Ancient Greek theater. The interior forms a unity for the purpose of enchantment of togetherness. The form coerces the spectator to be intimately bound up with the spectacle. Moreover, the architecture creates an effect of physical oppression.

Both inside and outside, Poelzig's habit of doggedly repeating the same motif can be noted. Similarly, his drawings give the impression that architectural form was created through repetitive strings of ornament.

The exterior was given a vertical emphasis and in its "wallness" creates a looming, alien presence. The foyers impress the spectator as caves. The main foyer was painted green. Walls and ceiling merge to envelop the spectator. The amphitheater, painted yellow, provided a liberating experience. Consequently, cave and tower became the favored Expressionist architectural motifs.

Social considerations partly determined this design. The powerful, vulgar formal effects were intended to dazzle the populace, not the elite. Inside, the seating arrangement eliminated a hierarchical plan, and tickets were cheap due to the large auditorium.

The Schauspielhaus was conceived as a work of art. It consisted of powerful emotion, and addresses itself exclusively to the emotions.

## GOETHEANUM II, STEINER, DORNACH (1924-28)

This is the second building on the site. It is a piece of concrete sculpture. Angled or broken planes lead from layer to layer. The building seems to be subject to a play of forces emerging from inside and outside it.

The most diverse functions are combined here under one form and roof. The style has been termed "organic functionalism."

The building is dualistic, polarized between the cubical auditorium block in the east and the entrance part in the west. The auditorium is shaped as an unadorned block, whereas the entrance side opens itself to the approaching visitor in multiple formations. The western side seems to grow out of the eastern block into a multitude of organic forms.

The protrusions and recessions of the exterior form express the breathing of a living body.

The design derives from the belief that art (and architecture) can only be appearance, not reality. Art (and architecture) that aims to realize this appearance ultimately is only a basic real thing. Both nature and human rationality have an urge to form and produce. In between these two is the human urge to play. This urge to play is at the base of artistic work. The artist recognized the tendencies of natural production in natural objects and assists to bring this tendency into reality. Such artistic creations bring ideas and sense reality together into the appearance. Art works reveal a higher reality in reality.

# ROMANTICISM AND TRADITIONALISM

The rational, machinist language of modern architecture excluded the representation of traditional imagery, that is, expressions of power and ideology of the state. Favorite historical styles were Gothic (in U.S., skyscrapers) and Classical (in a restrained style).

## URBAN PLAN, LUTYENS, NEW DELHI (1912-31)

Lutyens possessed this traditionalist faculty for invention along historicist lines. However, he never accepted Modern architecture. The design problems involved in this imperial capital included the integration of a vernacular cultural tradition with a humanist/Classicist style.

King George V decided in 1911 to move the Indian capital from Calcutta to Delhi, which had been the capital under the Moghul emperors. Old Delhi was a walled city. The plan of the new city resulted from the superimposition of a narrow rectangular grid for administrative buildings and a hexagonal grid for residential areas. Two hexagons overlap and coincide with the major east-west axis of the plan. This scheme intends to present the entire site at Delhi as a vast landscaped part, where the street grids connect the plain, the low foothills, the river, and surviving historical monuments from the earlier cities. The government buildings of New Delhi constitute the focus of this composition. Ultimately, this makes the new capital a garden city.

## VICEROY'S HOUSE, NEW DELHI (1920-31)

The government buildings are raised on seventeen-foot platforms. The Viceroy's House is set back 1200 feet from the two Secretariat buildings. This serves as official residence, but also as administrative center, and focus of the whole urban scheme. The design is on a Roman scale. King's Way, the avenue leading to the Viceroy's House is flanked by parks and canals. The road rises as it passes between the two Secretariat buildings, letting the Viceroy's House appear slowly from the top down. Between the Secretariats and Viceroy's House is the Jaipur column, a huge marble pillar.

Viceroy's House is a large horizontal building with a dome. The dome symbolizes Imperial rule. The lower walls are of red sandstone, the upper parts of cream sandstone, making it into a lush Indian combination. Lutyens combined European monumental Classical tradition with Indian features. The lines of the building appear modern, with dominating broad horizontals and massive walls that are broken by openings to create a composition of light and shade. The order was based on Doric, but fashioned as Delhi Doric. The walls are articulated in horizontal setbacks. Moghul features are used to cool the building by creating areas of shade. Overhanging cornices are one such detail. On the parapet level are small cupolas surrounding the central dome. The dome combines geometrical form with Oriental features, especially the Stupa railing. The garden front has lots of openings to allow cool breezes into the interior.

The interior provides, primarily, apartments for the viceroy's use. Inside, movement patterns align the building with the geometry of the entire plan of the city. There is a great staircase courtyard.

The gardens are inspired by Moghul traditions, and are mostly pattern-making with stones, water, and flowers.

## WOOLWORTH BUILDING, CASS GILBERT, NEW YORK (1911-13)

The period between the two World Wars was one of strong contrasts: ingenious inventions vs. looking backward; new industrial aesthetic vs. historicism. It was a boom period for building investments. The ruling economic policy was a laissez faire attitude. Anxiety-laden probing and apocalyptic utopianism characteristic of the European development were totally absent in the U.S.

The historicist decoration serves here to terminate the suggested upward movement.

The Woolworth Building's central tower is fifty-five stories, or 761 feet high. Two lower building parts flanking this tower are thirty stories high. It uses Gothic details to express its height. This style was set from the beginning, based on the Victoria Tower of the Houses of Parliament, London. There are hardly any horizontal features in this glass and terracotta curtain wall.

Up to the twenty-eighth floor, portal arches provide bracing to the steel structure.

On its completion, it was called "Cathedral of Commerce." The building was renovated in 1980-81.

## CHRYSLER BUILDING, VAN ALEN, NEW YORK (1928-30)

The next step lay in the stripped Gothic forms leading eventually to Art Deco articulations. The New York Zoning law of 1916 required the setbacks for light, which became characteristic for the forms of skyscrapers.

Walter P. Chrysler wanted to erect a distinct corporate identity and a suitable monument to his own career as a self-made man. There are hubcap friezes and eagle-head and radiator cap gargoyles. The top of the building was influenced by Expressionist design. The interiors are sumptuous, and employ expensive materials.

Being mostly the expression of Chrysler's attitude as a self-made entrepreneur, this was the swansong of 1920s skyscraper design.

## ROCKEFELLER CENTER, HOOD ET. AL., NEW YORK (1931-39)

This design took into consideration criticism leveled at earlier skyscrapers, namely that they completely disregarded their context. Here, a sunken plaza and roof gardens attempted to modify this lack. Square footage that would have been allowed under zoning regulations was sacrificed to increase the aesthetic quality of the entire complex. Building heights were staggered, and open space was provided on the ground.

The whole is a complex of office buildings, theaters, shops, and so on, and public spaces. It was erected in several stages. The buildings are arranged in a balanced asymmetry.

## TOTALITARIAN ARCHITECTURE DURING THE 1930S

In Italy, Russia, and Germany, totalitarian regimes came to power during the 1920s. These governments devoted considerable interest to the expressive quality of architecture, especially to how it could be used to legitimize their position. A persistent theme was the reinforcement of nationalist ideology through the use of earlier nationalist styles. A theme that unifies the architecture of totalitarianism is the rejection of Modern architecture.

With the National Socialist advent to power, Modern architecture disappeared from Germany. There had been right-wing criticisms earlier on, so that the stage for its demise was set when the Nazis assumed power in 1933. Functional approaches were still used where it made sense, for example, in factories or for welfare projects. In domestic architecture, the favored style became the Heimatstil. The Nazis' ideal was the peasantry, not the industrialized urban culture of Modern architecture.

For public structures, the style chosen derived from the works of Schinkel, Gilly, and Langhans. Their forms were abstracted. This choice allowed the hierarchization of public buildings, which in turn expressed the political hierarchy.

## ZEPPELIN FIELD, SPEER, NUREMBERG (1936)

After Troost's death in 1934, Albert Speer took over his position. Previously, Speer had organized the Party rallies. Speer favored a monumental scale deriving from Babylonian, Egyptian, and Classical prototypes. This area for the national Party rallies was laid out to hold 240,000 people. The field was surrounded by spectator stands. These centered on the orator's desk, from which Hitler addressed the crowds. Colonnades ran behind this.

## NEW CHANCELLORY, SPEER, BERLIN (1937-8)

Only the buildings designed for Hitler himself had any real meaning.

Inside, this building did not consist of space, but of voids. In this respect, there was no difference between this interior and a highway.

## PLAN FOR BERLIN, SPEER (1937-40)

Hitler's great dream was to rebuild Berlin as an imperial city, a heritage of his reign. This was begun in 1937, when he and Speer replanned Berlin with long avenues, axis, and a stage scenery borrowed from Paris, Ancient Rome and Washington. The replanning was based on an enormous avenue. Focal point was the Great Hall, a huge domed structure. Meant as a pantheon to Nazism, it was so large that it could have contained St. Peter's in Rome. This was a reworking of Boullée's design for a large spherical auditorium. Facing this building at the other end of a long boulevard was a triumphal arch in honor of Hitler.

Nazi architecture was primarily traditional, and used this tradition as a political instrument. Architecture was justified only through assimilation to propaganda. Predominantly, it was a celebratory architecture of buildings with ritual character. Only through this practice was an absolute style possible. Speer's buildings are *only* colossal, and express "overcoming" at all cost. Stone, the material of his buildings, predominated as style, and since decoration was futile in such colossal structures, made them into planned ruins. Stone also squashed any sense of structural technology. This was mostly just primitive tectonics.

# F.L. WRIGHT'S SECOND CAREER

## FALLINGWATER (KAUFMANN HOUSE), F.L. WRIGHT, BEAR RUN (1937)

This design dramatized the structural possibilities of reinforced concrete in the tiers of cantilevers above the waterfall. This design continues the natural landscape, but also expresses the potential of concrete in the seamless boxes. This structure is so dominant that it makes the bands of sash windows disappear. This design combines two sorts of romanticism, romanticism about nature and romanticism about scientific feats of construction. The building was used as a summer and weekend house.

The exterior massing is more complex and open than in the earlier prairie-houses. One gets the impression of a cross over a square. There is a play of masses and voids, horizontality and verticality, rough and smooth surfaces, and anchoring and cantilevered parts. Inside, fluid spaces contrast the water flowing outside.

The whole building's structure is anchored to the native rock and a solid core of masonry in the back, built up of great pylons of native stone. The choice of materials offers a striking contrast.

There are surprisingly few spaces inside. As this house was intended for a weekend retreat, the interior could be rather open. There is a unified living area on the main floor, with canopy slabs that shoot out in four directions, in a sense the only real separation of spaces. A stair leads down to a pool in the river. The three bedrooms upstairs are generally large suites with terraces. A small portion is given over to service functions.

## GUGGENHEIM MUSEUM, F.L. WRIGHT, NEW YORK (1943, 1956-59)

This building represents a bold attempt to create a design expressive of the sculptural freedom possible with reinforced concrete. The design was completed in 1943-45; actual construction took placed in 1956-59 after modifications of the original design. The floor plan too is part of the spatial continuum of this structure. It can indeed be described as "space contained by space." Wright's first concept was a horizontal building. Being considered too expensive to build because of the cost for the necessary land, the spiral was chosen as the tool to turn this horizontal building vertical. The continuous spiral is the climax of Wright's intentions of uninterrupted interiors. The form combines four themes running through Wright's whole work: the circle, the cantilever, the interpenetrated form, and the walled building enclosing a large unitary space surrounded by balconies.

The first scheme for the Museum was exhibited in a model of 1945. The interior rotunda goes back to Schinkel's Altes Museum; the exterior form to the Ancient Mesopotamian ziggurat.

The exterior form of the spiral is determined by two interlocked cones, the exterior spiral walls lean outward, and the interior ones inward.

The final structural scheme was worked out in three stages. The 1945 model represents the first stage. A ring of thin columns provides major support for the cantilevered floors on the interior circumference. Additional support comes from the tower and some piers beneath the lowest ring of the floor, and possibly through the curving and folding of the floor planes. On the outside, struts in the window area add support of the upper floors. In the second stage, the interior ring of columns is eliminated. The exterior struts are placed in seven-foot intervals. In the third stage, these struts were eliminated, and a series of radiating vertical ribs replaced them, ribs that partly separate the spiral rings into a series of gallery spaces. These ribs become progressively wider toward the top.

The spiral floor rings were poured of concrete in sections, measuring the distance between the ribs. The inside parapet was of plaster, and hung to the inside floor cantilever end; in the edge between it and the floor was hidden a utility duct. The exterior parts of the floors were of sprayed concrete.

Between 1985-92, Gwathmey/Siegel designed an addition to Wright's building.

FIGURE 36–1. Einstein Tower, Potsdam, Exterior.

FIGURE 36–2. Goetheanum, Dornach, Exterior.

**FIGURE 36–3.** Transformer Station, Dornach.

**FIGURE 36–4.** Viceroy's House (now the President's House), New Delhi.

**FIGURE 36–5.** Woolworth
Building, New York.

**FIGURE 36–6.** Guggenheim Museum, New York,
Exterior.

**FIGURE 36–7.** Guggenheim
Museum, Interior.

# Chapter 37

# Structuralist Architecture

In mid-20th-century architecture, there was also a movement in which extra-Modernist ideas were accommodated within a Modernist format. There were architects who did not want to follow either the functionalist or the expressionist extremes. They wanted a synthesis of the technological and organic trends. They achieved this by fulfilling function optimally and, at the same time, expressing that function in an easily recognizable way.

The basic element of structuralism is the acceptance of the existence of a collective system within which each individual is capable to partake. This derives from F. de Saussure's linguistic model in which "langue" is the collective system within which each individual expresses him/herself with "paroles." Language is an unconscious reality, which "structures" speaking. This model was then applied in the most varied fields, always leading to the search for existing orders in reality. This order was to be discovered through the analysis of existing phenomena. The basic tenet of structuralism is that man is the same always and everywhere. A structure is a totality of relationships within which individual elements can change but always are dependent from the whole. Human beings, as elements, lose their position of autonomous "creators" to the overall structure, and become decentralized subjects. Extreme structuralists posit that the "I" is no longer important, but rather the order into which life is imbedded.

In terms of architectural form, this meant the greatest possible dissolution of the undifferentiated total form. This led to an aesthetic of number or quantity. Smaller forms were not to be laid out as subdivisions of a larger whole, but as individual constitutive units. It can be called a style of "extreme articulation," that is, the varieties of the interior are extremely articulated in the exterior shape. In addition, the formulation of in-between elements became important. In part, structuralism is an expression of structure and space together. Clearly, functional – biological, psychological, or social – schemes are replaced by the creation of a formal structure. Structuralist architecture simply imposes form on content, claiming that this is universal.

It is interesting, that the two bastions of structuralism, Holland and Japan, are at the same time two countries with a rather high population density.

## ALVAR AALTO (1898-1976)

Began working in the 1920s as a member of the tradition of a Doricist sensibility, using simple, classical forms that were inspired by French Revolutionary Classicism. He then briefly associated himself with functionalism. The Sanatorium in Paimio (1929-32) is largely based on the intention to provide the best possible cure for tuberculosis. Rooms are exposed to the Southern sunny side, walls are painted in white, a healthy color, and the building has good mechanical equipment. The use of reinforced concrete and the arrangement of windows in bands are International Style features. Thus, Aalto was interested in creating buildings to serve the needs of active, sensual human beings. He designed buildings oriented toward "creature comforts." His forms and details are normally geared to visual aesthetic sensibility, and to the senses of hearing, touch, and sensations.

During the early 1930s, Aalto was hired by the Finnish timber industry to design furniture. This brought about his deviation from pure functionalism. He became interested in natural materials, wood, and began using round forms in his designs, inspired by his use of bent plywood or laminated wood for his furniture designs.

### Villa Mairea, Noormarku (1938-39)

A trademark of this design is the use of undulating curves on the outside. These enclose a free-form shape. Traditional Modernist features are seen in the flat roof, the use of crisp and simple volumes, and the plain surfaces. The materials used, however, are outside the scope of the International Style, and create a rich texture. Throughout, the building exhibits naturalistic imagery, sensory richness, and spatial and formal fluidity.

After World War II, in an effort to improve housing opportunities, Scandinavian design followed an anti-technological, humanist design approach. This was partly inspired by the horrors produced by technology during the war. The new style used in the various housing schemes was Neo-Empiricism, or People's Style. These developments greatly influenced Aalto's architecture after World War II.

### Civic Center, Säynätsalo (1949-52)

At Säynätsalo, Aalto was originally commissioned to design a town hall containing the council chamber and a few offices. He won the competition for this design in 1949. He convinced his clients to enlarge this project to include a library, apartments, and shops. The buildings are informally grouped in a U-shape and arranged around an interior court. This is a traditional element of the typology of the city hall. The main part of the building, the council chamber, is contained in a higher cubical volume with a slanting roof. This acts as a pivot for the whole plan. By not completely enclosing this court, a relationship with the surrounding nature is permitted. The level is a few feet above street level to create an abstract atrium. This arrangement imitates the image of an old farm village (re: Aalto's 1941 description of a "Karelian House"). The final design is not imposing, but rather serves as a stage for human activity. The main function of these buildings is to serve as background.

The façades are of brick and are articulated only by subtle changes in the surface texture and the fenestration. Through the uniformity of the building materials and the fact that plants and grass are allowed to grow within this structure, the whole is made to look like an old temple ruin. The ceiling of the council chamber is supported by a particularly shaped truss, which physiognomically suggests the action to support the roof.

An interesting interpretation of this design comes out of the application of the information theory. This theory states that signals have an information content through their potential for making selections. They give power to discriminate among or select from the alternative suggested by them. This theory seems to have been used by Aalto in the design and placing of the council chamber. An approaching viewer's expectations are consistently frustrated. First, the screen of trees and the unusual shape of the highest volume are confusing, especially the cantilevered steps seen from the southeast. Once at the main entrance to the complex, the council chamber is suggested by the slanted roof; the speaker sitting at the lower side, controlling both sight and acoustic lines. However, the materials and form of this part are the same as those of the other parts. Once inside the courtyard, several turns have to be made before one stands before the doors to the chamber. Inside the chamber, again the expected arrangement is confusing, as the speaker sits at a right angle to the slant of the roof.

There is a tendency in Aalto's work to saturate the viewer with these communicative devices. He uses the associational richness of already operative and socially legitimized iconographic types, but renders them totally profuse. One of these types used for the council chamber at Säynätsalo is the medieval/Renaissance city crown. However, this hierarchical symbol is then contradicted by giving the whole the appearance of a civic monument. Thus, his buildings sometimes do not seem to be straightforward, or acknowledge the harshness of the world into which they are built.

# LOUIS KAHN (1901-74)

Born 1901 in Estonia, came to the States in 1905 and studied under Paul Cret in Philadelphia. He received a Beaux-Arts training. After graduating in 1924, he worked for many years in other architects' practices, before starting his own office in the early 1950s. He was already in his 50s when he received his first commission.

# DESIGN PHILOSOPHY

Kahn differs from orthodox Modernism in his treatment of function. He explores the essence of the building's intended use, and then designed a form that was an organic entity to be used by human beings. First, Kahn studied the activities that had to be accommodated in a building and placed the most care on how to arrange these activities inside. Once this arrangement was worked out, he enclosed it in a physical frame. In this frame, he clearly separated between the spaces in which human activity would take place, and those spaces that were occupied by the mechanical and support systems: stairs, bathrooms, plumbing, wiring. This was separation into served and servant spaces.

Kahn achieved the union of the classical tradition of architecture with modernism. He presented anew the timeless architectural elements of column, wall, beam, and truss. He also celebrated the wall, after a period of preponderance of the metal skeleton. His designs depended on tectonics. He did preserve the modern emphasis on the easy handling of material load. This feature was also influenced by his exposure to Ancient architecture on a trip to Europe during 1950-51. A further Modernist residue is his emphasis on primary geometric forms. This followed his proposal that each building be made up of self-constituted elements, bodies, or spaces. In most of his designs, Kahn showed himself to be a master of monumentality. He was called the architect of the great occasions, of institutions, churches, synagogues, museums, universities, and capital cities.

Kahn created buildings based on a strong and expressive theme. He was interested in the question of "what the building wants to be." Louis Kahn viewed the purpose of architecture as elevating human institutions and human activity to an almost metaphysical plane. This intention was especially suited to monumental building tasks, such as a Parliament Building. He was also interested in the problem of light. He usually surrounded the main spaces with an in-between zone. Kahn's forms are so primitive that one is tricked into believing the buildings had been standing there for eternity. The same impression is created by the use of "weathered" surfaces.

## RICHARDS MEDICAL CENTER, PHILADELPHIA (1957-64)

The commission was to provide research facilities on a narrow site, which immediately suggested tall buildings. The medical research center was constructed from 1957 to 1961, the biology addition from 1961 to 1964. The original design included both parts.

The design premise rests on Kahn's ultimate philosophy, namely that the spaces containing the activities of the building are its ultimate reality, and thus, the design should start with these. Three principles guided the particular form of the Richards Medical Center. First, scientists work alone or in small groups. Second, they work in a potentially dangerous environment. Third, the site demanded a vertical arrangement. These premises were translated into clusters of studios, not a big warehouse, into a separation of laboratories and office spaces, and into a tower form. These premises define the form of the building. In the subsequent design part, the architect gives tangibility to the form by making it visible as a harmony of systems and uses.

Three stacks of research studios were grouped in a radiating pin-wheel configuration around a mechanical tower.

The basic division of this building is into served and servant spaces. The studio spaces are the served parts, the added utility towers the servant ones. Dominating features are the added stair or utility towers, with completely solid walls. This gives the center a medieval look, although it also evokes images of grain elevators. The studios are on cantilevered floors and are extensively glazed. Together, these form a sharp counterpoint of solid and void. The studio spaces are basically horizontally arranged, the towers vertically. The utility towers mostly serve for air intake and stairwells. The stairwells are those with the cleaved tops. The whole forms an assembly of various parts, however, not in any type of fusion. As the vertical utilities are housed in the towers, the studio floors are devoid of vertical dividers.

The towers were poured on the site. Later, they were faced with brick. The studio stacks consist of precast elements, complexly notched and slotted so as to fit together. Principal support occurs through eight columns of H-shape, placed on the exteriors, dividing each facade into three equal parts. The floors consist of precast trusses laid sideways into four columns, with the other trusses inserted into these, resulting in a grid of nine squares. Then the cantilever beams on the exteriors were set, finishing the square of the whole floor. Thus, the floors were basically space frames, which also housed the utility cords, tubes, and cables.

The building is designed around its use, not vice-versa (-the uses being stuffed into a pre-set exterior). Typologically, the complex imitates the old form of a medieval hill town, bristling with menacing defensive towers.

## JONAS SALK INSTITUTE, LA JOLLA (1959-65)

Here, Kahn was allowed to express his ceremonial predilections. The research part is formed by two parallel laboratory wings with open, uninterrupted spaces inside. These are three stories high, with one story below ground level. On the outside, closed stair towers are added, to the inside the scientists' cubicles are added.

The whole complex suggests a palace from which the main building – the corps de logis – has been removed. The main building has been replaced by a liberating vista into the open expanse of the ocean. Construction is again of reinforced concrete frame and Vierendeel trusses.

# NOTRE-DAME-DU-HAUT, LE CORBUSIER, RONCHAMP (1950-55)

Other Modernist architects also began to believe that architecture was more than a useful appliance. They proposed that it was primarily a vehicle for conveying communal values expressible in no other way. In most cases, building technology was not up to their formal demands, and the world had to wait until after World War II to see some of these designs realized. In general, these are buildings, which consider the site, the function, and the structure, in addition to realizing meaningful form. In terms of individual buildings, they were planned more as organisms.

Le Corbusier radically changed his architecture during the late 1930s. A result of this is his pilgrimage chapel at Ronchamp. Here, Corbusier molded space, and began reintroducing surface textures. The site had been used since the 12th century and was revered for a statue of the Virgin Mary. The existing building was destroyed during the War.

In his design, Corbusier wanted to integrate the existing site and environment. He created the building as a visual echo of the landscape ( = visual acoustics), as a sculptural response to the site. The whole building consists of complicated curves and highly irregular surfaces. The southern wall tapers toward the top and is perpendicular only at its eastern edge. The details are rather crudely shaped and finished. The final form was no longer suggestive of utilitarian efficiency, but evoked a number of images. Corbusier himself mentioned a clamshell as the source for his roof. The commission required a church seating 200 people, with provision for larger gatherings on festive days. For this purpose, an outdoor chapel was added to one side. The statue of the Virgin Mary is placed in the wall between indoor and outdoor chapels on a revolving plate. The plan was evolved from his modular system, although the outer walls and the roof are curved. Three chapels adjoin the main church space. Each terminates in an apse surmounted by a tower. Nevertheless, spatial openness and continuity are preserved inside.

The building is held up by a structural frame of reinforced concrete members. The open grids were filled in with rubble and masonry, and then sprayed with a layer of rough stucco. The roof is left in raw concrete. The actual and symbolic structures are not the same. The interesting aspect of this building is the great contrast between outside and inside. A score of windows are dug into the walls, but the glazed area is only three percent of the total surface. Similarly, the interior evokes a feeling of closedness and protection, whereas the exterior reaches out.

# QUERINI-STAMPAGLIA FOUNDATION, CARLO SCARPA, VENICE (1961-63)

In his work, Scarpa successfully integrated tradition and modernity. Some of his details recall Wright, but he was also influenced by local masonry traditions and craftsmanship. He kept distant from theory and ideological debates. He ignored especially the Rationalist design theory. Instead, he sought a balance between objects and memory, art and craft, as well as tradition and culture. His main belief is that a building is no more than a drawing at full scale.

This was a renovation. Scarpa focused on the dialectics between existing conditions and the new intervention. The new (floor) does not touch the old (walls) on the ground floor entry. This in-between space lets the high tide and the flood waters in, and elevates the new floor to a floating pavilion within the palazzo.

# ALDO VAN EYCK (1918-)

In his thinking, van Eyck is against the use of polarities. He rather favors the possibility to have two opposing elements play together. Already in 1959, he complained that architects courted technology and ran after progress. He demanded a new orientation back to the eternal elements of human existence. Generally, he identifies the built artifact with those it shelters. "Architecture," in his opinion, "need do no more than assist man's homecoming." These ideas were partly influenced by the humanistic concerns of Dutch Modern architecture.

Three concerns govern the design of his buildings: (1) he uses anthropological data as a base for architecture; (2) he establishes a formal order through geometry and symbolic elements; (3) he emphasizes integrated and object-oriented architecture.

He was heavily influenced by his study of primitive residential settlements.

### ORPHANAGE, AMSTERDAM (1957-60)

Does not seem to be a narrative building at first sight. The references to history are too general.

This is a single-story building of brick and reinforced concrete. It was planned for 150 children and intended to be a home, not a school or workplace. It avoids the traditional monumental forms for such institutions, and replaces it with a small-scale pavilion system.

This novel aspect is found in the plan. The whole was built additively out of identical cells. The fundamental unit was a domed square, thirteen feet square. A larger unit, also domed, covered the area of nine small units. A total of eight family units were provided, each consisting of living room, garden, kitchen and bedrooms. In addition, there were a central assembly room, two staff homes, and administrative offices. The whole arrangement is a space cluster in which individual cells coalesce together to form an organism. The intention was to create places, not spaces.

The plan attempts to combine advantages of a centralized organization with those of a decentralized one, or to provide both for the individual and the collective. Unity and diversity were reconciled. Living rooms are housed in the large units; corridors, playrooms, and bedrooms in the small ones. The plan is based on an additive principle, creating in the end "labyrinthine clarity." It is assembled of "bricks of space," not in the free-flowing manner of De Stijl. Similarities to this movement's aesthetic are found in the regularity of the plan. This, however, also refers to North African villages.

The strict formal organization of this design expresses his wish for a superior, new order of life. Van Eyck indeed goes to extremes in attempting to humanize abstract form. Here, he mainly individualized the monolithic image of the International Style. Van Eyck here saw it as his task to suggest, to a society without forms, the possibility for more beneficial social coexistence. The orphanage is structured as an open network of cells around the core. It is arranged so as not to disintegrate into an endless pattern of individual units. Here, architecture functions as a physical matrix for forming a community of human beings.

This design also shows another eternal theme, namely that of the excavation process. The building surface is eroded away in parts.

Ground floor walls are of light brown brick, window frames of black steel, and concrete is left open both inside and outside. An interesting element is the beam design, which evokes allusions both to a beam and a wall, as a section is cut out.

# HERMAN HERTZBERGER (1932-)

His design theory is close to the linguistic model. He accepts the idea of an imaginary museum, that is, an unconscious collection of forms, from which the architect can select adequate details and shapes. The architect actually selects from two fields of collective knowledge, one relating to archetypal behavior of human beings, the other to this unconscious museum of forms.

In detail, he considers forms to be polyvalent. This means that each form must provide room for individual interpretation. He is not interested in form as providing shelter, but as carrier of meaning. Forms need to have the potential to be transformed into identifiable units. Moreover, he is interested in the social ramifications of an architectural task.

## CENTRAAL BEHEER, APELDOORN (1968-72)

In plan, this is a cluster of spatial elements. In fact, structure and space are identical here. The building consists of a structural support system with infill. The arrangement was based on research that showed that in this company most activities were carried out by small groups, thus eliminating solutions providing large open office areas. There are 400 spatial units, each capable of accommodating up to four workstations. The whole building houses 1,000 employees. Four units are joined, in a cruciform plan, with communal areas. A number of individual units are joined by connecting bridges and decks, which function as a street network in the air. Floating modules are placed within an overall structural unity. The units leave cross-shaped empty spaces running through the whole interior. The whole complex is divided into four larger clusters around a central lobby with entrances from all four sides. The spaces are flexible and not overscaled.

There is thus a hierarchy of individual and open spaces. The setting achieves a balance between personal identity and controlled awareness of others. Each cubicle gives the feeling of privacy, and the communicative views give the one of collectivity. The dominant impression of the interior is that of the defined workspace and its personalization. The scale of the building is domestic, not institutional.

The main intention was to build a "house" for 1,000 people. Colors used on the inside are gray concrete and concrete block, dark timber and straw-colored stucco. The central lobby uses motifs from urban spaces, such as a clock from a clock tower. As with van Eyck's orphanage, the intention here was to break down the traditional monolithic building without losing the organizational principles and abstraction (i.e. the repetition of industrial materials). The materials are concrete, concrete blocks, and glass blocks.

The main characteristic of the exterior is the revelation of the process of assembly. The whole was developed from inside out. The staggered exterior presents a loose outline that pokes fun at the very idea of a façade. The building gives an impression of fundamental unfinishedness. It could be expanded without much formal change. This building has no entrance or back façade, and denies tradition. This is not Modernist analytical functionalism.

# PARTICIPATORY ARCHITECTURE

The basic philosophy of this development is that a building is only constituted in its relationship to the user.

## STUDENT HOUSING, LUCIEN KROLL, LOUVAIN (1969-73)

Kroll received this commission on the recommendation of the students. The complex belongs to the University of Louvain, and contains student housing, restaurants, shops, a school with kindergarten, and other communal services. The students were involved in planning and design from the beginning. This was partly influenced by the desire to create additional support for his unconventional designs against a rather traditionally oriented bureaucracy.

The whole complex is divided into individual blocks, which form a topographically laid-out group. No apparent geometrical system was used. In fact, this architecture could be interpreted as taking a stance against perfection. One could even go so far as to call it the work of wood butchers.

The whole building offers numerous sensual stimuli: various colors, forms, materials, and textures. It looks as if a storm has blown away part of the siding. Heterogeneity seemed to govern this variety. The freedom allotted to the individual elements seems to threaten the whole with disruption and chaos. Esthetic systems are seen slamming into each other. An Italian hill town sits on a sky lodge, which nestles up to a steel-and-glass office building to turn into a rubble canyon. The surfaces are articulated in zones. Plasticity is suggested through material and color contrasts. Seemingly, there is no precisely placed façade. Instead, this consists of an imitation of an organic structure, like an animal skin, which is subject to a process of growth and change and contains additional microcosmic organisms. Thus, the exterior appears to be influenced by vegetative principles. Kroll operates on the other side of all conventions. His works are not characterized by allusions to historical meanings. He rather uses a vocabulary that derives its meaning from the differences shown.

In part, the approach to this commission followed the metabolist/megastructural direction. Elements strictly determined by the architects were the communal facilities and the structural system, consisting of façade piers and irregularly placed piers inside. The arrangement of rooms and façades was created in cooperation with the students. Only the areas behind the more regular façades were designed without the expressed consultation of students, and followed traditional interior planning.

The surrounding area was originally laid out following the same principles as the architecture. Heaps of debris and stones were left on which eventually vegetation was to grow. In 1978, this approach was changed into a formalized arrangement.

Participation by the workmen can also be noted, not only in the use of materials, but also in the two large figures which were designed and built by them.

In this design, form is conceived in relation to the reaction of human beings. The conglomeration of materials and shapes expresses a pluralistic society.

# RALPH ERSKINE

Erskine advocated a regionalist position in the early 1960s. He had gone to Sweden because this country's social welfare system attracted him. There, he was confronted by harsh climate. Design solutions that would alleviate these adverse conditions began to preoccupy him.

In the Arctic, certain factors must be considered. There is a huge temperature change between the seasons, which also produces mood changes in the people. There is also a contrast between indoors and outdoors. Furthermore, there is geographical isolation. In consequence, cities need to be more attractive than those in warmer areas; they need to form extensive communities with many activities, they should cluster to emphasize and form a human milieu in the desert, and they should also emphasize urban features that enhance human communication, such as public squares. To counter the cold climate, a reduction in exterior surface by combining individual elements into large complexes helps.

He designed a shopping center in Lulea that was so successful that ten years after its completion, admission had to be charged to reduce the number of shoppers.

## BYKER WALL, NEWCASTLE (1968-75)

This commission brought worldwide recognition to Erskine, after he had worked on the fringe of the international scene, in Sweden, for decades. The success of this development derived mostly from the fact that the prospective residents were allowed to participate in the design. The architect's office was housed in an existing funeral parlor. Among the main concerns was to preserve the existing social infrastructure. In contrast to earlier housing developments, this one has a lower density, a result of residents' involvement. Erskine advocates a meaningful, expressive approach to architecture, which is based on ad hoc-ism, that is, on the combination of past and present systems. The whole evokes the image of a shanty town.

The Byker Project had existed before. Parts of it were destroyed to make room for new construction. The whole site was shaped into a series of public spaces and outdoor gardens around the buildings. Winding streets with squares lead to the wall. With the exception of the 3-9 story winding wall, all houses are two-story single family homes arranged in groups or rows. At the request of the tenants, a complete separation of car and pedestrian traffic was carried out. Inside the wall, a pergola follows its line, using fragments from earlier buildings as seats. The garden side of the development is treated in the theme of ruins in the garden. The lower houses are laid out in a picturesque arrangement. The street side evokes the image of a factory and a swimming bath in the wall. This resulted above all from the preservation and integration of 19th century buildings.

The smaller houses are arranged into villages, each with its own communal facilities.

The use of color was based on the residents' preference. The outside of it is an ad hoc assemblage of colors, brick patterns, windows, air conditioning equipment, and shed roofs. The wall is the most controversial part of this complex. Residents say that Byker is beautiful in spite of the wall. It is meant to protect the interior from wind and noise. On the street side, it has a closed appearance. On the inner side, it is open. Balconies (crows' nests or life boats) and wooden arcades add improvisational elements.

# JAMES STIRLING (1926-92)

Stirling has gone through the important transformations in post-World War II architecture. He began as a member of New Brutalism, and adhered to the theories of Team 10. He came to postmodernism through the influence of Hans Hollein (a colleague at Düsseldorf) and Leon Krier (worked for him beginning in 1968).

## NEUE STAATSGALERIE, STIRLING, STUTTGART (1977-84)

In Stirling's designs of the 1970s, the earlier articulation of function (such as at Leicester) was transformed into large complexes broken up into various individual parts. Eventually, this resulted in the treatment of a group of buildings as an urban landscape. Here, the building is laid out on a few terraces. Bands of different-colored stone reinforce this layering. This particularizes an architectural program into a scenic landscape.

Stirling treated his building as a connector between traditional and Modernist Stuttgart. It is located at one of the fast-traffic connectors laid out to modernize the bombed city after World War II. The actual design combines Modernist and traditional features. Abstract and representational features serve as icons for these two "styles." A number of elements are introduced to disrupt this axial arrangement. The steel and glass façades interrupt the masonry pattern and forms of the façades. These guitar-shaped curves refer to Cubism and Purism. A few Egyptian features can be detected (cavetto cornice and split through center). The elevator inside refers to pithead gear. All these elements make the building look at once like a ruin and a reconstruction. The whole is a collage of jokey references to historical details, and could be called Modernist Mannerism in its clashing juxtapositions of forms, images, and materials.

The overall form of the new complex was determined by the U shape of the existing building. In a reference to Schinkel's Altes Museum, Stirling arranged the gallery spaces in three wings along the perimeter of the complex, and set an open cylinder in the middle of the courtyard. An open passageway with ramps ran through this part. The protruding cylinder suggests Corbusier's Parliament building in Chandigarh as a source.

On the ground floor, spaces are arranged in a free-plan manner, with continuous columns marking their expanse. The exhibition galleries on the upper level are discrete spaces linked in a linear, traditional manner.

**FIGURE 37–1.** Salk Institute, La Jolla, View of office wing framing central courtyard.

**FIGURE 37–2.** Salk Institute, View of fountain at end of central courtyard.

**FIGURE 37–3.** Notre-Dame-du-Haut, Ronchamps.

FIGURE 37–4. Neue Staatsgalerie, Stuttgart, aerial view.

FIGURE 37–5. Neue Staatsgalerie, entrance terrace.

# Chapter 38

# Post-War International Style

From 1945 until ca. 1960, mainstream architectural development followed mostly the principles established in the International Style between the two World Wars. As before, it was an architecture generated by functional use and the necessary structural needs. The International Style had a hard time being accepted by the American people. This was most probably not the result of the design principles of the International Style, but of the new materials proposed by it. The three design principles established by Hitchcock and Johnson in 1932: (1) a concern with volume rather than mass, (2) the open expression on the outside of the underlying regular support skeleton, and (3) the elimination of applied decoration, were accepted by many people. However, the use of new industrial materials was the feature rejected by many. This situation changed after World War II. For about twenty-five years the machine became the predominant theme in the U.S. The automobile continued its road to victory, private homes became totally mechanized in household and kitchen activities, and the war had shown to everyone the power and potential of the machine. Moreover, the high output of industry during the war continued but, instead of producing weapons, factories produced machinery for peaceful uses. Elaborate highway systems and urban planning governed by a clear distribution of various uses became the predominant features of the layout of space. With the acceptance of the machine also came the acceptance of modern, or more accurately, International Style architecture. For a while, the International Style became synonymous with the corporate state and with middle-class culture. Buildings with exteriors of regular, modular façades were thought to best represent democracy, a social system based on the association of people in which everyone was equal to the other. Of course, the elevation of the International Style to the position of dominant architectural style was greatly helped by the forced emigration of the European founders of this movement: Gropius, Mies van der Rohe, and Mendelsohn. For these people, the United States was the Promised Land, the land of freedom, in which everything was possible. Furthermore, the American building technology was at such an advanced level that the machinistic, and sometimes megalomaniac, dreams and fantasies of these architects could be fulfilled. Lastly, the concept of functional architecture become more accepted in the U.S.: people wanted buildings that served them well, rather than buildings that showed off their social and financial status. Some American architectural offices were large, and the International Style was uniquely feasible for this anonymous type of design.

## SEAGRAM BUILDING, MIES VAN DER ROHE & PHILIP JOHNSON, NEW YORK (1954-58)

After World War II, in the U.S. Mies was finally able to realize his earlier dream of a glass tower. In turn, they would become symbols of modernization and urban renewal in cities across the U.S. In the Seagram Building, due to unlimited funds, Mies perfected this system. Glass curtain walls are hung in front of the structural skeleton. The Seagram building is luxurious. Even if the Seagram building looks like an industrially mass-produced structure, it is actually almost totally hand-made, and uses precious materials. Its cost per square foot of office space was roughly twice that of comparable space in midtown Manhattan skyscrapers. The client wanted a sumptuous building as corporation headquarters. On the advice of the CEO's daughter, the later architect Phyllis Lambert, it was decided to commission a distinguished architect. Based on a list provided by Philip Johnson, Mies was chosen. Johnson was later called in by Mies as collaborator.

In terms of space, Mies uses nondescript, universal space. Since functions change quite rapidly, it is not feasible to always design a new container for each change. He proposed to turn Sullivan's slogan "Form follows function" upside down by constructing practical and economical space into which the function is fitted.

The Seagram Building is basically a glass and steel tower. It rises as a sheer, dark cliff of bronze links and gray amber glass. This tower is set back ninety feet from the lot line facing Park Avenue. The building meets the earth firmly, as it is raised off the ground on a few two-story steel columns, which form the structural skeleton. This skeleton is set slightly behind the façade planes, except at the corners. The façades are fastened to the structural columns. They consist of a grid of metal I-beams and horizontal members, into which the glass panes are set. The absence of traditional horizontal window mullions creates some psychological discomfort for people inside. The vertical direction is emphasized over the horizontal. The I-beams, custom-made of bronze, are welded to the outside of the façades. They are narrowly spaced, and strengthen the wall-like character of the enclosure. The rectangular panels filling in the open spaces of the grid are all lined with a molding. Interestingly, with the change from the cruciform column to the H-shaped column came a merging of the vertical supports with the wall. This indicates a change from Mies's earlier "universal" space to the significance of the frame, or from Modernism to Traditionalism.

The ground floor is occupied by a two-story glass-enclosed lobby. The steel columns transform this part into a monumental portal. The empty plaza in front is symmetrically arranged. The massing of the building forms a T on its side. The small addition at the back of the office tower serves partly to house elevators and other mechanical services. This, however, goes only up to the tenth floor, where offices fill it. In addition, this added tower serves as a spine, to brace the whole against lateral forces. A lower addition, in the form of an upside-down T is attached to the back of the whole complex.

Quite interestingly, because Mies's designs mostly depend on technology, they cannot be looked on as establishing a clear signature style for Mies; rather, his forms have been copied infinitely, a sign for the culture of total commodification after World War II.

# ENGINEERING FACULTY BUILDING, STIRLING, LEICESTER UNIVERSITY (1959-63)

This building combines a Modernist and brutalist functionalism with references the High Victorian brick architecture. The design literally fits and fulfills the program, not even hiding the required water tank 100 feet up in the air. The building consists of two parts, a tower and a workshop wing. The latter has industrial roof skylights facing north, at a 45° deviation to the building axis. The tower has two lecture halls jutting out of it on the ground level. Above the smaller one is a tower of four floors of laboratory space. Over the larger one is a six-story tower of offices.

FIGURE 38–1. Seagram Building, New York.

FIGURE 38–2. Seagram Building,
Corner detail.

# Chapter 39

# Postmodernism

In 1966, Robert Venturi published his book, *Complexity and Contradiction in Architecture,* which was a study of the ambiguities of Mannerist, Baroque, and Rococo architecture. He had spent 1954-6 in Rome conducting historical studies. This study of historical examples illustrated Venturi's theory of design that refuted virtually every canon of the Modern Movement. It attacked the "simplistic" design philosophies of the Modern Movement – exemplified with his take-off on Mies' dictum: "Less is a bore." In this respect, it was an iconoclastic pamphlet. Venturi explained why Baroque and Rococo forms delight people, and why the pure International Style forms do not. In general, Venturi was discontent with the "boring" results produced by Modernism. Instead, he proposed that architectural design should incorporate the complexities and contradictions inherent in construction, history, and life. Venturi used a wide array of historical buildings to make his case, thus, partly revising the views of historic architecture.

Complexity and contradiction also result from the quality of each building to exist simultaneously as reality and as carrier of meanings. In this respect, most buildings allow double readings, and may serve a number of different functions.

In 1972, Venturi followed with *Learning from Las Vegas.* Here, Las Vegas was analyzed as a phenomenon of architectural communication. The main theory was that an architecture, which was simply concerned with space, form, and structure, was out of touch with present life. Venturi elaborated on the distinction between the "duck" and the "decorated shed," favoring the latter. He stated that architecture depends in its perception on past experience and emotional associations. Sources for architectural imagery can be found in the architecture of the urban sprawl and in history. In general, symbolism and associationism are more easily understandable elements of architecture than expression.

## GUILD HOUSE, VENTURI, PHILADELPHIA (1960-65)

The same type of whimsy is used in Venturi's larger buildings; however, it is coupled with a straightforward realism. The Guild House is an apartment building for the elderly, containing ninrty-onr units. It is very plain, making no pretense to being any better than the surrounding structures. In fact, it takes up the shape and exterior from the public housing projects done during Roosevelt's public works program in the 1930s. Standard industrial elements are used for windows, balconies, brickwork, and finishes. In contrast to 1930s projects, however, Venturi's building is not in the form of a cubical box. Instead, the front façade steps forward in stages, which is the same system as used in Renaissance and Baroque palaces. The actual street façade steps back like the garden fronts in those palaces, whereas the garden front of Guild House is of the flat plane one normally associates with street façades.

The plans do not consist of regular rectangular rooms, but show the same irregularity as used in Venturi's house for his mother. The rooms are arranged around the bends of zigzagging hallways in an overall symmetrical plan. Small, one-room apartments are on the rear side, two-room apartments on the front side.

Windows are sized and arranged for functional needs. The street façade on the ground floor level is of glazed subway tile. The entrance is bisected by a thick column (partly, this serves as a sun breaker). Above the entrance are supergraphics. The protruding entrance pavilion is emphasized by balconies and a large segmental window, forming an abstract pediment: giant order. The top part of this pavilion houses a lounge for television viewing. Venturi actually symbolizes the life-style of the elderly by placing a gold-plated antenna on top of the building. This protruding façade of the building is treated as a billboard. Its two-dimensional quality is brought out by the two slits on top and the fact that the round window almost touches the top cornice. This aspect establishes this building as a decorated shed. The façade seems applied; it does not appear to result from the spatial configuration it shields. The façade is a thin pastiche attached to a floor-slab-column structure (Le Corbusier's Domino House). The façade refers to Palladio's Villa Zeno.

Again, Venturi plays some jokes: the center of the entrance is blocked by a column, the most impressive window indicates the TV room, there are slits in the parapet wall on top, and a line of white tile separates an illusory attic story from the rest of the house, while splitting every window it encounters.

Venturi thus created an "inclusive" architecture that responded sympathetically to neighboring buildings, and accepted the messy and chaotic quality of human life. Moreover, he treated architecture as a vehicle for signs. Here, Venturi used primary (the name) and secondary (the TV antenna) signs, and coupled them with expressive features.

With these early-60s works, Venturi had brought architecture back into the context of representation and information, which dealt a much heavier blow to Modern architecture than his advocacy of complexity and contradiction. Nevertheless, this was a literary conception of architecture, with emphasis on imagery, not on formal integration.

# CHARLES MOORE

A different emphasis of this "inclusive" outlook is illustrated by some designs of Charles Moore: he had a strong feeling for the environmental role of architecture. He affirms values of pluralism. In his opinion, architecture is the "making of places" and its excellence resides in its ability to communicate and engage the individual's mind. He has developed the interview with the client into an art. Moore depends in his architecture on the unexpected juxtaposition of decontextualized forms to effect a unique and exciting synthesis. Moore's theory was that the architect acts to reinforce a sense of place by accepting what is already on the site, what already constitutes the place. Moreover, architecture should meet the most marginal human needs, as well as the anthropologically constant ones.

He is an architect who knows how to use modest means to create complex, exciting spaces that combine surprise with familiarity.

# CONDOMINIUM I, SEA RANCH (1965-72)

In 1965, he was hired to develop ocean front property north of San Francisco. Moore devised a style consisting of clusters of angular, rough units: groups of shed-roofed pavilions, sheathed in rough siding left to weather, enclose small courtyards, and echo the rugged coastal cliff in their overall craggy silhouette. This is an example of redwood cabin regionalism.

This building demonstrates the beneficial potential of a contextual and typological approach in architectural design. Moore has achieved an accurate representation of popular consumer taste by going directly to his user. Moreover, he has a view of architecture as an integrated discipline, one that emphasizes environmental as well as psychological effects of buildings and spaces. No one will misread Condominium I, because it is inherently a part of its place and expresses its function in a straightforward way. For Moore, form and decoration of a building must reflect its use pattern and respond to its context. Sea Ranch presents an ecologically sound architecture. The building has entered a limited partnership with the landscape, reacting formally to the prevailing wind pattern. Moore also understood that a house must establish "a territory for habitation, physical and metaphorical." People need to know where they are in space, in time, and in the order of things. Not just the image is important, but the making of a place. Condominium I is at once castle, compound, and promontory. The exterior is of rough wood, the interior of smooth wood. In this manner, architecture meets anthropologically constant human needs. The facade elevations are heavily dependent on the use of jagged roofs and bay windows. The volumes indicate the intended "destruction of the box."

Whereas the exterior responds to the environment, the interiors of the houses are more in tune with contemporary life styles, by introducing supergraphics to imitate urban interiors: contrast between inside and outside. The supergraphics also point to the impact of advertising on architecture. Rooms should be considered as empty stages for human habitation. They need to accommodate elements of ritual that are part of the human drama. The interior arrangement must also respond to the climatic and topographical characteristics of the area. At Sea Ranch, the individual spaces that protrude as "saddle bags" (aediculae) from the main building volume result from such considerations. As well, some humorous jokes should be played. These are played out in the supergraphics inside, which combine with the fact that architectural games are conducted inside barn-like exterior shapes. In this way a building engages the viewer, making him/her intuitively aware of the forces that have influenced architectural design since the beginning of mankind. Generally, Moore promotes design of a dwelling to consider "the need to be inside something that motivates (the user)." The design should proceed from the space of the room to the pattern of the house to the outside domain of the environment. Moore engages the fundamentals of architecture and dwells in the realm of architecture. For Moore, the facade is the place where inside and outside meet. Usually, in his houses, neither side dominates exclusively. In his architectural vocabulary he appeals to common sense.

## PIAZZA D'ITALIA, MOORE, NEW ORLEANS (1975-80)

This is a telling example of postmodern architecture, as it creates a fiction in a straightforward way. This was a public square intended to become the center of a predominantly Italian section of New Orleans. It was meant as a symbol of friendship between Italy and New Orleans, and honors the achievement of the Italian community, which comprised fifteen percent of this city's population. It was the first phase in a large-scale renovation project. The fountain partly cuts into the space intended for a projected building.

Moore tried to create a sense of place by using forms evoking historical allusions. The whole is in circular form. The Piazza d'Italia consists of a semi-circular façade made up of the different orders. In the center of the circle is a fountain in the shape of Italy. A few column screens serve as backdrop for a topographic map of Italy. The screens are painted in rust, yellow, and orange. Each section contains one of the five Italian orders. Moore invented a sixth one, the Delicatessen order. Through hydraulics, water streams and jets are also used to recreate Classical details: columns, egg-and-dart friezes, acanthus leaf capitals, and wetopes. The addition of neon lights modernizes this structure. The fountain basin plays the part of the Mediterranean. Sicily is in the center, as most residents were from this island. The fountain is dedicated to St. Joseph, patron of family life, and also contains a rostrum that can be used as a pulpit on the Saint's feast day. Water flows imitate the Arno, Po, and Tiber rivers. Concentric circles articulate the floor surface.

Special entrance features lead into the plaza from the two main streets bordering the site. One is a pergola, the other an archway. There is also a campanile on one street, which serves primarily to connect the new insertion with the existing buildings and their scale.

The project mixes classical details with supergraphics and water. All the classical orders are present, and provide the boot of Italy with a symbol of the past glory of this nation. Added to this are a few humoristic touches. Moore uses public imagery, and plays on the real, historical use of these images, turning metopes into wetopes.

# AT&T BUILDING, PHILIP JOHNSON, NEW YORK (1978-84)

This design was criticized as romantic the minute it was published. Its creative power and stylistic integration were denigrated; only its grandiose and monumental scales were seen as redeeming features. The pediment was first seen as satirical, then either defended as a stunning visual feature or a dollhouse doorway. The shaft was criticized as too repetitive. The building was alternately criticized for occupying its entire site and not leaving enough room for views, and praised for adding diversity to New York's homogenized skyscraper architecture.

This building rises straight up from the sidewalk. Its base measures 100 x 200 feet and it is 600 feet tall. It is a steel-frame building with pink granite cladding that rises as a shear cliff without setbacks. Here, the International Style glass box is rejected in favor of a historicizing design. Only thirty percent of the surface is glass. The building is divided into the traditional three parts. It combines a Renaissance base with a historicizing 1920s skyscraper and a Chippendale Top. The entrance was derived from Brunelleschi's Pazzi chapel and Alberti's Sant'Andrea in Mantua, the top from a Chippendale highboy and Boullée. The top pediment measures 30 feet in height and is broken by a circular opening, an "orbiculum." The entrance is 110 feet tall and has an arched portal flanked by rectangular openings between massive piers. However, these historical allusions form but a superficial compendium, an addition so to speak to a Modernist steel frame. Behind the building is a glass-covered galleria connecting the AT&T building to an addition, initially intended to house a museum of communication.

The lobby is 70 ft high and lined in granite. Its floor consists of black and white tiles laid in a geometric pattern. Inside is a statue by Evelyn Longman, The Genius of Electricity, which originally stood on top of the old AT&T headquarters. For the size of this statue, the lobby is rather narrow.

The design demonstrates an elastic reach into the past. A permanent reassurance from the past cannot come from literal, exact copying of a previous style, but requires a more complex architectural vocabulary. Since the world gets more diffuse, architecture must become more orderly in form and more pluralistic in style. Johnson fails to produce this, since he combines the amorphous volume of a glass skyscraper with the form of a classical temple portico that is scaled against no scale, or a delicate stone surface pattern with glass, or a notch at the apex. All this is unbalanced and idiosyncratic, but may add a measure of self-mockery to this design. Nevertheless, as the means of interchange became more sophisticated, there is a need for something more generic.

Interestingly enough, Johnson's position can be seen as Modernist. Just as the Modernist has seen development as consisting in a break with the past, so Johnson felt he needed to radically break with Modernism.

# PUBLIC SERVICES BUILDING, GRAVES, PORTLAND, OR (198-82)

In the later 1970s, Graves broke with the formal canon of the New York Five. He criticized Modernist architecture for having suppressed the duality between technical and symbolic attitudes, and consequently dismembered the cultural language of architecture. Graves called instead for figurative, that is, symbolic and anthropomorphic forms. He introduced historical motifs into the modernist language. He became increasingly preoccupied with naturalistic metaphors. Above all, he is concerned with a type of anthropomorphic symbolism. Especially his use of color testifies to this. He uses color to create metaphorical landscapes, that is, colors are used as they appear in nature: blue = sky or water, green = plants, yellow = sun, and red = walls (inspired by Etruscan architectural practice). Graves adheres to ornamentalism in architecture. Graves distinguishes between two forms in the language of architecture: first, a common language inherent to architecture, consisting of pragmatic, constructional, and technical requirements of building; second, a poetic language external to architecture, attempting to express the myths and rituals of society. This language should be sensitive to figurative, associative, and anthropomorphic attitudes of a culture. He distinguished between the internal and the external aspects of a building. Internal aspects relate to the physical framework of a structure, external ones to the decoration or embellishment of this structure. Whereas the internal aspects are generally guided by technological solutions, Graves thinks that the external aspects should partake of the figurative, associative, and anthropomorphic attitudes of a culture. The external aspects of a building should express ritual and symbol. Furthermore, Graves begins to use fragments of historical buildings, again to evoke associations and to turn the experience of architecture into an exciting activity.

For the Portland commission, design-build teams were invited to prepare designs. Cost overruns and delays of completion were charged to these teams. Graves's design was chosen because it alone provided all needed spaces at the total cost specified, in addition to being energy-efficient and highly original. Graves was asked to remove some ornamentation.

In Portland, features from Art Deco were used, together with references to Greek, Roman, and Renaissance features. There is also a reference to French Revolutionary Classicism. In addition, the setting was included, especially three government buildings opposite and flanking the new addition.

In his Portland Building, Graves reintroduced the two languages in his intention to express the public nature of the site and programme. This is accomplished in the façades, which hide a purely utilitarian interior of municipal offices and rental space. The façades are divided into three parts. On the main ones, dark green (or turquoise) is used for the parts close to the ground. The giant paired columns act as a sign for a portal and reinforce the sense of passage through the building. They are topped by a giant keystone, which houses a belvedere. The municipal offices are housed behind a glass façade, attempting both to mirror and to accept the city outside. They are meant to symbolize the collective, public nature of the activities taking place behind it. The rental floors are behind the lintel-like surface at the top. The side façades are articulated by similar colonnades, indicating the idea of passage. The stylized garlands are meant to tie these columns together, and are a classical gesture of welcome.

By letting different guidelines determine interior and exterior articulation, Graves has destroyed the elementary integrity of architecture. Architecture is experienced empathetically, in what might be called a pre-semiotic state of perception. That physical presence is architecture's primary meaning. Although Graves claims to have considered figurative, associative, and anthropomorphic attitudes in the design of the exterior aspects of this building, these are esoteric, because they are neither native and vernacular, nor were they handed down through an historical typology. The façade reveals a layered interweave of mural, trabeated, and arcuated structure, together with illusion. The façade design allows multiple readings.

By explaining his façades in symbolic terms, Graves opens himself to a literary critique of his scheme. In this respect, he does not follow the accepted distinction between literature and language. Literature treats words as motifs in a structure of words for their own sake. Language treats words as signs or symbols. While Graves's decorative details work adequately as signs, he did not pay attention to how they would function within the entire "word" structure of the façade. Graves mixes parts of different stylistic and typological origin. There is a Modernist glass wall that fills out the void created by the primitive hut of four corner posts supporting the roof plane. A material, which rejects physicality, is combined with the massive forms characteristic of the architecture of the early high cultures. It becomes quickly apparent that even these massive parts lack the mass that would impress the onlooker. This is not the architecture of power as exemplified by the Ishtar Gate of Ancient Babylon. The posts and roof plate are punctured by small windows announcing an interior of totally different proportions from those suggested outside. The incompatibility of these features is enlarged by Graves's "titanic struggle with the keystone," and the theme of the building as mask. This design is indeed a work of bricolage. The meanings are considered abstract enough to be general, and still recognizable and comprehensible. The building has elicited quite a few nicknames in Portland. Graves associates this activity with identifying with the building. In the end result, it does not make much difference whether Michael Graves designs a teapot or a building. He has no concern for scale, as for him creating architecture is synonymous with enlarging a drawing. His anorexic features may produce imaginary readings of his building, but fail to create a physical space.

# AUTONOMOUS ARCHITECTURE

This trend was initiated by A. Rossi and O.M. Ungers as a response to functionalism. This development is different from the American, in its approach to formal references to the everyday world (Pop art and Venturi's complexities), and in the wit and lighthearted polyvalence. Instead, this movement attempted to renew the significance of historical typology, claiming that architecture has an autonomous language of its own. The term "rational" is generally associated with Classical and normative. It can be seen as a reaction against the infantilism of pop architects and those proposing spontaneous expressionism. It also strongly disapproves of the political involvement of architects. It was strongly influenced by structural linguistic studies. Its main theoretical component is that values of architecture are independent of ideology. Rationalists see modernism as a storehouse of ideas, although only on a formal level. Other historical forms can serve as inspiration, although not as models, only as types. Architectural forms, though, constitute only a limited repertory. Rationalism can be divided into two camps: contextualism and abstract Modernism.

Rationalism also produced a novel architectural drawing style. The drawing is limited to thin outlines, and the projects are presented as pure volumes, without pedestrians drawn in.

## CEMETERY, ROSSI, MODENA (1971-83)

Aldo Rossi sought the archetypal in building forms, the primordial ideas. Such intentions led him to primary structures that superficially resemble the Classical styles. He reaches to the beginnings of modernism, aiming to transcend the one-sidedness of functionalism. He generally establishes a type by stripping his forms of all ornament. His work consists mostly of a small repertory of classically derived elements assembled in eccentric ways. His projects generally have a magico-metaphysical greatness and consist of light-drenched corporeality.

An important part of Rossi's design approach concerns typology. His typology is related to life. The forms and shapes are so self-evident that they cannot be changed. Their functions have been solved, and no longer present any problems. In fact, they have become part of the form. Rossi has attempted to reduce the multiplicity of forms to a few forms marked by typical characteristics. This approach runs the risk of burdening the forms with problematic connotations.

At Modena, great use was made of geometry's rich potential of symbolic connotations. The whole design exudes the character of a monument. The strict axial symmetry, the prominence of centrally placed structures and the surrounding wall seem to belong to the ruins of a historical vocabulary. Rossi's complex is placed next to an existing Neo-Classical cemetery. Together with formal similarities to the surrounding buildings, this constitutes its contextualism.

The cemetery is conceived, based on a Rationalist definition of death, namely as disruption of life. The images conjured up by the various buildings are those of a deserted house with empty windows and a factory with smokestack where work has been disrupted.

The typological form is characterized by straight passages with porticoes along which the graves are arranged. Along the walls are two stories of columbaria, in the center are the burial vaults, and the cone represents the collective grave. The cube is totally empty, and this is even shown in the shadow it throws. The cone forms a geometric contrast; it is fitted as an assembly hall with concentric circles of stepped seats.

Various levels of meaning are assembled here. Ideal forms, not impaired by ornament or intermediary buildings, are used, so that a high degree of autonomy is achieved. The design is also fitted into its context. A distinct typology is recognized.

# MARIO BOTTA

## SINGLE-FAMILY HOUSE, RIVA SAN VITALE (1972-3)

Beautifully located on a steeply sloping lake-shore, this house is laid out in tower form, and establishes a dialectic counterpart to the surrounding mountains. The building dominates its relationship with the immediate context. The natural surroundings are only allowed inside the house through memory and recollection. These recollections become mere shreds when confronted by the strong materials inside. The tower appears virtual, as it is only defined by its corner supports and roof slab. Inside and outside interpenetrate through several terraces and balconies. Bearing walls are in cement blocks laid without joints, painted white inside, which support the concrete floor slabs. Window and interior wall frames are of black iron. The entrance bridge is of red iron, and the floors are covered with red terracotta tile.

Here, architecture is commenting on architecture. The building has an archaeological quality. In fact, it refers typologically back to the "roccoli," which were part of the country estates of wealthy families. Freestanding towers standing on free ground, they were used to enjoy country life and catch birds. It is isolated from the rest of the village. The iron trellis bridge combines the technological with the martial.

### SECONDARY SCHOOL, MORBIO INFERIORE (1972-77)

For Botta, each building must interact closely with the spatial and historical territory into which it is inserted. There should be a mutual exchange and impact between building and built, and natural environment. The historical and local values provide the balance between human beings and nature. In this commission, Botta attempted to bring out these cultural and physical values through an analytical exposition. He emphasized the identity of the site, its history, and its collective memory. Formal characteristics of the site topography – the course of a creek, the edge of the forest, and a nearby church – determined siting, size, and orientation of the new building, to establish a spatial connection between new and existing. The concept of the built territory that is rich in identification potential is, therefore, contrasted to anonymous urban sprawl and its destruction of historical and local values. The intention is to establish a new ordering system that will provide a structure for future building.

Here, a bridge typology is used, although the finished building looks like a series of stacked pavilions. In this respect, the building is part of the megastructural urban projects Botta was presenting during the 1970s. The project intended to create a sense of place that enhanced the awareness of the historical and environmental qualities of the site. The "bridge" marks the boundary between the built area of the village and the mountainous and agricultural surroundings.

Each "bridge" element contains three-story pavilions in its four corners. On the ground floor are teacher's study rooms and entrances, on the second floor are classrooms, and on the third special laboratory spaces.

# CASA TONINI, REICHLIN & REINHARDT, TORRICELLA (1972-74)

This is a precise, regular building. It is primarily a neo-Palladian design, above all in its choice of cubical shape and the focus on the central bay. The nine-square grid plan is but the typical Palladio plan, as distilled by Rudolf Wittkower. The source of the Villa Rotonda is clearly visible. Built for a mathematician and derived from the Renaissance, the building asserts that the dignity of architecture lies in numbers and geometry. The main focus of the design lies in its form as a centralized building and the primacy accorded to the main central hall. Everything else in this design is subordinated to these two principles.

Historical details are quoted in a stripped-down manner. They are transformed through a Modernist outlook. The hard-edge reinforced concrete skeleton and other contemporary materials, as well as the functional use of these details – cornice becomes gutter, arch becomes window and chimney flue – modernize the historical model. The exterior shows its materials openly, appealing to Brutalism. These materials are also used to express plan and interior arrangement, as well as the proportional system of this building.

Inside, elegance reigns supreme. Historical references are more openly acknowledged. The central bay, extending through the entire height, becomes a public square onto which the upper floors offer a view. Light enters through its protruding pyramidal roof and the four cross arms linking it to the outside.

The design expresses the subjects of living in the country and a discourse on architectural types and rules. It asserts that architecture has an autonomous language of its own. Renaissance themes are used, however with slight distortions. A particular theme is that of a house within a house.

The building tries to address its broader geographical and cultural context. The arch behind this building frames a view of church towers and mountain peaks.

# GERMAN MUSEUM OF ARCHITECTURE (1979-1984)

An existing villa was converted to be used as a museum. It was gutted and surrounded by a loggia on the street side, ambulatories on the sides, and a hall rooms in back on the garden side. This hall is covered with a glass vaulted roof. A space is left for an existing tree to serve as a symbolic courtyard. The shell of the villa sticks out from this horizontal pedestal of new construction. Ungers inserted a central core inside that rises up from a simple baldachin on ground level to partially enclosed walls on the upper levels until it forms a simple hut on top. As this core evolves and changes as it rises, it illustrates the development of architecture from pillared shelter to primitive hut. The plan is strictly modular, and decoration is lacking from the new walls in- and outside.

FIGURE 39–1. Piazza d'Italia, New Orleans, Aerial view.

FIGURE 39–2. Piazza d'Italia, View of arch.

**FIGURE 39–3.** AT&T (Now Sony) Building, New York.

**FIGURE 39–4.** Public Services Building, Portland.

FIGURE 39–5. Public Service Building, Portland, Street façade with statue of Portlandia over the entrance.

FIGURE 39–6. Cemetery, Modena, exterior.

FIGURE 39–7. Cemetery, Modena, exterior.

FIGURE 39–8. Casa Tonini, Toricella.

FIGURE 39–9. German Museum of Architecture.

FIGURE 39–10. German Museum of Architecture, interior.

# Chapter 40

# Deconstructivist Architecture

## BACKGROUND

One of the eternal qualities of architectural form is its basis on geometric purity. Pure form is the goal of architectural design, providing stability and order.

Deconstructivist architecture deviates from this goal. It attacks the traditional system of architecture. Pure form is disturbed. Deconstructivist projects challenge the values of harmony, unity, and stability. They propose instead a view of structure which states that flaws are intrinsic to it. Thus, buildings are not dismantled, but impurities within are revealed: the form is interrogated.

## FORMAL ARCHITECTURAL SOURCE

For this purpose, formal strategies developed in Russian Constructivism are employed. The post-1968 attempt to exploit the political potential of art led to the renewal of this earlier example of a cultural revolution. Russian architects had broken the classical rules of composition by using pure forms to produce skewed geometric compositions. Simple forms were placed in conflict, to create an unstable, restless geometry. After the 1917 revolution, architects and artists turned increasingly toward architecture for its functional aspects, that is, its close relation to society. It was deemed extremely valuable to advance revolutionary goals. The social revolution required an architectural revolution. Constructivist projects were characterized by pure forms that seemingly destroy the structural framework. This was meant as an expression of dynamism, rather than instability. This style was based on an admiration for the machine, technology, and industrial materials.

## SOCIETY

Post-industrial society is a post-humanist society. The human world has increasingly become informatized and telematized through electronic communication technology. The subject is no longer self-constituting, and the anthropocentric world-view no longer applies. We have lost the sense that we have external foundations by which to ground our judgments and choices. Deconstructionist architecture attempts to address, and compensate for, this loss of center through the creation of self-referential architecture. Technology has overwhelmed nature. Modern thought has discovered unreasonableness in reason, and logic has been found to contain the illogical.

## PHILOSOPHY

Deconstruction is philosophy after the end of metaphysics. There are no longer any "last words" that universally determine human endeavor. Instead, multiple structures determine behavior; pluralism of languages, models, and methods is practiced. The basic philosophical question becomes the constitution of the self. According to Jacques Derrida, we are constituted by language, and are multilingual.

Another source is the French literary and philosophical movement known as deconstruction. Its main theory is that a literary text does not have a unifying wholeness or fixed meanings, but several asymmetrical and irreconcilable ones. Instead of interpreting books historically and biologically, the rules of language become more important in this task. Literary texts are no longer seen as expressing only anthropological metaphors. Narratives are no longer just about psychological or social conflicts, but can be merely descriptions of actions and events. Reading a novel is a creative appropriation, not just a reproduction.

Deconstruction derives ultimately from the incredulity in reason and its single-minded trust in rational industrialism. Martin Heidegger's questioning of technology and his promotion of human values not only undermined the system of philosophy produced by the Enlightenment, but also instilled doubt in Modernism's reliance on industrial technology and universal solutions in some architects of the 1950s and 1960s. Among them was a group of English architects who called themselves Archigram. They produced mostly utopian visions of a world of lattice frames, tubes, capsules, cells, spheres, and robots. These were meant for a society oriented toward high-technology recreation. Their designs follow closely the concept of "the house as machine." Theirs was a technological style embodying the optimism of Pop and of space travel.

## CENTRE POMPIDOU, PIANO & ROGERS, PARIS (1971-77)

High Tech architecture pushed Modernist technology to its limits, in an effort to make it more spectacular. The Pompidou Center uses logic, technology, mechanical service, structure, and construction, and displays them openly. The building houses a museum of modern art, a public library, an industrial design center, and an institute for acoustic and music research and coordination.

A competition was held in 1971, to which 681 entries were submitted. In the selection process, the jury eliminated designs that were aggressively geometric, eclectic, and/or banal. The winning design was chosen because it was none of these, dealt sympathetically with the site and program, promised to be novel, and emphasized flexibility.

Most competition projects dealt with the program by articulating the various requirements into different elements. Volumes and surfaces were used for expressive purposes and the whole could be integrated into its environment. Piano & Rogers's scheme was unique in ignoring these problems and presenting a solution in which a single building was made so flexible that it could accommodate the various functions. The structure, circulation, and service elements were pulled to the outside to make the façades more interesting. Fundamentally, the building derives from Mies's American phase (his universal spaces and the containers they engendered) and the intention to present it as a servicing mechanism. This resulted in a building that was crudely inserted into its context.

The definite design (fourth overall, including competition) was done in spring, 1973. In October 1974, the steel construction was begun, and in June 1975, the structure was complete.

This building is assembled as a megastructure. It consists of thirteen bays of trusses with a span of 150 feet. The main span was partly balanced between two short cantilevers. This system is similar to one evolved by a 19th c. German engineer called Gerber; hence the cantilevers were called gerberettes. The perimeter space is used to stabilize the whole in every direction. The structure is on the outside. Circulation is on one of the longer sides, mechanical services on the other. Structure and construction are the decoration of the building.

## AUSTRIAN TRAVEL AGENCY, HOLLEIN, VIENNA (1978)

A different questioning of Modernist intention focused on the meaning of architectural forms. This travel agency consisted of an interior remodeling. Hollein created an artificial environment that recounts tales of travels in different ways. The whole treatment of the interior is intended to suggest the fairy tale meaning of travel. The interior is designed as a theater stage. The message is easily understood because it is conveyed in a popular code.

Hollein used details from Ancient architecture, but inserted symbols for the technological age into these fragments. Tourism is symbolized through stereotypes: a pyramid points to Egypt, palm trees to the desert, an exotic land, or the 19th century (re: the kitchen columns in Nash's Brighton Pavilion). An actual proscenium with a stage set by Serlio serves as theater ticket counter. The set is a blown up woodcut by Serlio and the draped curtain is of metal. International travel is indicated by two soaring eagles in front of a painted sky. Ship travel is suggested by frozen ship flags (they are kept behind glass). A pavilion in the lobby seems taken from a stage set. In its forms it actually points to colonial architecture (India).

## CITY MUSEUM, HOLLEIN, MÖNCHENGLADBACH (1972-82)

This design was conceived as an architectural landscape. It is molded into a hill and gives the impression of being part of it. The administration building is a low high-rise on top. Its undulating wall repeats the undulating hill terraces. Diagonally across is another building.

The whole hilltop is laid out in imitation of an Ancient temple district. Each building is formed and shaped according to its function, not according to an overlying principle. This design approach treats the museum in terms of the house as a city.

## Gehry House, Gehry, Santa Monica (1979)

During the 1970s, Gehry began using skewed grids, reverse perspectives, intersections, and collisions of various parts, as well as postmodern spatial devices such as demi-forms and elaborate confusion. His own house is part of this phase.

This house is a renovation of an existing 1920s two-story gambrel-roofed clapboard suburban dwelling. The original house is embedded in several interlocking additions of conflicting structures. It is wrapped around and punctuated by corrugated metal and wire mesh fences. These are cheap materials. The design intention was to show these additions as coming out of the original house. Three types of space were created. At the back are small rooms, such as stairs, bedrooms, bathrooms, and closets. Second, the spaces of the old house, namely living room and master bedroom. Third, the spaces created by the new wrapper. The building is presented as unfinished and provisional. The production process is presented. The materials and the design also express the rough urban environment of Los Angeles. While being an expression of urban realism, it also puts up a false front in the form of a "fortified" exterior intended to hide the sumptuous house behind.

The first addition is made up of forms that twist out from the existing building. Doing this, they remove the skin and expose the structural frame of the original and the new. Various parts are ripped away. Studs and foundations are exposed to show the "reality" of construction. A glass cube is used to bring light into the kitchen. Together with the corrugated steel façade, it forms the wrapper, which encloses the new space. This wrapper articulates the new space of this house, one of multiple perspectives that cause one to feel suspended and tipped in various directions. Thus, one no longer feels like the traditional standing and stable viewer who was the center of the space. We can no longer use our conventional coordinates to orient ourselves in this hyperspace. Instead, perceptual shock is constantly maintained, and one begins to consider reality to be what one sees, not what one knows from memory. Hence, this space leads one to re-stimulate perception and refresh one's experience away from the habitual. The interior blocks the photographic point of view. Through the wrapper, the old house becomes an image (of the past).

The second stage breaks down the back of the complex.

The third addition consists of forms that appear to have escaped from the house through the break in the back. These forms are then presented in various stages of twisting.

Ultimately, in its unfinished state and its choice of materials, the Gehry House may reflect daily life in the United States, especially poverty, homelessness, and crime on the streets. The glass cube, through its allusion to Russian Constructivism, can be seen as an allegory of multinational capitalism, as the opposite image of America. The house attempts to combine these two views on a strictly spatial level.

## Wexner Arts Center, Eisenman, Columbus (1983-89)

In this center for progressive art, Eisenman intended to challenge art, instead of providing a neutral background for it. Architecture here questions the ordinary.

This design combines deconstruction with the fragmented, but nevertheless postmodernist reconstruction of the armory. The building invents its site. It is a work of dissimulation, that is., it attempts to recreate its reality artificially. It aims to demonstrate the aesthetic for this place for avant garde art, and intends to enhance its surroundings in a powerful manner. It tries to create an artificial place for invention, working along the notion of fiction.

A thin, 516-foot-long cage of steel columns and beams rises five stories high. This cage breaks through two existing buildings. Parts of these buildings protrude into the cage, and some support columns are eliminated, making the whole distorted, fragmented, and looking structurally unsafe. As this grid is the most visible part of the new building, it actually simulates scaffolding. It serves to initiate the grid language of the building, and is a pedestrian walkway. The grid – in various forms and dimensions – has invaded everything in this design and is the organizing principle of the plan of this building. The crossing of two grids in the building makes it an event. The grid refers to the city grid, the grid in modern art, and the grid of architectural structure. In this building, grids invade everything, dissolving in this way the conventional distinctions between walls, floors, and ceilings.

The design responds to history and the context. The Center continues the existing street grid alignment of Columbus, the flight path of the Columbus airport, and the historic grids used to survey Ohio. This line intersects with an asymptotic axis touching the oval of the campus plan. It rejects the campus grid of Ohio State University, although it aligns with the football stadium. In this, the design expands the notion of contextual response, although the meeting of the two lines is artificial.

The partly rebuilt armory demonstrates the power of traditional imagery and the importance of history. In its fragmentation and shifting, it questions the possibility of preserving the past. It is thus a dissimulated reconstruction of history. Within the composition, it serves also as a counterpoint to the modernist and grid features, highlighting the latter further. The cuts through which it is fragmented correspond to grid lines in plan.

In its entirety, the design makes the site become architecture, not the building proper. The massing concept is that of an archaeological earthwork. The essential elements are scaffolding and landscape. The white steel cage is like temporary scaffolding, but here made the central part of the permanent building. Scaffolding refers to the future, when stone has to be protected from the effects of pollution. Landscaping is treated as excavating, revealing the history and geography of the site. The plinths over the library mix characteristics of architecture and landscape. They suggest portions of the earth thrusting up, and allude to Indian burial mounds. The wild flowers and grasses point to the flora of Ohio. These plinths overturn the traditional concept of the ground as a horizontal datum for the building, by emerging into the domain usually reserved for the building. The same is expressed by the scaffolding.

The design also questions the notion of functional form, through details such as a suspended column in the staircase and windows that are placed on the floor.

## PARC DE LA VILLETTE, TSCHUMI, PARIS (1984-95)

Tschumi won the competition for a master plan and the "structuring" elements of this park in 1983. The final design was worked out in 1985. It consists of an array of scattered structures linked by a complex series of gardens, axial galleries, and meandering promenades. The major part consists of thirty garden buildings, or follies, which house galleries, studios, and restaurants. There is no beginning and no end to this plan.

In this design, Tschumi intended to show that architecture was not an autonomous discipline. The design was to present an organizing structure that was independent of use and without center, order, or hierarchy. He did this through acts of transposition, superimposition, combination, and "cinematic" landscape. Concepts from one field were transposed to another. In this step, concepts were rid of their inherent contextual problems. This contextual logic was at the heart of Tschumi's method. The whole is an essay in the deviation of ideal forms. He acknowledged that architecture does not have the power to affect socioeconomic change, and hence treated it as an artistic medium. The seductive power that architecture gains in this treatment could dissolve traditional ideology. Architecture is here portrayed as creating an event.

As an urban park, this design formulates a new type. It does not aim to contrast enclosed nature to the city, but wants to be part of the city. It can be looked upon as a large discontinuous building that overlaps with the city and existing structures on the site. This building explores concepts of superimposition and dissociation. The pavilions were intended to be read as fragments remaining from the explosion of a single building. The design derived from the understanding that the culture of the 1980s is one of disruptions, dissociations, and disjunctions. This is no longer the culture of the unified, centered, and self-generative subject, but rather a culture of madness. Architecture must therefore cease to think in terms of principles of formal composition but rather of questioning structures. This design aims to be an image for a future architectural organization that sees itself as related to cultural developments.

The basic design comprises operations of repetition, distortion, and superimposition, as opposed to traditional composition, hierarchy, or order. The main principle consists of the superimposition (layering) of three autonomous ordering systems: points, lines, and surfaces. These constitute objects, movements, and spaces. The points are established by pavilions laid out in a grid formation. The grid was chosen because of its ubiquity in history and the fact that it cannot be tied to an individual inventor. The lines include the grid of these pavilions, a set of classical axes (the north-south one links the two existing subway stations), and the path of thematic gardens. This one mimics a filmstrip thrown casually on the ground. The sound track is a pedestrian walkway, the image track a series of framed gardens. There are also lines formed as alleys of trees, articulating circle, square, and triangle ( = Bauhaus forms). The surfaces are pure geometric figures, any surface left after the programmatic requirements were satisfied. Each of these systems begins as an idealized structure with its own internal order, but when superimposed, encounters distortion, reinforcement, or indifference. The resulting disjunction questions the individual systems from without, rendering limits important. The goal was to displace the opposition between programme and architecture, that is, it attacked the traditional cause-and-effect relationship between form and function, structure and economics. Programme, form, and ideology played integral roles in this design. Form and function do not derive from one another, and can be exchanged. The traditional cause-and-effect relationships that determined architectural forms are here replaced by a system favoring contiguity and superimposition.

Tschumi's plan uses the device of layering. The coexistence of multiple systems produces a potential for multivalence of meaning, spatial complexity, and discoherence. The interaction produces encounters of reciprocity, conflict, and indifference.

Each system is also distorted within itself. Galleries defined by axes are twisted and broken. The pure figures of the surfaces are warped. Each of the cubes is decomposed into a number of formal elements, which are then recombined.

In the follies, Tschumi wanted to show that signs have no definitive transcendental meaning. This attitude decentered architecture and liberated it from its metaphysical meaning. Contrary to the conventional meaning of (architectural) folly (extravagant display of eclectic styles), Tschumi connected this term to programme: regulated juxtaposition of unprecedented programs. The basic folly is a 10 × 10 × 10 m cube, or a three-story neutral space. In each folly, the cube remains legible, so that these pavilions form a clear identifying symbol for the park just like the metro entrances. They started as self-referential, independent systems. But, the dismembered elements of the cube are embedded in each other in unstable assemblages. The cubes are distorted by elements that were extracted from it. The intention of the follies was to bring architecture back to degree zero, that is, a prose made of abstract, neutral, useless, and meaningless volumes. Architecture is pushed to its limits, to make space for pleasure, especially the pleasures of the uses to which the follies are put. The follies reject the idea of presence, especially the notion of the present object or part having a clear meaning. Thus, the follies do not have a predetermined signifying feature. Instead of dealing with a universal symbolic repertory, this park constantly produces new meaning. The follies are either for hedonistic or for educational purposes. They are placed at 120 meter intervals.

The point of departure for the follies is the opposition between reason and chance, or reason and madness. The follies are not primarily designed as functional spatial organizations or spaces formed according to technocratic norms. Instead, each provides a space for pleasure, with norms deriving from these pleasurable activities. Consequently, technological/technocratic norms become fiction.

This project is derived from Tschumi's interpretation of the present city as a fractured space of accidents. At La Villette, he created architecture without subordination to traditional rules of hierarchy, function, and order. The plan also subverts the notion of border on which "context" depends. The whole is a conjunction of irrationalities. It aims to unsettle memory and context. It aims to be architecture that means nothing and wants to be signifier rather than signified. It is pure trace or language play. Meaning comes through interpretation; it is not resident in the object. It is, however, not anti-autonomy or anti-structure. It is "différance" in space and time: an architectural element functions when it collides with a programmatic element in the movement of bodies.

A number of well-known architects are to design small gardens which are laid out along the "cinematic promenade," since it consists of a montage of images laid out as on an unrolled filmstrip. One function of the design is to make visitors enjoy the pleasure of wandering in a "weave."

## VITRA FIRE STATION, HADID, WEIL AM RHEIN (1987-1993)

The design intended to be an organizing center for the Vitra manufacturing complex. The building was to draw its axes together and give the complex a skyline. This small building had to alleviate the monotony of the existing factory complex.

For Hadid, the factory lacked a coherent structure, and she decided to invent her own landscape. She began with studies of the surrounding landscape, to really understand how to make a space out of this no-space. These drawings depict abstract views from a low-flying airplane. The landscape curves to the horizon, and is covered with a geometrically structured relief. Within this structure are a few disturbing lines, which turn out to be the tilted planes, shaping the fire station. These colliding planes suggest a slow movement, the release, production of a danger. Traces of this geological shifting are shown in the finished building, for ecample, in the triangular whole in the center of it.

This building represents its function in spatial terms. The building awaits the fire to put its full potential to extinction of the danger. The forms are held visually in tension. A simple function is turned into an event. The building is of tellurian and cosmic origin, involved both in releasing and subordinating danger.

The fire station is designed as the edge of the corridor extending from the factory entrance. The starting point for designing the building was a series of layered screening walls. The uses inhabit the spaces in between these walls. These in turn are punctured and broken according to functional requirements, the primary one being the movement of the fire engines.

The necessary spaces are arranged in a linear manner and housed in three beam-structures. On ground level, one beam contains shower and changing areas, the other a fitness room. A stair is positioned in the intersection of these two beams, leading to the third one upstairs, located between two terraces. A triangular roof slab supported on steel columns juts out from this form over the entrance. A shed for the fire engines terminates the building on one side. The forms suggest some mode of transportation, wings, fins, or wheel skirts.

## BERLIN MUSEUM EXTENSION FOR JEWISH MUSEUM, BERLIN (1989, 1992-98)

Libeskind won the 1988 competition. His design began with the addresses of famous Jewish people of the past, which he plotted on a map of Berlin and connected with straight lines, forming an imaginary topographical matrix. Laid over this was a hexagonal form, an elongated Star of David. This first dimension was put together with a second one, the incomplete third act of Schönberg's opera "Moses and Aron." After having completed the first two acts, Schönberg was unable to finish the third, because Hitler rose to power. Libeskind was interested in this absence, this power of incompletion. In addition, Walter Benjamin's "Einbahnstrasse," a collection of urban essay fragments, played a role. From this, Libeskind composed his scheme titled "Between the Lines," namely the meandering line of the building, and a broken empty line cutting through this building. This second line, left in unfinished concrete, denotes the empty history of Berlin's Jews. Hence, the museum is built around an empty space. The lines indicate flows of thoughts, organization, and relationships. The result is a forceful, expressive sculpture in reinforced concrete assembled of ramps, broken planes, and interpenetrating forms. Libeskind's concept combined visible and invisible elements into a whole.

The museum was to be for all Berliners, past, present, and future. This required a rethinking of the building type away from placing the viewer in a passive relationship to the form. The spaces inside the museum are to be construed as "open narratives," Libeskind says, "which in their architecture seek to provide the museum-goer with new insights into the collection and, in particular, the relation and significance of the Jewish Department to the Museum as a whole." Instead of merely housing the collection, in other words, this building seeks to estrange it from the viewers' own preconceptions. Such walls and oblique angles, he hopes, will defamiliarize the all-too-familiar ritual objects and historical chronologies, and will cause museum-goers to see into these relations between the Jewish and German departments as if for the first time. All that is required is for the museum curators to work within the grain of the building, rather than against it. The built form makes possible a formal spatial arrangement appropriate to historical context, narrative requirement, and object display simultaneously.

The extension is separate from the existing building. A connection is provided underground. Once in the addition, a stair leads straight through the entire building, giving visitors absolute choice of path through the museum. This main gallery-linking stairway climbs like Jacob's ladder through the entire building. There are also galleries that lead to the Tower of the Holocaust, an apocalyptic void that is an interior void turned 180° and materialized, and the E.T.A. Hoffmann Garden. The two structures of the museum are interwoven, with the Jewish section maintaining its independence within the whole scheme. Narrow passages are bridges, which are marked with Benjamin's sixty stations, and cross the empty sections inside. The museum extension can be exited back through the basement, or through the garden.

The extension is connected to the existing museum through an underground passage. As we enter the museum, in fact, the very plane of the ground on which we stand seems to slope slightly. It is an illusion created in part by the diagonal slant of narrow, turret-like windows, cut at thirty-five-degree angles across the ground-line itself. For, on the "ground-floor," we are actually standing just below ground level, which is literally visible through the window at about eye-level. Only the earth line in the half-buried window establishes a stable horizon. Because the upper floor windows are similarly angled, our view of Berlin itself is skewed, its skyline broken into disorienting slices of sky and buildings.

The walls inside and out are criss-crossed by glazed slits. These offer views to the actual places in which the events commemorated in the museum happened, but also form a graphic background to the exhibits. The elevation of the museum, both externally and internally, is penetrated by an angular system of sealed transparent openings. This fenestration is characteristic of all the building. Externally the zinc cladding, sealed and riveted, is pierced where deemed appropriate. The positions of these openings are defined, Libeskind suggests, in terms of a plotting of the lines of connectivity between individual places of Jewish importance on the Berlin city map. "I did build the museum on the basis of addressing points, for example of connections between Berliners and Jews who lived around Lindenstrasse." They also deny a rational understanding of this building. The rooms inside are narrow and loftlike. The exhibition halls themselves are spacious but so irregular in their shapes, cut through by enclosed voids and concrete trusses, that one never gains a sense of continuous passage. The final floor area is 110,000 square feet.

The voids symbolize the loss in human beings, thoughts, and ideas, which the holocaust caused to Berlin. It is twenty-seven meters high and runs the entire length of the building, over 150 meters. It is a straight line whose impenetrability forms the central axis. The void is traversed by bridges, which connect the various parts of the museum to each other. In fact a total of six voids cut through the museum on both horizontal and vertical planes. Of these six voids, the first two are accessible to visitors entering from the sacred and religious exhibition spaces. According to the architect's specifications, nothing is to be mounted on the walls of these first two voids, which may contain only free-standing vitrines or pedestals.

The third and fourth voids cut through the building at angles that traverse several floors, but these are otherwise inaccessible. Occasionally, a window opens into these voids, and they may be viewed from some thirty bridges cutting through them at different angles, but otherwise they are to remain sealed off and so completely "unusable space" jutting throughout the structure and outside it. The fifth and sixth voids run vertically the height of the building. Of these, the fifth void mirrors the geometry of the sixth void, an external space enclosed by a tower: this is the Holocaust void, an architectural model for absence. This concrete structure itself has no name, Libeskind says, because its subject is not its walls but the space enveloped by them, what is "between the lines." Though connected to the museum by an underground passageway, it appears to rise autonomously outside the walls of the museum and has no doors leading into it from outside. It is lighted only indirectly by natural light that comes through an acutely slanted window up high in the structure, barely visible from inside.

The interior of the building is thus interrupted by smaller, individual structures, shells housing the voids running throughout the structure, each painted graphite-black. They completely alter any sense of continuity or narrative flow, and suggest instead architectural, spatial, and thematic gaps in the presentation of Jewish history in Berlin. The absence of Berlin's Jews, as embodied by these voids, is meant to haunt any retrospective presentation of their past here. Moreover, curators of both permanent and temporary exhibitions will be reminded not to use these voids as "natural" boundaries or walls in their exhibition, or as markers within their exhibition narratives. Instead, they are to design exhibitions that integrate these voids into any story being told, so that when mounted, the exhibition narrative is interrupted wherever a void happens to intersect it. The walls of the voids facing the exhibition walls will thus remain untouched, unusable, outside of healing and suturing narrative. Libeskind has also contrived to establish the memory trace of the Berlin cinematic landscape/streetscape of the 1920s. The acute angularity and tonal contrast familiar to followers of Robert Wiene's *Das Cabinet des Dr. Caligari* (1919-20) is readily identifiable, especially at those points where the void crosses the galleries.

Implied in any museum's collection is that what you see is all there is to see, all that there ever was. By placing architectural "voids" throughout the museum, Libeskind has tried to puncture this museological illusion. What you see here, he seems to say, is actually only a mask for all that is missing, for the great absence of life that now makes a presentation of these artifacts a necessity. The voids make palpable a sense that much more is missing here than can ever be shown. As Bendt has aptly noted, it was the destruction itself that caused the collection to come into being. Otherwise, these objects would all be part of living, breathing homes – unavailable as museum objects. This is, then, an aggressively anti-redemptory design, built literally around an absence of meaning in history, an absence of the people who would have given meaning to their history.

The only way out of the new building is through the Garden of Exile. "This road of exile and emigration leads to a very special garden which I call the E. T. A. Hoffmann Garden," Libeskind has said. "Hoffmann was the romantic writer of incredible tales, and I dedicated this garden to him because he was a lawyer working in a building adjacent to the site." Hoffmann was a writer who was chosen to represent exile and emigration of Berlin Jews to New York, Tel Aviv, and elsewhere. The Garden of Exile consists of forty-nine concrete columns filled with earth, each 7 meters high, 1.3 x 1.5 meters square, spaced a meter apart. Forty-eight of these columns are filled with earth from Berlin, their number referring to the year of Israel's independence, 1948; the 49th column stands for Berlin and is filled with earth from Jerusalem. They are planted with willow oaks that will spread out over the entire garden of columns into a great, green canopy overhead. The columns stand at ninety-degree angles to the ground plate, but the ground plate itself is tilted at two different angles, so that one stumbles about as if in the dark, at sea without sea legs. We are sheltered in exile, on the one hand, but still somehow thrown off balance by it and disoriented at the same time.

**FIGURE 40–1.** Gehry House, Santa Monica, entrance façade.

FIGURE 40–2. Wexner Arts Center, Columbia, entrance to campus.

FIGURE 40–3. Wexner Arts Center, entrance with scaffolding.

**FIGURE 40–4.** Wexner Arts Center, entrance lobby with suspended column.

**FIGURE 40–5.** Parc de la Villette, Paris, view of canal, pavilion, and elevated walkway.

**FIGURE 40–6.** Part ce la Villette, pavilion.

**FIGURE 40–7.** Vitra Fire Station, Weil am Rhein, exterior.

FIGURE **40–8.** Vitra Fire Station, exterior.

FIGURE **40–9.** Jewish Extension to Berlin Museum, view of Garden of Exile and façade.

# Chapter 41

# Contemporary Developments

Modern architecture, exploiting new materials, is still very strong. Deconstruction has primarily helped break the tyranny of "four walls, a floor, and a roof." The strongest impact by far, however, has been the computer. It has changed the essence of space. Experiential space – through virtual means – has become more important in design than the old conventions and formal details. The computer has had strong impact because it facilitated the modeling of three-dimensional space. It has also changed the essence of space, as experiential space – through virtual means – has become important. Conceptions of architecture as craft have also gained value, either in high-tech, or in more "primitive" forms of constructions.

## UNITED STATES HOLOCAUST MEMORIAL MUSEUM, INGO FREED, WASHINGTON (1993)

This was an emotional programme, but also a contradictory one, as it had to represent horror through beauty. Its functions were remembrance, study, and learning. To prepare himself for this task, the architect visited concentration camps. The images that persisted after these visits were bridges, brick, and steel.

This building was intended to be a resonator of memory. It was meant to stir memories. The main entrance is in limestone, to integrate it with the existing context. The western facade interweaves brick and limestone, while the Hall of Remembrance is again in limestone.

A four-story entrance hall, the Hall of Witness, is the center of the building and serves as transition from everyday life to the ghost world of the Holocaust. Its brick walls are interwoven with steel structures, and support a skewed steel-and-glass roof. A wide stairway leads to a simple arched opening into the second floor.

The northern side of the building consists of four brick towers. One of the towers contains a three-story room with a collection of a thousand photographs, and is called the Tower of Faces.

On the second floor is the hexagonal Hall of Remembrance. Underneath it is the Meyerhoff Theater. Its walls are inscribed with the names of the twenty most important concentration camps. The vertical joints are articulated as glass slots.

The interior of the building is laid out according to a path, leading from the Hall of Witness through the exhibition, the bridges and tower rooms to the Hall of Remembrance, and then back again to the Hall of Witness. There are two ways to see the exhibits. One is to take the elevator to the fourth floor and then proceed down to the Hall of Witness; the other is the reverse. On the second level are also exhibition spaces. The fifth floor is reserved for scholars, and contains a library, the glass bridges, and four joined towers, which contain the research rooms. The fourth floor has the names of the towns from which the victims originated. The third floor has typical first names of the victims.

The building works as a memorial, which also contains the museum of the Holocaust.

The design wavers between abstraction and representation. On the whole, it demonstrates a minimalist design approach.

# MUSEUM OF TECHNOLOGY CULTURE, ASYMPTOTE, NEW YORK (1999-2005)

This museum is to show the evolution of technology from the Machine Age to the World Exhibitions and the late-20th-century cyberage. The focus is on documenting the rise of information technology. It is to emphasize technology and its relation to the human condition.

This is a hybrid structure that combines the typology of the convention center with that of the hangar and the sports stadium. Its design involved dis-programming, by combining public events with the cultural programming of the art museum.

The building has a skin of high-tech cladding that can be used as screens for digital video displays. This gives the building an ephemeral, liquid appearance. Technology is treated as art. It is 300 meters in length.

Inside, ramps connect the various exhibitions and parts. The tallest part contains eight floors. Through sliding walls and floors, the interior can be adapted to different needs.

The lightweight steel skeleton was designed using computer modeling.

# DODGER STADIUM, LOS ANGELES (1999)

Here, new polymers are used to construct a pneumatic roof for this stadium. This skin is permeable and can change from opaque to transparent. Inside, an electronic display board encircles the entire field. There is also a rail vessel that circles around the spectators and gives access to shops and restaurants.

# CALPUTTA SOGN BENDETG, SUMVIGT (1985-88)

Peter Zumthor's oeuvre, not large but very varied, is a rigorous meditation on essence. Each building is a reflection on relationships of site and function, on individuals to society, and on humankind to the phenomenal world and our perceptions of it. Zumthor is Swiss, and while his buildings have some affinities with what is often called Swiss Minimalism, they are in some respects different from the mainstream work of the school, perhaps because he lives in a comparatively remote part of the country, so that he is able to pursue his own ideas with few distractions. The relative isolation has not made him provincial but more profound. While his buildings always respect their surroundings, they are never meekly contextual, but play their part in the conversations of the places from which they partly take their essence. They always provide appropriate volumes in which to contain their functional requirements, but they are far from being merely utilitarian. With great but unforced originality, they offer lyrical interpretations of human requirements that ennoble the quotidian. He believes that "the language of architecture is not a question of a specific style. Every building is built for a specific use in a specific place and for a specific society. My buildings try to answer the questions that emerge from these simple facts as precisely and critically as they can."

Because he adopts quite different strategies for each task, materials and constructions vary widely. Materials are always carefully chosen as part of the imaginative strategy, and are used with great understanding of their tectonic and symbolic qualities. Perhaps because of his training as a cabinetmaker, the highest qualities of craftsmanship are always attained. For example, the little chapel sitting in its field at Sumvitg is made warm and welcoming and the space is comforting and numinous simultaneously.

# THERMAL BATH, ZUMTHOR, VALS (1996)

Nothing could be a greater contrast with this than the thermal baths at Vals where stone and steam and shafts of light remind us of the thermae of the Ancients. Light and its proper handling, dramatic or delicately graded, is a key element in all his work. It is always handled with imagination and innovation, but his buildings are deeply sensuous at many levels and play upon the senses of smell, touch and hearing as well as sight.

# FOOTBRIDGE OVER THE MUR; MARCEL MEILI , MARKUS PETER, JÜRG CONZETT; MURAU (1996)

This is a three-dimensional junction connecting paths from three different directions: it connects the train station and river walk to the pedestrian and bicycle crossing. The structural frame is visible and was designed to accommodate these requirements. It consists of two vertical hollow boxes with laminated horizontal beams on top and bottom. The horizontal parts function as roadbed and roof. This system allowed the elimination of conventional structural system needed for timber construction. The result is a calm interaction between material, form, and site. A long window in the vertical beam in the center allows oblique views to the town.

**FIGURE 41–1.** United States Holocaust Memorial Museum, Washington, View of entrance plaza with auditorium.

**FIGURE 41–2.** Chapel of St. Benedict, Sumvigt, exterior.

FIGURE 41–3.  Chapel of St. Benedict, interior.

# GLOSSARY

**abacus**
The flat slab inserted between the top of the capital and the entablature.

**aedicule**
Generally a niche in the wall framed by columns and pediment. Window and door openings can also be accentuated in this manner.

**agora**
An open area in the city used for market and civic functions and gatherings.

**ambulatory**
An aisle surrounding the apse or sanctuary space of a church. This is used for processions.

**antis**
Columns that are placed between two spur walls, usually at the entrance to the cella in a Greek temple.

**apse**
The semicircular or polygonal termination of an elongated room.

**arcade**
A series of arches supported on piers or columns.

**archivolt**
The stepped arches on top of the entrance into a Christian church.

**ashlar**
Cut blocks of masonry with flat faces and square edges.

**balustrade**
A barrier formed of turned posts supporting a rail.

**basilica**
A church divided into nave and aisles. This derives from the Ancient Roman meeting hall.

**battered**
The face of a wall, which inclines toward the top.

**buttress**
Narrow thickening of a wall to reinforce it.

**cella**
The main interior space of an Ancient temple.

**chevet**
The eastern end of a church consisting of choir, apse, and ambulatory.

**Classicism**
Any reuse of forms and principles of Ancient Greek and Roman architecture.

**clerestory**
Windows placed directly underneath a ceiling or vault.

**coffer**
Stepped rectangular or polygonal carvings into the underside of a dome or vault.

**corbel**
A system of vaulting achieved through projecting each layer of stones beyond the lower layer.

**crossing**
The square bay formed by the intersection of the nave and the transept in a church.

**crypt**
The space underneath the choir in a church, usually containing sarcophagi or relics.

**cyclopean**
A masonry wall built of large irregular stones.

**dolmen**
Prehistoric tombs consisting of upright and horizontal megaliths.

**dome**
A semispherical vault over a circular space.

**donjon**
The tower of a castle.

**entablature**
The horizontal beam above the columns in an Ancient Ttemple;. Cconsists of the architrave and the frieze.

**exedra**
A semicircular addition to a rectangular space.

**flying buttress**
Round arches in Gothic cathedrals connecting the buttresses to the vaults, transmitting the thrust of the vaults.

**hypostyle**
A hall with a roof supported by rows of columns.

**jamb**
The vertical posts framing a doorway.

**kiva**
A hole in the ground serving as a ceremonial conduit to the underworld.

**loggia**
A gallery beside a house with a vault supported by a series of columns.

**mastaba**
An Ancient Egyptian tomb consisting of a square stone or brick mound over an underground chamber.

**megalith**
A large irregular block of stone.

**megaron**
The typical plan of an Ancient Greek house consisting of the main room with a hearth surrounded by four columns, preceded by a guard-room, and a portico, usually with columns in antis. This was also used for Ancient temples.

**metope**
The square sculptural panels set in between the triglyphs of the Doric order.

**mihrab**
The prayer niche in a mosque.

**narthex**
The vestibule of a church, usually reaching across the entire width of the building.

**opisthodomos**
The treasury room added in the back of an Ancient temple.

**parterre**
The rectangular areas in a garden filled with geometric patterns.

**pendentive**
A concave triangular area facilitating the transition from the square plan of the walls to the circular support for the dome.

**peristyle**
A covered gallery supported on columns surrounding a garden or open court.

**piano nobile**
The main floor of a house, containing the public spaces.

**portico**
The main façade of an Ancient temple, or any façade consisting of columns supporting a pediment.

**post-and-lintel**
A support frame consisting of vertical posts and a horizontal beam.

**pronaos**
The vestibule of an Ancient temple with columns in antis.

**propylon**
A gateway formed of two pylons flanking a square passage.

**prostyle**
Having free-standing columns in front.

**pylon**
The rectangular, tapering blocks flanking the entrance to an Egyptian temple.

**qibla**
The wall toward, which the faithful pray in a mosque. Usually pointing to the direction of Mecca.

**stylobate**
The tree-stepped platform on which an Ancient temple is constructed.

**tambour**
The circular or polygonal section of walls underneath a dome.

**tholos**
A beehive-shaped chamber.

**trabeation**
A structural system consisting of posts and lintels.

**transept**
A rectangular space inserted between nave and choir in a church, projecting on both sides.

**triforium**
The section of the wall in a Gothic cathedral between gallery and clerestory, usually divided into three arches.

**triglyph**
In the Doric entablature, the pieces set in between the metopes, usually with three vertical incisions.

**trilithon**
A structure consisting of two upright and one horizontal stone block.

**trumeau**
The central post bisecting the entrance doors to a cathedral.

**truss**
Timber posts fastened together to form the support structure for a roof, or three-dimensional space frame.

**tympanum**
The arched area above the entrance to a cathedral, usually surrounded by a series of archivolts.

**vierendeel**
A structural skeleton consisting of individual members forming a grid, without diagonal bracing.

**westwork**
The western façade of a Romanesque church consisting of two towers flanking the main entrance.